Praise for *The Great Arab Conquests*

"[*The Great Arab Conquests*] states historical truths most nonexperts, general readers and politicians ignore."—*Philadelphia Inquirer*

"Kennedy tells a remarkable tale with skill and authority."
—*The Economist*

"Weighing the sources carefully, Kennedy has composed a vivid and plausible narrative of events that continue to shape the daily news."—*Milwaukee Shepherd Express*

"*The Great Arab Conquests* does a splendid job of showing how the core territories of early Christianity fell under Muslim power."
—*Books & Culture*

"Brings to resonant life the dazzling achievements of the military machine Muhammad created. . . . A major achievement of scholarship and readability."—*ForeWord*

"Will likely become a standard account of the conquests for many years to come."—*First Things*

"Kennedy here brings history to glowing life and, in the process, illuminates a part of our present in rich and meaningful ways. Unforgettable."—*January*

"An extremely valuable addition to the discipline. . . . Highly recommended."—*Choice*

"Kennedy vividly introduces the formative establishment of Islam."—*Booklist*

"A welcome addition to Islamic studies and history shelves."
—*Midwest Book Review*

THE
GREAT ARAB
CONQUESTS

How the Spread of Islam
Changed the World We Live In

HUGH KENNEDY

DA CAPO PRESS
A Member of the Perseus Books Group

Cataloging-in-Publication data for this book
is available from the Library of Congress.

First Da Capo Press edition 2007
First Da Capo Press paperback edition 2008
Reprinted by arrangement with Weidenfeld &
Nicolson, a division of The Orion Publishing Group
HC: ISBN: 978-0-306-81585-0
PB: ISBN: 978-0-306-81740-3

Published by Da Capo Press
A Member of the Perseus Books Group
www.dacapopress.com

Da Capo Press books are available at special discounts
for bulk purchases in the U.S. by corporations, institutions,
and other organizations. For more information, please
contact the Special Markets Department at the
Perseus Books Group, 2300 Chestnut Street, Suite 200,
Philadelphia, PA, 19103, or call (800) 810-4145, extension 5000,
or e-mail special.markets@perseusbooks.com.

10 9 8 7 6 5 4 3 2 1

for CJG

CONTENTS

✣

List of Illustrations and Maps   viii

Acknowledgements   xxv

Preface   1

Foreword: Remembrance of Things Past   12

1. The Foundations of Conquest   34
2. The Conquest of Syria and Palestine   66
3. The Conquest of Iraq   98
4. The Conquest of Egypt   139
5. The Conquest of Iran   169
6. Into the Maghreb   200
7. Crossing the Oxus   225
8. The Road to Samarqand   255
9. Furthest East and Furthest West   296
10. The War at Sea   324
11. Voices of the Conquered   344
12. Conclusion   363

Notes   377

Bibliography   398

Index   409

LIST OF ILLUSTRATIONS

The old Empires
1. Emperor Justinian I and his retinue; mosaic *c*. AD 547.
2. A dish depicting King Yazdgard III (632–51) hunting; Sasanian school, seventh century.
3. Mushabbak Church, Syria.
4. A Zoroastrian fire-temple in Konur Siyah, Fars, Iran.
5. Taqi-kisrā, Iraq; the arch of the great palace at Ctesiphon.
6. The ruin of the Marib dam, Yemen.
7. A seventh-century Sasanian helmet.
8. A seventh-century Sasanian sword.
9. The arms and armour of Byzantine troops, as depicted on the 'David Plates'.
10. A swing-beam siege engine in operation, from an early eighth-century wall-painting; tile fragment and modern sketch.

Landscapes and cities of the Conquests
11. Wadi Du^cān.
12. The Syrian desert.
13. The ancient Roman walls of Damascus.
14. Jerusalem seen from the Mount of Olives.
15. The Zagros Mountains.
16. The walls of Bishapur.
17. Sistan.
18. Central Iranian landscape.
19. The ramparts of old Samarqand.
20. Old Bukhara seen from the walls of the citadel.
21. The Tashtakaracha Pass in the mountains south of Samarqand.
22. The view from the ancient walls of Balkh to the Hindu Kush.
23. Cordova, Spain.

24. Toledo, Spain.
25. The Ribat of Sousse, Tunisia.
26. A modern reconstruction of a Byzantine dromon.
27. Tyre, Lebanon.
28. The site of early Muslim Basra, Iraq.
29. The centre of old Kūfa, Iraq.

The Conquests remembered
30. The Prophet Muhammad preparing for his first battle against the Quraysh of Mecca at Badr in 634; early fourteenth-century Persian manuscript.
31. The assassination of Chosroes II in 628; fifteenth-century Persian manuscript.
32. The battle of Qādisiya; fifteenth-century Persian book painting.
33. The Legend of the True Cross, by Piero della Francesca (*c*. 1415–92).

LIST OF MAPS

1. The world on the eve of the Muslim conquests, *x*
2. Limit of Muslim rule in 750, *xii*
3. Syria and Palestine, *xv*
4. Iraq, *xvi*
5. Egypt, *xvii*
6. Iran, *xviii*
7. North Africa, *xx*
8. Transoxania, *xxii*
9. Spain, *xxiii*

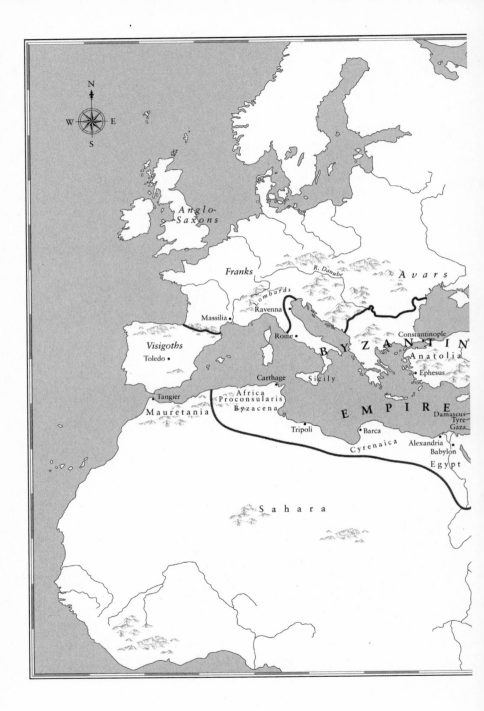

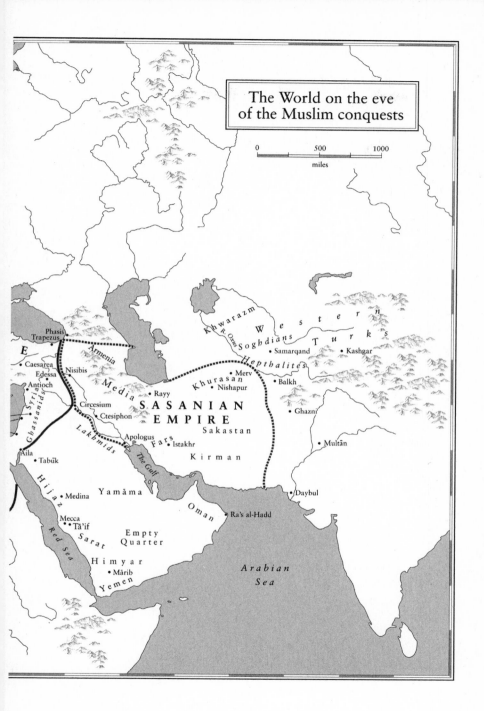

The World on the eve
of the Muslim conquests

0   500   1000
miles

Phasis
Trapezus
E
Caesarea   Armenia
Edessa   Nisibis
Antioch   Media
Syria   Circesium   Rayy
Ghassanids   Ctesiphon
Lakhmids   Apologus
Aila Tabūk   Istakhr   Fars
Hijaz   Medina
Mecca Tā'if
Sarat   Empty
Red Sea   Quarter
Himyar
Mārib
Yemen

Khwarazm
R. Oxus   W e s t e r n
Soghdians   T u r k s
Samarqand   Kashgar
Hepthalites
Merv
Khurasan Nishapur   Balkh

SASANIAN
EMPIRE   Ghazni
Sakastan

Kirman   Multān

The Gulf   Daybul

Yamāma   Oman   Ra's al-Hadd

Arabian
Sea

Anglo-
Saxons

Bretons CAROLINGIAN
EMPIRE

⚔ Poitiers
732

AQUITAINE
Narbonne
719–20

Lombards

AVAR
KHANATE

Constantinople

AL-ANDALUS
711–14
• Toledo

BYZANTINE

Sardinia

• Cordova

Sicily

Carthage
698
M
Qayrawān
670
• Pantelleria

Crete

⚔ Ghazwat al-Sawārī
Battle of the
Masts 655

Tangier
708

U

⚔

Subaytila
647

S

L

Tripoli
647

I

Barqa
644
M

Alexandria
641

• Ghadāmis

Babylon
al-Fustāt
641

Egypt

Fazzan

Tibesti

MAKU
Dongola •

Aïr

Bornu-
Kanem

AL

Darfur

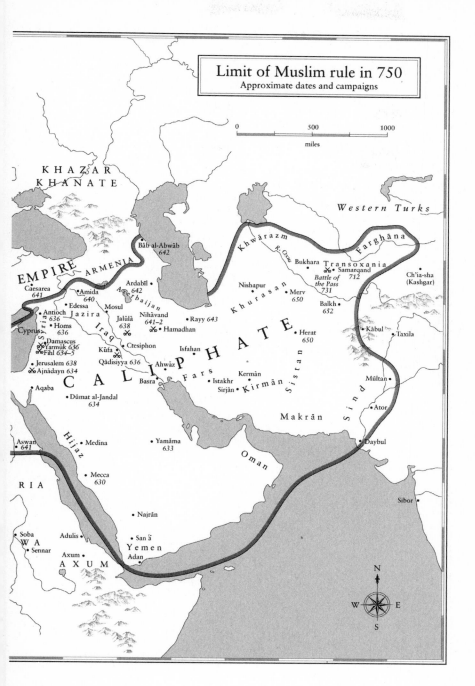

Limit of Muslim rule in 750
Approximate dates and campaigns

0   500   1000
miles

KHAZAR
KHANATE

Western Turks

Bāb al-Abwāb
642

Khwārazm
R. Oxus
Farghāna

Bukhara
Transoxania
Samarqand
Battle of
the Pass
731
712

Ch'ia-sha
(Kashgar)

EMPIRE
ARMENIA

Caesarea
641
Amida
640
Ardabīl
 Azerbaijan
642

Nishapur
Merv
650

Edessa
Mosul

Antioch
636
Jazira
Jalūlā
638
Nihāvand
641–2
Rayy 643
Hamadhan

Khurasan

Balkh
652

Homs
636

Damascus
Yarmūk 636
Fihl 634–5

Kūfa

Ctesiphon

Isfahan

Herat
650

Kābul
Taxila

Cyprus

Syria

Iraq

CALIPHATE

Jerusalem 638
Ajnàdayn 634

Qādisiyya 636
Ahwāz

Fars

Istakhr
Sirjān
Kermān
Kirmān

Sistan

Mūltan

Aqaba

Dūmat al-Jandal
634

Basra

Makrān

Ator

Hijaz

Aswan
641

Medina

Yamāma
633

Oman

Daybul

RIA

Mecca
630

Sibor

Najrān

Soba
WA
Sennar

Adulis

Axum

Sanʿā
Yemen
Adan

AXUM

N
W E
S

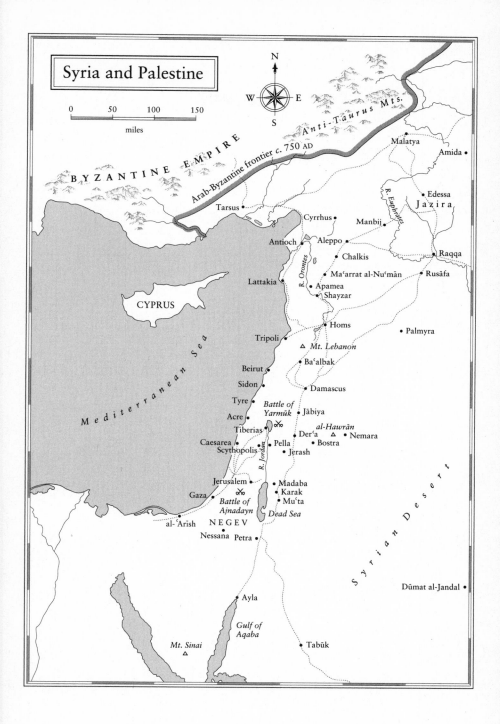

Syria and Palestine

0   50   100   150
miles

N
W E
S

B Y Z A N T I N E   E M P I R E

Anti-Taurus Mts.

Arab-Byzantine frontier c. 750 AD

Malatya
Amida •

Tarsus •

Cyrrhus •

Manbij •

Edessa •

R. Euphrates

J a z i r a

Antioch •

Aleppo •

Chalkis •

Raqqa •

Lattakia •

Ma'arrat al-Nu'mān •

Rusāfa •

R. Orontes

Apamea •
Shayzar •

CYPRUS

Homs •

Palmyra •

Tripoli •

△ Mt. Lebanon

M e d i t e r r a n e a n   S e a

Ba'albak •

Beirut •

Sidon •

Damascus •

Tyre •

Battle of
Yarmūk   Jābiya •

Acre •

al-Hawrān

Tiberias •

Der'a •   △ Nemara

Caesarea •

Pella •   Bostra •

Scythopolis •

Jerash •

R. Jordan

Jerusalem •

Madaba •

Gaza •

Karak •

Battle of
Ajnadayn

Mu'ta •

Dead Sea

al-'Arīsh

N E G E V

S y r i a n   D e s e r t

Nessana •   Petra •

Dūmat al-Jandal •

Ayla •

Gulf of
Aqaba

Mt. Sinai
△

Tabūk •

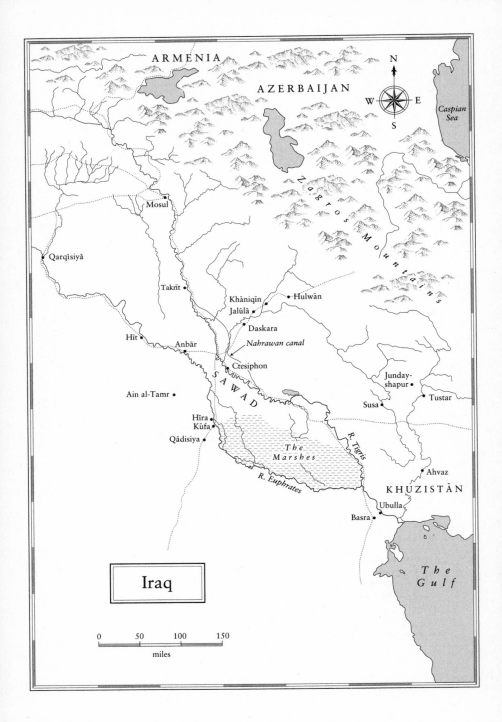

ARMENIA

AZERBAIJAN

N

W E

S

Caspian
Sea

Zagros Mountains

Mosul

Qarqīsiyā

Takrīt

Khāniqīn • Hulwân

Jalūlā

Daskara

Hit

Anbār

Nahrawan canal

Ain al-Tamr

S A W A D

Ctesiphon

Junday-
shapur

Susa • Tustar

Hīra
Kūfa

Qādisiya

*The
Marshes*

R. Tigris

Ahvaz

KHUZISTĀN

R. Euphrates

Ubulla

Basra

Iraq

*The
Gulf*

0   50   100   150

miles

Egypt

Iran

N

W · E

S

Mughan
Steppe

Caspian
Sea

Dihistān

Gūrgān

• Gurgān

Gīlān

Daylam

KHŪ

Qazvin •

Tabaristān

• Bistām

Azerbaijan

Elburz Mts.

Rayy •

Qumis •

Asadābād •

• Hamadhan

• Qumm

• Bisitun

• Nihāvand

Great Salt Desert

Zagros Mts.

• Isfahan

Sūs •

Junday-shapur

• Tustar

Khuzistan

• Rāmhurmuz

Basra •

Arrājar •

• Rashahr

Jannāba •

• Bishapur

• Istakhr

Kāzirūn •

Shīrāz •

• Sīrjān

• Tawwaj

Fars

Bam •

• Jūr

Kirmān

Darabjind •

Sīrāf •

The Gulf

Hurmuz •

Abarkavan
Island

Julfar •

0   50   100 150 200

miles

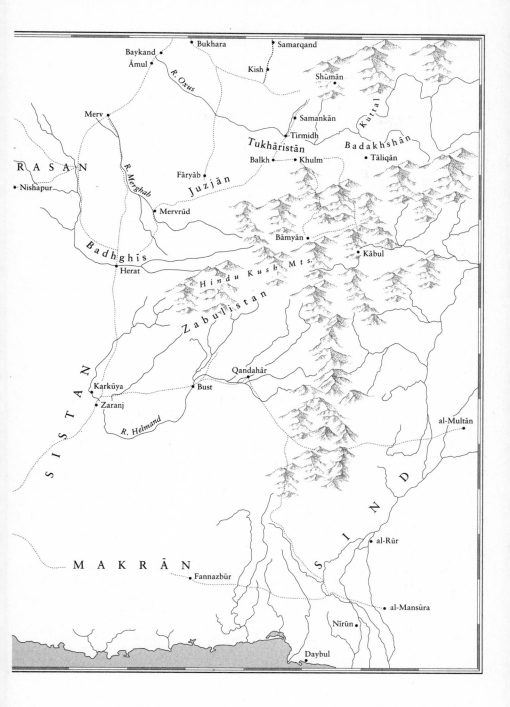

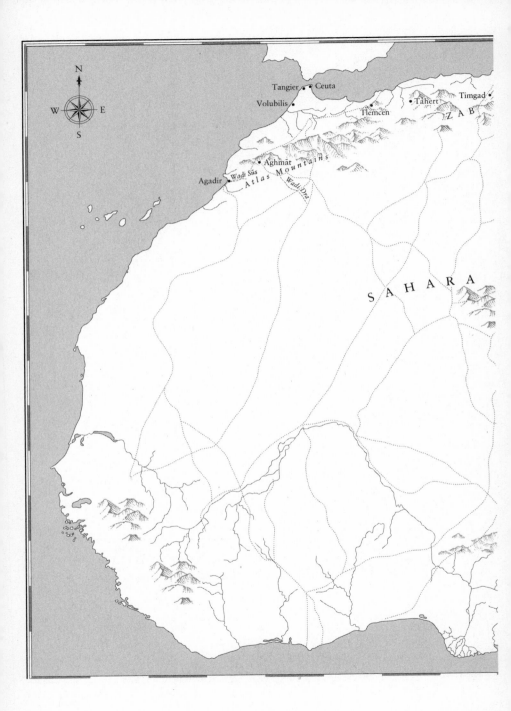

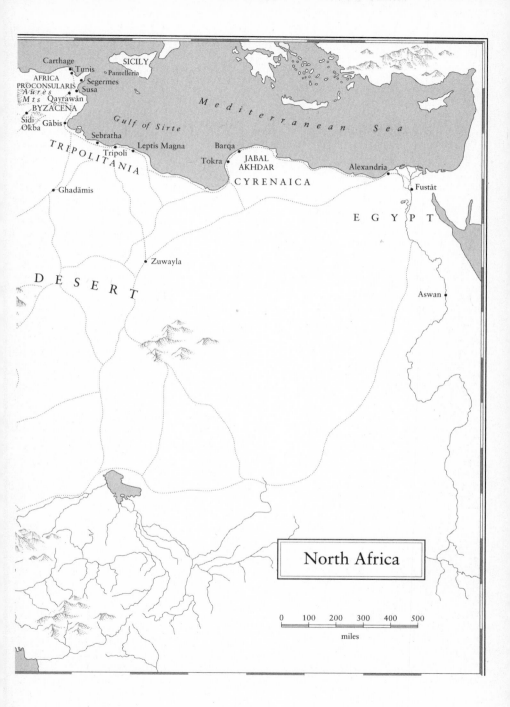

Carthage
Tunis
SICILY
AFRICA
PROCONSULARIS
Segermes
Pantelleria
Aures
Mts
Susa
Qayrawān
BYZACENA
Sidi
Okba
Gābis
Sebratha
Gulf of Sirte
M e d i t e r r a n e a n   S e a
Leptis Magna
Barqa
Tokra
JABAL
AKHDAR
Alexandria
TRIPOLITANIA
Tripoli
CYRENAICA
Fustāt
Ghadāmis
EGYPT
Zuwayla
DESERT
Aswan

North Africa

0   100   200   300   400   500

miles

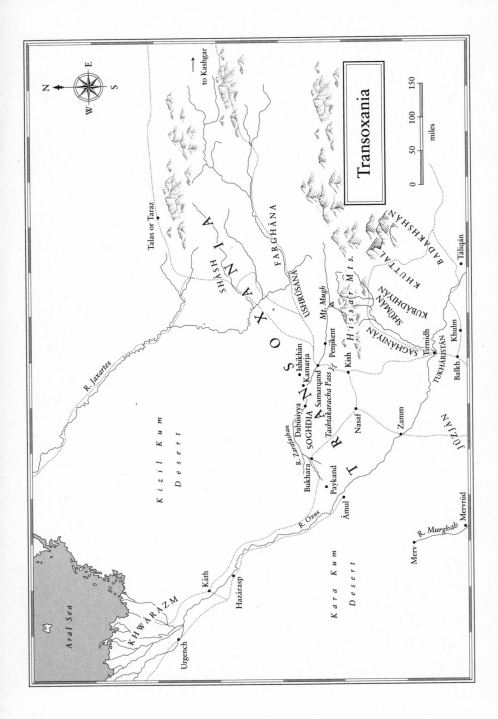

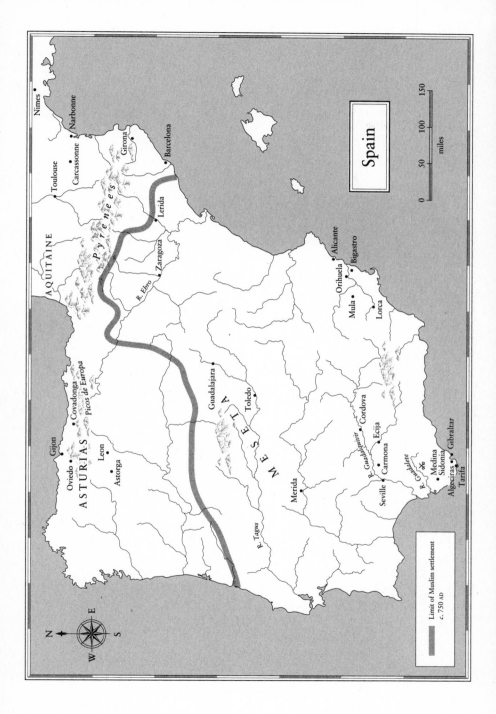

Spain

0 50 100 150
miles

Limit of Muslim settlement
c. 750 AD

Nimes
Narbonne
Carcassonne
Toulouse
AQUITAINE
Girona
Barcelona
Lerida
Zaragoza
R. Ebro
Pyrenees
Alicante
Bigastro
Orihuela
Mula
Lorca
Gijon
Oviedo
Covadonga
Picos de Europa
ASTURIAS
Leon
Astorga
Guadalajara
Toledo
MESETA
R. Tagus
Merida
Cordova
Ecija
Guadalquivir
Carmona
Seville
Guadalete
Medina Sidonia
Gibraltar
Algeciras
Tarifa

N
E
S
W

ACKNOWLEDGEMENTS

I owe many debts of gratitude to people who have helped me and supported me in the writing of this book. The book owes its whole existence to Georgina Capel of Capel & Land who first suggested that I should tackle the vast topic of the early Muslim conquests, and my thanks go to her. I am extremely grateful to the Leverhulme Trust for the award of a research fellowship which enabled me to prepare this work. I am grateful, too, to my colleagues in the School of History in St Andrews who have, over the years, provided such a supportive intellectual environment and so much good friendship. I would also like to thank Penny Gardiner, my editor at Weidenfeld & Nicolson. This is the third book we have worked on together and I owe much to her skill and enthusiasm, and also to Tom Graves for his work on the illustrations. Above all I must acknowledge the contribution of those friends and family who have sustained me in the self-absorbing and sometimes obsessive work. I am very grateful to them all for their patience and understanding.

PREFACE

❧

In the 680s a monk called John Bar Penkāyē was working on a
summary of world history in his remote monastery by the swift-
flowing River Tigris, in the mountains of what is now south-east
Turkey. When he came to write about the history of his own times,
he fell to musing about the Arab conquest of the Middle East, still
within living memory. As he contemplated these dramatic events he
was puzzled: 'How', he asked, 'could naked men, riding without
armour or shield, have been able to win . . . and bring low the proud
spirit of the Persians?' He was further struck that 'only a short period
passed before the entire world was handed over to the Arabs; they
subdued all fortified cities, taking control from sea to sea, and from
east to west – Egypt, and from Crete to Cappadocia, from Yemen to
the Gates of Alan [in the Caucasus], Armenians, Syrians, Persians,
Byzantines and Egyptians and all the areas in between: "their hand
was upon everyone" as the prophet says'.[1]

For John Bar Penkāyē, pious monk that he was, the answer was
clear: this was God's will. Nothing else could account for this wholly
extraordinary revolution in the affairs of men. Now, thirteen centuries
later, in a world where divine intervention is, for many people, not an
entirely satisfactory explanation of major historical changes, this book
is an attempt to suggest different sorts of answers to John's question.

This work concerns three major themes. The first is the story of
the events of the Muslim conquests in so far as we can reconstruct
them. The form of the book is unashamedly narrative. It is a tale of
how a small number (it is unlikely that any of the Arab Muslim armies
consisted of more than 20,000 men and many were much smaller) of
determined and highly motivated men were able to cover vast distances, through rugged and inhospitable lands, to conquer major
empires and kingdoms and to rule their lands. It is a tale of bravery

and daring, but it is also a tale of cruelty and destruction. I hope that this work will, while being true to the evidence, give some impression of these stirring events.

The second theme is that of the settlement of the Arabs after the conquest, where they lived and how they exploited the enormous resources that had fallen into their hands. This, in turn, raises the issue of how the Arabs were able to maintain their own identity and culture in a sea of strange and often hostile people, and at the same time provide an environment that encouraged many of the conquered people to convert to Islam and, in the Fertile Crescent, Egypt and North Africa, to adopt Arabic as their native tongue. This process is essential to understanding the creation and preservation of an Arab Muslim identity that still dominates many of the lands conquered in this period.

Finally, this is also a book about memory and the creation of memories. We have almost no perfectly contemporary records or descriptions of the Muslim conquests. All the accounts passed down to us have gone through several stages of editing and revision, and the addition of new and sometimes spurious information. Other historians have tended to dismiss much of this material because it is not an accurate record of 'what actually happened'. In reality, it is extremely interesting as an expression of social memory, of how the early Muslims reconstructed their past and explained the coming of Islam to the areas in which they now lived. The investigation of the foundation myths of the early Islamic community can tell us much about the world-view of the Muslims in the first century of Islam.

I have attempted to give an account of the history of the Arab Muslim conquests of the Middle East and the wider world as they occurred between the death of the Prophet Muhammad in 632 and the fall of the Umayyad caliphate in 750. The starting date is fairly obvious. Although the roots of the conquests lay in the policies and actions of Muhammad in his lifetime, it was not until after his death that Muslim armies began to invade lands outside the Arabian peninsula. The terminal date is more arbitrary, missing out, as it does, on some important conquests – of Sicily and Crete, for example – but in broad terms, the boundaries of the Muslim world as they were established by 750 remained largely unchanged until the expansion into India around the year 1000.

The Arab conquests had a major impact on human history and the results of these tumultuous years have shaped the world we all live in today. Yet there is nothing inevitable about the Arab/Islamic identity of the Middle East. In the year 632, Islam was confined to Arabic-speaking tribesmen living in Arabia and the desert margins of Syria and Iraq. Most of the population of Syria spoke Greek or Aramaic; most of those in Iraq, Persian or Aramaic; in Egypt they spoke Greek or Coptic; in Iran they spoke Pahlavi; in North Africa they spoke Latin, Greek or Berber. None of them were Muslims. In Egypt and North Africa, lands we now think of as clearly Islamic, there were no Muslims and effectively no Arabic speakers, and the same was true of Iran and Afghanistan. The scale and the speed of the transformation are astonishing; within a century of the Prophet's death, all these lands, along with Spain, Portugal, Uzbekistan, Turkmenistan and southern Pakistan (Sind), were ruled by an Arabic-speaking Muslim elite, and in all of them the local population was beginning to convert to the new religion.

The speed of the Muslim conquests is amazing, but there have been other rapid conquests of vast areas in the course of human history which are in a sense comparable. The conquests of Alexander the Great or Genghis Khan immediately come to mind. What makes the Arab Muslim conquests so remarkable is the permanence of the effect they had on the language and religion of the conquered lands. Spain and Portugal are the only countries conquered at this time where the spread of Islam has been reversed; by contrast we now think of Egypt as a major centre of Arab culture and of Iran as a stronghold of militant Islam.

Clearly so swift and massive a change needs historical investigation, yet the approachable literature on the subject is very restricted. This is partly because of territorial boundaries in the historical profession. The fundamental reference work, *The Cambridge Ancient History*, for example, ends with volume xiv, which takes us up to the assassination of the Byzantine emperor Maurice in 602. *The Cambridge History of Islam* starts off, naturally, with the life and preaching of Muhammad. The gap is reflected much more widely in the way in which history is taught and researched in modern universities: classical/ancient history is separated from medieval/Islamic history. This in turn is partly a consequence of the linguistic divide: historians tend to divide on one hand into those who are competent in the use of Latin and Greek sources, and on the other those who use Arabic and Persian; few, of whom I am certainly not one, feel equally competent and proficient in all.

The nature of the sources has also discouraged historians from trying to give a bold and clear narrative of these world-shaking events. Historians may enjoy controversy over interpretations and approaches, but when it comes to the dates and order of important events, everyone craves certainty. In the story of the great Arab conquests, there are fundamental questions of fact, the order of events in the conquest of Syria, for example, or the date of the battle of Qādisiya in Iraq, about which we simply cannot be certain. In this book I have attempted to construct a plausible narrative of the main events, but it would be wrong to claim that this is the only possible reconstruction, or to hide the fact that I have made choices and judgements that are sometimes based as much on probability and likelihood as on firm evidence.

There is also what one might, to use a popular contemporary cliché, call the elephant-in-the-room syndrome: the subject is simply so large and so obvious that scholars are reluctant to tackle it, preferring to work on smaller projects around the edge of the room where they feel comfortable in their own discipline. It may be impossible, it may be rash and foolish to try, but this book is an attempt to describe and investigate this particular historical pachyderm.

In doing so, I am standing on the shoulders of giants. This work shamelessly plunders and exploits the excellent scholarship of the last few decades. At the risk of being unduly selective, I would single out Fred Donner's *The Early Islamic Conquests*, Mike Morony's *Iraq after the Muslim Conquest*, Walter Kaegi's work on military history, Dick Bulliet on conversion to Islam, Robert Hoyland on non-Muslim views of early Islam and Larry Conrad and Chase Robinson on historiography. I have also depended on works of older generations of historians, who still have much to teach us – Hamilton Gibb on the Arab conquests in Central Asia, Vasili Vladimirovich Barthold on Turkistan, Alfred Butler on the Arab conquest of Egypt. My debts to these, and to other scholars living and dead, will be readily apparent to anyone familiar with the field.

This is a narrative history, heavily dependent on narrative sources. The nature and formation of these stories are discussed at some length in the Foreword, but I should say a few words about how I have treated them. The narratives of the early Muslim conquests are replete with confusion and improbability, and are often impossible to accept at face value. Modern authors have tended to approach these in two ways: either to dismiss them as hopelessly inaccurate and not worth the attention of serious historians; or to cherry-pick them for incidental details, names, places, etc. I have tried to do something slightly different: to read and use the stories for what they are trying to tell us; to work with the flow, so to speak, rather than against it, to surf the waves of the narrative and be carried along with it. This does not mean accepting the early Arabic accounts as accurate records of 'what actually happened', but accepting them as reflections of seventh- and eighth-century Muslim social memory and using them as such.

A particular case in point is the use of direct speech. The early Arabic accounts are full of records of conversations and oratorical set pieces and I have often quoted these in direct speech. This should not be taken to mean that I believe that these words were actually spoken on the occasion described. There are, however, good reasons for taking this approach. The speeches are often the means whereby different points of view are articulated in the sources. Descriptions of councils of war, for example, allow the author to discuss the issues and choices that faced the Muslim armies, to show why they did what they did and to explore the roads not taken. The second reason is to reflect the nature of the Arabic material and be true to it, especially for readers who are unfamiliar with the field, and to give texture and variety to what might otherwise be a bald and unexciting narrative.

This book is an attempt to tell the story of one of the most important changes in world history, a change whose results have profoundly affected the world in which we live today. I have tried to make it accessible, even entertaining, to student and general reader alike. No doubt scholars in the future will produce works that are fuller, more profound and more elegant; but if this work gives rise to wider reflections on these momentous events, it will have served its purpose.

TERMS AND CONDITIONS

This book is concerned primarily with the conquest of the central Islamic lands by Muslim armies in the century that followed the death of the Prophet Muhammed in 632. In order to clarify the issues it is important to attempt to define some terms. 'Conquest' may seem at first a fairly uncontentious term, implying the subjection of one party to another through the application of military force. In reality, however, things may be more complicated. The Arabic sources use the term conquest (*fath*) to describe the taking over of the lands of the Byzantine and Persian empires. The *fth* root in Arabic implies 'opening', but in the conquest literature it clearly implies the use of force. Conquest can, and did, take many different forms. At one extreme it meant the brutal and violent sack of a city, the pillaging of its wealth and the execution of many or all of its defenders. The sacking of Istakhr in Fars or Paykand in Transoxania are clear examples of this. But conquest was often a more peaceful process. The people of town and country would agree to the imposition of terms, usually involving the payment of tribute and the promise that they would not aid the enemies of the Muslims. The terms were agreed to because of the use, or threat of the use, of force. At the other extreme, conquest might be little more that the sending of a message accepting overlordship. Many of the more mountainous areas of Iran, North Africa and Spain must have been 'conquered' without an Arab ever having visited the area, still less settling down to rule and tax it. 'Conquest' meant different things to different people in different places at different times.

Conquest, Settlement and Conversion

The early Muslim conquests meant the imposition of a new political and religious elite on the lands conquered. The conquest was often followed by a process of settlement in which numbers of Arabs, many from nomad backgrounds, took up permanent residence in the conquered territories, often in specially founded new towns. While conquest and settlement took place comparatively quickly, and in the central Middle East were largely complete by 650, the conversion of the subject people to Islam was a slow and long-drawn-out process, and it was not until the tenth and early eleventh centuries that the majority of the population was converted to Islam. Conquest and settlement took only a decade; conversion of the majority took three hundred years.

Arabs and Muslims

The term Arab can only be usefully and simply defined as anyone whose mother tongue is Arabic. In 632 Arabs inhabited the Arabian peninsula and the Syrian desert and its margins. As the conquest proceeded, however, more and more people became Arabic speakers and numerous men who had no 'Arab blood' in their veins nonetheless spoke Arabic as their native tongue. In many areas where assimilation between conquerors and conquered advanced most rapidly, the differences between Arab and non-Arab had become very blurred by the end of the first Islamic century.

In 632 almost all Muslims were Arabs, and in the early years of the conquests we can use the terms Arab and Muslim interchangeably to describe the armies of the conquest. When we move into the late seventh and early eighth centuries, however, such a usage would be misleading. Arabs formed only a proportion of the Muslim armies that conquered North Africa, Spain and Central Asia. What defined these armies was not their Arabness, even if the leaders were Arabs and the language of command and administration Arabic, but their identity as the armies of Islam – that is, religious identity had replaced the ethnic.

If not all Muslims were Arabs, likewise not all Arabs were Muslims. Before the coming of Islam, large numbers of Arabs had been converted to Christianity, especially in those areas of the Syrian desert which bordered on Byzantine territory. Some of them retained their Christian faith after the conquests, and their status proved a problem for the Muslim jurists of the eighth century: should they be treated as subject people and obliged to pay the hated poll tax or should they be treated as Muslim Arabs? In some cases a compromise was reached whereby they just paid the alms tax, but at twice the rate of their Muslim counterparts.

Romans and Byzantines

Historians are accustomed to talking about the Byzantine Empire to describe the Eastern Roman Empire. It is a convenient term to designate the Christian, Greek-speaking and -writing empire of the seventh and eighth centuries. It is also completely out of touch with the language of the people at the time. No one at that or any other time ever described themselves in normal life as 'Byzantines'. They themselves knew that they were Romans and they called themselves as such, though they used the Greek term *Romaioi* to do so. Their

Muslim opponents also knew them as *Rūm*, or Romans, and this term was often extended to include the Latin Christian inhabitants of North Africa and Spain. Despite the violence it does to the language of the sources, I have, with some reluctance, accepted the general scholarly usage and refer to Byzantines and the Byzantine Empire throughout.

Kharāj *and* Jizya

The Arab conquerors always demanded payments in cash from the people they conquered. In later centuries, this public taxation was divided by the Islamic lawyers into two distinct categories, *kharāj* or land tax and *jizya* or poll tax, paid only by non-Muslims. At the time of the conquests, however, the terms were much more blurred and *jizya* was used to describe any sort of tax or tribute.

Christian Churches

At the time of the Muslim conquests there were five major churches or sects in the Middle East, each one claiming to be 'orthodox'. In North Africa and Spain the church was Latin-speaking and looked to Rome rather than Constantinople for leadership and doctrinal authority. There was no schism between this church and the Greek Orthodox, that would come later, but there was a different ecclesiastical culture. Then there was the Melkite (meaning 'royal') Greek Orthodox church supported (usually) by the imperial government in Constantinople. This was also known as the Chalcedonian church because it followed the doctrines on the nature of Christ adumbrated at the Council of Chalcedon in 451, and the Diophysite church, because it believed in the two natures, human and divine, within the person of Christ. Within the eastern Empire the main opposition to this established church came from the Jacobite Monophysite communities in Syria and the Monophysite Copts in Egypt, all of whom believed in the single and indivisible nature of Christ. They were known as Jacobites in Syria after the missionary Jacob Baradaeus (d. 521) who was the effective founder of the separate Monophysite ecclesiastical hierarchy. The Nestorian Church, named after its founder Nestorius (d. *c.* 451) who had been Patriarch of Constantinople before being deposed for heresy, was opposed to both the Monophysites and the Diophysites. Persecution had largely eliminated the Nestorian Church from Byzantine territory but it continued to flourish in the lands of the Persian Empire, especially Iraq, where Nestorians constituted the majority of the population. Finally, there was the Monothelite sect supported by the emperor Heraclius and his government. There is an old Scottish story about the stranger who approaches a small town and asks a local man how many churches there are in it, Scotland having almost as many different sects as the late antique Middle East. The local replies, 'Well, there used to be two but then we had a union so now there are three'. This is essentially what happened during the reign of Heraclius. In an effort to bridge the damaging gap between the Monophysite and Diophysite churches about the nature of the incarnation, Heraclius and his theological advisers came up with a subtle compromise formula called Monothelitism. Inevitably this pleased neither party, and his attempts to enforce this new doctrine in the Middle East and North Africa simply provoked more discontent.

NOTES AND BIBLIOGRAPHY

I have used endnotes sparingly in this work to avoid over-burdening the text with scholarly apparatus. I have contented myself with noting the main sources used, the origins of direct quotes and the most relevant secondary literature. In the case of the two primary sources I have depended on most, the *History of the Prophets and Kings* by Ṭabarī and the *Conquests of the Lands* by Balādhurī, I have given references to the original Leiden editions. Readers who wish to consult the English translations will find the references to the editions in the margins of the translated texts.

The bibliography is similarly restrained. A full bibliography, including all the literature on late antiquity and early Islam, would run to thousands of titles. My intention has been to confine myself to the works I have made best use of and those that I consider will be most relevant and accessible to the reader who wishes to explore the subject further.

A Note on Transliteration and Names
There are now standard and acceptable ways of transliterating Arabic letters in Latin script. I have not adopted any of these in their entirety.

For a non-Arabist, it is not very helpful to be able to distinguish between the two types of *h* or *s* or *t* and readers who do know the language will in any case be aware of these. Arabic has both long and short vowels and these I have indicated in most cases. It does seem to me helpful to know, for example, that the name of the great conqueror of Syria, Khālid b. al-Walīd is pronounced Khaalid b. al-Waleed, rather than, say Khaleed b. al-Waalid. Put simply, ā is pronounced as a long aa, ī as an ee and ū as an oo and the stress falls on these long syllables.

I have also marked the Arabic letter ᶜayn as ᶜ when it comes in the middle of words. The ᶜayn is a consonant peculiar to Arabic whose pronunciation can only be learned by imitation. It is perhaps most helpful to think of it as a gutteral prolongation of the previous vowel. The symbol ' (Arabic *hamza*) is a simple glottal stop.

Arabic names come from a variety of different traditions. Some are biblical in origin: Ibrāhīm is Abraham, Ishāq is Isaac, Yūsuf is Joseph, Mūsā is Moses and Yahyā is John. Some names like Umar, Amr, Uthmān and Alī were purely Arabic without any religious con- notations. There were also names describing the holder as a slave (*abd*) of God in any of His names, most commonly Abd Allāh but also others like Abd al-Malik (slave of the King), Abd al-Rahmān (slave of the Merciful).

Men were named after their fathers, thus Ibn (usually abbreviated to 'b.') Fulān (Fulān meaning 'so and so'). We also find men called Ibn Abī Fulān, 'son of the father of so and so'. Women were known as Bint Fulān, 'daughter of so and so' or, more commonly, as Umm Fulān, 'mother of so and so'. In the early days of Islam, most Arabs would also have had a tribal name or *nisba* such as Tamīmī (from the tribe of Tamīm) or Azdī (from the tribe of Azd).

The spelling of place names presents problems of a different sort. In general I have used conventional English names where they exist, thus Damascus not Dimashq, Aleppo not Halab etc. In the case of names like Azerbaijān, where there is a modern equivalent, I have preferred the forms used by the *Times Atlas of the World*. In the case of older and more obscure Arabic names, Yarmūk or Qādisiya for example, I have transliterated the Arabic, using the spellings given in Yāqūt's thirteenth-century geographical dictionary, the *Muᶜjam al-Buldān*.

Coins

The conquest narratives place great emphasis on the dividing up of money and the payment of taxes. At first the Muslims used the coins already in circulation in the areas they conquered, notably the Sasanian silver *drachm*, known in Arabic as the *dirham*. The *dirham* was a thin silver coin slightly over 2 centimetres in diameter and weighing about 3 grams. The Muslims began to mint these, at first with counter-struck Sasanian models, by the 660s. More valuable was the gold *dīnār*, a small coin about a centimetre in diameter based on the Byzantine *nomisma* which began to be minted during the caliphate of Abd al-Malik (685–705). From this time, all Islamic coins were purely epigraphic, with Arabic inscriptions but no images. In both North Africa and Spain, some early Muslim coins carried Muslim formulae translated into Latin.

FOREWORD:
REMEMBRANCE OF THINGS PAST

⚜

Our understanding of the Arab conquests of the seventh and eighth centuries is based on written and, to an extent, archaeological sources. At first glance these sources look abundant; vast numbers of pages of Arabic chronicles describe these triumphs in loving and admiring detail. The conquered people, particularly the Christian clergy of all denominations, contribute a different view, while the mass of archaeological evidence, especially from the lands of the Levant, gives us yet another. On closer investigation, however, none of these sources is as clear or easily usable as it first appears: all have to be sifted and used with care, and, despite the length of the narratives, there are still many aspects of the conquests about which we have virtually no information at all.

Any historical enquiry is inevitably shaped by the nature of the source material on which it is based. Partly this is a question of reliability, or 'can we believe what we read?'. At its most simple it is a matter of asking who wrote a text, what they wanted to convey and whether they were biased in favour of one side or another. The ways in which the sources define the enquiry, however, go much further than considerations of reliability and party prejudice. The interests of the authors and compilers of texts determine what questions we can ask. For example, in investigating the Arab conquests we can ask what battles were fought and who participated in them. If we want to look in more detail at the face of battle, however – why one side prevailed and the other was defeated – we come up against a wall of ignorance because the writers on whom we depend were simply not interested in pursuing these questions. The level and area of discussion are defined by the ancient authors, and there are many roads down which we simply cannot go. It is not possible to write a history of the Muslim conquests full of those tidy battle maps beloved of most historians of warfare, in which divisions of foot soldiers are shown clearly in square black boxes while bold arrows show how the cavalry manoeuvred around them. If this book does not discuss many of the questions that are normally dealt with in military history – commissariat and the supply of provisions, for example – it is not because these topics are uninteresting, but rather because we have no information that would enable us to answer them. An understanding of the scope and limitations of the documents is crucial to understanding the strengths and weaknesses of my account of the Arab conquests.

The Arab conquests of the Middle East directly affected the lives of millions of people, many of them literate in a part of the world in which the culture of writing had been developed for millennia. Yet very few of them thought to write down what they had seen and experienced. The number of contemporary accounts of those crucial decades, the 630s and 640s, can be counted on the fingers of one hand; even the ones that we do have are fragmentary and very slight.

The lack of contemporary eyewitness accounts does not mean that we have no historical evidence at all for what went on in these momentous decades. On the contrary, we have a vast number of narratives that purport to tell us what happened. The problem for the historian is that they are mostly episodic, discontinuous and frequently contradict each other – and sometimes themselves. It is often impossible to know what to believe and accept as a reasonably accurate account of events that actually happened. In a way more interesting, however, is what they offer in terms of the attitudes and the memories different groups preserved and cherished about what had gone on.

The Middle East conquered by the Muslims in these early decades was a multicultural society, a world where different languages and religions coexisted and intermingled in the same geographical area. After the success of the conquests, the language of the new elite was Arabic. Even for government, however, the existing administrative languages – Greek in Syria and Egypt, Middle Persian (Pahlavi) in Iraq and Iran, Latin in Spain – continued to be used for the business of government. After a couple of generations, however, this began to change. Around the year 700, sixty or more years after the earliest conquests, the Umayyad caliph Abd al-Malik (685–705) decreed that Arabic and Arabic alone was to be used in the administration. The decree was surprisingly effective. From this time, anyone wanting a position in the expanding bureaucracy of the Islamic state, whether they were Arab or non-Arab by descent and upbringing, needed to be able to read and write in Arabic. The inscriptions on the new style, image-free coins and the roadside milestones were all in Arabic. There was no point for most people in learning Greek or Pahlavi because there were no career opportunities in them. It was around this time, in the early eighth century, that the Arabic traditions of the conquests began to be collected and written down.

The momentous events of the seventh and eighth centuries inspired an extensive Arabic-language literature which claimed to describe what had happened then. But the memories and narratives of the Muslim conquest were more than the records of 'old forgotten far-off things and battles long ago'. They were the foundation myths of Muslim society in the areas that generated them. They were developed because they helped to explain how Islam had come to the land and to justify the defeat and displacement of the previous elites. These accounts did not deal with ethnogenesis, the birth of peoples, as Latin historians of the early medieval West did, but rather with the birth of the Islamic community. They preserved the names of the heroes who had led the armies of the conquest and were the founding fathers of the Islamic state in their area; the names of the companions of the Prophet, men who had met and heard Muhammad and brought with them a direct connection with his charisma; the names of the caliphs who had turned Islamic armies in their direction.

These narratives do provide information about the course of events, and just as interestingly they show how these events were remembered by later generations, how they saw the beginnings of the community in which they lived. Looked at as a form of social memory, the distortions and legends that can seem at first sight an obstacle to our understanding can be seen instead as reflecting the attitudes and values of this early Muslim society.

In the form in which they have come down to us, these accounts were edited in the ninth and early tenth centuries; that is, between 150 and 250 years after the events. The Arabic narratives are rarely simple accounts written by a single author and telling a straightforward account of events. They are actually multi-layered compositions that have gone through different stages of editing and elaboration for different purposes at different times. At the risk of oversimplifying a complex process, the narratives seem to have gone through three stages of development. The first was oral transmission of traditional stories of heroic deeds in battle. Such traditions were often preserved within tribes and kinship groups or among Muslims who had settled in particular areas. In part they may have preserved these memories as their predecessors had treasured accounts of the battles of the Arab tribes in the years before the coming of Islam. The ancient tradition of recording the triumphs and tragedies of pre-Islamic warfare certainly coloured the way in which the battles of the first Islamic conquests were remembered. Like their ancestors in the *jāhiliya* (time of ignorance) before the coming of Islam, they composed and preserved poems and songs to celebrate heroic deeds. As well as these ancient, traditional themes, the Muslims could also remember their victories as clear evidence that God was on their side, the deaths of their enemies and the vast quantities of booty they amassed all being evidence of divine favour: no one could question the essential rightness of what they had done. They also preserved, elaborated and even made up accounts to serve new purposes, to justify claims to stipends or rights to enjoy the proceeds of taxation. Men who could prove that their ancestors had participated in the early conquests felt entitled to salaries from public funds; the inhabitants of cities might hope for lighter taxation because they had surrendered peacefully to the Muslim armies. In short, the stories of the conquests were preserved, not because of interest in producing a clear historical narrative, but because it was felt to be useful. Correspondingly, material that was not useful, the exact chronology of events, for example, was consigned to oblivion.

The next stage was the collection and writing down of this oral material. It is not easy to say exactly at what stage this occurred because Arabic, like English, uses expressions like 'He says (in his book)' so verbs of speech may actually refer to writing, but the process was certainly begun during the eighth century. These collections seem to have been made for antiquarian reasons, to preserve the record of the early years of Muslim rule in Iraq or Egypt when the memories were fading and there was a risk that much of this important story would fall into oblivion. The practical considerations that had led to the preservation of these traditions in the first place had, by now, become largely irrelevant, but of course the collections assembled by these editors necessarily reflected the purposes of the earlier narrators.

The ninth and early tenth centuries saw a vast explosion of writing and book production. The introduction of paper to replace parchment (dried animal skins) as the main writing material[1] meant that writing became both quicker and cheaper. Historical writing increased as part of this, reflecting a growing demand for historical information, both in the circles around the courts of the caliphs and among the wider literate society of Baghdad and the rest of Iraq. In Baghdad, where there was a real book trade, it became possible to make a living writing for a wider public, not just for a rich patron. Knowledge became professionalized, in the sense that men could make a career out of it.

Knowing your history, being an authority, could lead to an appointment at court. The historian Balādhurī, whose *Book of Conquests* is one of the main sources on which we rely, seems to have made a living as a *nadīm* or 'boon-companion' at the Abbasid court. Every boon-companion was expected to bring some knowledge, expertise or talent to the party: some were poets, some authorities on quaint or unusual Arab vocabulary or the characteristics of different geographical areas. Surely Balādhurī owed his position to the fact that he knew so much about the conquests and other areas of early Islamic history, for he was a great authority too on the genealogies of the ancient Arab tribes. This was all despite the fact that he does not seem to have come from an important family and was not himself a descendant of the participants. The greatest of these compilers was Tabarī (d. 923). He was a Persian who came from a landowning family in the area along the south shores of the Caspian Sea. He spent most of his adult life in Baghdad and became a great authority on two of the most important areas of Muslim learning, the interpretation of the Koran and the history of Islam. He seems to have lived a quiet bachelor life, subsisting off the revenues of his family estates, which were brought to him by pilgrims from his homeland as they came through Baghdad on their way to Mecca and Medina. He made it his task to collect as much as he could of the writings of his predecessors and edit them into one mighty compilation. He also attempted, with considerable success, to order it. He adopted an annalistic framework in which the events of each year were recorded under the number of the year. He was not the first Arab writer to use this method, which may in turn have been inherited from the Greek tradition of chronicle writing, but no one else had used it to present such a vast amount of information. In many ways, his work made the individual publications of his predecessors redundant and virtually all later accounts of the history of the early Islamic world in general, and of the Muslim conquests in particular, were based on his mighty opus.

Much of the material found in these early Arabic narratives of the conquests takes the form of vivid stories about events. These are not recounted in a continuous prose, as a modern historian would present them, but rather in short anecdotes known in Arabic as *akhbār* (singular *khabr*). Tabarī, and other editors of the ninth and tenth centuries, made no effort to streamline this formula and produce a single linear account. Each of these *akhbār* is a distinct self-contained account, sometimes only a few lines long, sometime three or four pages, but seldom more. The several anecdotes are often grouped together, discussing the same event, or very similar events, but the details are changed: events happen in different orders; different people are credited with the same heroic deeds; the names of the commanders of Arab armies in the great battles of the conquests are not the same. The editors of the ninth and tenth centuries usually avoided making judgements about which of these accounts might be correct. They are frustratingly undecided in their approach and often seem to be simply presenting all the evidence and implicitly inviting the reader to make up their own mind.

In many cases the editors give their sources in some detail in the form of an *isnād*, 'I was told by X who was told by Y who was told by Z who was an eyewitness'. This device was really the equivalent of footnotes in modern academic writing, citing reputable sources. This *isnād* was designed to prove that the material was genuine, and to do that it was important that all the names in the list were men (or occasionally women) of good standing who would not appear to be the sort of people who might sink to making things up. It was also important to show that the people in the chain of information had lived at the right times, so that it would have been possible for them to have communicated this information to the next generation. By the tenth century a whole academic discipline had developed, producing vast biographical dictionaries in which one could look up the details of all the individuals in the chain to check on their credentials.

Modern readers will note immediately that there are some obvious problems with this procedure because it provides few ways of ensuring the reliability of the material, problems of which the people at the time were very well aware. There was clearly a mass of fabricated material about these events in circulation, but the editors of the ninth and tenth centuries had exactly the sort of problems we do in trying to sort out truth from things that were simply invented.

The authors of the original anecdotes of the conquests and the editors were extremely interested in certain sorts of information, annoyingly uninterested in other things. They include numerous verbatim speeches, supposedly made by great men, often before battle is joined. These are reminiscent of the speeches put into the mouths of Greek and Byzantine commanders by classical historians in the same situation. The Arabic narratives, however, often include a number of speeches made by different participants in what is presented as a council of war: the Arabic sources give a picture of a more consensual, or perhaps more debated, process of military decision-making. Obviously, in the absence of stenographers or tape recorders, such speeches are very unlikely to be a true record of what was said. On the other hand, they are certainly authentic documents of the eighth or early ninth century, if not of the seventh. They must reflect the attitudes of the Muslims at that time to these events: the historian cannot simply dismiss them.

Another characteristic of these anecdotes is what has been described as onomatomania, the obsession with knowing the names of the participants involved in events. Of course, this applies only to Arab Muslim participants: the Arabic sources give us versions of the names of the most important enemy generals but that is as far as it goes, opposing armies being simply an anonymous mass. The listing of Arab names is done with loving care and precision, a really scientific delight in identifying men, the tribes from which they came and the groups in which they fought. The problem for the historian is that these lists frequently contradict each other. Furthermore, there are some examples in which later versions of the story seem to have access to more names than earlier ones do. This is deeply suspicious for modern historical sensibilities. The anecdotes seem to grow details as they are handed on from one generation to the next. It is clear that some of this detail is elaborated in response to questions like 'Who were the main commanders at the battle of Nihāvand?' No narrator would like to confess ignorance; better to make up some plausible names than reveal the limitations of your knowledge. In other cases, the names are clearly preserved by the descendants and fellow tribesmen of the participants. In the seventh century it was a matter of considerable practical importance. If your father or grandfather had participated in those first glorious battles, Qādisiya in Iraq or Yarmūk in Syria, you benefited in both money and status. By the mid eighth century these relationships had largely lost their practical value. No one, except the members of the ruling family and, sometimes, the descendants of the Prophet and Alī, continued to benefit from this system. By this time people got paid because of the military or bureaucratic jobs they did rather than what their forefathers had done. Nevertheless, being related to these early heroes still carried some social cachet. Among the English aristocracy there is still, according to some, prestige to be derived from the belief that 'My ancestors came over with the Conquest', meaning in this case the Norman conquest of England in 1066. Something of the same snobbery, if you like, may have been present among some of these status-conscious Muslims.

Another subject of consuming interest to the early historians was whether towns and provinces had been conquered peacefully (*sulhan*) or by force (*anwatan*). In the early years after the conquests this was an issue with major practical implications. If cities were taken by peaceful agreement, the inhabitants were usually guaranteed their lives and properties and they were only required to pay in taxation that global sum which had been recorded in the treaties. If they had been taken by force, on the other hand, then their property was forfeit and the levels of taxation much higher. Perhaps most importantly and onerously, the non-Muslim inhabitants would have had to pay the poll tax. We know very little about how towns and townspeople were taxed in the first century of Muslim rule (almost all our material relates to the taxation of rural areas and agricultural land), but the nature of the conquest may have made a significant difference to both the tax status and the security of property of the inhabitants in the early years. Deciding how a city had been conquered and what tribute had been paid could be a matter of crucial practical importance, and it is a subject of obsessive interest to the early historians. In the nature of these things, however, the truth of the matter was often quite unclear.

Conquest was often a messy business; some people resisted, others capitulated. In recording it almost everyone had a vested interest in one version of events or another. A variety of convenient fictions were elaborated to explain the confusion. One, of which Damascus is the most striking example, is that different parts of the city fell in different ways at the same time. So in Damascus in 636 we have the Arab general Khālid b. al-Walīd storming the East Gate, while at the very same moment another commander, Abū Ubayda, was making an agreement with the inhabitants of the western sector. The two armies met in the city centre. In this way, the issue of whether Damascus had been taken by force or had surrendered peacefully remained debatable. Another useful explanation was that places were conquered twice; the first time the inhabitants made a treaty and were accorded the privileges of peaceful surrender, but later they rebelled and the area had to be reconquered by force. Antioch in Syria and Alexandria in Egypt were two places where this is recorded. This may of course have happened, even if the 'rebellion' was simply a refusal or inability to pay the tax agreed, but we cannot overlook the possibility that such accounts are attempts to reconcile differing versions which are themselves a reflection of disputes over taxation and the fiscal status of conquered areas.

Like the issue of who had participated in the conquests, the issue of peaceful or violent conquest no longer had the same resonance when the compilations on which we rely were put together in the ninth and tenth centuries. There is no evidence that the taxation of different areas was determined by the nature of a conquest that had occurred at least two centuries before. By this time these debates were of largely antiquarian interest, or rather they formed part of the general political culture with which bureaucrats and boon-companions were supposed to be familiar. We should not, however, overlook the fact that the survival of this material in the sources long after it had ceased to be of practical utility strongly suggests that it originated in the early years after the Muslim conquest: no one would have had any incentive to make it up at a later date. The details must have been preserved at a time in the early formative years of the Islamic state when they still had a real, practical purpose.

The writers and compilers of these early traditions also seem to have been obsessed with the question of the distribution of booty after a city or area had been conquered. There was never any doubt that pillage was acceptable and the victors were fully entitled to the spoils of war. The point at issue was how it should be divided up among the conquerors. Should everybody get the same amount? Should horsemen get more than foot soldiers? Should men who had participated in the campaign but not the actual battle get a share as well? If so, how much? How much should be sent to the caliph in Medina as his share? This interest certainly reflects the delight with which many of these rough-and-ready Bedouin soldiers seized and made use of the accoutrements of civilized life, but the stories are really about justice and fairness (but only among the conquerors, of course). They like to recount how the booty was divided up justly and transparently, in an open field after the battle before the eyes of all. Such narratives are clearly part of a cult of the 'good old days' when the Muslims were all brave and pure of heart and justice was done under the stern gaze of the caliph Umar (634–44). These 'good old days' were cherished and developed in a later world which seemed to have lost this early innocence, when the descendants of the original conquerors felt that they were being marginalized and excluded from what they saw as their just rewards. These ancient memories of better times were doubly precious as affirmations from the past and pointers to a better future.

If the historians show keen interest in some aspects of the conquests, they are much less concerned with others which may seem to our eyes much more important. The account of the battle of Qādisiya in Iraq, that marked the decisive end of Persian power in Iraq in Tabarī's *History*, takes up some two hundred pages in the English translation, yet the course of the battle remains frustratingly obscure. Admittedly it is very difficult to be certain about the actual progress of the military action even in more recent conflicts, but this vagueness makes it almost impossible to provide convincing answers to the crucial question of why the Byzantine and Sasanian armies which tried to prevent the Arab invasions of their territory performed so badly. We are sometimes told in bald and stark terms that the fighting was hard but eventually the Muslims prevailed. Sometimes too their opponents are driven into rivers or ravines and large numbers are killed in that way. There are a number of reports that both Byzantine and Sasanian troops were chained together to prevent them fleeing from the battlefield; this is not real historical information but a topos to show how the Muslims were inspired by faith while their opponents were coerced by tyranny.[2] This may have been true, but the stories as presented tell us nothing about the real military reasons for defeat.

Perhaps even more exasperating for the modern historian is the vagueness about chronology. This is a particular problem of the earliest phases of the conquests. We are given dates ranging over three or four years for the great victories of Yarmūk and Qādisiya. The ninth- and tenth-century editors were quite happy to keep it that way and simply admit that there were these many different opinions. In the absence of corroborative accounts from outside the Arabic tradition, we are often quite uncertain as to the true date of even the most important events in early Muslim history.

So what can a modern historian, attempting to reconstruct the course of events and analyse the reasons for the success of Muslim arms, make of all this? Since the nineteenth-century beginnings of scientific research in the field, historians have wrung their hands and lamented the disorganization of the material, the apparently legendary nature of much of it and the endless repetitions and contradictions. Alfred Butler, writing on the conquest of Egypt in 1902, lamented the 'invincible confusion' of the sources while some of the material he dismissed simply as 'fairy stories'.

Historians have long been aware of the confused and contradictory nature of much of this material, but in the 1970s and 1980s a much more wide-reaching challenge was mounted to the reliability of any of these traditions. Albrecht Noth in Germany observed how many of the conquest narratives were formulaic set pieces, topoi, which appeared in numerous different accounts and were transferred, as it were, from one battlefield to another. Accounts of how cities fell to the Arabs because of the treachery of some of the inhabitants are found in so many different cases and are expressed in such similar language that they can hardly all be true. At almost the same time, Michael Cook and Patricia Crone in London argued that the sources for the life of Muhammad and early Islam more generally were so riddled with contradictions and inconsistency that we could not be certain of anything; the very existence of Muhammad himself was questioned.[3]

The result of this critical onslaught was that many historians, even those not convinced by all the revisionist arguments, have been reluctant to take these narratives seriously or to rely on any of the details they contain. I am of a different opinion. There are a number of reasons why we should return to this material and try to use it rather than dismissing it out of hand. The first is that Arabic accounts can sometimes be checked against sources outside the Arabic literary tradition, the Syriac Khuzistān Chronicle, for example, or the Armenian history of Sebeos, both accounts written by Christians within a generation of the events they describe. They are much shorter and less detailed than the Arabic accounts but they tend to support the general outlines of the Arabic history. On occasion they even support the detail. For example, the Arabic sources say that the heavily fortified city of Tustar fell to the Muslims because of the treachery of some of the inhabitants, who showed the Muslims how to enter through water tunnels. Such elements have often been dismissed as formulaic and valueless since we find similar accounts of the conquests of other towns and fortresses. In this case, however, the local Khuzistān Chronicle, a Syriac Christian source quite unconnected with the Muslim tradition, independently tells more or less the same story, suggesting strongly that the city did fall in the way described. This implies that the Arabic sources for the conquest of Tustar, and perhaps by extension for other areas too, are more reliable than has been thought.

We can go further with the rehabilitation of the Arabic sources. Many of them can be traced back to compilers in the mid eighth century, men like Sayf b. Umar. Sayf lived in Kūfa in Iraq and died after 786. Beyond that we know nothing of his life, but he is the most important narrative source for the early conquests. Medieval and modern historians have suspected that he fabricated some of his accounts, but the most recent scholarship suggests that he is more reliable than previous authors had imagined. He is certainly responsible for collecting and editing many of the most vivid accounts of the early conquests.[4] Sayf was writing little more than a century after the early conquests and it is possible that some of the participants were still alive when Sayf was a boy. Furthermore, the later conquests in Spain and Central Asia were still under way in his lifetime. Sayf was as close in time to the great Muslim conquests than Gregory of Tours was to the early Merovingians or Bede to the conversion of the Anglo-

Saxons, both sources on which historians have always relied for the reconstruction of these events.

There is a further dimension to these sources, the dimension of social memory. James Fentress and Chris Wickham have pointed out how traditional accounts, which may or may not be factually accurate, bear memories of attitudes and perceptions which tell us a great deal about how societies remember their past and hence about attitudes at the time of their composition.[5] The conquest narratives should be read as just such a social memory. In this way the early Arabic sources are very revealing of the attitudes of Muslims in the two centuries that followed the conquests. If we want to investigate the *mentalités* of early Islamic society, then these sources are of the greatest value. The tendency among some historians has been to denigrate the narratives: if instead we try to go with the narrative flow, to read them for what they are trying to tell us, they can be much more illuminating.

One of the key issues that the sources address is the difference between the Arab Muslims and their opponents, their differing habits, attitudes and values. The Arab writers do not analyse these issues in any formal sense but instead explore them in narrative. Let us take, as an example, one narrative among the hundreds that have come down to us from the eighth and ninth centuries. It comes in the *History of the Conquests*, compiled in its present form by Ibn Abd al-Hakam in the mid ninth century.[6]

The story begins with an account of how the Muslim governor of Egypt, Abd al-Azīz b. Marwān (governor 686–704), came to Alexandria on a visit. While he was there he enquired whether there were any men still alive who remembered the conquest of the city by the Muslims in 641, at least half a century previously. He was told that there was only one aged Byzantine, who had been a young boy at the time. When asked what he recollected from that time, he did not attempt to give a general account of the warfare and the fall of the city but instead told the story of one particular incident in which he had personally been involved. He had been friends with the son of one of the Byzantine patricians (a generic term the Arabic sources use for high-ranking Byzantines). His friend had suggested that they went out 'to take a look at these Arabs who are fighting us'. Accordingly the patrician's son got dressed up in a brocade robe, a gold headband

and a finely decorated sword. He rode a plump, sleek horse while his friend the narrator had a wiry little pony. They left the fortifications and came to a rise from which they looked down on a Bedouin tent outside which there was a tethered horse and a spear stuck in the ground. They looked at the enemy and were amazed by their 'weakness' (meaning their poverty and lack of military equipment) and asked each other how such 'weak' men could have achieved what they did. As they stood chatting, a man came out of the tent and saw them. He untied the horse, rubbed it and stroked it and then jumped up on it bareback and, grabbing the spear in his hand, came towards them. The narrator said to his friend that the man was clearly coming to get them so they turned to flee back to the safety of the city walls, but the Arab soon caught up with his friend on the plump horse and speared him to death. He then pursued the narrator, who managed to reach the safety of the gate. Now feeling secure, he went up on the walls and saw the Arab returning to his tent. He had not glanced at the corpse or made any effort to steal the valuable garments or the excellent horse. Instead he went on his way, reciting Arabic, which the narrator reckoned must have been the Koran. The narrator then gives us the moral of the tale: the Arabs had achieved what they had because they were not interested in the goods of this world. When the Arab got back to his tent he dismounted, tied up his horse, planted his spear in the ground and went in, telling nobody about what he had done. When the story was over, the governor asked the man to describe the Arab. He replied that he was short, thin and ugly, like a human swordfish, at which the governor observed that he was a typical Yemeni (south Arabian).

At first glance this story is hardly worthy of serious reading, let alone retelling. The Muslim conquest of Alexandria was an event of fundamental importance, marking as it did the end of Byzantine rule in Egypt and the extinction of 900 years of Greek-speaking rule in the city. The historian devotes two or three pages to it. He tells us nothing of the nature of the siege, if there was one, where the armies might have been deployed or any of the military details we would like to know. This trivial anecdote occupies almost all the space he allows for the event. Furthermore there is no real evidence that it is true, in the sense of describing an event that actually occurred, and even if it was, it would not be very interesting: the protagonists are anonymous and the death of one man had no significant effect on more general events. On further consideration, however, this anecdote is quite revealing. For a start the telling of it is put into a historical context. It may not be a true record of what happened in 641 but it does appear to be a genuine artefact of the late seventh century. The Umayyad governor wanted to find out more about the circumstances in which the province he now ruled over became part of the Muslim world. Like the historians and compilers of his generation, he was engaged in recovering and recording these memories before they disappeared for ever. The story itself stresses some familiar themes. The Byzantines are wealthy and complacent, unused to the rigours of warfare. Furthermore the text shows sharp divisions of class and wealth between the son of the patrician and the narrator. The Arab, by contrast, lives a life of privation and austerity in his tent. Unlike the upper-class Byzantine he is an excellent horseman, having a close and affectionate relationship with his mount and being able to leap on to it and ride bareback. He is also, of course, a skilled and hardened spearsman. After the death of the patrician, he shows his religious zeal by reciting the Koran and his lack of concern for material goods by not stopping to strip the corpse of his victim. The governor's concluding question about the appearance of the man allows the narrator to describe a small, wiry, ill-favoured individual. In a way, this is a surprisingly unflattering portrait, but it too makes a point; the man is described as typically Yemeni. Most of the Arabs who conquered Egypt were of Yemeni or south Arabian origin. The governor, in contrast, came from the tribe of Quraysh, the tribe of the Prophet himself, a much more aristocratic lineage. However, the author who is said to have preserved this anecdote was himself a Yemeni, from the ancient tribe of Khawlān. Khawlān were not Bedouin in the traditional sense but inhabited an area of villages in the mountainous heart of Yemen. Their descendants, still called Khawlān, live in the same area today. Khawlānis played an important part in the conquest of Egypt and were prominent among the old established Arab families of Fustāt (Old Cairo) in the two centuries that followed. The author clearly developed the anecdote as a way of emphasizing the important role of his kinsmen, and of Yemenis in general, in the conquest of the country they now lived in.

The anecdote is also making a point about the ways in which the Muslims thought of themselves as different from, and more virtuous than, the Christians who surrounded them and who were certainly at this stage much more numerous. It makes a political point too about the role of Yemenis in the conquests and the way in which the governor should respect them for their achievements at this time. The final redactor, Ibn Abd al-Hakam, in whose work we find the story, was writing at a time in the mid ninth century when these old Yemeni families were losing their influence and special status as Turkish troops employed by the Abbasid caliphs of Baghdad came to take over military power in Egypt. By pointing out the heroism of this early generation, he is making a point about the rights and status of his own class in his own day. The story has clearly been refashioned along the way, but it preserves a social memory of the hardiness, piety and Yemeni identity of the conquerors. This memory was preserved because it was valuable to those who kept it alive, but it also reflects the reality of the environment, if not the detail, of the conquests themselves.

The Arabic historiography also varies greatly in quality and approach. In general, the accounts of the first phases of the conquests, from the 630s to the 650s, are generally replete with mythical and tropical elements, imagined speeches and dialogue and lists of names of participants. They are correspondingly short of details about topography and terrain, equipment and tactics. The accounts of the conquests of Egypt and North Africa owe something to a local historiographical tradition, but in both cases this tradition is disappointingly thin. The conquests of the early eighth century are very differently reported. The accounts of the expeditions in Transoxania, collected and edited by the writer Madā'inī and published in Tabarī's *History*, are by far the most vivid and detailed we have of any of the major campaigns of the period. They are full of incident and action, heat and dust, and recount the failures of Arab arms just as fully as the successes. Nowhere else can we get as close to the reality of frontier warfare. The account of the conquest of Spain in the same decades is in striking contrast. The narratives are thin, replete with folkloric and mythical elements, and date, in their present form, from at least two centuries after the event: the best endeavours of generations of Spanish historians have failed to penetrate the confusion.

Alongside the newly dominant Arabic, there were other, older cultural traditions which produced their own literature. Of course,

some people continued to write in the old high-culture language of
Greek. The most famous of these was John of Damascus, the most
important Greek Orthodox theologian of the eighth century. He came
from a family of bureaucrats of Arab origin who worked for the
Umayyad administration in Damascus in the same way as their
ancestors had worked for the Byzantines. But St John, as he came to
be known, belonged to the last generation to use Greek as a primary
language of business, and he was no historian. We have no surviving
local Greek historiography of the Arabic conquests. Of course, people
continued to write history in Greek across the Byzantine frontier,
where Greek endured as the language of government. It is interesting,
however, that the main Greek account of this period, written by the
monk Theophanes in Constantinople, seems to be dependent for its
information on Arabic or Syriac accounts, translated into Greek.
There is no independent Byzantine tradition to provide a check on
the Arabic narratives.

For the historian of this period, the Syriac tradition is more important than the Greek. Syriac is a written dialect of Aramaic, a Semitic
language, not very different from Hebrew and Arabic but using its
own distinctive script. For centuries it was the common vernacular
speech of the Fertile Crescent, understood alike by subjects of the
Byzantine emperor in Syria or the Persian King of Kings in Iraq.
Christ and his disciples would have spoken it in their everyday lives.
It is still spoken in a few places, notably the small Syrian town of
Ma'lūlā, a largely Christian community isolated, until recently, in
a rocky mountain gorge north of Damascus. With the coming of
Christianity to Syria, the Bible was translated into Syriac, and in many
rural areas far away from the Greek-speaking cities of the coast, the
church liturgy and all religious writing was in Syriac, the language the
local people could understand.

The Syriac historiography of the early Muslim world comes mostly
from an ecclesiastical background. As in early medieval Europe, most
of the chroniclers were monks or priests, and their concerns were first
and foremost for the monastery and the world around it. They are
interested as much in unseasonably harsh weather and rural hardships,
both of which directly impinged on the life of the monastery, as they
are in wars and the comings and goings of kings. Above all they are
concerned with the politics of the Church, the great deeds of famous

saints, the rivalries for ecclesiastical office, the evildoing of corrupt and, worst of all, heretical churchmen. In this world of village, mountain and steppe, the arrival of the Arabs is viewed with the same apprehension as frost in May or the coming of a plague of locusts: they are a burden imposed by the Lord on the faithful which is probably a punishment for their sins and, in any case, has to be endured with as much stoicism as possible. Perhaps strangely to modern eyes, there are no exhortations to the local people to arm themselves and attack their oppressors. The moral is rather that people should remain faithful to their Church and God would preserve them.

There is a literature of resistance but it is an apocalyptic literature. These writings look forward to a day when a great king or emperor will destroy the domination of the Arabs and usher in a coming of the end of the world. Present hardships and tyranny will be ended, not by the human agency of those who are being oppressed, but by divine and superhuman intervention. This writing is in many ways weird and wacky and the twenty-first-century reader may easily wonder how anyone believed it or even took it seriously. But it does provide an essential insight into the thought world of that great mass of the people of the Fertile Crescent who were conquered and submitted to these new alien invaders. Helplessness and fatalism, learned from generations of distant and unresponsive rule, seem to have deterred such people from taking up arms in their own defence: better to rely on prayer for the present and the coming of a long-promised just ruler for the future.

There were other non-Muslim traditions of historical writing. In the remote fastnesses of the Caucasus mountains, the Armenians continued a tradition of historical writing which lasted from the coming of Christianity in the fourth century all through the Middle Ages. For the time of the Muslim conquests, the chronicle of Sebeos provides a few tantalizing pages of information which largely corroborate the broad outlines of the Arabic tradition.[7] For the conquest of Egypt there is the Coptic chronicle of John of Nikiu, bishop of a small town in the Nile Delta and a contemporary eyewitness.[8] This survives only in an Ethiopic translation, some of the narrative is lost and much of the rest is muddled and confused. For Spain there is a Latin chronicle produced in the south in the area under Muslim rule and known, from the year of the final entry, as 'the Chronicle of 754'. Finally the eighth century saw the emergence of an Arabic-language Christian chronicle-writing tradition which drew on both Christian and Arabic traditions. These chronicles are sometimes nearly contemporary with the events they describe and the information that they give us is invaluable, but their brevity and fragmentary nature mean that they leave many questions unanswered.

Although the Christian chronicles are often frustratingly short, vague and confused they do provide both a check and an antidote to the material found in the much more voluminous and apparently more polished products of the Arabic tradition. The Arabic sources are almost exclusively interested in the doings of Muslims. The only infidels who get speaking parts in the chronicles are the Byzantine emperors and Persian generals whose deliberations form a prelude to their inevitable defeats. An outsider reading Tabarī's vast *History of the Prophets and Kings*, for example, would have very little idea that the vast majority of the population of the lands ruled by the caliphs in the eighth and ninth centuries were not Muslim, still less any understanding of their concerns and the effect that the coming of the Arabs had on them. As long as they paid the money agreed, and were not actively hostile to the new regime in any way, their doings could be, and were, completely ignored in the narratives of the ruling elite.

The written sources are extensive but very problematic. Can we supplement them by turning to the archaeology? Surely the unemotional testimony of mute material remains can give us a more balanced account than these overwrought stories? To an extent this is true, but the archaeology, like the written records, has its limitations and in a way its own agenda.

To begin with it is clear that there is no direct archaeological testimony to the conquests themselves. No battlefield has yielded up a harvest of bones and old weapons, there is not a single town or village in which we can point to a layer of destruction or burning and say that this must have happened at the time of the Arab conquests. All the archaeological evidence can do is provide a guide to longer-term trends, the background noise to the coming of the Muslims.

Another problem is the patchy nature of this evidence. There has been a great deal of excavation and survey of sites in Syria, Jordan and Palestine/Israel accompanied by a lively critical debate about the evidence and its interpretation. Across the desert in Iraq, the position is very different. Political problems over the last thirty years have meant that the sort of investigation and questioning which have been so fruitful in the Levant have simply never happened on any large scale. The same is true to some extent in Iran. Here the Islamic Revolution of 1979 brought a virtual halt to excavation and survey and, though a new generation of Iranian archaeologists are beginning to take up the challenge, the debate about the transition from Sasanian to Islamic rule in the cities of Iran has hardly begun.

One area in which the archaeology has illuminated the coming of the Muslims is the question of the state of population and society in the Middle East at the time. Again Syria and Palestine provide the best example. There has been a lively debate in recent years about the fate of Syria in late antiquity. There is little doubt that the whole of the Levant enjoyed a period of almost unprecedented economic and demographic growth in the first four decades of the sixth century. The question is whether this flourishing continued until the coming of the Arabs almost a hundred years later. There are no records or statistics that will tell us this and the narrative sources can only provide glimpses. The archaeological evidence from towns and villages suggests, however, that the second half of the sixth century and the beginning of the seventh was a period of stagnation, if not absolute decline. Cities do not seem to have expanded and some, like the great capital of the east at Antioch, can be shown to have contracted, consolidating within a reduced circuit of walls. The evidence is often ambiguous: very rarely does the archaeological record demonstrate that a certain place or building was clearly abandoned. We can see that the great colonnaded streets, bath-houses and theatres of antiquity were invaded by squatters or turned over to industrial use as pottery kilns. It is less clear what this means for the prosperity of the town: did it become a half-abandoned ruin-field or was a plentiful and vigorous population simply using the city in different ways and for new purposes? Much of the evidence can be read both ways.

Furthermore, the archaeology has been bedevilled by contemporary political concerns. There is one commonly held view that Palestine in particular was a flourishing and wealthy area until the coming of the Arabs destroyed this idyll and reduced much of the area

to desert. Such views have been espoused by Zionists and others who
have used the fate of Palestine to suggest or even argue that the Arabs
were destructive rulers who are, by implication, unworthy to rule the
area today. This view has been challenged, not least by other Israeli
archaeologists, who have demonstrated that, at least in some cases,
the changes and decline popularly associated with the coming of the
Arabs had been well under way before. There is also evidence of
development of markets (in Bet She'an and Palmyra, for example) and
bringing of new lands under cultivation along the desert margins of
Syria. The archaeological evidence is problematic and ambiguous,
contested territory, and its interpretation often owes more to the
preconceptions of the investigator than to hard science.

We are on firmer ground when looking at the constructive aspects
of early Muslim rule.[9] It is generally much easier to determine when
buildings were constructed than when they fell into disuse. We can see
the footprint of Islam in many of the cities that the Arabs conquered
as mosques were constructed in many urban centres. Mosques, like
churches, can be easily identified from their plans, the rectangular
enclosure, the columned prayer hall and above all the mihrab, or
niche, which points the worshipper in the direction of Mecca. Literary
sources tell us that mosques were constructed shortly after the conquest in many cities. There is, however, no surviving archaeological
evidence for this. It is not until the very end of the seventh century,
at least sixty years after the conquests, that the first testimony of
Muslim religious architecture appears with the construction of the
Dome of the Rock in Jerusalem after 685. Within a hundred years of
the conquests, there were mosques in Damascus, Jerusalem, Jerash,
Amman, Ba'albak in Syria, Fustāt in Egypt, Istakhr and possibly Susa
in Iran. There must have been mosques in Iraq and other parts of
Iran, indeed historians and Arab travellers tell us about them, but
nothing seems to have survived to give archaeological confirmation.
The religious buildings in Jerusalem (the Dome of the Rock) and
Damascus (the Umayyad Mosque) have both miraculously survived
the thirteen centuries since they were built to demonstrate more
eloquently and forcefully than any literary text the wealth and power
of the early Islamic state. The Umayyad-period mosques at minor
settlements like Ba'albak and Jerash show how Islam had spread into
the smaller towns of Syria. The mosques show that Islam was in the

ascendant a hundred years after the initial conquests, but they tell us nothing about the course of those conquests or the reasons for Muslim victory.

If the mosques are a clear indication of the arrival of a new order, it is more difficult to tell how the everyday life of the population might have changed. In many areas the picture is one of continuity. The Muslim conquest did not, for example, bring in new kinds of pottery to Syria. Local ceramics, everyday cooking- and tableware, continued to be produced under Muslim rule as they had been under Byzantine government. Not surprisingly, the incoming Arab conquerors simply purchased and used what they found. It was not until two or three generations later that the first Muslim styles appeared, and even then they were fine wares, for court and elite use. The pottery of everyday life remained largely unaffected. There is, however, one change in the ceramic record which we can observe, and that is the disappearance of large-scale pottery imports into Syria from across the Mediterranean Sea. In late antiquity there had been massive imports of the tableware known to archaeologists as African Red Slip, which was manufactured mostly in Tunisia. This had been distributed as a sort of piggyback trade along with the grain and oil that the province exported throughout the Roman Empire. The disappearance of this ware from the markets of the lands conquered by the Muslims indicates a break in commercial contacts which reflects the picture that we have in the written sources of the eastern Mediterranean as a zone of conflict rather than a highway of commerce. Again, the archaeology can be used to demonstrate the long-term effects of the conquests, but not the course of events at the time.

The Arab conquests of the Middle East are among the epoch-making changes in human history. The sources we have for understanding these tumultuous events are hemmed in by many limitations. We cannot always, perhaps ever, find answers to the questions we most want to ask, yet by treating the evidence with respect, and working with it, we can come to a fuller understanding of what was happening.

1

THE FOUNDATIONS OF CONQUEST

⊶⟊⟊⊷

The Muslim conquests of the Middle East originated in Arabia, and most of those who fought in the first phases of the conquest came from the Arabian peninsula or the Syrian desert that lies to the north. At no time either before or after the Muslim conquests did the inhabitants of these areas conquer huge empires beyond the vague and shifting frontiers of their homeland. For the first and only time, the coming of Islam mobilized the military energies and hardiness of the peoples of the Arabian peninsula to invade the world that surrounded them. What sort of place was it that produced these warriors, and what sort of men were they that they could create this massive revolution in human history?

The Arabian peninsula is vast. A straight line from the south-east point of Arabia at Ra's al-Hadd in Oman to Aleppo at the north-west corner of the Syrian desert is over 2,500 kilometres long. Relying on animal transport, a journey along this route would take well over a hundred days of continuous travel. Coordination of men and armies over so vast a distance was not easy, and it was only the particular circumstances of the early Islamic conquests that made it possible.

Much of Arabia is desert, but all deserts are not the same. If the Inuit have a thousand words for different sorts of snow, the nomads of Arabia must have almost that number for different sorts of sand, gravel and stones. Some desert, like the famous Empty Quarter of central southern Arabia, is made up of sand dunes, a landscape where no one can live and only the hardiest, or most foolish, pass through. But most of the desert is not quite like that. The surface is more often gravel than sand, desolate but easy to traverse. To the outsider, most desert landscapes look formidably bleak. The land is often flat or marked by hills – low, rolling and anonymous – with the few plants in the wadis (dry river beds) thorny and unappealing to most of us. This landscape looks very different to the Bedouin who inhabit it. For them, the rolling hills all have their names and identities – almost their own personalities. The gullies of the wadis, whether flat or stony, each offer different possibilities. The desert landscapes of Arabia were well known to their inhabitants and, we can almost say, cherished. The poets of ancient Arabia delighted in naming the hills and valleys where their tribes had camped, fought and loved. For them, the desert was a land of opportunity, and a land of danger.

The Arabic-speaking nomads of the desert are conventionally known in English as Bedouin and this is the terminology I shall use. Arabs are recorded in the desert from Assyrian times in the early first millennium BC on. They were a permanent feature of the desert landscapes, but for the settled people of the Fertile Crescent, on whose writings we rely for information, they were very much the 'Other' – noises off, sometimes intruding on to the settled lands to pillage and rob, but always to return, or be driven back, to their desert fastnesses. The Arabs had little political history and in ancient times their chiefs lived and died without leaving any traces for posterity, save in the memories of their fellow tribesmen and followers. In the third century AD we begin to find Arabs making a more definite impression on the records. It was during this period that Queen Zenobia, from her base in the great oasis trading city of Palmyra, deep in the Syrian desert, created a kingdom that encompassed much of the Middle East. It took a major campaign by the Roman emperor Aurelian in 272 to bring this area under Roman control again. Zenobia's empire was transitory but, for the first time, Arabic speakers had demonstrated their ability to conquer and, briefly, control the cities of the Fertile Crescent.

In the rocky landscapes south-east of Damascus, where the black basalt rocks of the fertile Hawrān give way to the gravel and sand of the Syrian desert, stood the Roman fort at Nemara. Nemara was one of the remotest outposts of the Roman world; far away from the porticoes and fountains of Damascus, it was a lonely outpost, almost lost in the scorching empty desert that stretched all the way to Iraq. Outside the walls of the fort lay a simple grave with an inscribed tombstone. It was written in the old Nabataean script of Petra, but the language is recognizably Arabic. It commemorated one Imru'l-Qays, son of Amr, king of all the Arabs, and extolled his conquests as far away as the lands of Himyar in Yemen. It also tells us that he died

'in prosperity' in AD 328. The tombstone is extremely interesting: a
lone document of the period, it shows the development of the idea of
the Arabs as a group with their own separate identity, distinct from
Romans, Nabataeans and others. We do not know whether Imru'l-
Qays died of old age, in his tent, or on a hostile raid against Syria, on
a peaceful trading mission to the Roman world or, as some Arab
sources suggest, as a convert to Christianity. His resting place sym-
bolizes both the separate identity of the early Arabs and their close
interactions with the Romans and Persians who ruled the settled lands
that bordered their desert homes.

In the sixth century AD, this nascent Arab self-awareness developed
further. At this time the Fertile Crescent was dominated by two great
empires, the Byzantines in Syria and Palestine and the Sasanian Persians in Iraq. Both of these great powers had problems with managing
the nomad Arabs along the desert frontiers of their domains. The
Romans had, with typical Roman efficiency, erected forts and built
roads so that their troops could guard the frontier, the *limes*, and keep
the rich cities and agricultural land of the interior safe from the
depredations of the nomads. This system was hard to maintain; it was
difficult to keep men to garrison remote forts like Nemara and it was
above all expensive. If we knew more about the Sasanian Persians, we
would probably find that they were encountering similar problem
themselves.

During the course of the sixth century, both great powers tried to
find alternative ways of managing the desert frontier, and they turned
to client kingdoms. In effect they used Arabs to manage Arabs. On
the frontiers of Syria the Byzantines worked through a powerful
dynasty known to history as the Ghassānids. The Ghassānid chiefs
were given the Greek administrative title of phylarch and were paid
subsidies to keep the Bedouin friendly. Through a mixture of payment,
diplomacy and kinship alliances, the Ghassānids managed the desert
frontier, acting as the interface between the Byzantine government
and the nomads. They also became Christians, albeit of the Monophysite sect, which was increasingly regarded as heretical by the
authorities in Constantinople. The Ghassānid chiefs lived an attractive
semi-nomadic lifestyle. In the spring, when the desert margins are
vivid green with new herbage, they would camp at Jābiya in the Golan
Heights and the tribal chiefs would come to visit, to pay their respects

and, no doubt, to receive their cash. At other times they would hold court near the great shrine of the warrior St Sergius, at Rusāfa in the northern Syrian desert.[1] They did not settle in the Roman town but built a stone audience hall about a mile to the north. They would pitch their tents around this and Arabs would come on pilgrimage to the shrine of the saint and visit the Ghassānid phylarch.

A thousand miles away across the Syrian desert to the east, the Lakhmids, managers of the desert margins for the Sasanian kings, also held court. The Lakhmids seem to have been more settled than the Ghassānids and their capital at Hīra, just where the desert meets the richly cultivated lands along the lower Euphrates, was a real Arab town. Like the Ghassānids, the Lakhmids were Christians. They were also great patrons of the earliest Arabic literature. Poets and story-tellers flocked to their court, and it was probably here that the Arabic script, soon to be used for recording the Koran and the deeds of the early conquerors, was perfected. A strong Arab identity was emerging, not yet ready to conquer great empires, but possessing a common language and, increasingly, a common culture.

Many Arabs lived as Bedouin in tribes, following a nomadic lifestyle and living quite literally in a state of anarchy, of non-government. These nomads depended on their flocks, above all on sheep and camels. The different sorts of animals led to different patterns of subsistence. Camel-rearing was the life-support system of the nomads of the inner desert. Camels can survive for two weeks or more without water, and this gave the Bedouin the capacity to move far away from the settled lands and take advantage of scattered grazing and remote water sources in areas where none of the armies of the imperial powers could hope to pursue them. Ovocaprids, sheep and goats, are much less self-sufficient. They need to be watered every day, cannot survive on the rough, sparse herbage that can sustain camels and need to be taken to market when the time comes for them to be sold and slaugh-tered. Sheep nomads lived within striking distance of the settled lands and had a much closer interaction with the settled people than the camel nomads of the inner desert. The camel nomads were more completely independent. Almost immune from attack in their desert fastnesses, they were the real warrior aristocracy of the Arabs.

Tribes, rather than states or empires, were the dominant political forces in the desert, and sometimes reading accounts of the early years of Islam and the great conquests, it is easy to get the impression that tribal loyalties and tribal rivalries were as important in motivating the Arabs to fight and conquer as the new religion of Islam or the desire for booty. But in reality, tribal loyalties were more complex and varied than at first appears. The Arabs pictured themselves as living in tribes. Each tribesman believed that all the members of the tribe were descended from a common ancestor and called themselves after him, so the tribe of Tamīm would call themselves, and be called by others, the Banū Tamīm. In reality this self-image was a bit misleading because large tribes like the Tamīm never met together and had no single chief or common decision-making process. The crucial choices about where to camp, where to find grazing and how to avoid the enemy were made in much smaller tenting groups, even by individual families. Furthermore membership in tribes was not entirely determined by biological descent. Men could and did move tribe to attach themselves to new groups. A successful leader might find that his tribe had increased in number quite dramatically while a failed chief would find his men slipping away. Because they thought in biological links, however, men would not say that they changed tribe but rather that they must have been in some way part of that kin all along.

Indeed, without kin a man and his family could not survive in the desert. This was an almost unimaginably harsh environment. Beasts might die, grazing fail, wells dry up and enemies pounce. There was no police force, not even a corrupt and inefficient one, no ruler to whom the victim could appeal: only the bonds of kinship, real or fictional, could protect a man, offer help in times of need, offer protection or the threat of vengeance in time of attack. A man without kin was lost. In some ways the early Muslim leadership set out to destroy or at least reduce the loyalty to tribe. The Muslim community, the *umma*, was to be a new sort of tribe, based not on descent but on commitment to the new religion, the acceptance that Allāh was the one true God and that Muhammad was his prophet. The *umma* would offer the protection and security that people had previously been given by their tribe. In reality it was not easy to dismantle the tribal loyalties that had served men so well for so long. In the early years of the conquests, men fought in tribal groups and gathered round their tribal banners on the field of battle. During these wars, members of the tribe of, say, Tamīm must have fought alongside fellow tribesmen whom they had never met and possibly had never heard of before. When they were settled in the new military cities in Basra and Kūfa in Iraq or Fustāt in Egypt, they were placed in tribal groups. When it came to the struggle for resources, for salaries and booty, tribal rivalries acquired a fierce and brutal intensity which they had seldom had in the more open and scattered society of the desert. Far from being diminished by the new religion of Islam, tribal solidarities were in some ways reinforced by the events of the conquest. It would be wrong, however, to overestimate the role played by tribes. In reality tribal loyalties were crucially important to some people at some times, literally a matter of life and death, but at other times they were disregarded, ignored and even forgotten.

Tribes were led by chiefs, normally called *sharīf* (pl. *ashrāf*) in early Muslim times. Leadership within the tribe was both elective and hereditary. Each tribe or sub-tribe would have a ruling kin, brothers and cousins from whom the chief would normally be chosen. While there was no formal election, tribesmen would offer their loyalties to the most able, or the luckiest, member of the ruling kin. Chiefs were certainly chosen for their ability as war leaders, but bravery and skill in battle were far from being the only qualities required. A chief needed to be a skilled negotiator, to resolve quarrels between his followers before they got out of hand, and to deal with members of other tribes and even the imperial authorities. Chiefs also had to have intelligence – the sort of intelligence which meant that they knew where the fickle desert rain had recently fallen, and where they could find the small but succulent patches of grazing that would mean their followers and their flocks could eat and drink well. To do this, a successful chief needed to keep an open tent. The famed hospitality of the Bedouin was an important part of a complex survival strategy: guests would certainly be fed and entertained but in exchange they would be expected to provide information about grazing, warfare and disputes, prices and trading opportunities. Without these informal communication networks, news of the coming of Islam could never have spread through the vast, nearly empty expanses of desert Arabia, and the armies that were to conquer the great empires could never have been assembled.

With a very few exceptions, all adult male Bedouin could be described as soldiers. From an early age they were taught to ride,

wield a sword, use a bow, travel hard and sleep rough, finding their
food where they could. In conditions of tribal competition there were
no civilians. The Bedouin lived in tents, painted no paintings and built
no buildings: they are virtually invisible in the archaeological record.
They did, however, excel in one major art form: their poetry. The
poetry of the Arabs of the *jāhiliya* (the period of 'ignorance' before
the coming of Islam) is a unique and complex art form. Among later
Arab critics it has often been held up as a model of poetic form, to be
admired rather than imitated. Some modern scholarship has questioned its authenticity, but the general consensus is that at least some
of the material offers a witness to the ideals and mindsets of the pre-
Islamic Arabs.

Later Arab commentators emphasized the central importance of
poets to this society. An Arab literary critic writing in the ninth century
noted that 'in the *jāhiliya* poetry was to the Arabs all they knew and
the complete extent of their knowledge', and Ibn Rashīq, writing in
the mid eleventh century, describes the importance of the poet to his
kinsmen:

> When there appeared a poet in the family of the Arabs, the other
> tribes round about would gather to that family and wish them joy of
> their good luck. Feasts would be got ready, the women of the tribe
> would join together in bands, playing on lutes as they did at weddings
> and the men and boys would congratulate one another: for a poet was
> a defence to the honour of them all, a weapon to ward off insult to
> their good name and a means for perpetuating their glorious deeds
> and establishing their fame for ever.[2]

The poet, in fact, performed a number of important functions, encouraging tribal solidarity and *esprit de corps*, defending the reputation of
his group and preserving their memory for posterity.

The poetry is firmly set in the Bedouin desert environment. Much
of it adheres to the fairly strict formula of the *qasīda*, a poem of perhaps
a hundred lines, spoken in the first person, describing the loves and
adventures of the poet, the excellence of his camel, the glories of his
tribe or patron. The virtues of which he boasts are the virtues of a
warrior aristocracy. He is brave and fearless, naturally, he can endure
great hardships, he has admirable self-control and he is an irresistible

lover and a great hunter. Poets are often subversive, even outlaw characters, seducing other men's wives with shameless enthusiasm, and they often see themselves as loners, one man and his camel against the world. There is no sign of formal religion, no mention of a deity, just the power of blind fate, the threatening beauty of the desert landscape.

For an example of the battle poetry of the period we can turn to a poem ascribed to Āmir b. al-Tufayl. He was a contemporary of the Prophet Muhammad and he and his tribe had pastures in the Hijaz around the city of Tā'if. Much of his life seems to have been spent in battle and, though he himself died a peaceful death, his father and numbers of his uncles and brothers are said to have been slain in tribal conflicts. In one of his poems he revels in a dawn attack on the enemies of his tribe:

> We came upon them at dawn with our tall steeds, lean and sinewy
>   and spears whose steel was as burning flame
> And swords that reap the necks, keen and sharp of edge, kept carefully
>   in the sheaths until time of need
> And war-mares, springing lightly, of eager heart, strongly knit
>   together, not to be overtaken
> We came upon their host in the morning, and they were like a flock
>   of sheep on whom falls the ravening wolf
> And there were left there on ground of them Amr and Amr and
>   Aswad – the fighters are my witness that I speak true!
> We fell on them with white steel ground to keenness: we cut them to
>   pieces until they were destroyed;
> And we carried off their women on the saddles behind us, with their
>   cheeks bleeding, torn in anguish by their nails.[3]

Or again,

> Truly War knows that I am her child
> And that I am the chief who wears her token in fight.
> And that I dwell on a mountain top of glory in the highest honour
> And that I render restive and distrest
> Mail-clad warriors in the black dust of battle.
> And that I dash upon them when they flinch before me,

In an attack more fierce that the spring of a lion
With my sword I smite on the day of battle
Cleaving in twain the rings of the strongest mail.
This then is my equipment – would that the young warrior
Could see the length of days without fear of old age!
Truly the folk of Āmir know
That we hold the peak of their mount of glory
And that we are the swordsmen of the day of battle,
When the faint hearts hold back and dare not advance.[4]

These, then, were the values held by many of the Bedouin who participated in the early Muslim conquests. The poets glorify swiftness and strength in battle and the excellence of their riding animals. There is also a strong emphasis on individual valour. The poetic warrior is defending his tribe, laying waste rival tribes; but perhaps most of all he is concerned for his own bravery and reputation. The armies of Islam would have taken into battle many of these same ideals, especially the concern for reputation of both individual and tribe. Consciously or unconsciously, they would have been aware of the warrior poets of the *jāhiliya* as role models.

This poetry also affected the way in which they remembered the events and hence the way we can attempt to understand them. There is no concern for overall strategy, for a general account of the progress of battle, but endless interest in individuals and their encounters with the enemy.

While much of Arabia is desert, the peninsula also includes some surprisingly varied landscapes. In the highlands of Yemen in the south-western corner, and parts of Oman in the south-east, high mountains attract enough rainfall to allow permanent agriculture. Here the people lived, as they still do today, in stone-built villages perched on crags, cultivating crops on terraces on the steeply sloping hillsides. The people of the villages were grouped into tribes, like the Arabs of the desert, but they were not nomads. It is impossible to know what proportion of the Arabs who joined the armies of the conquests came from these settled communities. In modern times, the population of small Yemen is almost certainly higher than the whole of vast Saudi Arabia, and we can be certain that many of the conquerors, especially those who went to Egypt, North Africa and Spain, came from groups who were not Bedouin at all but whose families had cultivated their small but fertile fields for generations.

The people of the settled south had a very different political tradition from that of the Bedouin of the rest of the peninsula. From the beginning of the first millenium BC, there had been established, lasting kingdoms in this area, and temples built with solid stone masonry, great square monolithic columns, palaces and fortresses, and a monumental script had been developed to record the doings of founders and restorers.[5] This was a society in which taxes were collected and administrators appointed. In the heyday of the great incense trade in the last centuries BC, a whole string of merchant cities existed along the edge of the Yemeni desert, caravan cities through which the precious perfumes, frankincense and myrrh were transported by trains of camels from the rugged southern coast, where the small scraggy trees that produced the precious resins grew, towards Mediterranean ports like Gaza, where the markets were. This was also a society that could organize massive civil-engineering projects like the great dam at Marib. Here, on the sandy margins of the Empty Quarter, the rain-water from the Yemeni highlands was collected and harvested, distributed through an artificial oasis to provide drinking water and to irrigate crops.

By the end of the sixth century, when Muhammad began his preaching, the glory days of the south Arabian kingdoms were well in the past. By the first century AD, the incense trade had shifted as improved navigation and understanding of the monsoons meant that the maritime route up the Red Sea became the main commercial thoroughfare. The last of the ancient kingdoms, Himyar, was based not on the old trade routes of the interior but on the towns and villages of highland Yemen. By the late sixth century, Himyar itself was in decay and the great Marib dam had been breached, never to be repaired again, the oasis abandoned to wandering Bedouin. The last dated inscription in the old south Arabian script was set up in 559. With the end of the kingdom of Himyar came foreign rule, first by the Ethiopians from the 530s and then by Persians. Some men could still read the old monumental inscriptions, folk memories remained of old kingdoms, and the final breach in the late sixth century of the Marib dam was recognized as a turning point in the history of the area.

There were scattered towns in other parts of the Arabian peninsula and networks of markets and traders. In the hilly areas of the Hijaz in western Arabia there were small commercial and agricultural towns, including Medina and Mecca, and it was the inhabitants of these small Hijazi towns who were the elite of the early Muslim empire. There were settled communities, too, in the great date-growing areas of Yamāma on the Gulf coast. Most of these towns and markets were mainly used for the exchange of the wool and leather of the pastoralists, and for the grain, olive oil and wine that were the main luxuries. From about AD 500, however, a new economic dynamic began to emerge, the mining of precious metals in the Hijaz.[6] Why it began at this time, and not before, is unclear: possibly chance discoveries set off a wave of prospecting. Both archaeological and literary evidence show that this mining was increasing in importance around the year 600 and that some of the mines were owned and managed by Bedouin tribes like the Banū Sulaym. The production of precious metals greatly increased the prosperity of the area. Bedouin, or at least some Bedouin, now had enough money to become important consumers of the produce of the settled lands. Groups of merchants emerged to import goods from Syria, setting up networks between the tribes to allow their caravans to pass in peace.

The most important of these new trading centres seems to have been Mecca. Mecca is situated in a barren valley between jagged arid mountains, a very discouraging environment for a city, but it seems to have had a religious significance that attracted people. A shrine had grown up around a black meteoritic stone. The people of the town claimed that the shrine had originally been founded by Abraham and that it was already extremely ancient. Around the shrine lay a sacred area, a *haram*, in which violence was forbidden. In this area members of different hostile tribes could meet to do business, exchange goods and information. A commercial fair developed and Bedouin came from far and wide to visit it: shrine and trade were intimately linked.

At the end of the sixth century, the shrine and the sacred enclosure were managed by a tribe called Quraysh. They were not nomads but lived in Mecca. They looked after the sanctuary and, increasingly, they organized trading caravans from Mecca to Syria in the north and Yemen in the south. They developed a network of contacts throughout western Arabia and sometimes beyond: some of the leading families were said to have acquired landed estates and property in Syria. These contacts, this experience of trade, travel and the politics of negotiation, were to prove extremely important in the emergence of the Islamic state.

The nomads and the merchants and farmers of the settled areas had subtle symbiotic relations. Some tribes had both settled and nomad branches, some groups lived as pastoralists or farmers at different periods, and many did a bit of both. The Bedouin depended on the settled people for any grain, oil or wine they needed. They also depended on them to manage the shrines and fairs where they could meet and make arrangements for the passing of caravans that supplemented their meagre income. In many ways, the Bedouin were used to accepting the political leadership, or at least the political guidance, of settled elites. On the other hand, the settled people needed, or feared, the Bedouin for their military skills. When they were managed as the Ghassānids and Lakhmids managed the Bedouin of the Syrian desert, they could be a useful military support; when mismanaged or neglected, they could be a threat and a source of disruption and mayhem. It was this symbiosis of settled leadership and nomad military power which formed the foundation of the armies of the early Muslim conquests.

This is not the place to give a full account of the life of Muhammad and his teaching, but some knowledge of his life and achievements is essential for understanding the dynamics of the early conquests. He was born into an honoured but not especially wealthy branch of Quraysh in about 570. In his youth he is said to have made trading expeditions to Syria and to have discussed religion with Syrian Christian monks, but much of the story of his early life is obscured by pious legend. It was probably around 600 that he first began to preach a religion of strict monotheism. The message he brought was very simple. There was one god, Allāh, and Muhammad was his messenger, passing on God's word, brought to him by the angel Gabriel. He also taught that after death the souls of men would be judged, the virtuous going to heaven, a green and delightful garden, the wicked going to a burning, scorching hell. Muhammad began to attract followers, but he also made enemies. Men did not like to believe that their revered ancestors would burn in hell and, more practically, they saw this new preaching as an attack on the shrine at Mecca and the prosperity it brought. Muhammad found himself increasingly unpopular.

By 622 matters had come to a head but Muhammad was saved by an invitation from the people to Medina, about 320 kilometres to the north. Medina was a town but a very different sort of town from Mecca. It had no shrine and the people lived in scattered settlements in a fertile oasis, farming wheat and dates. Medina was a city in crisis: tribal feuds and rivalries were making life unpleasant and dangerous but no one seemed able to put an end to the feuding. It was at this point that they invited Muhammad, an outsider from the prestigious tribe of Quraysh, to come and mediate between them. Muhammad and a small group of followers travelled from Mecca to Medina. Their journey was described as a *hijra*, or emigration, and the participants as *muhājirūn*, while the supporters of the Prophet in Medina were called *ansār* or helpers. The year of the emigration, 622, marks the beginning of the Islamic era. Among the small group of *muhājirūn* were Abū Bakr, Umar and Uthmān, who were eventually to be the first three successors of the Prophet, and his cousin and son-in-law Alī. The *hijra* marks the moment when Muhammad passed from being a lonely prophet, 'a voice crying in the wilderness', to being the ruler of a small but expanding state.

From the very beginning, Muhammad was a warrior as well as a prophet and judge, and the Islamic community expanded through conflict as well as preaching. The Quraysh of Mecca were determined to crush him and Muhammad gave as good as he got by attacking the trading caravans, the lifeblood of the rulers of Mecca. In 624, by the well of Badr, the Muslims inflicted a first defeat on the Meccans, taking a number of prisoners but not capturing the caravan, which safely made it to the city. Two years later the Meccans defeated Muhammad's forces at Uhud, and the next year they made an attempt to take Medina itself. The Muslims were able to defeat this at the battle of the Khandaq (Trench) and a sort of stalemate ensued. A truce was made with the Meccans at Hudaybiya in 628 and in 630 Muhammad was able to occupy the city and most of the Meccan aristocracy accepted his authority. In the two years between his occupation of Mecca and his death in 632, Muhammad's influence spread far and wide in Arabia. Delegations arrived from tribes all over the peninsula, accepting his lordship and agreeing to pay some form of tribute.

We can see something of how the Muslims at the time of the great conquests regarded the legacy of the Prophet in the speeches said to have been made by Arab leaders to the Sasanian shah Yazdgard at the time of the conquest of Iraq. For one of these men,[7]

> There was nobody more destitute than we were. As for our hunger, it was not hunger in the usual sense. We used to eat beetles of various sorts, scorpions and snakes and we considered this our food. Nothing but the bare earth was our dwelling. We wore only what we spun from the hair of camels and sheep. Our religion was to kill one another and raid one another. There were those among us who would bury their daughters alive, not wanting them to eat our food ... but then God sent us a well-known man. We knew his lineage, his face and his birthplace. His land [the Hijaz] is the best part of our land. His glory and the glory of our ancestors are famous among us. His family is the best of our families and his tribe [Quraysh] the best of our tribes. He himself was the best among us and at the same time, the most truthful and the most forbearing. He invited us to embrace his religion ... He spoke and we spoke; he spoke the truth and we lied. He grew in stature and we became smaller. Everything he said came to pass. God instilled in our hearts belief in him and caused us to follow him.

Another[8] stressed the military and political aspects of his achievement:

> All the tribes whom he had invited to join him were divided among themselves. One group joined him while another remained aloof. Only the select embraced his religion. He acted in this way as long as God wished but then he was ordered to split with the Arabs who opposed him and take action against them. Willingly or unwillingly, all of them joined him. Those who joined him unwillingly were eventually reconciled while those who joined him willingly became more and more satisfied. We all came to understand the superiority of his message over our previous condition, which was full of conflict and poverty.

It is most unlikely that either of these speeches was actually made as described but they are still very interesting. The account as it has come down to us was probably elaborated in the first half of the eighth century, within two or three generations of the Prophet's death and while the Muslim conquests of Spain, Central Asia and India were still continuing. They show how the early Muslims remembered Muhammad leading them out of poverty and internal divisions. They stress the importance of his descent from Quraysh and of his new religion, which most of them accepted, if not with enthusiasm, at least peacefully.

Muhammad's military campaigns were, in one sense, the beginning of the Muslim conquests. His example showed that armed force was going to be an acceptable and important element first in the defence of the new religion and then in its expansion. The Prophet's example meant that there was no parallel to the tendency to pacificism so marked in early Christianity. The history of his campaigns was well remembered by the early Muslims and it has been argued[9] that the records of his military expeditions, both those he participated in himself and those he dispatched under the command of others, were the basic material of his earliest biographies. At the same time, diplomacy was certainly more important than military conquest in the spread of Muhammad's influence in the Arabian peninsula. It was the network of contacts he derived from his Quraysh connections rather than the sword which led people from as far away as Yemen and Oman to swear allegiance to him. Military force had ensured the survival of the *umma*, but in the Prophet's lifetime it was not the primary instrument in its expansion.

The teachings of Islam also introduced the idea of *jihād*.[10] *Jihād* or Holy War is an important concept in Islam. It is also one that has from the beginning aroused continuing controversy among Muslims. Fundamental questions about whether *jihād* needs to be violent or can be simply a spiritual struggle, whether it can only be defensive or can legitimately be used to expand the frontiers of Islam, and whether it is an obligation on Muslims or a voluntary activity that may be rewarded with spiritual merit, were all open to debate.

The Koran contains a number of passages instructing Muslims as to how they should relate to the unbelievers and different passages seem to give different messages. There is a group of verses that recommend peaceful argument and discussion with non-Muslims in order to convince them of the error of their ways. Verse 16:125, for example, exhorts Muslims to 'Invite all to the way of your Lord with wisdom and beautiful preaching: and argue with them in ways that are best and most gracious: For your Lord knows best who has strayed from His path, and who receives guidance'. A number of verses suggest that at least some Muslims were very reluctant to join military expeditions and they are rebuked for staying at home and doing nothing when they should have been fighting 'in the path of God'. The number and urgency of these exhortations suggests that there was a quietist group among the early Muslims who were, for whatever reason, reluctant to fight aggressive wars for their new religion.

In some passages those who do not fight are shown to be missing out on the temporal benefits of victory as well as rewards in the life to come. Verses 4:72–4 make it clear to them:

> Among you is he who tarries behind, and if disaster overtook you [the Muslim force], he would say 'God has been gracious unto me since I was not present with them'. And if bounty from God befell you, he would surely cry, as if there had been no friendship between you and him: 'Oh, would that I had been with them, then I would have achieved a great success. Let those fight in the path of God who sell the life of this world for the other. Whoever fights in the path of God, whether he be killed or be victorious, on him shall We bestow a great reward.'

Other verses stress only the spiritual rewards. Verses 9:38–9, for example, read, 'O believers! What is the matter with you that when it is said to you, "March out in the path of God" you are weighed down to the ground. Are you satisfied with the life of this world over the Hereafter? The enjoyment of the life of this world is but little when compared with the life of the Hereafter. If you do not march forth, · He will afflict you with a painful punishment, and will substitute another people instead of you. You cannot harm Him at all, but God has power over everything.' Here we find the idea, expressed in so many pious conquest narratives, that the rewards of the afterlife were, or at least should be, the motivating factor for the Muslim warrior.

There are also passages that suggest a much more militant and violent attitude to non-Muslims. The classic statement of these views in the Koran comes in verse 9:5: 'When the sacred months are past [in which a truce had been in force between the Muslims and their enemies], kill the idolators wherever you find them, and seize them, besiege them and lie in wait for them in every place of ambush; but if they repent, pray regularly and give the alms tax, then let them go their way, for God is forgiving, merciful.' This verse can almost be considered the foundation text for the Muslim conquests, and its terms are echoed in numerous accounts of the surrender of towns and countries to Muslim arms. It is somewhat tempered by other verses, such as 9:29: 'Fight those who do not believe in God or the Last Day, and who do not forbid what has been forbidden by God and His Messenger [Muhammad], and those among the People of the Book who do not acknowledge the religion of truth until they pay tribute [jizya], after they have been brought low.' This verse, and others like it, make it clear that the People of the Book (that is Christian and Jews who have revealed scriptures) should be spared as long as they pay tribute and acknowledge their position as second-class citizens.

Muslim commentators have worked hard to reconcile these apparently different views. The dominant opinion has come to be that the verses advocating unrestricted warfare on the unbelievers were revealed later than the more moderate ones urging preaching and discussion. According to the religious scholars, this meant that the earlier verses were abrogated or replaced by the later ones. The militant verses, especially 9:5 cited above, therefore represent the final Muslim view on Holy War. It would, however, be wrong to imagine that the argument was cut and dried at the time of the early Muslim conquests, and it was not until almost two hundred years after the death of the Prophet that the definition of *jihād* began to be formalized by such scholars as Abd Allāh b. Mubārak (d. 797).[11] The Koran certainly provided scriptural support for the idea that Muslims could and should fight the unbelievers, but at no point does it suggest that they should be presented with the alternatives of conversions or death. The alternatives are conversion, submission and the payment of taxes, or continuing war. In short, the Koranic exhortations can be used to support the extension of Muslim political power over the unbelievers wherever they are, but they cannot be used to justify compulsory conversion to Islam. Koranic discussions of fighting also made it clear that religious rewards, that is the joys of paradise, were more important than material success. In these ways, the Koran provided the ideological justification for the wars of the Muslim conquests.

The potentially confusing messages of the Koran seem to have been simplified into a rough-and-ready rule of thumb which provided a justification for the wars of conquest. When the Bedouin addressed the Sasanian King of Kings one of them explained what they were doing. When Muhammad had secured the allegiance of all the Arabs, 'he ordered us to start with the neighbouring nations and invite them to justice. We are therefore inviting you to embrace our religion. This is a religion which approves of all that is good and rejects all that is evil'. It was, however, an invitation that was difficult to refuse:

> if you refuse, you must pay the tribute (*jizā*). This is a bad thing but not as bad as the alternative; if you refuse to pay, it will be war. If you respond positively and embrace our religion, we shall leave you with the Book of God and teach you its contents. Provided that you govern according to the rules included in it, we shall leave your country and let you deal with its affairs as you please. If you protect yourself against us by paying the tribute, we will accept it from you and guarantee your safety. Otherwise we shall fight you.[12]

This was how *jihād* was interpreted during the early eighth century, and probably before.

Along with an ideology of conquest, the Muslim *umma* in the last years of the Prophet's life also produced an elite capable of leading and directing it. The inner circle was composed of men who had supported Muhammad in the early days at Mecca and who had joined him in the *hijra* to Medina in 622. Among them were the first caliphs Abū Bakr (632–4), Umar (634–44) and Uthmān (644–56). It was under the direction of these men that the initial conquests took place. They are all given distinct characters by the Arabic sources, Abū Bakr the grave and affable old man, Umar the stern, puritanical unyielding leader and Uthmān rich and generous, but fatally weakened by his predilection for appointing his own kinsmen to high office. None of these men actually led the Muslim armies in person and, apart from Umar's probable visit to Jerusalem, none of them seems to have left Medina, the political capital of the new state, at all. How much control they actually exercised over their distant armies is very difficult to tell. The Arabic sources consistently portray Umar, during whose reign the most important of the early conquests took place, as the real commander. We have numerous accounts of how he wrote to commanders in the field telling them what to do, how he received booty and eminent prisoners at Medina and behaved as a very 'hands-on' commander-in-chief. Modern historians have tended to doubt this, seeing the image as an idealization of the early Islamic state in general and Umar in particular. In reality, the commanders on the ground must have exercised much more autonomy than the texts suggest.

Communication across the vast distances penetrated by the Arab armies are unlikely to have been as swift and continuous as the Arabic tradition suggests, but there clearly was a substantial degree of control from the centre. Commanders were appointed and dismissed on the caliphs' orders and there is no example in the literature of a commander rebelling against his authority or defying his orders. This is in marked contrast with both the Roman and Sasanian empires, which were at different times effectively disabled by the rebellions of generals and governors against their rulers. The Muslim conquests were far from being the outpouring of an unruly horde of nomads; the campaigns were directed by a small group of able and determined men.

The political leadership of the early Islamic state was composed almost entirely of the *muhājirūn*, those members of the Quraysh in Mecca who had originally supported Muhammad: the *ansār* of Medina were largely, but not entirely, excluded from military command. It is unlikely, however, that the conquests would have been so successful without the military leadership and expertise provided by the rest of the Quraysh of Mecca. From about 628 onwards, more and more leading Qurashis pledged their allegiance to the Prophet. In return, many of them were rewarded with important positions in the new order. When the conquests began under Abū Bakr, he turned to this group to find many of his commanders. Among them was Khālid b. al-Walīd, who was sent by Abū Bakr to suppress the dissent in Yamāma in eastern Arabia and then on to lead the Muslim armies in Iraq and Syria. Another man from the same background was Amr b. al-Ās, an influential Qurashi who agreed to come over to Muhammad in 628 'on condition that my past sins [i.e. his resistance to Muhammad] be pardoned and that he give me an active part in affairs: and he did so'.[13] Amr was typical of the new elite who considered themselves to be socially superior to many of those who had been Muhammad's earliest supporters. He had inherited an estate, famous for its grapes and raisins, near Ṭā'if and, in an incautious moment, he told a messenger sent by the caliph Umar that his, Amr's, father had been dressed in a garment of silk with gold buttons while Umar's father had carried firewood for a living.[14] Amr went on to play an important role in the conquest of Syria before leading the Muslim armies into Egypt. Perhaps the most striking example of the recruitment of old enemies into the new elite was the family of Abū Sufyān. Abū Sufyān was a rich Meccan of the old school and a dyed-in-the-wool opponent of Muhammad and his new religion. His sons were quick to see the possibilities of the new order and converted to Islam, one of them, Muʿāwiya, serving as one of Muhammad's secretaries. Muʿāwiya and his brother Yazīd were dispatched with the early Muslim armies to Syria, where their father already owned landed estates. Yazīd became governor of the newly conquered territories before succumbing to plague, but Muʿāwiya survived to become first governor of Syria and then, from 661, caliph. He can also claim to be the founder of Muslim naval power in the eastern Mediterranean.

Among the towns of the Hijaz is the ancient city of Ṭā'if, high in the mountains near Mecca. Ṭā'if was a walled and fortified city surrounded by orchards and gardens, a place of retreat from the scorching heat of the Meccan summer. It was dominated by the high-status tribe of Thaqīf, who were the guardians of the town shrine, dedicated to the goddess al-Lat. Like many of the Meccans, the Thaqafis, as members of the tribe were called, pledged their allegiance to Muhammad in the last four years of his life. They were to become junior partners to the Quraysh in the Islamic project, especially important in the conquest and early administration of Iraq.

The members of this new elite were emphatically not Bedouin. They came from urban and commercial backgrounds. They prided themselves on the virtue of *hilm* – that is, self-control and political understanding. This was in marked contrast to the Bedouin, whom they considered excitable and unreliable, useful for their military skills and hardiness but needing to be to be controlled and led.[15] But the partnership, the complementarity, was the key to the success of the early Arab conquests, the result of the urban elite of the Hijaz using and directing the military energies of the Bedouin to achieve their aims.

When Muhammad died in 632 the whole future of the Islamic project hung in the balance. For a few weeks it was touch and go whether this new community would survive and expand or simply disintegrate into its feuding constituent parts. The future history of much of the world was decided by the actions of a small number of men arguing and debating in Medina. Muhammad had left no generally acknowledged heir. He had made it clear that he was the 'seal of the Prophets', the last in the great chain of messengers of God which had begun with Adam. It was quite unclear whether he could have any sort of successor at all. Different groups within the community began to assert their own needs. The *ansār* of Medina seem to have been happy to accept Islam as a religion but they no longer wished to accept the political authority of the Quraysh: after all, these men had come to them as refugees, had been welcomed into their city and were now lording it over them. It was particularly galling that new converts from the Quraysh, men who had vigorously opposed the Prophet when they themselves were fighting for his cause, now seemed to be in very influential positions. They met together in the shelter of the portico of one of their houses and debated, most apparently favouring the idea that the *ansār* should be independent and in control of their home town.

While the debate rumbled on and ideas were tossed around, other people were moving with speed and efficiency. Before the *ansār* had come to any firm conclusions, Umar b. al-Khattāb had taken the hand of Abū Bakr and pledged allegiance to him as *khalīfat Allāh*, the deputy of God on earth.* After this dramatic gesture, both the Quraysh and, more reluctantly, the *ansār* felt obliged to accept Abū Bakr's leadership. This at least is the account in the traditional Arab sources, and it has the ring of truth. It was essentially a *coup d'état*. In doing this, Umar was making a number of points. He was saying that there should be one successor to the Prophet who would lead the whole community, Quraysh and *ansār* alike. He was also saying that the leader would be chosen from the *muhājirūn*, the early converts from Mecca. Mecca would be the religious focus of the new religion, but political power

---

* The Arabic word *khalīfa* is the origin of the English 'caliph', the title by which the rulers of the early Islamic state are normally known in English. The caliphs also had the more formal title of *Amīr al-mu'minīn* or Commander of the Faithful.

was based in Medina and it was from Medina that the first two caliphs directed the great conquests.

In many ways the elderly Abū Bakr was the perfect choice. No one could dispute his loyalty to the Prophet and he shared with Alī the honour of being the first converts to the new religion. He had been the Prophet's companion when he made the dangerous *hijra* from Mecca to Medina in 622. He also seems to have been tactful and diplomatic, but perhaps his most important quality was his knowledge of the Arab tribes of Arabia, their leaders, their interests and their conflicts. These qualities were to be extremely valuable in the crucial two years of his short reign.

Umar's coup ensured that Abū Bakr and the Quraysh were going to control the nascent Muslim state, but there were much wider problems in the rest of Arabia. The spread of Muhammad's influence in the peninsula had largely occurred peacefully: tribes and their leaders had wished to be associated with this new power and some of them had agreed to pay taxes to Medina. Muhammad's death brought all this into question. Many of the leaders who had pledged allegiance felt that this had been a personal contract and that it lapsed with his death. Others felt that they should be allowed to be Muslims without paying the taxes or acknowledging the political authority of Medina. Yet others saw this as an opportunity to challenge the primacy of Medina. Among the latter were the numerous tribe of the Banū Hanīfa of Yamāma in eastern Arabia. They now asserted that they too had a Prophet, called Maslama. They boldly suggested that the peninsula should be divided into two zones of influence; the Quraysh could have one and they should have the other. Other tribes in north-east Arabia chose to follow a prophetess called Sajāh. Muhammad had shown how powerful a position a prophet could hold and how much benefit it could bring to his or her tribe. It was not surprising that others tried to follow his example. The Muslim sources refer to all these movements as the *ridda*, a term that usually means apostasy from Islam but in this context meant all types of rejection of Islam or the political authority of Medina.

The new Islamic leadership decided to take a bold, hard line on these developments. They demanded that those who had once pledged allegiance to Muhammad now owed it to his successor and the Medina regime. No one could be a Muslim unless they were prepared to pay taxes to Medina. In making this decision, they set in motion the events that were to result in the great Arab conquests: if they had decided to let other areas of Arabia go and consolidate the new religion around the shrine in Mecca, or if they had decided that it was possible for men to be Muslims without acknowledging the political authority of Medina, or if they had decided not to use military force to assert their authority, the conquests would never have occurred in the way they did.

Having made this decision, the leadership set about enforcing it with ruthless efficiency. Any one group that would not accept rule from Medina was to be brought into line, by force if necessary. The Meccan aristocrat Khālid b. al-Walīd was sent to crush the Banū Hanīfa and the other tribes of north-east Arabia and other expeditions, almost all led by Qurashis, were sent to Oman, south Arabia and Yemen. They were helped by the fact that many of the tribesmen of the Hijaz and western Arabia remained loyal to Medina and agreed to serve in the armies.

These *ridda* wars were effectively the first stage of the wider Islamic conquests. Khālid b. al-Walīd moved directly from crushing the Banū Hanīfa to supporting the Banū Shaybān in their first attacks on the Sasanian Empire in Iraq. Amr b. al-Ās was sent to bring the tribes of southern Syria into line and continued to be a leading figure in the conquest of the entire country.

The dynamics of these first conquests were significant. The Islamic state could never survive as a stable Arab polity confined to Arabia and desert Syria. The Bedouin had traditionally lived off raiding neighbouring tribes and extracting payment in various forms from settled peoples. It was a fundamental principle of early Islam, however, that Muslims should not attack each other: the *umma* was like a large and expanding tribe in the sense that all men were members of the same defensive group. If all the Arabs were now part of one big family, raiding each other was clearly out of the question.[16] The inhabitants of the settled communities were also fellow Muslims. A peaceful, Muslim Arabia would mean abandoning both of the traditional nomad ways of surviving. The alternatives were stark: either the Islamic elite were to lead the Bedouin against the world beyond Arabia and the desert margin, or the Islamic polity would simply disintegrate into its warring constituent parts and the normal rivalries and anarchy of desert life would reassert themselves once more. Once the *ridda* had been subdued and the tribes of Arabia were brought once more under the control of Medina, the leadership had no choice but to direct the frenetic military energies of the Bedouin against the Roman and Sasanian empires. The only way of avoiding an implosion was to direct the Muslims against the non-Muslim world.

The conquests started before the *ridda* was finally over, tribes being encouraged to join the Muslim cause and accept the authority of Medina in order to be allowed to participate in these campaigns. Soon there was a continuous procession of nomads to Medina wanting to be enrolled in armies and willing to accept the orders of Umar and the Islamic leadership.

They were dispatched in armies of fighting men. The early Muslim conquests were not achieved by a migration of Bedouin tribesmen with their families, tents and flocks in the way that the Saljuk Turks entered the Middle East in the eleventh century. They were achieved by fighting men under orders. Only after the conquest were the families allowed or encouraged to move from their desert camping grounds and settle in the newly conquered areas.

The numbers we are given for the forces vary wildly and are unlikely, at this early stage in Islamic history, to be very reliable. Muslim sources tell us that the combined might of the armies that conquered Syria was around 30,000 men,[17] but these seldom came together and operated for most of the time in smaller groups. The forces that conquered Iraq seem to have been significantly smaller, and the Arabic sources quote between 6,000 and 12,000 men.[18] The numbers in Egypt were smaller still: Amr's initial force was between 3,500 and 4,000 men, though they were soon joined by 12,000 reinforcements. These numbers may be unreliable but they look realistic and are fairly consistent. This was not a horde that overwhelmed the opposition by sheer weight of numbers; indeed, at the crucial battles of Yarmūk in Syria and the Qādisiya in Iraq, it is possible that they were outnumbered by their Roman and Sasanian opponents.

The military equipment of the Arab armies was simple but effective. They had no technological advantages over their enemies, no new weapons or superior arms. When the Mongols conquered much of Asia and Europe in the early thirteenth century, it is clear that mastery of the art of mounted archery was a major factor in their success. It gave them fire power and mobility that were vastly superior to those of their opponents. By contrast, the Arabs seem to have enjoyed no such advantages.

We have a clear idea of the equipment of Roman soldiers from statues and sculptures of battles, which enable us to reconstruct the equipment with some confidence. Equally, we have a clear picture of the mounted warriors of the fourteenth- and fifteenth-century Islamic worlds from the superbly meticulous Persian manuscript illustrations of the period. In the case of the early Arab military, however, we have almost no visual evidence at all. There is no reliably dated archaeological evidence of Arab military equipment from this period, no surviving swords or armour. Instead we have to rely on incidental mentions in narratives and poetry which, except in exceptional circumstances, rarely provide detailed descriptions.[19]

The soldiers of the early Muslim armies were normally expected to provide their own weapons, or acquire them in battle. Military equipment was one of the most sought-after items of booty when an army was defeated or a city taken. A lively market in weapons and armour frequently ensued. There was no question of any uniform: each man would dress in what he could find, and what he could afford. They were also expected to provide their own food most of the time. There was no supply train, no lumbering carts loaded with victuals to hamper the progress of the army. Instead, each man would be expected to carry his own supplies or acquire them on the road. The soldiers in the Muslim army that invaded the Byzantine Empire in 716–17 were ordered by their commander to take two *mudds* (about 2 kilos) of grain each on the backs of their horses. In the event they did not need them because they acquired enough through raiding. They built huts for the winter and cultivated the land so that later in the campaign they could live off what they had sown.[20] Travelling light and living off the land, the Muslim forces were able to cover vast distances, feats that would never have been possible if they had had creaking wagonloads of supplies to haul along with them.

The principal weapon was the sword.[21] The early Arab sword was not the curved scimitar of popular imagination but a broad, straight, two-edged blade with a small hilt. It was contained in a leather or wooden scabbard and usually worn on straps around the shoulders, not on a belt. Surviving examples from the late Sasanian period have blades about a metre in length. These weapons must have required considerable strength and dexterity to use. The best swords seem to have been imported from India, though Yemen and Khurasan also had reputations as centres for the manufacture of high-grade weapons. Swords were certainly expensive and precious, given names, handed down in families and celebrated in poetry. The sword, wielded at close quarters, was the weapon of the true hero. They also seem to have been widely used, and it is possible that the growing wealth of parts of the Arabian peninsula in the late sixth and early seventh centuries had allowed more of the Bedouin to acquire these prestigious weapons.

Along with swords there were also spears. The long *rumh* was essentially an infantry weapon with a wooden shaft and a metal head, allowing it to be used as a slashing as well as a stabbing weapon. The shorter *harba* appears in the early Islamic period and may have been used on horseback, though there is no evidence of the use of heavy lances in mounted warfare. We also hear reports of the use of iron bars, maces and, of course, sticks, stones, tent-poles and anything else that came to hand. There were also bows and arrows, and archery was highly esteemed. The sources talk of 'Arab' bows and 'Persian' bows, and it is likely that the Arab ones were lighter and simpler. There is no indication that the Muslim armies had crossbows at this stage although they certainly did by the ninth century.

Chain-mail body armour[22] was worn, although the number of men who could afford it must have been quite small: in 704 it was said that in the whole vast province of Khurasan there were only 350 suits of mail for about 50,000 warriors. Coats of mail were handed down from one generation to another, and new ones, brilliant and shiny, were extremely valuable. Head protection came in two forms. There was the *mighfar*, known in the history of Western armour as an aventail. This was essentially a hood of chain mail which was extended down at the back to protect the neck. Alternatively, there was a rounded helmet known as a *bayda* or egg. A fully equipped warrior must have been quite well protected, at least as much as the Norman warriors of the Bayeux tapestry, but most of the rank and file must have been much less fortunate, fighting in cloaks and turbans which would have left them very vulnerable.

We have very few detailed descriptions of the face of battle in this period and no military manuals from the time of the early Muslim

conquests, but sometimes the sources give pieces of advice which
provide some idea of tactics. In 658 an army of inexperienced Iraqis
was invading Syria in one of the numerous Muslim civil wars of the
period. A wily old Bedouin leader took it upon himself to give them
some advice.[23] He urged them first to make sure that they had access
to a good water supply. Their Syrian opponents were marching on
foot but the Iraqis were mounted, and they should use the mobility
this offered to station themselves between their enemies and the water.
He then went on: 'Do not fight them firing arrows at them and
thrusting at them in an open space for they outnumber you and you
cannot be sure that you will not be surrounded.' They should not
stand still or form a traditional line of battle because their opponents
had both horsemen and foot soldiers and each group would support
the other in close-quarter combat. If the line was broken, it would be
disastrous. Instead, they should keep the advantages offered by their
mobility and divide the army into small squadrons (*katā'ib*), each of
which could support the others. If they preferred to remain on horseback they could, but they could also dismount if they wished. The
emphasis on fighting on foot is interesting: having horses or camels
was very useful for mobility, reconnaissance and, in this case, seizing
control of battlefield advantages such as the water supply, but battles
were usually decided by foot soldiers fighting at close quarters. They
would throw away their spears and fight with swords, often ending up
by wrestling their opponents to the ground. The lack of stirrups, at
least in the early conquests, probably gave the foot soldier a comparative advantage. The Syrian army of the late seventh and early
eighth centuries, which was victorious in this battle as in many others
of the period, seems to have specialized in fighting on foot in close
formation. When the troops were attacked by cavalry, they would
form a spear wall, kneeling with the ends of their spears in the ground
beside them with the points sticking up towards the enemy. They
would wait until the enemy were upon them, before rising up and
jabbing at the horses' faces. It required discipline and a good deal of
nerve to do this, but as long as the line held, it was very effective.
Such systematic tactics were foreign to the Bedouin traditions of
warfare with their accent on mobility and individual courage, but they
were probably employed in the later phases of the conquest by Muslim
armies operating in the Maghreb, and Central Asia.

Two innovations in military technology became widely diffused during the course of the conquests. Stirrups[24] were unknown to the mounted warriors of the ancient world. Precisely when and where they were invented is not clear. There are wall paintings from Central Asia, probably dating from the end of the seventh or the beginning of the eighth century, which show stirrups in use. Literary sources say that they were first used by Arab armies operating in southern Iran (mostly against other Arabs) in the 680s. By the eighth century they had been widely adopted. The importance of the coming of stirrups has been widely debated by historians. It has been suggested that in the Latin West they allowed the development of the heavily armoured knight with all the social and cultural results that flowed from it. It does not seem that this innovation had such far-reaching consequences in the Islamic world, though they would certainly have facilitated the long-range raids characteristic of the later phases of the conquests.

The second important military innovation of these early years of the conquests was the development of swing-beam artillery. Large pieces were known as *manjanīq*, smaller ones as *arrāda*.[25] These engines were known before the Muslim conquests, the first well-attested example being their use by the Avars at the siege of Thessalonica in 597. These swing-beam engines were operated by men pulling down on ropes at one end of the beam so that the other end swung up very quickly and shot the missile from a sling attached to its tip. The only recorded use of siege artillery in the first phase of the Islamic conquests (632–50) comes from the account of the Arab assault on the Persian capital of Ctesiphon/al-Mada'in, where the Arabs are said to have used twenty such devices constructed by a renegade Persian engineer on the orders of the Arab commander, Saʿd b. Abī Waqqās.[26] It is striking that siege engines are not mentioned at all in the accounts of the Arab conquest of fortified cities like Damascus, or the great Roman fortress at Babylon in Egypt, but it is impossible to tell whether this is because they were not used or simply because the sources do not mention them. In the eighth century we hear of Muslims using them to breach the walls of Samarqand in 712, and this information is clearly confirmed by the finding of a graffito showing the technology at work. At the same time we are told of an engine operated by 500 men which brought down the standard on the Buddhist shrine at Daybul in Sind.

In general, however, siege warfare seems to have been fairly basic; only in the long and hard campaigns in Transoxania in the early eighth century do we get the impression that systematic and prolonged siege operations were conducted.

The early Muslims had no secret weapons, no mastery of new military technology with which to overpower their enemies. Their advantages were simply those of mobility, good leadership and, perhaps most important of all, motivation and high morale.

The motivation of the warriors at the time of these early conquests is difficult to assess. Sir Francis Bacon said that Queen Elizabeth I of England did not like to make windows on to men's hearts and secret thoughts and to an extent historians are unable to. All we can do is speculate from what they said, or are alleged to have said, about what they thought they were doing.

The fullest and most articulate discussion of the motivations of the Muslims comes in the series of speeches said to have been made by Muslim emissaries to the Persian authorities, some of which we have already seen. The Muslims repeatedly stress that they are not interested in the affairs of this world; rather, it is the rewards of paradise that spur them on, as well as the belief that the Persian dead would not enjoy the same rewards: 'If you kill us, we shall enter Paradise; if we kill you, you will enter the fire.'[27] They were acting on God's direct orders: 'Now we have come to you by the order of our Lord, fighting for his sake. We act upon his orders and seek the fulfilment of his promise.'

The Muslim dead are frequently described as martyrs (shuhadā). According to Muslim tradition, the idea that those who died in the jihād were martyrs first appears in accounts of the battle of Badr (624), and it seems to have been generally accepted that those killed in the Holy War would go straight to paradise; on one occasion the site of a battle where many Muslims have been killed is described as smelling of sweet perfume. There are stories of men deliberately seeking martyrdom, or at least putting themselves in danger to achieve it: 'A member of the tribe of Tamīm called Sawād, who was defending his kinsmen launched an attack, courting martyrdom. He was mortally wounded after he began but martyrdom was slow in coming. He stood up against [the Persian commander] Rustam, determined to kill but was killed before he could reach him.' In this case, it is interesting to note the combination of desire for martyrdom with the obligations of tribal solidarity.[28] There are a few extreme examples, such as the man who deliberately removed his armour in battle so that he might be slain more quickly[29] and so achieve a martyr's reward, but these are exceptional: not unreasonably, most men wanted to enjoy the fruits of their victory in this world before passing to the delights of the next.

Another motive put into the mouths of early Muslim warriors is freeing the subjects of the Persians from their tyranny so that they can convert to Islam. 'God has sent us and brought us here so that we can free those who wish from servitude to the people of this world and make them servants of God, so that we can transform their poverty in this world into affluence and that we can free them from evil religions and bestow upon them the justice of Islam. He has sent us to bring his religion to all his creatures and to call them to Islam.'[30]

In general, however, conversion to Islam, or offering the opportunity for conversion to Islam, is not widely cited as a reason for fighting. More common is pride in Arabness and pride in the tribe. When Saᶜd, the commander of Muslim forces in Iraq, wanted to urge his men to great deeds, he appealed to their Arab pride: 'You are Arab chiefs and notables, the elite of every tribe and the pride of those who follow you.'[31] The speeches frequently contrast the austerity and honesty of the Arabs with the luxury and lying of the Persians. Pride in the achievements of the tribe remained an important motivating factor as it had in the *jāhiliya*. This comes out most clearly in the poetry, such as this anonymous verse celebrating the achievements of the tribe of Tamīm at the battle of Qādisiya:

We found the Banū Tamīm who were numerous
The most steadfast men on the field of battle.
They set out with a huge army in dense formation
Against a tumultuous enemy and drove them away, dispersed.
They are seas of generosity, but for the Persian kings, they are men
Like the lions of the forests: you would think they were mountains.
They left Qādisiya in glory and honour
After long days of battle on the mountain slopes.[32]

Or this poem celebrating the role of Asad:

> We brought to Kisra* horsemen from the sides of a high mountain
> And he confronted them with horsemen of his own.
> We left in Persia many a woman praying
> And weeping whenever she sees the full moon.
> We slaughtered Rustam and his sons
> And the horses raised sand over them.
> At the place of the conflict we left
> Men who will never move again.[33]

The delight in battle and slaughter come straight from the spirit of the pre-Islamic world. Individual glory and reputation remained important too. In one exhortation, the desire for paradise is combined with the old-fashioned desire for lasting fame in this world: 'O Arabs, fight for religion and for this world. Hasten to forgiveness from your lord and to a garden whose breadth is as the heavens and the earth, prepared for the God-fearing ones. And if the devil tries to discourage you by making you think of the dangers of this war, remember the stories which will be related about you during the fairs and festivals for ever and ever.'[34]

Desire for fame in this world was of course coupled with desire for wealth. One of the most consistent features of the early conquest narratives is the desire for booty and the delight in describing the riches that were obtained. The booty is usually described as money, portable goods and slaves; the acquisition of human booty was always important and in some areas, notably Berber North Africa, it seems to have been the dominant form of reward. Interestingly, given that these were pastoral people, animals are seldom mentioned, possibly because the warriors had largely abandoned their previous pastoral lifestyle. The concern for acquiring booty was matched by the concern for distributing it fairly. Many of these descriptions are no doubt didactic in turn and the fairness and justice with which it was done were certainly exaggerated, but the point remains valid.

The emerging Islamic state had the men, the military skills, the ideological conviction and the leadership to embark on a major

* Kisra, the Arabic form of Chosroes, was the generic name given to Persian kings.

campaign of expansion. Above all, the leaders of the new state were fully aware that it had to expand or collapse. For them there was only one possible course of action: conquest.

2

THE CONQUEST OF SYRIA AND PALESTINE

⚜

The lands of Syria and Palestine were all provinces of the Byzantine Empire, ruled from Constantinople. In 632, the year of Muhammad's death, the Byzantines also ruled much of the Balkans, southern Italy and Sicily, and North Africa. Romans and Byzantines had ruled the lands of the eastern Mediterranean for 600 years without interruption. When the Roman Empire in the west collapsed in confusion and chaos during the course of the fifth century, the richer provinces of the eastern and southern shores of the Mediterranean continued to flourish. The imperial authorities in Constantinople continued to collect taxes, maintain a regular army and send governors to rule the provinces. While towns in the west declined into villages, the cities of Syria were still being embellished with broad straight streets, markets, baths and, above all, with churches.

In both town and country, the landscapes of Syria were dominated by the legacy of a thousand years of rule by Greek-speaking elites imbued with classical learning and sensibilities. The mighty ruins of pagan antiquity dominated cities like Palmyra, Heliopolis (Ba'albak), Gerasa (Jerash) and Petra, as they do today. Smaller towns and villages boasted colonnades and porticoes which reflected on a smaller, but not necessarily cruder, scale the forms of Graeco-Roman architecture.

The great temples of Palmyra and Ba'albak may still have dominated the towns in which they stood, but they were for the most part roofless ruins. In Gerasa the court of the great temple of Artemis was used for pottery kilns, so that the great paved piazza that surrounded the shrine of the goddess was converted to noisome industrial use, while the temple itself was closed and barred, the haunt of snakes and demons. The lands of Syria and Egypt were profoundly Christian. Christianity had, after all, been founded in these lands and it was in Antioch that the followers of the new religion were first called

Christians. For the first three centuries after the coming of Jesus, Christians competed with other religions in the great bazaar of faiths in the Levant. There were Greek-speaking pagans who worshipped Zeus and Apollo, and Aramaic-speaking villagers who worshipped the same deity but called him Bel or Haddad after ancient gods who were already old when the Israelites first entered Canaan.

By the sixth century, however, Christianity was the majority religion in town and country, mountain and desert. There were important Jewish communities, especially in Palestine, and there were still regions and social circles in which classical paganism survived: men still made mosaics for the floors of their houses with images from the ancient legends and myths, though whether they still believed these or not is difficult to tell.

Christianity was also the religion of the governing imperial hierarchy, and this was significant for the shape of society. By the sixth century it would have been impossible for anyone who was not a Christian to hold an important government office. But the Christians of Syria were far from being a homogeneous group. During the sixth century, profound differences had emerged between different groups of believers. The main point of issue was the divinity of Christ and his incarnation: was Christ at one and the same time wholly human and wholly divine, or did he just have a single divine nature, his humanity on earth only appearing to be like ours? This apparently obscure theological debate aroused enormous passions because it reflected wider divisions in society. At the risk of greatly over-simplifying a very complex situation, it was generally the case that those who believed that Christ was wholly divine and wholly human (called Diophysites because they believed in two natures, or Chalcedonians, after the Council of Chalcedon in 451 where the doctrine was first adumbrated) were drawn from the Greek-speaking urban elites, while those who believed that Christ had only one, divine nature (Monophysites) were drawn from the Aramaic-speaking villages, the rural monasteries and the encampments of the Christian Arabs. There were regional variations too: in Palestine most of the Christians seem to have been Diophysites, while in northern Syria the two groups were probably more evenly balanced.

The imperial authorities were firmly Diophysite and regarded the Monophysites as subversives and heretics, persecuting them with intermittent ferocity. This meant that a significant proportion of the Christian population of Syria was alienated from the imperial government and would not necessarily see it as being in their interest to support the imperial church against outside invaders.

Until around 540 Syria had enjoyed a sustained period of prosperity and demographic growth. Everywhere villages were expanding and new lands along the desert margins were being brought under cultivation. From around 540, a century before the Muslim conquest, this happy picture began to change. In that year a new and vigorous strain of bubonic plague hit the entire area. The mortality was swift and terrifying. Towns, where the population was most dense, are likely to have been worst affected but villages too suffered as the epidemic spread. The people least affected were probably the nomads of the desert. The plague was spread by fleas living on rats. In the cities rats must have been as common as they are today; in the nomad camps there was little enough food for humans, never mind rodents, and no places for vermin to hide.

The plague returned with terrifying regularity throughout the remainder of the sixth century and into the seventh. In the absence of statistics, it is impossible to be certain of the impact it made on population levels. Historians estimate that the Black Death, the bubonic plague that ravaged the Middle East and western Europe in 1348–9, probably killed over a third of the population. There is no reason to think that the impact of the sixth-century plague was any less severe. Many of the once flourishing towns and villages of the area must have seemed empty and decaying. When the Muslim conquerors entered the cities of Syria and Palestine in the 630s and 640s they may have walked through streets where the grass and thorns grew high between the ancient columns and where the remaining inhabitants clustered in little groups, squatting in the ruins of the great palatial houses their ancestors had enjoyed.

Epidemic disease was not the only problem Syria faced during the second half of the sixth century. Relations between the Byzantine and Sasanian Persian empires were largely peaceful during the fifth and early sixth centuries. Both powers respected each other's borders and their zones of influence in the Syrian desert to the south and the mountains of Armenia to the north. In the mid sixth century, however, large-scale and very damaging warfare erupted between the two great powers. The Sasanian monarchs invaded Byzantine territory on a number of occasions. In 540 they sacked the great capital of the east at Antioch and in 573 they conquered the important provincial capital at Apamea. On both occasions they returned with a large amount of booty and transported large numbers of the population to new cities in the Persian Empire.

If relations had deteriorated in the sixth century, they became much worse in the seventh. In the year 602, the emperor Maurice and his entire family were assassinated by mutinous soldiers. Some years before, the emperor had given refuge to the young and energetic Sasanian monarch Chosroes II when he had been temporarily driven from his throne. Chosroes now used the death of his benefactor as an excuse for launching a devastating attack on the Byzantine Empire. His armies won a series of spectacular victories. In 611 Persian armies invaded Syria, Jerusalem fell to them in 614 and in 615 the Persians reached the shores of the Bosporus opposite Constantinople itself. In 619 they took Alexandria and all of Egypt was in their hands.

The Byzantine recovery was the achievement of the emperor Heraclius (610–41). He had been governor of Byzantine North Africa but in 610 sailed to Constantinople with his provincial army to seize the throne from the brutal usurper Phocas. His reign had been dominated by the struggle with the Persians. After many years, when Persian armies had seemed unstoppable, Heraclius had turned the tables dramatically when he launched an attack behind the enemy lines in 624. In a move of great daring and brilliant strategic vision, he had led an army from the Black Sea coast of Turkey, through western Iran and northern Iraq, sacking the famous fire temple at Shiz and the palace of Chosroes at Dastgard. With the death of his arch-rival Chosroes II in 628 and the subsequent divisions among the Persians as they struggled to find a new ruler, Heraclius was able to make a peace that re-established the old frontier between the two empires along the Khābūr river. In 629 he negotiated the withdrawal of Persian soldiers from Syria and Egypt and set about restoring Byzantine rule in the newly recovered provinces. On 21 March 630 he enjoyed his greatest moment of triumph when he returned the relics of the True Cross, taken by the Persians, to Jerusalem.

Although the Persians had been decisively defeated, the conquest of Syria and Palestine had a very damaging effect on Byzantine power in the Levant. Apart from the bloodshed caused by the warfare, it seems that many of the Greek-speaking elite emigrated to the security of North Africa or Rome.¹ The fighting had been very destructive, especially in the. towns, but perhaps more important was the loss of the tradition of imperial rule and administration. For most of the period of Muhammad's mission, Syria and Palestine were ruled by the Persians, not the Byzantines, and it was not until 630, a couple of years before the Prophet's death, that Byzantine control was re-established. Nonetheless, this control must have been very patchy, and there were probably many areas where Byzantine government hardly existed. Most younger-generation Syrians would have had no experience or memory of imperial rule, and no cause to be loyal to Constantinople. Even as Byzantine government was being slowly re-established, the religious differences that had divided Syria in the sixth century came to the fore again. The emperor Heraclius was determined to enforce religious conformity on a Christian population that in large measure rejected his doctrinal position.

Byzantine control over Syria had been established for more than half a millennium. If Islam had been born fifty years earlier, and the early Muslims had attempted to raid Syria and Palestine in the 580s not the 630s, there can be little doubt that they would have been seen off very quickly, as the provinces were firmly controlled by the government and the defences well organized. The coincidence that the first Muslim armies appeared in the area immediately after the traumatic events of the great war between Byzantium and Iran was the essential prerequisite for the success of Muslim arms.

Syria may have been ravaged by war and pestilence but for the Bedouin of Arabia it was still the source of wine, oil and grain. The districts around Gaza and Bostra, where the agricultural lands bordered the desert, were frequently visited by merchants from Mecca and other trading centres in the Arabian peninsula.

The country was familiar territory to the leaders of the early Islamic community and it was natural that it would be the first objective of the new Muslim armies. The tradition that the Prophet himself visited Syria before the start of his mission is ancient and well attested. A Syrian city, Jerusalem had been the first focus of prayer for the earliest Muslims, before the adoption of Mecca. Abū Sufyān, leader of the Meccan opposition to Muhammad, owned property in Jordan, including the village of Qubbash, in the fertile Balqā district south of Amman, which he used as a base for his trading activities.[2] The towns of Syria were the entrepôts along the desert margin and many members of the new Islamic elite had visited the country and knew it well. When Muhammad, at the end of his life, was looking for areas to provide new resources for the Muslims, it was natural that he looked north. Syria was very different in this respect from Iraq, which few of the new Islamic elite had visited before the conquests began and which was essentially unfamiliar territory.

The Muslim attacks on Syria had begun on a small and not very successful scale in the last two years of the Prophet's life. Visitors to Jordan, travelling south along the 'King's Highway', the ancient route that runs along the fertile ridges to the east of the Dead Sea, from Karak to Petra, are shown the tombs of the early Muslim heroes just south of the village of Mu'ta. The tombs, with their neat domes and groves of trees, are quite modern, but their position seems to be a genuine relic of the first encounter between Muslims and Byzantine forces. In 629 Muhammad had sent a raiding party in the direction of Syria, probably just looking for booty in the turmoil that followed the withdrawal of the Persian army. As the small band of Muslims rode north up the King's Highway, they were met by a detachment of Byzantine soldiers, mostly local Arab tribesmen, marching south down the road to re-establish Byzantine rule in the area. In a short clash at Mu'ta, the Muslims were defeated and forced to flee, several of the leaders being killed and buried in the tombs we still see today. Among the Muslims who fled to fight another day was Khālid b. al-Walīd, the 'Sword of God' who was later to play such an important role in the conquest of Syria.

The defeat at Mu'ta was a humiliation for the nascent Muslim state but Muhammad seems to have been undeterred and was still determined to pursue the project of raiding Syria. In 630 he sent a carefully planned expedition against Tabūk in the northern Hijaz which may have been a trial run for attacks on Syria. Among the commanders who gained useful military experience there was Amr b. al-Ās, the man who was to conquer Egypt for the Muslims a decade later. There can be no doubt that when the early Muslim high command embarked on the conquest of Syria, they were pursuing a policy already begun by their Prophet.

Immediately after Muhammad's death, the caliph Abū Bakr sent another expedition to Syria, an expedition that marked the beginning of the real conquest of the country. The sequence of events becomes extremely confused at this point. We have a vast mass of traditions about major battles and minor engagements and about the capture of cities. But the truth is that there is no way of reconciling the different chronological schemes that were elaborated by different Muslim editors, and there are very few external sources to give us any sort of guidance. As the great Muslim historian Tabarī complained when he was collecting the conquest narratives, 'in fact, one of the most annoying things about this study is the occurrence of such differences as the one I have noted above about the date of this battle. Such differences arose because some of these battles were so close together in time'.³ In the end, we can only be certain that campaigning began in earnest from 632 and that eight years later, in 640, all of Syria was under some sort of Muslim rule with the exception of the coastal city of Caesarea. The account that follows is based on the most generally accepted chronology, but it should be treated with considerable caution.

The objective of these early expeditions was to assert the control of Medina over the Arab tribes on the fringes of the settled land. On the western borders of the fertile land of Iraq and along the edges of the Nile valley in Egypt, the border between the desert and the sown is a comparatively firm line between one ecological zone and another. In Syria the distinction is much less clear cut. Moving east from the well-watered Mediterranean coast, the landscape becomes gradually more arid. At the line of the 200mm isohyet (the line beyond which there is less than 200mm annual average rainfall) settled agriculture is impossible without oasis irrigation. West of the line is a zone that can be used as pasture by the Bedouin or by dry farming. Many Bedouin have also been part-time farmers, cultivating small fields of grain as well as pasturing their animals. The policy of securing the allegiance of the Syrian Bedouin to Islam led the Muslims inexorably into conflict with the Byzantine imperial authorities and their Arab allies. It was a very conscious and deliberate policy move by the caliph Abū Bakr and the rest of the Muslim leadership: all nomad Arabs were to pledge their allegiance to the Muslim state and those who did not do it voluntarily were to be coerced.

Abū Bakr is said to have dispatched four small armies to operate independently in the frontier zones to the east of the Dead Sea and the Jordan valley, attaching banners to the spears of the leaders as a sign of authority. His choice of commanders was to be very important in the history of the early Islamic state. One of them was Yazīd, the son of Abū Sufyān, who took with him his brother, Muʿāwiya. As we have seen, the family already had properties in Syria and knew the area well. Yazīd was to be one of the leading Muslim commanders in the conquest, and this enabled him and his brother to establish the power of their family in Syria. Yazīd died of the plague before the conquests were finally complete, but his brother Muʿāwiya inherited his role. The power base he built up in Syria during and immediately after the conquests enabled him to establish himself as the first Umayyad caliph in 661 and rule the entire Muslim world from Damascus.

Another appointment with long-term consequences was that of Amr b. al-Ās, shrewd and cunning rather than a great warrior, the wily Odysseus of the early Islamic armies. His background as a merchant trading in Gaza had recommended him to the Prophet, who had chosen him to collect taxes from the tribes on the road from Medina to Syria. He chose to lead his men, said to have been about three thousand in number, many from Mecca and Medina,[4] to the area with which he was already familiar. He travelled along the Red Sea coast as far as the head of the Gulf of Aqaba then turned west, camping with his men in the great sandy depression between Jordan and Israel known as the Wadi Araba. From there they climbed up the escarpment to the plateau of the Negev before heading for the sea at Gaza. Here Amr began negotiations with the local military commander, probably demanding money, and there is a tradition that the Byzantine governor attempted to capture or murder him as they were parleying. Finally, on 4 February 634,[5] there was a battle in which Amr and his men defeated the small Byzantine army at a village called Dāthin, near Gaza, and killed its commander. The Arab victory made an immediate impression. News travelled fast, and we are told that a Jewish community near Caesarea openly rejoiced at the death of a Byzantine official and the humiliation of the imperial authority.[6]

The Muslim victory at Dāthin may have been on a fairly small scale but it alerted the Byzantine authorities to the new threat from the south. Overall command lay with the emperor Heraclius. He was around 60 years old at this time and was certainly no pampered denizen of the vast and luxurious palaces of Constantinople; rather, he was a man with a vast amount of military experience, well used to the hardships of campaign. He was also at the height of his powers and, even as the earliest Muslim raids on Syria began, had just celebrated a major triumph with the return of the True Cross to Jerusalem. Heraclius never led his armies against the Muslims in person (but neither did the Muslim caliphs lead the armies of Islam) but he remained behind the lines in Syria, in Homs or Antioch, directing operations, appointing generals and issuing instructions. The portrayal of Heraclius in the Arabic sources is very interesting.[7] He is renowned for his shrewdness and wisdom and his ability to foresee the future. In one story, Abū Sufyān, the Meccan aristocrat, tells how he saw Heraclius when he was visiting Syria with a group of merchants. 'We arrived there when Heraclius had just defeated the Persians and driven them out of his territory recapturing from them the great cross, which the Persians had stolen ... Heraclius then left Homs, which was his headquarters and walked on foot ... in order to pray in the Holy City. Carpets were spread for him and aromatic herbs were thrown on the carpets. When he reached Jerusalem, Heraclius prayed together with the Byzantine nobles.'[8] He is shown here victorious but modest and pious.

In a number of anecdotes, Heraclius is said to have recognized the greatness of Muhammad and would have become a Muslim if the Byzantine nobles had not been so hostile to the idea. To the Arabs, he was the key, symbolic leader of the Byzantine resistance to the armies of Islam, the ancient enemy. He is shown to be proud and autocratic but he also goes through moments when he alone of his advisers and courtiers can see how strong the Muslims are and recognizes that they are bound to prevail. The image the Arab sources give of Heraclius is not entirely unsympathetic: he is a tragic figure whose failure to embrace Islam meant that his career ended in humiliation and failure.

Up to this point, the Muslim attacks on Syria had amounted to little more than pinpricks along the frontier. The next phase of the conquest began with the arrival of Khālid b. al-Walīd and his men after the forced march across the desert from Iraq, where he had been raiding along the desert frontier. Khālid's march across the Syrian desert, with perhaps five hundred of his troops, has been enshrined in history and legend:[9] Arab sources marvelled at his endurance; modern scholars have seen him as a master of strategy.[10] The story is often told of how he crossed six waterless days of desert by making some of his camels drink more than their fill, binding their jaws so that they could not chew their cud, then slaughtering them one by one so his men could drink the water from their stomachs. At another stage, when Khālid and his men were stumbling along, suffering from extreme thirst, he asked one of his men, Rāfi, who had been in the area before, whether he had any idea about water. Rāfi said that there was water near at hand: 'Go on and look for two hummocks which look like two women's breasts and then go to them.' When they arrived he told them to search for a thorn bush like a man's buttocks. They scrabbled around and found a root but no sign of a tree, but Rāfi told them that this was the place and they should dig there. Soon they uncovered damp ground and small quantities of sweet water. Rāfi, greatly relieved by the discovery, said to Khālid, 'O Commander, by God, I have not come to this waterhole for thirty years. I have only been once before when I was a boy with my father.'[11] So, the account goes on, they prepared themselves and attacked the enemy, who could not believe that any army could cross the desert to them.

The trouble is that the accounts of this expedition, though vivid, are very confused. We can be certain that Khālid did cross the desert from Iraq to Syria some time in the spring or early summer of 634, that it was a memorable feat of military endurance and that his arrival in Syria was an important ingredient of the success of Muslim arms there. The problem is that some sources suggest that he went on the long southern route by Dūmat al-Jandal, while others are equally certain that he made the journey via Palmyra to the north. There are good arguments on each side and simply no knowing which version is correct.

The Arabic narratives give pride of place to Khālid as the commander who provided the most effective leadership, even after Umar had dismissed him from supreme command and replaced him with Abū Ubayda. It was Khālid who united the different Muslim armies on his arrival, it was Khālid who began the conquest of Damascus by opening the East Gate, and it was Khālid who devised the tactics that won the battle of Yarmūk. He then went on to take a leading role in the conquest of Homs and Chalkis (Ar. Qinnasrīn). His reputation as a great general has lasted through the generations and streets are named after him all over the Arab world. Despite his undoubted achievements, however, his reputation in the sources is mixed. He came from one of the most aristocratic families in Mecca and like many of people of his class he had been deeply suspicious of Muhammad with his preaching of social justice and simple monotheism. He had not been one of the early converts to Islam; indeed, he had been among the enemies of the Prophet, actually fighting against him at the battle of Uhud, but he converted to Islam soon after. Once converted he become staunchly Muslim and began to devote all his considerable military talents to the support of the new Muslim state. On Muhammad's orders, he destroyed one of the most famous of the old idols, the image of the goddess al-Uzza at Nakhla near Mecca. He enjoyed the confidence of the first caliph Abū Bakr and was entrusted with commanding the armies against the rebel Arab tribes in the *ridda* wars. He won great victories but also gained a reputation for ruthless and sometimes over-hasty reactions: on one occasion he massacred a whole group of Muslims by mistake and compounded the offence by immediately marrying the widow of one of his victims.[12] His later fame seems to have rankled with some early Muslims, notably the caliph Umar, who strongly believed that early commitment to Islam was essential for anyone who wished to be a leader, that late conversion did not suffice, and that a little humility would not go amiss. A story told of Khālid attempts to explain his life and rehabilitate him. In a dialogue with the Armenian general Jurjah immediately before the battle of Yarmūk, Khālid is made to justify his career and explain why he was popularly called the 'Sword of God'.

God sent us his Prophet, who summoned us, but we avoided him and kept well away from him. Then some of us believed him and followed him, whereas others distanced themselves from him and called him a liar. I was among those who called him a liar, shunned him and fought him. Then God gripped our hearts and our forelocks, guiding us to him so that he followed him. The Prophet said to me 'You are a sword among the swords of God which God has drawn against the polytheists', and he prayed for victory for me. Thus I was named the

Sword of God because I am now the most hostile of Muslims to the polytheists.

Khālid had been instructed by Abū Bakr to march as quickly as possible to aid the conquest of Syria, which had now reached a critical state. On Easter Day, 634 (24 April), he and his forces suddenly appeared and fell upon the Ghassānid Christian allies of the Byzantines, who were celebrating the festival amid the lush grass and spring flowers of the Meadow of Rāhit just north of Damascus.[13] He then turned south to join up with the other Muslim commanders already operating in Syria, who now seem to have been united under his command to face the challenge posed by the Byzantine imperial armies. They began with an attack on the city of Bostra.[14]

Bostra lies just north of the modern Syrian–Jordanian border in a flat but fertile landscape strewn with the black basalt boulders characteristic of much of the area. To the north of the city, and clearly visible from its walls, rise the volcanic hills of the Hawrān. Though the mountains are rugged, if not especially high, they contain, like many volcanic areas, patches of extremely fertile soil. The hinterland of Bostra was the closest area to Arabia which could supply the wheat, oil and wine the Bedouin desired. The city had become rich as a trading entrepôt, and it was widely believed that the Prophet himself had visited it in his youth and had been instructed in the mysteries of the Christian faith there by the monk Bahira. Bostra was also a political centre. When the Roman emperor Trajan had annexed the Nabataean kingdom in 106 and turned it into the Roman province of Arabia, he had moved the capital from distant Petra in the south to the more accessible (accessible from Rome, that is) city of Bostra. Built of tough, unyielding black basalt, the ruins of the ancient city of Bostra are among the most impressive in the Near East. The huge Roman theatre there still survives almost intact, forming the centre of a later medieval fortress. Columns and paving stones indicate the routes of ancient streets, and there are the remains of baths and a number of important Christian churches, including a magnificent round cathedral.

It is not clear whether the Byzantines had re-established an imperial presence in the city after the departure of the Sasanians. The city seems to have put up little resistance, and towards the end of May 634 it made peace with the Muslims, the citizens agreeing to pay an annual tax. It was the first major Syrian city to be taken by the invaders.

After the surrender of Bostra, the Muslim force marched west to meet up with Amr b. al-Ās. Amr, after his first victory at Dāthin, was now confronted by a large Byzantine force which had gathered south-west of Jerusalem on the road to Gaza. Khālid and the others crossed the Jordan valley without apparently encountering any resistance and met up with Amr and his men. The combined Muslim army is said in one source to have been about twenty thousand strong and was under the command of Amr, who is the only Arab general named in the sources, where his image is consistently one of shrewdness and intelligence. He is described spying out the enemy camp in person or sending agents to do so, while the Byzantine general writes to him as someone equal to himself in cunning.[15] The armies met at a place the Muslim authors called Ajnādayn, and a major battle developed. We have no detailed information about the nature of the conflict but it is clear that the Byzantines were defeated and that the remnants of their army withdrew to Jerusalem and other fortified sites. News of the victory of the Muslims spread far and wide, and it seems to be the battle referred to in the Frankish chronicle of Fredegar composed some twenty years later in France. He includes the interesting, and possibly true, detail that 'the Saracens' (the Muslims) offered to sell back to Heraclius the booty they had just taken from his defeated men but that the emperor refused to pay for any of these stolen goods.[16]

The contemporary Armenian chronicler Sebeos tells how the Byzantine forces were ordered by the emperor to remain on the defensive.[17] Instead, they left their camps by the river and took refuge in the city of Pella, on the east bank of the river. Pella was a prosperous city in the fertile lands of the Jordan valley and an easily defended acropolis rose above the classical streets and porticoes on the valley floor. Here they were attacked again. As usual, the course of battle is not entirely clear but some features seem to have been remembered. The Byzantine troops had crossed the Jordan valley from Scythopolis on the west bank and, in order to delay the pursuing Muslims, had cut some of the irrigation ditches, allowing the water to spill out and the flat lands of the valley bottom to become an ocean of mud.[18] The Muslims charged on, not knowing what the Byzantines had done, and many of their horses became stuck in the mire, 'but then God delivered them'. In the end, it was the Byzantines who were trapped in the mire and many were massacred.

The remnants of the Byzantine forces now withdrew to Damascus. The Muslims pursued them. The siege of Damascus became one of the set pieces of the conquest of Syria. To a remarkable extent we can retrace the progress of the siege because of the detailed descriptions of the sources and the preservation of the fabric of the city. The walls of old Damascus, Roman or earlier in origin and continuously restored since, are still largely intact. Only at the western end where the city expanded in Ottoman times is the old circuit breached. All except one of the ancient gates survive and they bear the same names today as they do in the early Arabic sources: it is an astonishing example of the continuity of urban geography and architecture through almost fourteen centuries. We are told that Khālid b. al-Walīd was stationed at the East Gate (Bāb Sharqī), Amr b. al-Ās at St Thomas's Gate (Bāb Tūma), Abū Ubayda at the now demolished Jābiya Gate on the west side and Yazīd b. Abī Sufyān at the Little Gate and Kaysān Gate on the south side.

The Muslims also took the precaution of stationing a force on the road north of Damascus. This proved a wise move because Heraclius, who is said to have been in Homs at this time, sent a force of cavalry to try to relieve the siege but they were intercepted and never made it.[19] Just how long the siege lasted is not clear. Disconcertingly, the Arabic sources give widely differing estimates, anything from four to fourteen months. The Muslims do not seem to have had any siege engines, or any equipment more sophisticated than ropes and ladders, and even the ladders had to be borrowed from a neighbouring monastery.[20] It seems that all the attackers could do against the substantial Roman walls of the city was to mount a blockade and hope that famine, boredom or internal disputes would cause the defenders to give up. When it became clear that no relieving force was going to appear, the defenders of the city began to despair. According to one account, the end came when a child was born to the *patrikios* (Byzantine commander) in charge and he allowed his men to relax and eat and drink to celebrate. Khālid b. al-Walīd, who was always on the lookout for opportunities and knew exactly what was going on in the city, decided to take advantage. He had ropes and ladders with him. Some of his men approached the gate using inflated animal skins to cross the moat. They threw their ropes around the battlements and hauled themselves up, bringing the ropes up after them so that they would not be seen. Then, at a given signal, with the cry of '*Allāhu akbar*' (God is great) they rushed the gate, killing the gatekeepers and anyone else who resisted.

Meanwhile, at the other end of the town, the Damascenes had begun opening negotiations for a peaceful surrender and Muslim troops began to enter the city from the west. The two groups, Khālid's men from the east and the others from the west, met in the city centre in the old markets and began to negotiate. Terms were made, leaving the inhabitants in peace in exchange for tribute. Properties belonging to the imperial fisc were confiscated for the benefit of all Muslims, becoming part of the *fay* (the communal wealth of the Muslim community).[21] As usual there was booty to be divided up and the commanders were careful to keep a share for those who had been stationed on the road north, for though they had played no direct part in the siege their presence had contributed to the victory and they had earned their booty. The complicated stories which evolved of the taking of Damascus, from two different ends in two different ways, may be an attempt to solve the thorny issue of whether the city was taken by force or by treaty (see above, pp. 18–20). In this case the authorities seem to have tried to reach a compromise that allowed it to be neither one thing nor the other.

The accounts of the fall of Damascus also reflect divided loyalties among the population. The city was a centre of imperial power with a military governor appointed by the emperor himself, but many if not most of the inhabitants were Christian Arabs. It is evident that many of them had split allegiances and that they felt closer to the Arabs outside the walls than they did to the Greeks and Armenians who composed a large part of the garrison. Whatever the explanation, it is clear that Damascus was spared the horrors of bombardment and sack. In the century that followed, the city became the capital of the whole Muslim world and entered what came to be its golden age.

Around the time of the fall of Damascus, and as usual the chronology is very uncertain here, the elderly Abū Bakr, the successor of Muhammad and first caliph of Islam, died in Medina. We know that his death occurred in July 634. What is less clear is what stage this was in the story of the conquest, but there are a number of reports that news reached the Muslim armies in Syria during the course of the siege. The new caliph was the austere and formidable Umar, who is portrayed in many accounts as the mastermind behind the conquests. There was no opposition to his succession among the forces in Syria but the new caliph had clear ideas about command. As we have seen, Umar disliked Khālid b. al-Walīd intensely. The fact that Khālid had fought so brilliantly for the Muslim cause against the *ridda* in eastern Arabia and again in Iraq and Syria did little to improve his standing with the new caliph. He now abruptly ordered that Khālid be removed from command and return to Medina. In one account, Abū Ubayda, now appointed as supreme commander in Khālid's place, was ordered to demand that Khālid should confess to being a liar. If he refused, as he was bound to do, his turban should be pulled off his head and half his property confiscated. Faced with this ultimatum the great general asked for time to consult, not as might be imagined with his friends or subordinates, but with his sister. She was clear that Umar hated her brother and if he admitted to being a liar he would be removed all the same. There was no point in trying to placate the caliph by admitting to crimes he did not believe he had committed.

In an interesting reflection on the power of the caliph and the unity of the Muslims, Khālid felt that he had no choice but to go to Medina. A Byzantine general in that position might well have raised a rebellion and called on his troops to support him in a bid for the throne. By contrast, the greatest general of the Muslim army meekly accepted dismissal and humiliation. When he arrived at Medina, Umar pursued his vendetta. Whenever he met Khālid he would taunt him: 'Khālid, take the property of the Muslims out from under your arse!', to which Khālid would meekly reply that he did not have any of the 'Muslims' property'. In the end a settlement was reached, with Khālid paying over most of his fortune so that he was left only with military equipment (*ʿuddat*) and slaves (*raqīq*). He was soon back in Syria, playing a major role in the battle of the Yarmūk and the subsequent conquests of Homs and Chalkis, where he finally settled. In the end Umar is said to have recognized that he had maligned the 'Sword of God' and that Abū Bakr, who supported Khālid, had been a better judge of men.[22] The great general died peacefully in 642, a brilliant, ruthless military commander, but one with whom the more pious Muslims could never feel entirely comfortable.

Meanwhile, the emperor Heraclius was preparing one more major effort to drive the Muslim invaders out of Syria. After the fall of Damascus he had retreated to Antioch in the north of Syria, the traditional capital of the entire area. Here he set about directing what was to prove his last campaign. The Byzantines assembled all the troops they could recruit. Arab sources give very large numbers, over 100,000,[23] but comparisons with other Byzantine armies of the period make it clear that this is a huge exaggeration, with numbers between 15,000 and 20,000 being more probable. The armies comprised a very diverse collection of men. There were Byzantine Greeks under the command of Theodore Trithurios, a large contingent of Armenians under Jurjah and the local Christian Arabs led by the king of the Ghassānids, traditional allies of the Byzantines, Jabala b. Ayham. The overall commander was an Armenian called Vahān. The different contingents would have spoken different languages – Greek, Armenian and Arabic – and they may have found it difficult to communicate with each other. There were also profound religious and cultural differences. The Greeks and Armenians would have come from settled, probably rural village backgrounds and were used to living and fighting in upland, mountain terrain. The Arabs, on the other hand, were nomads, used to the mobile traditions of desert warfare. All the troops came from Christian backgrounds but both Armenians and Christian Arabs were regarded as heretics by the orthodox Byzantines. How far these divisions really affected the performance of the Byzantine army is not clear, but the sources are awash with rumours of disaffection, of Jurjah converting to Islam at the hand of Khālid b. al-Walīd on the eve of battle and of the Christian Arabs going over to the Muslim side in the course of battle. The Arab sources also talk of the Byzantine soldiers being chained together so that they could not flee, but this is a story found in many accounts of the conquests, used to contrast the free and motivated Muslims with the serf-like soldiers of their enemies: there is no real evidence for such an impractical idea being put into effect, though it may be a distant reflection of the practice of infantry locking shields together to make a protective wall.[24]

The Byzantine forces probably assembled in Homs and marched south through the Biqa valley, past Baʿalbak with its great pagan temples – now almost empty of worshippers but still magnificent in their decay – and so to Damascus. In anticipation of the arrival of this force, the Arabs seem to have withdrawn from the city, allowing Byzantine forces to reoccupy it unopposed. We have no information on how they found the town but there are reports of tension between the Byzantine generals demanding supplies for their men, as was the usual Byzantine practice, and the local financial administrator, the Arab Mansūr, who maintained that the city did not have sufficient resources to feed them. Certainly the army did not use Damascus as a base but moved on south.

The Byzantine army assembled at Jābiya in the Golan Heights. This was the traditional summer pasture of the Ghassānids. According to the most probable reconstruction, it was now August 636 and the Golan would have provided much-needed food, water and pasture for the army. Meanwhile the Muslim forces prepared to oppose the Byzantines and hold on to their newly won gains. Their army also assembled in the Golan area, to the south-east of the Byzantines. The different Muslim armies had now come together under the command of Abū Ubayda, or possibly Khālid b. al-Walīd. Yazīd b. Abī Sufyān and Amr b. al-Ās both led contingents. According to Muslim sources, the Arab army numbered about 24,000. In view of the downward revision of the numbers on the Byzantine side, it is possible that the two armies were not very different in size.

The battle that ensued between the Christian and Muslim armies is generally known as the battle of Yarmūk and conventionally dated to the summer of 636.[25] The battle of Yarmūk is, along with the battle of Qādisiya in Iraq, one of the major conflicts that has come to symbolize the Muslim victories in the Fertile Crescent. As with Qādisiya, the Arab accounts are extensive and confused and it is difficult to be clear about exactly what happened. There is no contemporary or reliable account from the Byzantine point of view. Both sides are said by the Muslim sources to have been inspired by religious zeal. As the Byzantines remained in their fortified camp, preparing for battle, 'the priests, deacons and monks urged them on lamenting the fate of Christianity'.[26] On the other side, Khālid b. al-Walīd addressed his men: 'This is one of God's battles. There should be neither pride nor wrongdoing in it. Strive sincerely, seeking God in your work, for this day also has what lies beyond it [i.e. the afterlife]', and he went on to urge them to stick together and fight in unison.[27]

The River Yarmūk, a perennial watercourse, flows down from the plateau of the Hawrān to the Jordan valley, just south of the Sea of Galilee. In the course of its descent into the rift valley, it has gouged out a steep gorge, with high cliffs on each side. On the north side, it is joined by a number of smaller valleys, notably the Wadi al-Ruqqād. These steep ravines were to define the course of the battle and may have proved disastrous to the defeated when they attempted to flee from the scene. The actual site of the battle, between the Yarmūk gorge in the south and the Golan in the north, is a land of rolling, rocky hills, dotted with villages and farms. It was, in fact, good open country for cavalry manoeuvres, but it also provided some cover from rocks or trees for men to hide or set up an ambush. Since 1948 this site has been politically very sensitive, lying as it does on the border between Syria (north of the river), Jordan (south of the river) and the Israeli-occupied Golan. This has made access to the battlefield very difficult for historians. It was not always thus, however. Before the First World War, when the entire area was part of the Ottoman Empire, the battlefield was visited by the great Italian orientalist Leone Caetani, Prince of Sermoneta. He used his first-hand observations and knowledge of the Arabic sources to produce a geographical setting for the battle, which has formed the basis of the most plausible modern accounts.[28]

The battle of Yarmūk was a series of conflicts that probably lasted more than a month and culminated in a major battle towards the end of August.[29] The first encounters took place in the Jābiya region, after which the Muslims retreated east towards Darᶜa. There followed a period of waiting and skirmishing as the Byzantines prepared their army and tried to sow divisions in the Muslim ranks. It seems that the real fighting began when the Muslims feigned a retreat from their positions and lured elements of the Byzantine army into rough terrain, where they were ambushed. During the Muslim counter-attack, the Byzantine cavalry became separated from the infantry, enabling the Muslim cavalry to inflict great slaughter on the foot soldiers while the cavalry were making their way through the Muslim ranks.[30] Khālid b. al-Walīd is said to have organized the Muslim cavalry in a 'battle order which the Arabs had not used before'. He divided the cavalry into small squadrons (kardūs), between thirty-six and forty in number, apparently so that they would appear more numerous in the eyes of the enemy.[31] The Byzantines may also have been unsettled by a dust storm. The main Byzantine force was now driven west and hemmed in between the rugged valleys of the Wadi'l-Ruqqād and Wadi'l-ʿAllān, with the cliffs of the Yarmūk gorge behind them. Any prospect of retreat to the west was destroyed when Khālid b. al-Walīd took the old Roman bridge across the Wadi al-Ruqqād, and Muslim forces went on to storm the Byzantine camp at Yāqūsa on the road to the Sea of Galilee. As the enemy pressed home their advantage, the Byzantine forces were further demoralized by rumours that the Christian Arabs had defected to the Muslims. Morale broke and the Byzantine forces lost all cohesion. There are reports of exhausted and dejected soldiers sitting down, wrapped in their mantles, lamenting the fact that they had not been able to defend Christianity and waiting for death.[32] Others were driven down the cliffs into the wadis. The Muslims took very few prisoners.

The defeat on the Yarmūk was catastrophic for the Byzantines and news spread far and wide. In distant France, the author of the chronicle of Fredegar recorded it twenty years later as a terrible defeat. He has the Muslim army at 200,000 strong. According to him, the night before the battle 'the army of Heraclius was smitten by the sword of the Lord: 52,000 of his men died where they slept'. Not surprisingly, the survivors were seriously disheartened. 'When on the following day, at the moment of joining battle, his men saw that so large a part of their force had fallen to divine judgment, they no longer dared advance on the Saracens but all retired whence they came.'[33] Towards the end of the seventh century, the ascetic St Anastasius of Sinai in his remote monastery remembered it as 'the first and fearful and incurable fall of the Roman army'.[34]

In the aftermath of the victory, the Muslims continued to reduce the cities of Syria to obedience. One force, led by Abū Ubayda and Khālid b. al-Walīd, went north from Damascus to Homs, an important city in late Roman times.[35] They besieged the city through the winter (probably 636–7) despite the bitter cold and sorties by the Byzantine garrison. The defenders were convinced that the cold would force the Arabs, shod only in sandals, to give up the siege, though when spring came and they were still there, voices were raised in the city urging peace negotiations. According to another account, the Muslims were aided when the walls were badly damaged by an earthquake, a sure sign of God's favour to them. In the end the two sides made peace. As usual, the inhabitants were obliged to pay taxes to the Muslims, some apparently at a fixed rate, others at a variable rate according to their prosperity at the time. All their lives, property, city walls, churches and water mills were to be guaranteed to them except for a quarter of the church of St John, which was to be turned into a mosque.[36] At the same time we are also told that half the houses should be made available to the conquerors. The general leading the Muslim conquest of the city is said to have 'divided it up among the Muslims in lots so that they might occupy them [the houses]. He also settled them in every place whose occupants had evacuated it and every abandoned garden'.[37] Homs was an important centre on the fringes of the Syrian desert and it may have been thought that this was a suitable place for the Bedouin to settle. The city was probably the first in Syria to have a substantial Muslim population.

The clause about giving up a quarter of the church for use as a mosque may seem curious and perhaps improbable: after all, how could these two religions, whose followers had just been engaged in violent warfare, end up by sharing the main religious building in the town? We are told, however, that it also happened at Damascus, where the Muslims used half of the cathedral as the first mosque. Only at the beginning of the eighth century, sixty years after the conquest, were the Christians expelled and a purpose-built mosque constructed. Even then, compensation was paid and the Christians made a new cathedral in the church of St Mary, about half a kilometre east of the mosque, and this remains the cathedral of the Melkite (Greek Orthodox) community of Damascus to the present day. Interestingly, we find archaeological confirmation of this practice from a small town in the Negev, Subeita. Here there are two large, finely built Byzantine churches. In the narthex or porch of one are the foundations of a small mosque. We can tell it is a mosque because of the mihrab, the niche showing the direction of Mecca, which is clearly visible. All this evidence suggests that, after the political defeat of the Christian forces, the two religious communities could and did coexist, if not in harmony, at least in a measure of mutual tolerance.

The next city up the road to the north was Chalkis, which the Arabs called Qinnasrīn.[38] Whereas Homs is still one of the most important cities in Syria, Chalkis has virtually disappeared from the maps. Only recently have archaeological surveys and excavations in a little village just east of the Damascus–Aleppo road revealed the ancient site. Chalkis stood in the middle of a fertile, grain-growing plain; although an important administrative centre, it was never a very big city. The ancient acropolis can be distinguished, as can the early Islamic town, which lay outside the confines of the classical city: the Arabs settled outside the walls in what was effectively a new suburb, not in the city itself. After the fall of the city, Khālid b. al-Walīd decided to make it his home and he was joined there by his wife.

It was probably at around this time that the Muslims came into contact with one of the less desirable aspects of Syrian life at the time, the plague. Among the victims were the overall commander of Muslim forces, Abū Ubayda, and Yazīd b. Abī Sufyān, whose position was inherited by his brother Muʿāwiya, later to be the first Umayyad caliph.[39]

Heraclius seems to have moved from Antioch after the battle of Yarmūk and settled in Edessa, where he tried to organize the defence of northern Mesopotamia and south-eastern Anatolia. He then moved on along the upper Euphrates before turning west, heading for Constantinople, the capital he had not visited for the last ten years. There is no evidence, as some have suggested, that he was disabled by senility or depression, but he must have been weary and painfully aware of the scale of the Byzantine defeat. Arab authors put a number of sad and resigned speeches into his mouth and Heraclius's farewell to Syria was widely reported. In one he is made to say, 'Peace be upon you, O Syria. This is the farewell after which there will be no reunion. No Byzantine man will ever return to you except in fear [as a prisoner] until the coming of the Anti-Christ. How sweet will be his deeds [because he will fight the Muslims] and how bitter their outcome for the Byzantines [because he will be defeated].'[40] In another version he just says as he goes through the passes in the Taurus mountains and looks behind him, 'Peace be upon you, O Syria [Sūriya]! What a rich country this is for the enemy!'[41] As he withdrew, he took with him all the garrisons from the districts along the new frontier, creating a sort of no man's land between Byzantine and Muslim territory at the north-eastern corner of the Mediterranean.[42] A later Syriac source, deeply hostile to everything Byzantine, says that Heraclius 'gave order to his troops to pillage and devastate the villages and towns, as if the land already belonged to the enemy. The Byzantines stole and pillaged all they found, and devastated the country more than the Arabs'. [43]

With the departure of the emperor, the remaining Byzantine cities were left to their own devices. Antioch, the ancient capital of Syria, put up little resistance and the remaining inhabitants seem to have made no effort to use the mighty walls the emperor Justinian had built around their city less than a hundred years before to keep the attackers out: probably there were just too few of them to defend the huge circuit. They are said to have rebelled against Muslim rule later, but this may mean only that they refused or were unable to pay taxes and had to be coerced into doing so. In other small towns, the surrender to the Muslim armies had an almost carnival atmosphere. At the little town of Shayzar on a bend of the Orontes river in central Syria the inhabitants came out to meet the Muslims with players of drums and cymbals, as was customary when greeting important visitors.[44] The same happened at Maʿarrat al-Nuʿmān and Apamea, once the proud capital of the Roman province of Syria II but now in deep decay after being sacked ferociously by the Persians sixty years before, in 573. It was not always as easy as that: when the people of Darʿa[45] in southern Syria came out to greet the caliph Umar with drumming and singing, carrying swords and bunches of myrtle, the puritanical monarch ordered that they be stopped. His general, Abū Ubayda, by now used to the customs of Syrian small towns, explained that it was their custom and if he stopped them doing it, they would think he was breaking the agreement the Muslims had made with them. Reluctantly, the grumpy caliph allowed them to continue.

The most vigorous resistance the Muslims encountered was in the cities of the Syrian and Palestinian coasts. These had always been the areas in which Greek civilization was most firmly established and most deeply entrenched. It was also because the Byzantines were able to resupply and reinforce these towns from the sea. The Byzantine forces in Palestine had largely withdrawn to Egypt, but Gaza and Caesarea still held out. Gaza had been the scene of the first encounter between Amr b. al-Ās and the Byzantines at the very beginning of the conquest, and it seems that he now returned to the city and succeeded in taking it. It was natural from that position that his thoughts should turn to Egypt, with which Gaza had such close connections.

Further up the coast, the strongest resistance was in the city of

Caesarea. While Gaza has been continuously inhabited and built over
so that very few traces of its classical past have survived, Caesarea is
largely deserted and the outlines of the ancient city, founded by Herod
the Great (73–4 BC) as a window on the Mediterranean world, can
still be seen. The city remained prosperous into the sixth century,
with new residential quarters laid out between the great monuments
of the classical period. Down by the harbour, an elegant octagonal
church overlooked the quays and docks. It seems that the city held
out for some years, possibly as late as 641, five years after the defeat
of the Byzantine forces at the battle of Yarmūk, and we are told that
it fell only when one of the Jewish inhabitants showed the Muslims
how to enter through a concealed water channel. It is said that the
man who led the conquering army was Muᶜāwiya b. Abī Sufyān. If so,
it was a first military triumph for the man who was to become, twenty
years later, the first Umayyad caliph and who was to rule the entire
Muslim world from his base in Damascus. Because they had resisted
so long and the city had been taken by storm, many of the inhabitants
were enslaved and taken to the Hijaz where, we are told, they worked
as secretaries and labourers for the Muslims (*fi'l-kuttāb wa'l-aᶜmāl
li'l-Muslimīn*).[46] Perhaps we see here the beginnings of the Muslim
appropriation of Greek culture, so characteristic of the early Islamic
period.

In Latakia, modern Syria's largest port, the inhabitants closed the
great gate of their city walls against the invaders. The Arabs are said
to have made a great effort and dug ditches deep enough to conceal a
man and a horse. Then they pretended to be retiring to Homs. When
night fell, they returned to their hiding places. In the morning the
inhabitants opened the gate to drive their cattle out to the pastures;
this was obviously a very agricultural town. The Arabs emerged suddenly from their hiding places and forced the gate, taking possession
of the city. Here the inhabitants were allowed to keep the whole of
their church and the Muslims built a new mosque for themselves.[47]
The cities of Lebanon, Beirut, Tyre and Sidon put up no resistance.
Only at Tripoli did the Byzantines hold out for a long time and,
supplied from the sea, the city was defended until the beginning of
the reign of the caliph Uthmān in 644. The Muslims built a small
fortress outside the walls to keep watch on the inhabitants and finally
they woke up one day to find that the defenders had all been evacuated

overnight in Byzantine ships.[48] Its fall meant the final end of Byzantine control of any part of the eastern seaboard of the Mediterranean.

There was one city whose conquest was more of symbolic than military importance, and that was Jerusalem. The city had great significance for the early Muslims, as the first focus for their prayers and later as the site from which Muhammad is said to have begun the famous night journey on which the secrets of the heavens were revealed to him. Jerusalem at the end of the sixth century was a thriving centre of pilgrimage and ecclesiastical administration. The walls enclosed roughly the same area as the Old City today. We have an unusual insight into the appearance of the cityscape because of a document known as the Madaba map.[49] This is a mosaic map of the Holy Land laid on the floor of a church in the little Jordanian town of Madaba, probably at the end of the sixth century. The city of Jerusalem figures prominently in it. We can see the classical colonnaded streets, which follow the same route as the main streets of the Old City do today. We can see the walls and tower and the great church of the Holy Sepulchre, marking the site where Christ was crucified, buried and rose again. We can also see the great New Church, the Nea, built by the emperor Justinian as part of his campaign to beautify the city. Excavation since 1967 has recovered the foundations of the church and the new street that led to it, confirming the accuracy of the map. There is one area of the city which the map does not tell us about, the Temple Mount. This is the vast platform where Herod's temple had stood and which had probably been empty since the Romans destroyed the temple in AD 70. Sixty years after the Muslim conquest, the Umayyad caliph Abd al-Malik was to build the Dome of the Rock on the spot, generally regarded as the third most holy place in Sunni Islam after Mecca and Medina. It would be fascinating to know what, if anything, Umar found on the site but, tantalizingly, the mosaic has been destroyed just at the point where the temple platform should be: if the accident of survival had spared another few centimetres of the ancient tesserae, we might have an answer to this question.

The man in charge of Jerusalem was the newly appointed patriarch, Sophronius. He was a Greek churchman, educated and sophisticated, with a lively contempt for the rude Bedouin. For Sophronius, the appearance of the Arabs was a sign of God's anger at the sins of the

Christian people. In a fiery sermon he berated them: 'Whence occur wars against us? Whence multiply barbarian invasions? Whence rise up the ranks of the Saracens against us? Whence increases so much destruction and plundering? Whence comes the unceasing shedding of human blood? Whence the birds of the heavens devour human bodies? Whence is the cross mocked? Whence is Christ Himself, the giver of all good things and our provider of light, blasphemed by barbarian mouths?' 'The Saracens', he went on, 'have risen up unexpectedly against us because of our sins and ravaged everything with violent and beastly impulse and with impious and ungodly boldness.'⁵⁰ This is the authentic voice of high Greek culture, appalled and dismayed about the Muslim conquest of Syria.

Despite his contempt and loathing for the Arabs, the military circumstances meant that Sophronius had no alternative but to negotiate with them. He did insist, however, that he would surrender the city only to the caliph Umar himself. The surrender of Jerusalem became the subject of history and legend, and a quarry of examples for those who wanted to argue points about Muslim–Christian relations.

The opportunity came when Umar visited Syria. As usual with the Arabic sources there is considerable confusion about when he did this and, indeed, whether there was one visit or several.⁵¹ The most likely scenario is that the caliph came to Jābiya in 637 or 638 and while he was staying there, dealing with a wide range of administrative matters, a delegation from the city arrived to make terms. They came on horseback, wielding swords, and some in the Muslim camp assumed they were hostile raiders. But the caliph, preternaturally wise as always, was able to reassure them that they were only coming to negotiate. The purported text of the agreement that was reached has come down to us:

In the name of God, the Merciful, the Compassionate. This is the assurance of safety [amān] which the servant of God Umar, the Commander of the Faithful, has given to the people of Jerusalem. He has given them an assurance of safety for themselves, for their property, their churches, their crosses, the sick and healthy of the city and for all the rituals which belong to their religion. Their churches will not be inhabited by Muslims and will not be destroyed. Neither they, nor the land on which they stand, nor their cross, nor their property will be damaged. They will not be forcibly converted. No Jew will live with them in Jerusalem.

The people of Jerusalem must pay the taxes (*jizya*) like the people of other cities and must expel the Byzantines and the robbers. Those of the people of Jerusalem who want to leave with the Byzantines, take their property and abandon their churches and crosses will be safe until the reach their place of refuge. The villagers [*ahl al-ard*, who had taken refuge in the city at the time of the conquest] may remain in the city if they wish but must pay taxes like the citizens. Those who wish may go with the Byzantines and those who wish may return to their families. Nothing is to be taken from them before their harvest is reaped.

If they pay their taxes according to their obligations, then the conditions laid out in this letter are under the covenant of God, are the responsibility of His Prophet, of the caliphs and of the faithful.[52]

There then follows a list of witnesses including Khālid b. al-Walīd, Amr b. al-Ās and the future caliph Muᶜāwiya b. Abī Sufyān.

Whether the text really is that agreed by Umar, or an ancient fabrication, we cannot be sure, but it gives a clear impression of how the Muslims should respond to their newly conquered Christian subjects. The fact that it bore the name of Umar undoubtedly gave it added weight and authority. The emphasis on the security of religion is not surprising, given the particular status of Jerusalem. Rather more unexpected is the provision that Jews are not to be allowed to settle in the city. This prohibition had been a feature of Roman law and the fact that a Muslim source records it suggests that the Christian negotiators had played a strong hand. Some of the clauses throw interesting light on the circumstances of the city. The provision made for Greek officials to leave points to an emigration of the upper and official classes, and the clauses about the country people who have come to the city are a clear reflection of contemporary circumstances.

Umar then visited the city in person. The fullest account of his visit is given in the Christian Arabic chronicle of Saᶜīd b. Batrīq, also known by his Christian name of Eutychius.[53] Writing in the eleventh century, he preserved traditions intended to show how Umar had safeguarded the position of the Christians in the Holy City. According to his account, Sophronius welcomed Umar to the city and the people were given guarantees about their property and freedom of religious observance. When it was the time for prayer, the patriarch suggested that the caliph should pray in the Church of the Holy Sepulchre itself, but Umar refused because he said that if he did, the Muslims would take it as a shrine and it would be lost to the Christians. He then issued a document in which the Muslims were forbidden to pray in the precincts of the church and, as a result, the church has remained in Christian hands ever since. Umar then requested a site to build a mosque and the patriarch took him by the hand to the rock on the platform where Herod's temple had once stood. The narrative is clearly fashioned to make it clear that the status of the Christians in Jerualem was based on the unimpeachable authority of Umar himself.

In the Arabic tradition, Umar was guided by one Ka'b b. Abhar, a Jew who was converted to Islam and is said to have introduced many stories and traditions about the Jews into the new religion. In response to the caliph's question, Ka'b suggested that the rock, which sticks up in the centre of the platform, should be the direction of their prayer on that day, but Umar rejected this, making it clear that God had reserved this role for the Ka'ba in Mecca. Umar was well aware that the site marked the position of the Jewish temple which had been destroyed by the Romans after the great Jewish rebellion in AD 70 and had been left as a rubbish tip in Byzantine times. He set about clearing the site himself and the people followed his example. He may have ordered the erection of a simple place of prayer. Certainly when the European Christian pilgrim Arculf visited Jerusalem after the Muslim conquest but before the beginning of the building of the Dome of the Rock in 685, he found a basic place of worship there. It is for this reason that the Dome is sometimes quite misleadingly referred to as the mosque of Umar (or Omar).

By 640 the whole of Syria, apart from one or two coastal towns, had come under Islamic rule. The northern boundary of Muslim rule was established at Antioch, the ancient city of Cyrrhus and Manbij. Garrisons were established and the local people enjoined to let the Muslims know of any approaching Byzantine forces. For the moment, however, the Byzantines were too devastated by defeat, the death of Heraclius in February 641 and the subsequent struggles for succession to the imperial title to be able to mount any sort of counter-offensive.

The completion of the conquest of Syria opened the way for

Muslim armies to cross the Euphrates and begin the conquest of the
Jazira. The Arabic word *jazīra* means 'island' but since the seventh
century the term has been used to describe the 'island' between the
Tigris and Euphrates rivers in the lands of modern Syria and Iraq. To
the north, the Jazira was bordered by the mountains of the Anti-
Taurus in south-east Anatolia, the border running more or less along
the modern Turkish frontier. The landscape is mostly flat open plains
and desert. A recent historian notes: 'the Jazira is rather like the
Mediterranean, an ocean of steppe punctuated by archipelagos of river
valleys and hills and settled unevenly on its shores'.[54] There is a natural
unity to this area and communications are quick and easy, but at the
time of the Muslim conquest it was divided between Byzantine territory in the west and Sasanian lands in the east, with the frontier near
the ancient city of Nisibis, more or less along the line of the modern
Syria–Iraq border. This division determined the way in which it was
conquered, Muslim forces from Syria taking the lands on the Byzantine side of the frontier, forces from Iraq taking the ex-Sasanian lands
further to the east.

In the river valleys there were a number of ancient cities of which
the most famous was Edessa. Edessa was one of the centres of early
Christianity. In the first century AD its then king Abgar is said to have
been the first monarch in the world to accept Christianity. Its great
cathedral, of which nothing now survives, was one of the most magnificent buildings in eastern Christendom. It was also an important
political centre, and Heraclius had made it his base in the final stages
of his campaign in Syria.

The conquest of the Jazira was an important stage in the consolidation of Islamic rule in the Fertile Crescent. If it had remained
in Byzantine hands it would have been a major threat to Syria and
Iraq. Despite its strategic importance and the antiquity of its cities,
the conquest of the Jazira is recounted in a very laconic fashion in the
Arabic sources, and such accounts as there are are more concerned
with the terms of capitulation than the course of the military campaign.[55] Most agree that the conquest was led by Iyād b. Ghanam,
who was ordered by the caliph Umar to lead a force of Syrian Arabs
across the Euphrates. According to one account he had just 5,000 men
with him,[56] but despite these small numbers he encountered little
serious opposition. It seems that the withdrawal of the Byzantine

imperial army left the local people with little choice but to capitulate and agree to the comparatively easy terms the Arabs were offering. Even at Amida (Diyarbakr), whose mighty city walls are one of the great glories of ancient and medieval military architecture, there seems to have been no resistance, and the same was true of the great castle the Byzantines had built in the sixth century at Dara to repel Persian attacks.[57] Edessa seems to have capitulated quickly on condition that the Christians could keep their cathedral but agreed not to build any new churches and not to aid the enemies of the Muslims. The city of Raqqa on the Euphrates also fell after a short resistance. The exact route of Iyād's army as it toured the province accepting the surrender of smaller cities cannot be determined, but it seems that he may have finished by raiding along the ancient road that led to Armenia before halting at Bitlis. He then returned to Syria, where he died.

Syria had been conquered by Arab armies recruited in the Hijaz. This did not, however, result in a vast influx of new immigrants from Arabia. The Quraysh and their allies in the Muslim elite knew Syria well and they wanted to keep control over its resources. They did not want to share it with a mass of impoverished Bedouin. These were encouraged to move to Iraq instead. In British army parlance it could be said that Syria was for the officers, Iraq for the other ranks. They did not found new Muslim towns as later happened in Iraq and Egypt. All the towns that were important under Muslim rule had been important in Roman times (though some cities, such as Scythopolis, which had been important in Roman times, declined and virtually disappeared in the Islamic period). At one stage there seems to have been a project to establish a new town at Jābiya in the Golan, the old summer camping ground of the Ghassānids. It was here that the caliph Umar had come to meet the leaders of the victorious armies on his visit to Syria. But Jābiya remained just that, a summer camping ground: no mosque was built there, no government palace and no plots were allotted to different tribes. Instead the Muslims seem to have preferred to settle in established towns. We have seen how houses in Homs were made available for them. At Chalkis and Aleppo what were effectively Bedouin suburbs were established outside the walls of the old cities.

In part this was possible because sections of the Byzantine elite had fled to Constantinople or further west, leaving space in the towns.

After the fall of Damascus, many people left the city to join Heraclius[58] and prominent Muslims were able to take up residence: Amr b. al-Ās owned several residences in Damascus and estates in Palestine. The treaty Umar made with the citizens of Jerusalem assumed that elements of the Byzantines would leave, either voluntarily or under coercion. It also looks as if many areas of Syria had been depopulated by plague and warfare and the Muslim conquerors had driven out many of the Byzantine inhabitants of the coastal cities.[59] It was hard to find men to garrison the port cities of the Mediterranean coast. Mu'āwiya was obliged to settle Tripoli with Jews, in the absence of any Muslims who could be persuaded to take up residence there. Muslims were also settled in villages around Tiberias and were sometimes given deserted agricultural land on condition that they brought it under cultivation. There is no evidence of great tribal migrations of the sort that are well attested in Iraq.

Something of the day-to-day working of the relationship between the Arab tribes and the inhabitants of the towns and villages can be seen from a group of papyri found in the little town of Nessana in the Negev.[60] Some of these are bilingual, Greek and Arabic, demand notes ordering the Christian people of the town to provide the Bedouin in the area with supplies of wheat and olive oil and, in some cases, cash. The payments seem to have been made directly to the tribal chiefs and there was no complicated bureaucracy involved. How the local people collected the supplies and divided up the burden seems to have been up to them. The documents, which date from 674–5, a generation after the conquest, show how simple and, in a way, informal the Arab occupation could be.

The pattern of Arab settlement in Syria had another consequence. In Iraq and Egypt the Muslim settlers in the towns were directly dependent on the state for their pensions, often their sole means of livelihood. In Syria, by contrast, many of the new elite had urban or rural properties off which they could live. Within a generation members of the Muslim elite in Syria were building themselves luxurious and imposing residences in the countryside, something, again, which seems to have been virtually unknown in Iraq or Egypt.

So, if there was no massive influx of Arabs sweeping away Graeco-Roman civilization, what actually changed in Syria as a result of the Muslim conquests? At the most obvious level, the government and administration were controlled at the top by Arabic-speaking Muslims, but at second glance even this change was not as dramatic as it might initially appear. For the first half-century, the bureaucracy continued to use Greek and was staffed in large measure by local Christians. There was a new elite religion, but it seems to have made little impact on the built environment. In Iraq, in the new towns of Kūfa and Basra, the mosque lay at the heart of the Muslim city; in Damascus at the same time the Muslims had to make do with a half-share of the cathedral church in the city centre.

There is little evidence, either, for the bedouinization of the countryside. The impression that the Arab conquests resulted in hordes of nomads coming in and ravaging the settled lands seems to have been generally untrue, although there may have been incidents of violence and destruction in the course of the invasions. In those fragile, marginal areas such as the Syrian steppe east of Homs, Transjordan and the Negev in southern Israel, areas where the boundaries between cultivated lands and the pastures of the nomads shifted according to political and cultural changes, the evidence suggests that the first century of Muslim rule saw an expansion of settled agriculture. Not until after 750, when the Syria-based Umayyads were overthrown by the Iraq-based Abbasids, did the boundaries of settlement retreat and the Bedouin areas expand.

The Muslim conquest of Syria did, however, have profound effects on the long-term history of the area. It brought to an end almost a thousand years of rule by Greek speakers with contacts in the Mediterranean world. From this point on, the most important links were not with Rome or Constantinople but with Mecca and Medina, and later with Baghdad and Cairo. The emergence of Islam as the dominant religion and Arabic as the near-universal language could not have occurred without the conquest. These deep changes in language and culture may have taken some time but they could not have occurred without the military conquests of the 630s.

3

THE CONQUEST OF IRAQ

ⵣ

A t last you see a thin, hard, dark line on the horizon. It takes twenty days' riding across the desert from the Muslim headquarters at Medina, days of scorching heat and fierce winds, painfully cold nights, huddled under a cloak or tramping on under the stars. This desert is not the sand dunes and palm-fringed oases of popular imagination, but a hard, bitter landscape of stones and gravel, low undulating hills and occasional gnarled and thorny trees. Then comes the longed-for line on the horizon which shows that the end of the journey is in sight. Over the next day or two, the line broadens out, the weary traveller can begin to pick out the trees and perhaps the houses of the settled lands. For this is the Sawād, the Black Lands of the alluvial plains of central Iraq. It is flat as far as the eye can see, a land of palm trees and grain fields made fertile by the waters of the Tigris and Euphrates. For centuries this had been one of the richest and most productive areas on earth.

For 400 years before the Muslim conquest, Iraq had been an integral part of the Sasanian Empire.[1] Sasanian was the name of the dynasty that had revived and renewed the empire of Iran in the third century AD. Along with the Byzantine Empire, the Sasanian was one of the great powers of the ancient world, but the states had very different imperial styles. At the risk of gross oversimplification, it could be argued that while the Byzantine Empire was controlled by a bureaucracy and a standing army, the Sasanian kingdom was ruled by a warrior aristocracy. When the emperor Justinian had himself and his consort Theodora portrayed in mosaic on the walls of a church in Ravenna, they were on foot, calm, elegant, dressed entirely in civilian clothes. When the Sasanian monarch Chosroes II had himself portrayed in stone carving in the grotto at Tāqi Bustān it was as a man of action, a mighty hunter, mounted on a horse in full armour or showing his skills as an archer.

The Sasanian monarch ruled as King of Kings, *Shāhānshāh*, reflecting the fact that the empire boasted a number of aristocratic families almost as ancient and famous as the Sasanians themselves. Their empire included all of modern Iran, Iraq to the west and much of Afghanistan and Turkmenistan to the east. The kings had a capital in the plains of Iraq at Ctesiphon, just south-east of modern Baghdad, but they seem to have spent much of their time on the move between one country estate and another, up and down the roads that led through the Zagros mountains from the plains of Mesopotamia to the highlands of Iran.

Whereas the upper classes of the Byzantine Empire tended to live in cities, in the Persian Empire they were based more in their country estates and palaces. The towns, too, seem to have looked very different from the cities of the Byzantine world. To begin with they were mostly built of mud brick or rubble masonry, they rarely had regular street plans and there had never been town councils to spend money on embellishing them. The typical urban settlement in Sasanian Iraq and Iran was a country town, possibly with a fortress and a walled city centre, known as the *shāhristān*, serving as marketplace and manufacturing centre but devoid of any pretensions to civic greatness or self-government.

The Byzantine Empire was overwhelmingly Christian in religion, whereas the state religion of the Sasanian Empire was Zoroastriansim.[2] Zoroastrians believed that there were two great powers struggling to dominate the world, a good god called Ohrmazd and a wicked one called Ahriman. The worship was centred on fire-temples, for fire was believed to be a sacred element which should be kept pure and not contaminated. The fire-temples were tended by a caste of priests known as magi: it is possible that the three wise men who came to visit the infant Christ were Zoroastrian priests. The magi were supported by the Sasanian shahs and the fire-temples were granted extensive landed estates for their maintenance. Whereas in Byzantine Christianity the main churches were in the centres of population and were designed to accommodate large congregations who gathered to join in worship, the most important fire-temples seem to have been found in remote rural locations, and the small domed chambers that sheltered the sacred fires were certainly not designed to welcome large numbers of worshippers. The impression is of an elite-established religion, secure in its wealth and hierarchical structure but with little popular appeal. There were no Zoroastrian hermits to compare with the heroic ascetics of the Christian world and, as far as we know, no great Zoroastrian preachers whose words could move men to intense and passionate devotion. This was especially true in Iraq, where there were large Christian and Jewish populations. There were no major fire-temples in Iraq and it seems that the faith was confined to Persian administrators and soldiers.

Christianity had spread far in the Sasanian Empire. Iraq, the wealthiest and most populous part of the empire, was probably largely Christian, though there was a significant Jewish population as well.[3] Most of the Christians belonged to the Nestorian, eastern Syrian church, which was regarded as heretical by the Byzantine authorities. This had some benefits for the churches under Sasanian rule because it meant that they were not tainted by connection with the Byzantine Empire. The fact remained, though, that a large proportion of the population of the Persian Empire did not share the religion of the ruling Persian aristocracy and that there could be no common bond against the claims of Islam.

Much of the revenue that sustained the splendour of the Persian monarchy was derived from the rich agricultural lands of Iraq.[4] Members of the royal family and the great aristocratic dynasties had extensive and productive estates cultivated by large numbers of peasants who lived in serf-like conditions.[5] There was a vast social and economic gulf between the aristocracy and the people who tilled their lands. In theory at least, intermarriage between social groups was strictly forbidden. The upper classes were exempt from the hated poll tax, which merchants and peasants were obliged to pay to the Sasanian shah. The aristocracy wore crowns, golden belts and armbands and the tall conical hats called *qalansuwa*. Rustam, the Persian general who led the army against the Arab invaders, came from this background and his *qalansuwa* is said to have been worth 100,000 silver dirhams. Below the greater aristocracy was a larger group of *dehqāns*, a word that might usefully be translated as 'gentry'. These lesser landowners were the pillars of the Sasanian bureaucracy and taxation system.

The aristocracy was Persian speaking but most of the population talked Aramaic. These Aramaeans[6] were the farmers and peasants who made the land so productive. Some Aramaeans might aspire to gentry status, but entrance to the aristocracy was impossible. They did not normally serve in the army, which was mostly recruited from Persians and people like the Armenians with a strong warrior tradition. The despised Aramaean peasants were unlikely to risk their lives to defend their masters.

There is an interesting description of the Persian army at the beginning of the seventh century in the *Strategikon* attributed to the Roman emperor Maurice (582–602). He begins by stressing that the Persians are servile and obey their rulers out of fear, an idea that is also found in the Arabic sources. They are also patriotic and will endure great hardships for their fatherland. In warfare they prefer an orderly approach to a brave and impulsive one. They prefer to encamp in fortifications and 'when the time for battle draws near, they surround themselves with a ditch and a sharpened palissade'. When facing lancers they like to choose broken terrain and use their bows so that the enemy charge will be broken up. They also like to postpone battle, especially if they know that their opponents are ready to fight. They are disturbed when attacked by carefully drawn-up formations of infantry and they do not themselves make use of spears and shields. Charging against them is effective because 'they are prompted to rapid flight and do not know how to wheel suddenly against their attackers as the [nomad] Scythians do'. They are also vulnerable to attacks on the flanks and from the rear and unexpected night attacks are effective 'because they pitch their tents indiscriminately and without order inside their fortifications'.[7] The description is interesting because it fits well with the narrative accounts of battles that we have from Arabic sources, notably the emphasis on fortifications and defensive warfare and generally playing safe. These conservative tactics may have put the Persians at a grave disadvantage against the more mobile, adventurous Arabs.

The great war between the Byzantines and the Persians which had so damaged the Roman Empire in the first three decades of the seventh century had also been a disaster for the Sasanians.[8] At first Persian arms had been almost entirely successful. In 615 the Persian army had reached the Bosphorus opposite Constantinople, and in 619 Persian troops entered Alexandria and completed the conquest of Egypt. The tide began to turn in March 624 when the emperor Heraclius took his fleet to the Black Sea and began the invasion of Armenia and

Azerbaijan. The Persians were now outflanked and were forced to withdraw their army from Anatolia to face the emperor, who was now attacking from the north. In 627 he swept through north-western Iran, before descending to the plains of northern Iraq and defeating the Persian army at Nineveh (12 December 627). It was the greatest military disaster that the Sasanian Empire had ever suffered. Chosroes retired to the capital at Ctesiphon, leaving his palace at Dastgard to be sacked by the Romans. Here he began the search for scapegoats to blame for the spectacular reversal of fortunes that had occurred. He seems to have decided on the execution of his most important military commander, Shahrbarāz, but before he could act there was a coup. Chosroes was assassinated early in 628 and his son, who had agreed to his father's murder, ascended the throne as Kavād II.

Kavād immediately set about negotiating a peace with Heraclius in which all prisoners were to be released and the pre-war frontiers restored. And all might yet have been well had the new king not died within the year, probably of the plague. He was succeeded by his infant son, Ardashīr III, but the general, Shāhrbarāz, refused to accept this and in June 629 seized the throne. This was the first time in four centuries that a man who was not a member of the Sasanian family had tried to take the throne, and there was considerable resistance. After just two months, he, too, was murdered and, since Chosroes II had left no other sons, the throne passed to his daughter, Būrān, who, although apparently an effective ruler, died, of natural causes, after a year. There then followed a bewildering succession of short-lived rulers until finally Yazdgard III, a grandson of the great Chosroes, was elevated to the throne in 632.

The details of these intrigues are not in themselves important. The overall effect was decisive, however. The Sasanian Empire had been ravaged by an invading army and any idea of its invincibility had been destroyed. Archaeological evidence suggests that many settlements in the richest part of Iraq were abandoned as a result of the war.[9] Furthermore the house of Sasan, the mainstay and *raison d'être* of the state, had been torn apart by feud and murder. It is more than likely that Yazdgard, if he had been given time, would have restored royal control and prestige. But the year of his accession was the year of the death of the Prophet Muhammad: Arab tribes were already taking advantage of the chaos to make inroads on the settled lands of Iraq, and Khālid b. al-Walīd, the Muslim general, was on his way. In these circumstances, it is surprising not that the Persians were defeated by the Arabs but that they fought with such determination.

In many places the border between the irrigated lands and the desert is clear and precise: you can virtually stand with one foot on either side of this environmental frontier. But the frontier was no barrier to human movement and communication. The Arab tribes that roamed the desert areas along the west bank of the Euphrates had a long tradition of interaction with the settled, mostly Aramaic-speaking inhabitants of the Sawād.[10] These might be peaceful – the exchange of the meat and skins that the Bedouin produced for the grain, wine and fine textiles of the settled lands. Or they could be more violent, with nomads demanding and extorting taxes, using their mobility and their military skills to terrorize the villagers. Some nomads also took military service with the Sasanian government, or, more simply, accepted subsidies from the authorities for not using their military power against the settled people.

One such tribe were the Banū Shaybān, who seem to have been concentrated in the desert lands east of the old Arab town of Hīra. Some of the shaikhs of the tribe had palaces in the city. Like many tribes the Banū Shaybān were far from united and different lineages competed to assert their leadership. At the time of the death of the Prophet, the old leaders were being challenged by an upstart, called Muthannā b. Hāritha, from a minor branch of the tribe. Muthannā was trying to make his reputation by leading anyone who would follow him in raids on the settled lands; by establishing himself as a successful collector of booty, he could expect to attract supporters who would accept him as a great tribal leader. For some years before the arrival of the first Muslim army in 633 he had been raiding the frontier lands, not settling or conquering but asserting the nomads' rights to tribute.

Muthannā may not have been a man of deep, or any, religious conviction, but circumstances meant that he became one of the earliest Muslim commanders in Iraq. The dominant clan of the Banū Shaybān had followed the prophetess Sajāh and opposed the Muslim armies in the *ridda* wars. Muthannā could see his chance. When the Muslim armies under Khālid b. al-Walīd approached Iraq, he and his followers joined up with them, while the old leaders of Shaybān opposed them and were marginalized and excluded. Members of the same tribe were both the earliest supporters of the Muslims in the conquest of Iraq and their fiercest enemies. Tribal politics interacted with religious motivation in diverse and complex ways and Muslim leaders often took advantage of local rivalries to attract new supporters to the cause.

Khālid b. al-Walīd, Meccan aristocrat and supremely competent military commander, had been led to the borderlands of Iraq as a natural continuation of his work in subduing the *ridda* in north-eastern Arabia. From the time of the Prophet's death, it had been the policy of Medina that all Arab nomads should be subject to Muslim rule and the tribes of the Euphrates area were to be no exception.

Khālid probably arrived at the frontiers of Iraq in the spring or early summer of 633.[11] The Muslim force he brought with him was small enough, perhaps around a thousand men,[12] but they were a well-led and disciplined group. He seems to have roamed along the frontier, no doubt mopping up any resistance he encountered among the Bedouin and defeating the Persian garrisons of the frontier forts.[13] He then reached the ancient city of Hīra. Hīra was a fairly small city – one later Arab source estimated the population at 6,000 males,[14] say 30,000 overall. It was not a compact town and there is no indication that it was ever walled; rather it was an extended settlement, where Arab chiefs lived in fortified palaces scattered among the palm trees.

One such palace was excavated in 1931 by an expedition from Oxford.[15] The building was surrounded by a wall of fired brick and was on two storeys, the lower of which incorporated windowless cellars. In the interior, which was constructed in mud-brick, there was a court-yard surrounded by rooms. The excavators uncovered a number of stucco decorative panels with patterns on them, either abstract or vegetable, suggesting that the inhabitants lived in some style. Most of the population of the town were Arabs, many with family connections with the Bedouin in the nearby desert. Many of these Arabs were also Christian and there were famous monasteries and churches in among the houses. It was the seat of a Nestorian bishopric. The excavators discovered the remains of two basilica-planned churches built of brick, for, as in most of Mesopotamia, there was no good building stone available. The interiors were plastered and decorated with religious paintings, only small fragments of which survive.

Little fighting was necessary to persuade the inhabitants to make terms; the Arab notables fortified themselves in their palaces and peered over the battlements while the Muslim troops roamed the open spaces between them.[16] Then negotiations were opened. The Arab notables were ready to make peace in return for a tribute and promises that neither their churches (*bayᶜa*) or palaces (*qusūr*) should be harmed.[17] The tribute collected was the first that was ever sent from Iraq to Medina: it was just the beginning of a waterfall of wealth which was to flow from the Sawād to the capitals of the caliphs: Medina, Damascus and later Baghdad.

Khālid did not rest with the conquest of Hīra but moved on north to Anbār, another Arab town on the borders of the desert, and then west to the oasis town of Ain Tamr (Spring of the Dates). In each of these he encountered resistance, from Persian troops but also from the local Arabs, many of whom, like the people of Hīra, were Christian.

Many prisoners are said to have been taken in these early raids. As usual they were kept as slaves for a while, often being obliged to do hard manual labour; we are told of one man forced to become a gravedigger. Many of them were later freed, becoming *mawāli* (non-Arab Muslims) of Arab tribes and entering the Muslim community as full members. Among those said to have been taken prisoner at this time was Nusayr, whose son Mūsā b. Nusayr was to lead the Muslim conquest of Spain in 712.[18] This was typical of the way in which the Muslims won over many of the people they conquered and incorporated them into their military forces to make further conquests.

So far Khālid's attacks on Iraq had been little more than unfinished business from the *ridda*. His objective was to secure the allegiance of the Arab tribes to the Muslim government in Medina. The defeats of the Persian frontier forces and the tribute taken confirmed his credibility as a military leader. As yet, he had not penetrated far into the settled lands, nor had he encountered the full might of the Persian army. He was never to do so because orders arrived from the caliph Abū Bakr in Medina that he should lead a force across the desert to aid the Muslim conquest of Syria, where resistance was proving unexpectedly strong: at this stage, Syria still had priority over Iraq among the Muslim leadership. He seems to have obeyed instantly.

The departure of Khālid left the remaining Muslim forces along the Iraqi border leaderless. For a while Muthannā seems to have taken over command, but when Umar became caliph he decided to send another army to the Iraqi borderlands to ensure the continued allegiance of the Arab tribes there. It was not a particularly impressive force, numbering at most five thousand and probably many fewer. Recruitment seems to have been difficult and we are told that men disliked going there 'because of the Persians' authority, might, power and glory and their victories over other nations'.[19] Many of them were recruited from the *ansār* of Medina, not noted for their military skills, and they were led by a man called Abū Ubayd, from the Thaqīf tribe of Tā'if, the little city in the hills near Mecca. Probably in late 634 Abū Ubayd, who had met up with Muthannā and his men, encountered a Persian force in a conflict that became known as the Battle of the Bridge. The Arabic sources give an unusually consistent account of the battle.[20] The Persian forces were led by Rustam, who had recently been appointed commander-in-chief. They were said to have been well equipped, their cavalry horses wearing chain mail (*tajāfīf*), horsemen bearing heraldic banners (*shuʿur*), and with a number of elephants.[21] With them they brought the great tiger-skin standard of the Persian kings, 40 metres long and 6 metres wide.[22] Between the two armies lay an irrigation canal with an old bridge which the people of nearby Hīra used to cross to reach their fields. Despite advice to the contrary, Abū Ubayd, who is portrayed as obstinate and very much afraid of being thought a coward, was determined to cross to meet the enemy. The elephants seem to have terrified the Muslims' horses and Persian archers did devastating work among the Muslim ranks. As usual in the wars of the conquests, the Muslims dismounted and began hand-to-hand fighting with swords. Abū Ubayd himself is said to have tried to attack one of the elephants, either by spearing it in the belly or cutting off its trunk, but the elephants responded by trampling him until he was dead. The loss of their commander led to a rout among the Muslims. It was at this moment that one of them decided to cut the bridge to stop the Muslims fleeing and make them stand their ground, or so he said.[23] As a result many more Muslims perished by drowning as they attempted to swim across the canal to safety. Only a small number of survivors remained to be rallied by Muthannā and retreat into the desert.

The Battle of the Bridge was the worst defeat the Muslims suffered in the early wars of the conquests. It might well have signalled the end of their campaigns against Iraq, which would have remained a largely Christian, Aramaic-speaking land under Persian rule. That this did not happen was due to two things – disarray among the Persian ranks and the determination of the new caliph, Umar, that the defeat should be avenged.

In the immediate aftermath of defeat, the surviving Muslim soldiers, led by Muthannā, who seems to have been quite severely wounded at the Battle of the Bridge and died shortly after, were reduced to doing what Arabs had so often done before, raiding along the desert margin when Persian power was too weak to prevent them. Umar's immediate response was to call on reinforcements. Manpower, however, was beginning to be a problem. The tribes of the Hijaz who had formed the core of early Muslim power were now widely dispersed, mostly in Syria, and the defeat had depleted their ranks still further. But Umar did not want to rely on men from those tribes who had, only a year or two before, challenged the Islamic leadership in the *ridda*. So he turned instead to tribesmen who had been more or less neutral in the war that had just ended. South of the Hijaz, towards the borders of Yemen, lay a mountainous area called the Sarat. It was from the villages and encampments of this area that most of the new recruits came, led by a rather larger-than-life tribal leader called Jarīr b. Abd Allāh al-Bajalī. Jarīr had good Islamic credentials, having converted to Islam a few years before the death of Muhammad and being hence entitled to the coveted status of Companion of the Prophet. On the other hand, he was a tribal leader, proud of his ancient lineage and high social status. He saw no good reason why the coming of Islam should undermine the power and prestige of a man in his position.

From the first, relations between him and Muthannā had been sticky, a rivalry that is reflected in the historical sources as supporters of each of them tried to exaggerate their hero's achievements.[24] And new dangers were appearing on the horizon, for while the Muslim forces were restricted to desultory raids, the new young Persian king, Yazdgard III, had become strong enough to assert his authority and mobilize his troops to get rid of those irritating Bedouin for good and all.[25] The Armenian Sebeos, the writer closest to the events (Sebeos was writing in the 650s, little more than a decade later), says the Persian army numbered 80,000, and he may have had good inside information since a number of Armenian princes came with contingents of between 1,000 and 3,000 men to join the imperial army.

In response, Umar began to organize another army. To solve the problem of command, he chose a man who was very much part of the early Islamic elite. Sa‘d b. Abī Waqqās came from the Quraysh of Mecca but he had also joined the Muslim cause early and was one of that small band of veterans who could claim to have fought beside the Prophet in his first victory at the battle of Badr in 624. He has a reputation in the Muslim tradition of being something of a hothead. When Muhammad was being verbally abused by his enemies in Mecca before the *hijra*, Sa‘d hit one of them with the jawbone of a camel and drew blood. In later life he delighted in his reputation as the first man to fire an arrow in the cause of Islam.[26] Neither Muthannā nor the newly arrived Jarīr could challenge his right to lead. The army he brought, however, was not especially impressive. Largely recruited in the Hijaz, Yemen and other parts of south Arabia, it was probably about four thousand strong when it left Medina in the autumn of 637, drawn from as many as ten different tribal groups.[27] Umar also ordered contingents from Syria to join these forces in Iraq, including, apparently, some of those who had previously left Iraq for Syria with Khālid b. al-Walīd. By the time of the confrontation between the Muslims and the main Persian army, Sa‘d's forces probably numbered between 6,000 and 12,000,[28] significantly smaller than the Persians: as the most important modern authority on the conquests notes, 'for all its importance, the Battle of Qādisiyya seems to have been a clash between two rather small armies'.[29]

The little town of Qādisiya lay among the palm groves on the very edge of the settled lands of Iraq. In later years pilgrims would assemble here before setting out on the long desert road to the holy cities of Mecca and Medina, and it was a natural point of arrival and assembly for Sa‘d's army. It was here that the fate of Iraq was to be decided.

The story of the battle of Qādisiya formed the basis of great legends.[30] The memory of the victory of a small, improvised and ill-equipped Arab army over the might of imperial Persia has provided inspiration for Muslims and Arabs down the centuries. In Saddam Hussein's Baghdad, the quarter along the Tigris that housed most of the government ministries was called Qādisiya. When in 1986 Saddam issued bonds to raise money for the war against Iran, they were called Qādisiya bonds. Less appropriately, the Iraqi official media often dubbed the 2003 second Gulf War as Saddam's Qādisiya. In all cases a conscious effort was being made to tap into popular memory of a time when the Arab armies had triumphed over enormous odds.

Despite the enormous importance of the battle and its iconic status, we know remarkably little about the actual course of the conflict, and many of the details are clearly formulaic. Even the year in which it occurred is quite uncertain. Arabic sources are typically contradictory about the dates, suggesting anything from 635 to 638,[31] with most historians settling for 636. On the other hand, recent research in the Armenian sources suggests that the climactic battle may have happened on the Orthodox Christmas Day (6 January) 638.[32] The descriptions of the battle run to some 160 pages in Ṭabarī's great *History*, and although full of events and details, give no clear overall picture. The Armenian sources make it clear that the Persians were disastrously defeated, but that the Armenian princes, naturally, fought with great bravery, two of the most important of them being slain, along with many Persian notables.

The Arab accounts begin with the recruitment and dispatch of the army from Medina, careful attention being paid to the names and tribal allegiances of those who participated. After the arrival of the army on the borders of Iraq there are accounts of embassies between the Arabs and the great king Yazdgard III. We are told of debates and councils of war among the Muslims, and the point is made repeatedly that they should not penetrate deeply into the irrigated lands and canals of the Sawād but should fight on the desert margins, so that if things should go wrong they could escape into the wilderness, so stressing the precariousness of the position of the Muslims.

We also hear of debates among the Persians. When the Muslim forces arrived along the edge of the desert and began to raid the settled areas, the local landowners sent messages to the new young king Yazdgard in the capital of Ctesiphon requesting help and protection. The king ordered Rustam to lead an expedition against them. Rustam had been one of Yazdgard's main supporters in the struggle for the throne. He was an experienced general and now became the effective regent of Iraq.[33] He is sometimes described in the Arabic sources as an Armenian, and the army he commanded certainly contained Armenian contingents led by their princes. Other sources say he came from Hamadhan or Rayy, and it seems as if his power was based in Media, west central Iran, while Yazdgard III had been supported first of all by the notables of Fars, further to the south. Regional rivalries may have undermined the Persian war effort. Rustam's image in the Arabic sources is of a man of wisdom, experience and a generally pessimistic disposition.[34] In the great Persian epic, the *Shahnāmah* of Firdawsi, composed around the year 1000, he is described as 'an astute, intelligent man and a fine warrior. He was a very knowledgeable astrologer who paid attention to the advice of priests'. Firdawsi also gives us the text of a long verse letter that Rustam is said to have written to his brother before the battle, foretelling defeat and the end of the Sasanian dynasty.[35]

> This house will lose all trace of sovereignty
> Of royal glory and of victory
> The sun looks down from its exalted sphere
> And sees the day of our defeat draw near
> Ahead of us lies war and endless strife
> Such that my failing heart despairs of life.
> I see what has to be, and choose the way
> Of silence since there is no more to say
> But for the Persians I will weep, and for
> The House of Sasan ruined by this war
> Alas for their great crown and throne, for all
> The royal splendour now destined to fall.

He finishes with a lament on his own impending death and an exhortation to loyalty to the doomed Persian monarchy:

> My grave is Qādisiya's battlefield
> My crown will be my blood, my shroud my shield.
> The heavens will this; may my death not cause
> Your heart to grieve too much at heaven's laws
> Watch the king always, and prepare to give
> Your life in battle so that he may live.

According to the Arabic sources, he urged the young King Yazdgard not to fight the Arabs unless absolutely necessary. He alone among the Persians recognized the military abilities and ideological commitment of the despised Bedouin and realized that they would be victorious.

The accounts of the embassies to the Persians and the debates that ensued are among the most interesting parts of the conquest narratives, not because they represent an accurate record of what actually took place but because of the insight they give us into the attitudes of early Muslims to the conquest. One of the fullest narratives[36] begins with Saᶜd telling a group of his advisers that he is sending them on a mission to the Persians. One of them suggested that this was showing too much respect and that only one man should be sent, so the speaker, Ribᶜī,* was dispatched on his own. He was taken under guard by the Persian authorities to meet with Rustam. Before he was brought in to face the general, the Persians agreed that they should try to overawe this Bedouin. They set out to demonstrate the wealth and sophistication of the Persian court. Precious objects (*zibrīj*) were displayed, cushions and carpets laid out. Rustam himself was seated on a golden throne and it was decorated with rugs (*anmāt*) and cushions embroidered with gold thread. The contrast between this and the condition of Ribᶜī, who came in on a shaggy, stumpy horse, is played up in the sources.[37] His sword was finely polished but covered in a scabbard made of shabby cloth. His spear was bound with camel sinews. He had a red shield made of cowhide 'like a thick round loaf of bread' and a bow and arrows.

Instead of being overawed, the Bedouin was defiant. His appearance was deliberately provocative. He was, we are told, 'the hairiest of the Arabs', and he did nothing to smooth out his image. His coat was the covering of his camel in which he had made a hole, and he tied it round his waist with reeds. His headdress was the girth-rope of his camel tied around him like a bandana. On his head he had four locks of hair, which stuck up 'like the horns of a goat'. His behaviour was as uncouth as his appearance. Instead of dismounting as ordered, he rode his horse on to the carpet, and when he did get down, he tore open two cushions to use them to tether his animal. When told to lay down his arms, he adamantly refused, saying that the Persians had invited him and they could take him as he was or he would go away

* Ribᶜī b. ᶜĀmir al-Tamīmī.

again. When he was finally brought in to the presence of Rustam his behaviour was proudly destructive: he used his spear to make holes and gashes in the carpets and cushions so that none of them was undamaged. When asked why he did it, he replied, 'We do not like to sit on this finery of yours.'

Rustam then asked him what had brought him here and Rib'ī replied with a short homily:

> Allah has sent us and brought us here so that we may free those who desire from servitude [*ibādat*] to earthly rulers and make them servants of God, that we may change their poverty into wealth and free them from the tyranny of [false] religions and bring them to the justice of Islam. He has sent us to bring His religion to all His creatures and to call them to Islam. Whoever accepts it from us will be safe and we shall leave him alone but whoever refuses we shall fight until we fulfil the promise of God.

When Rustam asked him what the promise of God was, he replied, 'Paradise for him who dies fighting those who have refused to embrace Islam and victory for him who survives.' Rustam then asked him whether he was the chief of the Muslims and Rib'ī replied that he was not but that it did not matter because they were all parts of the same whole, 'and the most humble of them can make promise protection on behalf of the most noble'.

Rustam then asked for time for consultation and Rib'ī reluctantly granted three days, because that was the time the Prophet had allowed. When his uncouth visitor had gone, and Rustam was alone with the Persian nobles, he expressed admiration for Rib'ī's statement. The Persians were horrified that Rustam might be contemplating abandoning his religion on the advice of this scruffy lout. He replied that they should not look at his clothing but rather at his 'judgement, his speech and his conduct'.

The nobles then went and examined Rib'ī's weapons and criticized their quality, but he showed them that they meant business by drawing his sword from its rags 'like a flame of fire'. When it came to archery, his arrow penetrated the Persian shield while his leather one stood up to their arrow. Rib'ī then returned to the Muslim camp to give the Persians time to consider.

The Persians continued to argue among themselves about the proper response, and Rustam requested that Rib'ī return the following day. Instead the Muslims send another man, to make the point that they were all equal and united, and he too rode on the precious carpets and he defiantly offered them the three usual options: 'If you embrace Islam, we will leave you alone, if you agree to pay the poll tax, we will protect you if you need our protection. Otherwise it is war.' These three options were becoming the usual offer in negotiations between the Muslims and their opponents. Rustam suggested a truce. The Arab agreed, though only for three days, 'beginning yesterday'.

On the Persian side the arguments continued and Rustam asked for a third man to be sent. This was Mughīra b. Shuʿba, altogether a more important individual than the previous two and a man who was to play a major role in the conquest and settlement of Iraq. Once again the Persians attempted to overawe their visitor; they were in their gold embroidered robes and wearing crowns. In front of them was a carpet a bow-shot long, and no one could approach them without walking on it. As they might have guessed, Mughīra was unimpressed and showed his contempt by jumping up on the throne beside Rustam. He was violently removed by the Persians, to which he responded by giving a short sermon on equality, speaking through an interpreter, an Arab from Hīra. He argued that the Arabs treated each other as equals and he was appalled that they did not, concluding that 'a kingdom cannot be based on such conduct, nor on such minds as yours'. This too provoked an argument among the Persians: the lower-class people (sifla) said that Mughīra was right but the landowners (dahāqīn) said that he was saying what their slaves had always been saying and they cursed their ancestors for not taking the Arabs more seriously.

Rustam made a joke to try to soothe the differences in front of Mughīra. Then there was a more formal disputation, Rustam and Mughīra each making a short speech with the translator[38] standing between them. Rustam began by stressing the glory and prestige of the Persians. Even if they were defeated temporarily, Allāh would restore their glory. He went on to say that the Arabs had always lived in poverty and when they were afflicted by famine and drought they would seek help at the border. He knew that that was what they were doing now, so he would provide each of them with a load of dates and two garments so that they could leave: he had no desire the kill any of them or take them prisoner.

Mughīra roundly rejected this patronizing proposition. He said that all the Persians' prosperity was due to Allāh and that they had not been nearly grateful enough. The present position of the Arabs was not due to hunger or destitution but because Allāh had sent them a prophet. He went on to stress the religious position as the others had before. When he reached the sentence 'And if you need our protection then be our slave [abd] and pay the jizya humbly, otherwise it is the sword', Rustam lost his temper and swore 'on the sun' that dawn would not break the next day before he had killed them all. So negotiations were broken off. After Mughīra had gone, Rustam told the Persians that no one could withstand people of such honesty, intelligence and steadfastness of purpose.

Modern historians have tended to denigrate such set pieces in the Arabic texts; after all, they were written down a long time later, are full of conventional tropes and themes and cannot possibly describe real events and speeches. This account was passed down by at least two early narrators before being collected by Sayf b. Umar[39](d. after 786) and the chances are that it was composed in its present form within a hundred years of the events it purports to describe. It is also likely it was elaborated when Muslim forces were still expanding the boundaries of Islam in Spain and Central Asia. In a real sense it is an authentic document of the conquest mentality, and if we want to understand the mind-set of the early Arab conquerors, it is to such documents we must turn.

The most fundamental point conveyed in the text is, of course, that the Arabs were inspired by the knowledge that Allāh was behind them and the preaching of Muhammad. So far so predictable. What is more striking is the awareness of and attention to the cultural divisions between them and the Persians. The Persians are richly clothed and live among luxurious carpets and textiles, the Arabs are poor and ragged. The only part of the Arabs' equipment which is not old and scruffy is the bright blades of their swords. The Arabs are contemptuous of the wealth of their opponents. There is also the strong sense that the Arabs believed that they lived in a more egalitarian society in contrast to the more hierarchical Persian one, and that this was an important source of strength to them. Finally, there is the theme of the Persians recognizing the power and moral superiority of the Arabs. In this case Rustam quarrels with his courtiers while acknowledging this and they remain ignorant and contemptuous.

As the Arabs waited for the confrontation, they are said to have launched raids into the Sawād, driving back animals to be used for food. On one occasion a high-class Persian wedding party was ambushed, the men slain and the women taken captive. The Arabs are also shown as adept at spying, sneaking into their opponents' camp, cutting their tent ropes and stealing their mounts to spread alarm among the enemy.

There are numerous reports of the final battle at Qādisiya but the details are very confused and it is impossible to get an overall picture. Numerous short and disconnected Arab anecdotes tell us of the bravery of one man, the death of another, occasionally the cowardice of a third. Certain themes are consistent: the fact that the fighting continued for a number of days and nights, the fact that the Persians used elephants in the early phases of the conflict but that they were largely ineffective. It looks as if the most intense fighting was done on foot and those who were mounted got down to join in. One short Arabic account stresses the importance of archery in their success.[40] A soldier in the Persian army recalled, 'I took part in the battle of Qādisiya when I was still a Magian [he later converted to Islam]. When the Arabs sent their arrows against us, we began to shout "dūk, dūk" by which we meant spindles. These "spindles" continued to shower upon us until we were overwhelmed. One of our archers would shoot an arrow from his bow but it would do no more than attach itself to the garment of an Arab whereas their arrow would tear through a coat of mail and the double cuirass we had on.' The superior power of Arab archery may have been an important factor in the success of Muslim troops here.

It is clear from Muslim and non-Muslim sources alike that the Persians suffered a catastrophic defeat and that many Persian leaders, including Rustam himself, were killed. The *Shahnāmah* account has him dying heroically in single combat with Saᶜd b. Abī Waqqās,[41] but the Arab sources know nothing of this, observing tersely that 'his body was covered with so many blows and stabs that the identity of his killer could not be determined'.[42] After Qādisiya, central Iraq lay open to Muslim invasion.

In the aftermath of the battle, Muslim troops pursued the fleeing Persians through the canals and palm groves of the Sawād. Crossing the waterways could cause problems, but after the victory at Qādisiya, local Persian landowners wisely offered their help to the Muslims, like Bistām, the *dehqān* of Burs, who built pontoon bridges across canals and sent back intelligence about the movement of the Persian forces. The disintegration of the Persian command left many locals with little alternative but to make what terms they could with the invaders.

The Arab advanced guard caught up with the remnants of the Persian forces at Bābil, ancient Babylon. Here, by the mounds of the long-deserted capital of Hammurabi and Nebuchadnezzar, they defeated them 'in less time than it takes to slip off one's cloak'.[43] The surviving Persian commanders now scattered to try to coordinate resistance in the provinces. Fayzurān went to the little town of Nihāvand in the Zagros, 'where the treasures of the Persian king were stored', and began assembling an army. Hurmuzān fled south to the rich province of Khuzistān where he set about collecting taxes to finance resistance. Others fled along the main road to the capital at Ctesiphon.[44]

Along the road there were skirmishes and individual combats. Sayf b. Umar describes one such encounter between Shāhriyār, commander of a Persian rearguard force, and a Bedouin called Nā'il.[45] Both men approached on horseback:

each had his spear. Both were of sturdy build except that Shāhriyār was 'built like a camel'. When he saw Nā'il he flung his spear down in order to grab him by the neck. Nā'il did the same. They drew their swords and hacked at each other. Then they took each other by the throat and crashed down from their mounts. Shāhriyār fell on top of Nā'il like a ton of bricks and held him down under one thigh. He drew his dagger and started to undo Nā'il's coat of mail. Shāhriyār's thumb happened to land in Nā'il's mouth and Nā'il crushed the bone with his teeth. He noticed a momentary slackening in his opponent's assault and, attacking him furiously, whipped him off on to the ground, sat on his chest, drew his own dagger [*khanjar*] and tore Shāhriyār's coat of mail from his belly. Then he stabbed him in the abdomen and side until he died. Nā'il took his horse, his bracelets and his spoils.

After this triumph, Saᶜd rewarded Nā'il with the dead man's equipment:

'After you have put on this Persian's bracelets, cloak and coat of mail, I want you to mount his horse.' Bracelets were an important part of the accoutrements of Persian nobility[46] and Sa‘d warned Nā'il to wear them only when he was going into battle. This story gives rich detail and a good fight scene, and it repeats the two themes we saw in the *Shahnāmah*: the superiority of the Persians' military equipment and the Arabs' rejection of their luxurious and effeminate ways.

Persians built like camels were not the only hazards on the way across the Sawād. At one point the Muslims encountered a group of soldiers (*katība*) who had been recruited by Queen Būrān, who had sworn that the kingdom of Persia (*mulk Fārs*) would not perish as long as they lived. They had with them a tame lion, called Muqarrat, which belonged to the Persian king. The lion seems to have gone into battle for them but was slain by an Arab soldier who jumped down from his horse and killed it. After this loss, the resistance of the Persians crumbled.[47] The Muslims also came across large numbers of Persian peasants (*fallāhīn*) living in the villages along the Tigris. Many had been employed digging protective ditches for the Persian army, but they seem to have been unarmed and in no mood to resist. Shīrzād, a Persian *dehqān* who had come over to the Muslim side, persuaded Sa‘d that they should not be harmed as they were only underlings of the Persians (*‘ulūj ahl furs*) who would never pose any sort of threat; 100,000 of them are said to have had their names recorded, so that taxes could be collected from them, and allowed to go. As long as they paid their taxes and did not undertake any hostile activity, the Muslims had no quarrel with these people and certainly made no attempt to convert them to Islam: it was the Persian aristocracy and army who were the enemy.

The next strategic objective was the Sasanian capital at Ctesiphon, 160 kilometres, say three or four days' journey, across the Sawād to the north-east, and it was from there that King Yazdgard III had tried to direct the battle.

The Persian capital, which is generally known to western historians by the Hellenized name of Ctesiphon, was a sprawling collection of cities, a fact reflected in its Arab name of Madā'in, meaning 'the Cities'. The site straddles the Tigris, which brought both life-giving water and death-dealing floods to the cities; at times it shifted its course dramatically as it made its way through the flat lands of the Sawād, carving up city centres and isolating one suburb from another.

We have no detailed written descriptions of the city at this time, and archaeological excavation has been very patchy. The first major settlement seems to have been the Greek city of Seleucia on the west bank. From about 170 BC Ctesiphon became the winter capital of the Parthian kings of Iran. After they took the city in 224, the Sasanians continued to use it as a capital, although in practice the kings often resided on country estates in the hills. In about AD 230 Ardashīr I, the effective founder of the Sasanian dynasty, laid out a round fortified city on the west bank of the river, but in the middle of the fifth century the river shifted its course, cutting the round city in two. By the time the Muslims arrived, the main part of the city was established on the east bank, though there was still a significant settlement on the west. On the east bank there were palaces, gardens and residential areas where houses for the upper classes have been excavated, but there seem to have been no fortifications to speak of. The largely mud-brick houses have dissolved back into the Mesopotamian plain and the only major building to have survived the ravages of time is part of the great palace known as the Arch of Chosroes. This is the surviving fragment of a huge audience hall, probably built by Chosroes II (591–628) on a scale that far surpassed any other palaces constructed by the Sasanians or their Muslim successors. It has remained a source of awe to later generations and even in its sadly mutilated state still demonstrates something of the power and majesty of the great kings.

Despite the fact that it was the effective capital of the Persian Empire, Ctesiphon was in many ways a very un-Persian city. The vast majority of the inhabitants of the area were probably Aramaic speaking, and there were churches and synagogues but, it would seem, no major fire-temples.

Soon the Muslims approached the sections of Ctesiphon on the west bank of the Tigris. This part of the city was protected by earthworks, guards and other sorts of military equipment. The Muslims began to bombard them with siege engines (*majānīq* and *arrādāt*), which are said to have been constructed by Shīrzād on Saʿd's orders. The reference to siege engines may be anachronistic – there is no confirmation of this fact in other texts. It remains one of the earliest examples of Muslim forces using artillery against fortifications. It also attests once again to a strategic strength of the Muslims, their ability to recruit local troops and put their talents to good use.

The Persians continued to defend themselves behind their walls and they made at least one unsuccessful sally in an attempt to break the siege. There are also reports that Yazdgard III, still in the main part of the city on the east bank of the river, sent a message offering to make peace on the basis that the Tigris would form the frontier between the Arabs and the Persian Empire, the Persians holding all the land to the east of the river. The Arab negotiator is said to have replied that there would never be peace between them until the Arabs could 'eat the honey of Ifridūn [between Rayy and Nishapur in north-east Iran] mixed with the citrons of Kūthā [in Iraq]' – that is until they had conquered the whole of the lands of Iraq and Iran.[48] The next day, as the Arabs approached the walls again and began bombarding them with their catapults, there was an uncanny silence; no one appeared on the battlements. One man remained, who explained that the Arabs' self-confident rejection of the terms had led the Persians to abandon the city and evacuate to the east bank. Saᶜd now moved his men into the fortified enclosure to use it as a base.

Now the Tigris, swift flowing and treacherous, lay between them and the main part of the city. There was no bridge and people generally crossed the river by ferry, but the Persians had removed all the boats to the east bank. Crossing the river and attacking the fortified position was thus a very difficult proposition, but Saᶜd urged his men to try, pointing out that all the land behind them to the west was secure, so that they could save themselves if anything went wrong. Some local people showed the Arabs a place where the bottom of the river was firm and could be crossed on horseback. An advance guard, said to have been sixty men, volunteered to cross first to secure the quays so that the bulk of the army could land in safety. They divided their horses into a squadron of stallions and a squadron of mares, to make them more tractable, it was said, and plunged into the river: 600 more men prepared to follow them.

The Persians, meanwhile, saw what was happening and they too urged their horses into the water. A battle in mid-stream ensued. The Arab commander shouted to his men, 'Use your spears! Use your spears! Point them at those horses, aim at their eyes!' They fought hand to hand until the Persians retreated to the far bank. The Muslims caught up with them on the shore, killing many of them, and taking possession of the quays. The rest of the force followed closely so that the enemy would have no time to regroup: they rode through the waves, the dark waters of the Tigris throwing up white spume. The men kept talking to each other as they swam across, in close-knit groups, chatting as if they were marching on dry ground. They surprised the Persians in a way the latter had not thought possible.[49] We see the Arabic sources stressing the hardiness of the Arabs and their willingness to take risks that more conventional armies would avoid.

Stories about the crossing were later bandied around among the soldiers. All the Muslims made the crossing safely, according to one story, apart from one man, who slid off the back of his chestnut mare. 'I can still see it clearly before my own eyes,' the narrator went on, 'as the horse shook its mane free.' Fortunately a colleague saw he was in distress, urged his horse towards him, grabbed him by the hand and dragged him along until they reached the safety of dry land. The survivor paid his rescuer the ultimate compliment: 'Even my own sisters would not be able to give birth to someone like you!'[50]

More trivial incidents were remembered too. It was said that no one lost anything except for one man, whose cup, tied on with a frayed piece of string that broke, floated away in the water. The man swimming beside him remarked that it was God's decree but the owner remonstrated with him. 'Why just me? God would never take my only cup from among all the people in the army.' When they reached the other side, they met a man who had been in the advance guard which had established the bridge-head. He had gone down to the water's edge to meet the first people in the main force as they reached the shore. The wind and the waves had tossed the cup to and fro until it landed on the bank. The man retrieved it with his lance and brought it to the troops. Here the owner recognized it and took it from him, saying to his companion, 'Didn't I tell you . . .?' Such anecdotes, aside from being good stories, were opportunities for Muslims to remember how God had looked after their forebears.

Meanwhile in the city itself the Persians prepared to abandon their capital. Even before the Arabs had crossed the river, Yazdgard had sent his household away. Now he left himself, along the high road to Iran, catching up with the rest of his household at Hulwān. He travelled through a land ravaged by famine and plague, the same plague that caused such devastation in Syria.[51] The men he left in charge seem to have lost the will to resist. Soon they were loading the most precious and portable goods and as much as they could from the treasury on to the backs of their horses and mules. Persian women and children were evacuated too. However, they left behind vast quantities of clothes and all sorts of precious objects, as well as all the cattle, sheep, food and drink they had collected to sustain the siege that never happened.

The Arab armies seem to have met little opposition when they entered the almost deserted city. There was some short-lived resistance around the White Palace, but that was soon overcome. Sa'd then made it his headquarters and ordered that the great Arch of Chosroes should be made into the Muslims' place of worship. Early mosques needed very little fixed furniture, possibly a mihrab facing Mecca and a minbar, a pulpit for Friday sermons.[52] The huge arch must have made a grand setting for prayers, very unlike the simple enclosure and shelter of the mosques that the Muslims established in new cities like Kūfa and Basra in the years to come. This early conversion of an important piece of architecture into a mosque may have ensured its survival. Not only was the great arch preserved unharmed but the plaster statues (tamāthīl) that decorated it were left in place, even as the Muslims prayed beneath them.[53]

Then began the division of the spoils. The Arabic sources describe with great relish how the treasures of the Persian kings were divided up among the conquerors.[54] The stories stress two themes: the contrast between the rude simplicity of the Bedouin and the luxury and richness of the Persian court and the scrupulous care and honesty with which the booty was distributed.

There are stories about the recovery of the Persian royal regalia. According to one version, the Muslim advance guard was pursuing the retreating Persians along the road to the mountains. When they came to the bridge across the Nahrawān canal, the refugees crowded together to cross. A mule was pushed off into the water. With great effort the Persians struggled to retrieve it and the Arab commander observed: 'By God there must be something important about that mule. They would not have put in so much effort to get it back nor would they have endured our swords in this dangerous situation unless there was something valuable they did not want to give up.' The Arabs dismounted to engage the enemy, and when they had been routed the commander ordered his men to haul the mule out of the water with all its baggage. It was not until the party returned to the central collecting point in Ctesiphon that they opened the baggage and found it contained 'all the king's finery, his clothes, gems, sword belt and coat of mail encrusted with jewels. The king used to don all those when he was sitting in state'.[55] In another version, two mules are captured carrying baskets, one of which contained the king's crown, which could only be held up by two jewel-encrusted props (*istawāntān*), while the other contained his robes, woven with gold thread and encrusted with gems.[56] In a third account, the Arabs also found the king's swords, aventail (*mighfar*), greaves (*sāqā*) and armplates (*sāᶜidā*) and, in another bag, coats of mail that had belonged to the emperor Heraclius, the Turkish Khaqan, Bahram Chubin, and other foes of the Persian monarchs, kept as trophies.[57]

Another set of stories deals with the great carpet that adorned the royal palace. This was called the King's Spring (*Bahāri Kisrā*) in Persian. It was huge, about 30 metres square. The Persian court kept it for use in the winter, and when they wanted a drinking party, they could sit on it and imagine that they were in a garden with all the flowers blooming. The background was gold coloured, the brocade was inlaid, the fruits depicted were precious stone, its foliage silk and its waters cloth of gold.[58] The question then arose of what to do with this fantastic object. In a different situation, it would probably have adorned the palace of the new ruler as it had that of the old, and indeed some people suggested that the caliph Umar should have it, but the early Muslims were adamant about the fair distribution of the spoils. There was no alternative. It was sent as part of the tribute to the caliph in Medina. Here it was cut up into numerous different pieces. The Prophet's cousin and son-in-law Alī, who had played no active part in the conquests himself, received a fragment which he sold for 20,000 dirhams, and other members of the Muslim elite no doubt had their shares.[59]

After the conquest of the city, the rough-and-ready Bedouin troops experienced for themselves the grandeur of the Persian monarchy. The tribesmen scarcely knew what to do with the luxuries that had come their way. The precious camphor that had perfumed the court was mistaken for salt by the Arabs, who had never seen it, and used in their cooking.[60]

Meanwhile Persian rule was being challenged in the countryside as well. One story tells of a Persian cavalry man from Ctesiphon who was in a village that belonged to him when news came of the Arab invasion and the flight of the Persians. At first he paid no attention to it, for he was a very self-confident man, and went about his business until he came to a house where he found some of his serfs (*aᶜlāj lahu*), packing their clothes and preparing to leave. On being questioned they told him that they had been driven from their houses by hornets (*zanābīr*). His immediate response was to try to solve the problem; calling for a crossbow and clay bullets, and he began to fire at the insects, splattering them against the walls. He must soon have appreciated that there was more to it than met the eye and, realizing that his serfs were escaping from his control, he lost his nerve. He ordered one of them to saddle a mount for him. He had not gone far when he was met by an Arab soldier, who drove his spear into him and left him to die.[61] The defeat of Persian arms had clearly meant that the Persian ruling class were no longer respected and the peasants were no longer obeying their masters. The old order was coming to an end.

As the Persian forces retreated eastwards towards the mountains, the Muslim army, about twelve thousand strong, moved up the road behind them. When the Persians reached Jalūlā, they decided to make a stand. Jalūlā was a parting of the ways: beyond here the Persians of Azerbaijan and the north-west would go one way, those of Media and Fars another. If they were to make a stand it had to be here. The king moved on up through the Zagros mountains, leaving men and money with his general, Mihrān, while he himself avoided meeting the enemy in person. The Persians took up defensive positions at Jalūlā. As often, they seem to have preferred a static, defensive style of warfare, fortifying themselves and making occasional sallies, in contrast to the much more mobile tactics of the Arabs. At Jalūlā they created an earthwork enclosure, topped with pointed wooden stakes (*hasak min al-khashab*), later replaced by iron ones.[62] The Muslims built no fortifications but launched repeated attacks on their opponents. According to one account, the fortifications were breached when the Persians made a sortie and opened breaches in the defences to let their horses back in.[63] Soon a group of Arabs had established themselves within the stockade and they opened the way for others to follow. The victory was complete and the slaughter terrible.

And there was booty to be taken and divided. Among the more

notable trophies was a figurine of a camel, 'about the size of a young goat when it was stood on the ground', made of gold or silver, decorated with pearls and rubies, on it the figure of a man, similarly decorated.[64] There was also booty of a human sort. One of the Arab soldiers recalled how he had entered a Persian tent in which there were pillows (*marāfiq*) and clothes. 'Suddenly I sense the presence of a human form hidden under some covers [*farsh*], I tear them away and what do I find? A woman like a gazelle, radiant as the sun! I took her and her clothes and surrendered the latter as booty [to be divided up] but put in a request that the girl should be allotted to me. I took her as a concubine and she bore me a child.'[65] Such were the pleasures of victory, and the Muslims had no inhibitions about enjoying them.

The victory at Jalūlā secured Arab control over the Sawād. Muslim forces penetrated north of Qarqīsiyā on the Euphrates and Tikrit on the Tigris. The big question was whether they would go further, through the passes in the Zagros mountains to the Iranian plateau and beyond.

At the same time as the Sawād was being conquered, Arab forces were making their first incursions in southern Iraq. Military activities here followed roughly the same pattern as further north, beginning with raids by local tribesmen trying to take advantage of the weakness of the Sasanian defences. Soon Umar sent a commander, Utba b. Ghazwān, from Medina with reinforcements, probably only a few hundred men,[66] to make sure that any gains made came under the authority of the Muslim leadership. We are also told that the expedition was part of a broader Muslim strategy, to divert the Persians of southern Iraq and Fars from helping their compatriots further north.[67] Their first substantial conquest was the city of Ubulla. Ubulla (known to the ancient Greek geographers as Apologos) was at that time the leading port at the head of the Gulf. We are told little about the details of the conquest except that the Arabs found a new sort of bread made of white flour there.

From this base, expeditions went out to conquer the nearby towns and villages. As usual we have many details but no overall picture. Persian resistance was confined to local garrisons and *dehqāns* and there was no attempt to launch a major expedition against the invaders. As the various districts came under Muslim control, taxes were gathered and distributed among the conquering armies. Very few of the

Bedouin could read or write and the task of keeping the accounts was entrusted to one Ziyād, 'although he was only a boy with plaits on his head'. He was paid the substantial salary of 2 dirhams a day for his pains: it was the beginning of a glittering administrative career and the boy Ziyād grew up to be one of the founder figures of Islamic government apparatus.

After Utba died while returning from the pilgrimage to Mecca, he was replaced by Mughīra b. Shuᶜba. We have already encountered Mughīra as the man who dared sit with Rustam on his throne. He was chosen by Umar to lead the Muslims in southern Iraq because he was not a Bedouin but a man from the settled areas of the Hijaz. Although he had converted to Islam just two years before the Prophet's death, he could still claim the coveted status of 'Companion of the Prophet'. Mughīra was a tough and resourceful leader but his career was soon engulfed in a scandal that almost cost him his life.

He began an affair with a woman called Umm Jamīl, who was married to a man from the tribe of Thaqīf. Other members of the tribe caught wind of the affair and were determined to preserve the honour of their kin. They waited until he went to visit her and then crept up to see what was going on. They saw Mughīra and Umm Jamīl, both naked, he lying on top of her. They stole away and went to tell the caliph Umar. He in turn appointed the righteous Abū Mūsā al-Ashᶜarī to go and take over command in Basra and send Mughīra to him in Medina to be investigated. When he arrived Umar confronted him with the four witnesses. The first was emphatic about what he had seen: ' I saw him lying on the woman's front pressing into her and I saw him pushing in and withdrawing [his penis] as the applicator goes in and out of the make-up [kuhl] bottle.' The next two witnesses gave exactly the same testimony. Umar now turned to the fourth, the young Ziyād, who has already appeared doing the army's accounts. The caliph hoped that his would not be the testimony to condemn a Companion of the Prophet to death. Ziyād showed a talent for diplomacy and quick thinking which was to serve him well in the rest of his life. 'I saw a scandalous sight,' he said, 'and I heard heavy breathing but I did not see whether he was actually penetrating her or not.' Since the Koran stipulates[68] that conviction for adultery requires the unequivocal testimony of four witnesses, the case collapsed, and indeed we are told that Umar ordered that the other three witnesses be flogged for making unfounded allegations.[69] The story was often repeated by Muslim lawyers, for here was the great Umar, after the Prophet himself the most important law giver in Sunni Islam, making conviction for adultery very problematic indeed.

It now fell to Abū Mūsā al-Ashʿari, pious and effective, to lead the Muslim advance in the south, and it was he who commanded the Arab armies that conquered Khuzistān. After crossing the irrigated lands around the lower Tigris, where the city of Basra was soon to be founded, the Muslim armies naturally moved forward into Khuzistān. Khuzistān, named after an ancient but long-vanished people called the Khuzis, lay between the north-east corner of the Gulf and the southern Zagros mountains. It had been the land of the ancient Elamites, and the vast ziggurat they constructed at Choga Zunbil (Basket Hill), already 2,000 years old at the time of the Muslim conquest, still remains to bear witness to their power and wealth. The landscape of parts of the province was in many ways a continuation of the Mesopotamian plain, but as the land rose slowly towards the foothills, the endless flatness of Iraq changed into rolling hills and outcrops of rock became visible. Nowadays, Khuzistān, with its unlovely capital Ahvaz, is the centre of Iran's oil industry, but when the Arabs arrived it was agriculture and textiles which made the region among the most prosperous in the Middle East.

Khuzistān is watered not by the Tigris and Euphrates, which flow and stagnate through the plains well to the west, but by a number of smaller rivers, the most important being the Karun, which follows a winding, tortuous course through gorges in the southern Zagros to reach the plains. The melting snows on the mountains provide ample water in the spring for irrigated agriculture. In the piedmont below the steep mountains, the rivers cut deeply into the rolling hills and great weirs were necessary to raise the water level to fill irrigation canals. Some of these, like the Sasanian dam and bridge at Tustar, have left enough traces to show the massive scale of this irrigation activity.

The prosperity of Khuzistān seems to have increased significantly in Sasanian times. Cities like Tustar, Junday-shapur and Ahvaz were either founded or expanded. Rice and sugar grew well here but the area was famous above all for its linens and cottons. There was also a considerable Christian community and a number of bishoprics had been established. It was into this prosperous and well-populated area that the Arab forces moved next.

Like the history of the conquest of Iraq, the course of the conquest of Khuzistān is not at all clear, and the numerous stories about different encounters add to, rather than diminish, the confusion. There are, however, two differences. The first is that we can get a much clearer idea of the physical environment of the conquests. The cities and towns of seventh-century Iraq are little more than names to us. True, we have some idea about the topography of Ctesiphon and some fragmentary excavations from Hīra but towns like Ubulla and Qādisiya have completely disappeared, swallowed up in the alluvium of central Iraq or washed away by the constantly changing watercourses. In Khuzistān, where the rivers bite deeper into the rock, there is much more continuity and we can use the modern topography to help interpret the ancient sources. We also have a local source written shortly after the events of the conquest, which acts as some sort of check on the voluminous but very confused Arabic accounts. The so-called Khuzistān Chronicle was written in Syriac, the language of the Eastern Church, by an anonymous Christian author.[70] Most of the chronicle is very brief but the author, or one of the authors, takes some space to describe the conquest of his homeland by these new invaders. The source provides another voice, which corroborates many of the events in the Arabic sources, and thus we can be reasonably certain of the main outlines of the history of the conquest of this area.

The defence of Khuzistān had been entrusted to the general Hurmuzān, who had gone to the province after the fall of Ctesiphon. He put up a spirited and determined resistance, making treaties when it suited him, but also defying the Arabs when he felt strong enough.

The author of the chronicle begins by describing how the invaders took most of the fortified towns very swiftly, including the major city of Junday-shapur. Junday-shapur was a city with a bishopric and a considerable Christian population, and was famous as the home town of the Bukhtishu family of doctors, physicians to generations of caliphs. Sadly, the idea of a flourishing medical school here, entertained by historians since the nineteenth century, has had to be abandoned under the withering gaze of modern scholarship: certainly the Christian community here produced families of doctors, but there was no organized academy. The site is abandoned now, but aerial photography shows traces of both a round city and a square one, Sasanian foundations superimposed on each other. There were no natural defences and the Muslims seem to have had little difficulty in taking the city.

The conquest of the city provides the setting for one of those moralistic tales that seek to illuminate the virtues of the early Muslim. According to this story,[71] the city resisted vigorously until one day, to the great surprise of the Muslims, the gates were flung open and the city was opened up. The Muslims asked the defenders what had come over them, to which they replied, 'You have shot us an arrow with a message that safety would be granted to us. We have accepted this and set aside the tribute payments.' The Muslims replied that they had done no such thing, but after extensive enquiries they found a slave, originally from Junday-shapur, who admitted that he had indeed written such a message. The Muslim commanders explained that this was the work of a slave with no authority to make such an offer, to which the inhabitants replied that they had no means of knowing that and finished by saying that they were going to keep their side of the bargain, even if the Muslims chose to act treacherously. The Muslims referred the matter to Umar, who responded that the promise was in fact binding, for 'God holds the keeping of promises in the highest esteem'. The moral is clear: even the promise of a slave must be respected.

Soon, the Christian author goes on, only Susa and Tustar held out. Susa was one of the homes of the great Achaemenid rulers of ancient Iran; its palaces rivalled those of Persepolis in size and splendour. Alexander the Great sacked it, plundering its fabulous riches, and it was there that he arranged his famous mass wedding, when 10,000 Greeks and Persians were legendarily united in marriage. Later, in Sasanian times, it became an important Christian centre and, as a result, was destroyed by the Sasanian king Shapur II (309–79), who pursued an actively anti-Christian policy. It had recovered enough by the time of the Muslim conquest to put up some resistance, and the Muslims later built one of the earliest surviving mosques in Iran there. The site today is dominated by a castle, erected not by some medieval potentate, but by the French archaeological mission at the end of the nineteenth century to protect themselves against Bedouin attack. For the early Muslims, however, the most noteworthy feature of the town

THE CONQUEST OF IRAQ 129

was not the Achaemenid heritage but the fact that it housed the tomb of the prophet Daniel. The Muslims took the city after a few days and killed all the Persian nobles there. In the Arabic sources the fall of the city is described as a sort of miracle.[72] Apparently the Christian monks and priests had appeared on the battlements, taunting the attackers and saying that no one could take Susa unless the Antichrist was in their army. If he was not among them, they went on, the attackers might as well not bother and should go away now. One of the Muslim commanders, in fury and frustration, went up to one of the gates and kicked it. Instantly the chains snapped, the locks broke and it flew open. The inhabitants could only beg for peace.

They also seized the 'House of Mār [Saint] Daniel' and took the treasure that had been kept there on the orders of the Persian kings since the days of Darius and Cyrus, another example of the de-thesaurization of precious metals that so often accompanied the Arabic conquest. They also broke open the silver coffin and carried off the mummified corpse within: 'many said it was Daniel's but others claimed it was Darius'. Daniel was much revered and the emperor Heraclius is said to have tried to take the body away to join his great relic collection in Constantinople. Daniel, unlike many Old Testament figures, does not appear in the Koran and the initial Muslim impulse seems to have been to destroy the cult, the caliph Umar ordering that the body be reburied under the river bed. The Muslims had removed the signet ring, which carried a picture of a man between two lions, from the corpse, and Umar ordered that it be returned.[73] But Daniel soon became a cult figure for the Muslims too. Muslims began to make pilgrimages to the site and the tomb of Daniel still exists in the heart of the city, a tall whitewashed dome overlooking the river. This is a very early example of the way in which Islam appropriated and Islamized an ancient pre-existing cult.

With the fall of Susa, only Tustar remained. The city was situated on a rocky outcrop beside the river and was defended by a castle, remains of which still survive. The river had been dammed by a weir and a bridge, both massive engineering projects which are said to have been constructed by Roman prisoners of war after Shapur I defeated the emperor Valerian in 260. It is known to this day as Bandi Qaysar, or Caesar's dam, and Arab authors considered it one of the wonders of the world; much of it still exists. Behind the dam two tunnels were cut in the rock on which the city stood to lead water away to irrigate more fields to the south. The Khuzistān Chronicle describes it graphically: 'this Shushtra [Tustar] is very extensive and strong, because of the mighty rivers and canals that surround it on every side like moats. One of these was called Ardashīragān after [the Sasanian king] Ardashīr who dug it. Another, which crossed it was called Samīrām after the Queen and another Dārāyagān after Darius. The largest of them all was a mighty torrent which flowed down from the northern mountains.'

Hurmuzān determined to make a last stand here and, according to the Khuzistān Chronicle, Tustar held out for two years. In the end it was treachery not military force which led to the fall of the city; two men with houses on the city walls conspired with the Arabs: in return for a third of the spoils, they would let them in.[74] Accordingly tunnels were dug under the city walls and the Arabs were able to enter the walls through them. Hurmuzān retreated to the citadel (*qalʿa*) and was taken alive, but a local bishop, along with 'students, priests and deacons', was killed.

The story of the conquest of Khuzistān has a curious coda in the accounts of the fate of Hurmuzān.[75] As in the case of the wise but pessimistic Rustam, the defeated general at Qādisiya, the personality of Hurmuzān is elaborated to make certain points about the differences between Arab and Persian, Muslim and non-Muslim and the connections between the two. After his surrender at Tustar, he was brought to Medina to be presented to the caliph. Before he and his escort entered the city, they arrayed him in all his finery, his brocade and cloth-of-gold robes and a crown studded with rubies. Then they led him through the streets so that everyone could see him. When they reached Umar's house, however, they found he was not there, so they went to look for him in the mosque but could not find him there either. Finally they passed a group of boys playing in the street, who told them that the caliph was asleep in a corner of the mosque with his cloak folded under his head for a pillow.

When they returned to the mosque they found him as the boys had said. He had just received a delegation of visitors from Kūfa and, when they had left, he had simply put his head down for a nap. Apart from him there was no one in the mosque. They sat down a little way from him. Hurmuzān enquired where his guards and attendants were but was told he had none. 'Then he must be a prophet,' the Persian said. 'No,' his escort replied, 'but he does the things prophets do.' Meanwhile more people gathered round and the noise woke Umar up. He sat up and saw the Persian and the escort asked him to talk to the 'king of Ahvaz'. Umar refused as long as he was wearing all his finery, and only when the prisoner had been stripped as far as decency allowed and reclad in a coarse robe did the interrogation begin.

Umar asked Hurmuzān what he thought about the recent turn of events, to which the Persian replied that in the old days God was not on the side of the Persians or the Arabs and the Persians were in the ascendancy, but now God was favouring the Arabs and they had won. Umar replied that the real reason was that the Persians had previously been united while the Arabs had not. Umar was inclined to execute him in revenge for the Muslims he had slain. Hurmuzān asked for some water, and when it was given to him he said he was afraid he would be killed while he was drinking. The caliph replied that he would not be killed before he had drunk the water, whereupon Hurmuzān allowed his hands to tremble and the water was spilled. When Umar again threatened to kill him, the Persian said that he had already been given immunity: after all, he had not drunk the water. Umar was furious, but the assembled company agreed that Hurmuzān was right. In the end, he was converted to Islam, allowed to live in Medina and given a substantial pension. The story of Hurmuzān's trick is probably a folk motif grafted on to historical events, but it serves its purpose to illustrate the contrast between Persian pride and luxury and Muslim simplicity, the honesty of the Muslims and the integration of elements of the Persian elite into the Muslim hierarchy.

A notable feature of the conquest of Iraq, and one that certainly aided the Muslims, was the defection of substantial numbers of Persian troops to the Arab side and the willingness of the Muslims to incorporate these renegades into their armies and pay them salaries. Among these were the Hamra[76] (the Reds), some of whom defected to the Muslims before the battle of Qādisiya and participated in the division of the booty that had been taken from their old comrades in arms.[77] Others joined them afterwards and fought in the Muslim army at Jalūlā. Among them were 4,000 men from the mountains of Daylam, at the south-east corner of the Caspian Sea, who seem to have been an elite unit of the army (*jund*) of the Shahanshah. Many of them subsequently settled in the Muslim new town of Kūfa, where they had their own quarter.[78]

Another group of defectors were the Asāwira,[79] a group of 300 heavily armed cavalry, many of aristocratic origins. Yazdgard III had sent them on as his advance guard as he left Iraq for Iran but, perhaps because they had no faith in his leadership, they went over to the Muslim side and settled in Basra.[80] Like the Hamra of Kūfa, they too were given a privileged position in the Muslim forces.

The Muslims had now conquered a vast and wealthy country. They were a small number, probably no more than fifty thousand men among a much larger population. The question that confronted them was how they were going to hold it and exploit its resources. In the immediate aftermath of the victory in Iraq, the Muslims settled in two new, purpose-built towns, Kūfa and Basra. We are told that Umar ordered the Muslims not to disperse through the small towns and countryside of Iraq, nor to revert to a Bedouin lifestyle in the nearby desert. Instead they were to come together in newly constructed cities, which were to form their homes and their military bases.

We know much more about the foundation of Kūfa than of Basra and Sayf b. Umar gives a full account of what they did and why. Immediately after the fall of the Persian capital of Ctesiphon, the Muslim army had settled, or rather camped, there, as expeditions fanned out, east to Hulwān at the foot of the Zagros and north of Qarqīsiyā on the Euphrates. The climate in the old Persian capital was said to be unhealthy. Umar, we are told, noted that Arabs returning from there were looking worn out. Furthermore, they were putting on weight and their muscles were becoming flabby. One Arab commander arriving at the site asked, 'Do camels thrive in this place?' On being told that the answer was no, he commented that Umar had said that 'Arab tribesmen will not be healthy in a region in which camels do not thrive'.[81]

Two men were sent out to look for a site on the desert margins. Separately they prospected along the banks of the Euphrates from Anbār to the south until they came together at a place called Kūfa, close to Hīra. Here they found three small Christian monasteries with huts made of reeds scattered between them. Both men decided there and then that they had found what they were looking for. They both dismounted and performed a ritual prayer. One of them also recited a poem, remarkable for what appears to be its pagan imagery:

> O God, Lord of heaven and what it covers
> Lord of the earth and what it carries
> By the wind and what it scatters
> By the stars and what they topple
> By the seas and what they drown
> By the demons and what they delude
> By the spirits and what they possess
> Bless this gravelly site and make it an abode of firmness.

Sa'd came from Ctesiphon and clearly decided that this was to be the place. He explained its advantages to Umar thus: 'I have taken up residence on a site covered with pebbles; it is situated between Hīra and the Euphrates, one side borders on the dry land, the other borders on the water. Dry as well as tender thistles abound there. I have left a free choice to the Muslims in Ctesiphon and those who prefer to stay there I allowed to remain as a garrison.'

This, at least, is how the choice of the site was remembered in Tabarī's *History*. The word may never have been spoken as reported but the motives are convincing. Ctesiphon may well have been unhealthy for the Bedouin and their beasts and Kūfa provided much better pasture. There were probably other considerations as well. One was the need to maintain good communications with Medina, but perhaps the most important was to keep the Muslims together, manageable and militarily effective, rather than see them disperse and lose their coherence.

Most of the Muslims in Ctesiphon elected to move to the new site, and it has been plausibly suggested that the adult male population in this first phase of the growth of the city was around twenty thousand,[82] though this was soon to be swelled by new immigrants from Arabia, hoping for a share of the action. Along with the rest of their possessions, they are said to have brought with them the doors of their houses to hang on their new residences. The first houses were built of the local reeds, but after a fire that damaged many of them, they asked Umar's permission to build in mud brick (*laban*). This was granted on condition that no one built a house with more than three apartments (*abyāt*) and that the buildings did not become too high:

once again we see the emphasis on modesty and equality among the Muslims.

The new settlement was planned with some care by a man called Abū'l-Hayyāj, who has claims to have been the first Muslim city planner. Roads radiated out from a central point and men were settled in their tribal groups along these routes so that, initially at least, men of different tribes were established in the same area. It must have reinforced tribal solidarity and rivalries between tribes. Umar is said to have specified the widths of the streets: 20 metres for the main roads (40 cubits), with side streets of 15 and 10 metres; the smallest alleys were to be 3.5 metres and no passage was to be narrower than that.[83] This was to be a clearly laid-out city, not a tangle of winding alleyways where people settled and built as they wished.

In the middle was what can be described as a civic centre. The first building to be erected was the mosque, which sat in the middle of an open square. A mighty archer was called upon to stand at the centre and fire arrows in each direction: people were permitted to build their houses only beyond the places where the arrows had fallen. The interior of the square was left empty for people to meet.

The mosque itself seems to have been roughly square in shape, about 110 metres in each direction.[84] In its earliest phase it is said to have had no walls at the sides and a partial covering at one end. It was probably constructed very simply in reeds or mud brick. Sitting in the interior, you could look out and see the neighbouring Christian monastery of Hind and, further in the distance, the gate that led to the bridge of boats across the river.[85] Shortly after its construction, the treasury in the governor's palace was robbed and Saʿd made the decision to bring the mosque right up to the palace so that they shared a common wall. The fact that the mosque was frequented day and night was felt to be the best protection against theft. This new mosque may have been rather more substantial. At one end there was a roofed area about 100 metres long, 'whose ceiling resembled the ceilings in Byzantine churches', by which he presumably meant open beams supported by columns of marble.[86] The columns are said to have come from Christian churches.[87] It was not until Ziyād's governorate, in the time of the first Umayyad caliph Muʿāwiya, that the mosque was walled in. New pillars, 15 metres in height, were made of stone from Ahvaz, fixed together with lead centres and iron clamps.

If the mosque was simplicity itself, the palace was a more complex building, and it became the subject of a vigorous dispute. Sayf, as preserved in Ṭabarī, tells the story.[88] According to him, the citadel was built for Saʿd by a Persian from Hamadhan called Rūzbih b. Buzurgmihr, and it was made of fired bricks taken from an old palace of the pre-Islamic kings of Ḥīra. Because the palace lay in the centre of the city, in which there was a great deal of noise and commotion, Saʿd had constructed a wooden door with a lock on it. When the caliph Umar heard about this, he sent a man to burn the door down, abusing Saʿd for putting a barrier between himself and the ordinary Muslims, preventing them from entering any time they wished. The story is part of a polemical literature against rulers who attempted to separate themselves or put themselves above the rank-and-file believers. The story that Saʿd's palace was made of reused bricks may well be true, however.[89]

The primitive mosque of Kūfa lay on the site of the modern mosque of the town. This was the place where the caliph Alī was assassinated in 661, and it has long been a place of veneration to the Shia, so no archaeological excavation has been possible. The palace, however, was excavated in the 1950s and 1960s. Three main building phases were detected, all superimposed, an early one, an Umayyad one and an early Abbasid one. By the ninth century the building was essentially abandoned and occupied by squatters. The first phase was demolished to its foundations when the second Umayyad building was constructed. All that remains are outside walls with square bastions projecting at regular intervals. Was this the foundation of Saʿd's palace, as the excavator thought, or the building constructed by Ziyād a generation later at the beginning of the Umayyad period, as the main historian of the city believed? It is impossible to tell.

We can, however, be certain that within a generation of the foundation of the city, it had acquired two public buildings, the mosque and the palace, which shared a common wall. In this way the classic central architectural layout of the Islamic city had been established, a layout that had no direct parallel in pre-Islamic architecture and which was to persist for centuries to come. To this official complex, a third element was added, the markets.[90] It is clear that Kūfa was provided with souks from the very beginning: after all, the victorious Arab troops had to spent the dirhams they had been given as booty somewhere. At a fairly early stage they were also being paid salaries, and these too they would have spent on both necessities and luxuries. It was the noise from the markets which is said to have induced Sa{c}d to strengthen the walls and gates of his palace. We know nothing, however, of the shape or form of the early souks except that they came to occupy the open spaces around the mosque and palace. They do not seem to have been built structures until the late Umayyad period, a century after the foundation of the city. Before this, they were probably flimsy shelters, built of wood and reeds and roofed with mats. Nonetheless, the presence of the souks, in the heart of the town, surrounding mosque and palace, set the fundamental pattern for subsequent Islamic urbanism.

The Muslims operating in southern Iraq also founded a city on the margins of the desert at Basra. The accounts of the early settlement of Basra are very confused, though the Khuzistān Chronicle clearly ascribes it to Abū Mūsā al-Ash{c}ari, commander of the forces that conquered his homeland. It was also much smaller than Kūfa, perhaps only 1,000 men, as the army in the south was much smaller.[91] The site of the first city of Basra is now known as Zubayr and lies about 20 kilometres from the centre of the modern city. It was some distance from the river bank and canals were required to bring water to it. Although the location of the site is well known and much of it is open semi-desert, there have been no published excavations and no serious survey. If conditions were more peaceful than they are as I write, it would present a wonderful opportunity for students of early Islamic urbanism to explore the archaeology of this early military settlement.

It was in these new cities that early Islamic fiscal administration developed most precociously.[92] The inhabitants lived off the receipts of taxation, paid in cash as salaries (atā). At first this was supplemented by payments in kind, grain, oil and other foodstuffs (rizq), but this was gradually phased out and replaced by money. The names of those entitled to payments were entered in registers known as dīwāns. The administration of this system was very complex. In Basra, for example, there are said to have been 80,000 men by the end of Mu{c}a-wiya's caliphate in 680, each of whom was entitled to at least 200 dirhams per year. This required the collection and payment of 16 million dirhams, a massive task demanding skilled workers. The Muslims were forced to employ accountants and officials who had worked for the defeated Sasanians, and they brought with them the old Persian traditions of financial administration and bureaucratic practice.

Both the new towns, Kūfa and Basra, played an immensely important part in the history of the early Muslim world, first as military bases from which armies set out for the conquest of Iran and the east and then as cultural centres. Kūfa was also politically important, a major centre of resistance to the Umayyad caliphs of Damascus and the centre of the movement of support for the family of the Prophet which was to develop into Shiism. The foundation of Baghdad, only a few kilometres to the north, in 762 dealt a fatal blow to the prosperity of the city. By the ninth century it was in full decline and only the status of the ancient mosque as a place of pilgrimage kept the city alive. Basra in contrast was far enough away to escape the gravitational pull of Baghdad and remained the major port at the head of the Gulf. Although the centre of the city has shifted, Abū Mūsā al-Ashʿari's foundation has survived the centuries and is now the second-largest city of Iraq.

At about the same time, a force from Kūfa was marching up the Tigris towards the Jazira, accepting the surrender of towns and villages along the river banks and in the surrounding plains. When they came to the site where the city of Mosul now stands they found a castle, some Christian churches with a few houses near by and a settlement of Jews. Almost immediately after this small community was conquered, the Arabs set about developing a new town on the site, the origins of the modern city of Mosul. Plots for house building were distributed to the Arabs and the city grew rapidly to become one of the main urban centres of Iraq.[93]

The absolute chronology of events is very difficult to ascertain, but we can be reasonably confident that by the end of 640 Muslim forces had taken control of the irrigated lands of Iraq from Tikrit in the north to the Gulf in the south and as far east as the foothills of the Zagros mountains. Muslim settlement remained very patchy and was largely concentrated in the newly founded garrison cities at Kūfa, Basra and, on a smaller scale, Mosul. There was a garrison holding the old Persian capital at Ctesiphon and there were probably others of which we know nothing. The numbers of the conquerors were very small to subdue and hold this large and populous territory. The 20,000 adult males who first settled in Kūfa were surrounded by a population in the surrounding countryside which is thought to number half a million men.[94] Although the number of Arabs was swelled by new immigrants, they were always a very small minority and cannot, in the first generation, have comprised more than 10 per cent of the total. Their problems would have been compounded by the nature of the terrain, criss-crossed as it was with irrigation ditches and canals. It would certainly not have been possible to conquer and hold the land if the Muslims had been faced with determined popular resistance. In the event, however, the only serious resistance came from the Persian royal army. For reasons that are not entirely clear, this army failed repeatedly to hold its own against the Arab forces. In field battles at Qādisiya and Jalūlā, and cities like Ctesiphon at Tustar, the Sasanian forces were decisively defeated. With the collapse of the Persian army, the Arabs were prepared to make fairly easy terms with the rest of the population – they did not massacre townspeople and villagers, they did not seize their houses or their lands, they did not interfere with their religions and customs, they did not even settle among them. They demanded only that taxes be paid and that the people did not aid their enemies. Whether the taxes were higher or lower than they had been under the previous administration we cannot tell, but we can be certain that most people in Iraq thought that it was a bargain well worth making.

4

THE CONQUEST OF EGYPT

֍

The conquests of Syria and Iraq had followed on naturally from
the conquest of Arabia. In Syria, and to a lesser extent in Iraq,
there were already Arabs, both settled and nomad, either to be incorporated into the Muslim armies or subdued. It was logical, even
unavoidable, to move on from there to conquer, as the Muslim armies
did, the non-Arab peoples of the area.

Egypt was very different.[1] In the modern world we think of Egypt
as an Arab country, in many ways a political and cultural centre of the
Arab world. At the beginning of the seventh century, however, this
was not the case at all. There seems to have been no substantial Arab
settlement, no Arab tribes roamed the deserts and few Arab merchants
did business in the towns. The earliest Muslims certainly knew of it
but seem to have had few contacts there.

The story of the conquest is elaborated in the Arabic sources with
a mass of confusing detail.[2] Egypt in the eighth and ninth centuries
produced its own school of history-writing that was completely separate from the Iraqi tradition on which we depend for the history of
the conquests of the Fertile Crescent and Iran. The great Baghdad-
based historian Tabarī, who devotes hundreds of pages to collecting
the stories of the conquests of Syria, Iraq and Iran, dismisses the
conquest of Egypt in fewer than twenty.[3] A strong local tradition of
history-writing developed early in Egypt, however. Stories about the
Muslim conquest of the country were collected and written down by
a historian called Ibn Abd al-Hakam (c. 805–71) in the mid ninth
century.[4] He came from an Arab family whose ancestors had come
over with the conquest, and he sought to record and preserve the
memory of the great deeds of that time. He wrote at a time when the
old Arab aristocracy of Egypt was being replaced as the ruling elite
by Turkish soldiers brought in from the east, and his accounts are

tinged with nostalgia for the days when his family, and families like them, had ruled the land. He derived his information from a variety of works, now lost, which were composed in Egypt in the eighth and early ninth centuries[5] and were probably themselves based on local oral tradition and reflect a real early Islamic social memory about the conquests. It is useful to consider these texts as a separate body of literature and I shall refer to this material as the Egyptian-Arab writing.

At the same time, the Muslim conquest is recorded in a contemporary Christian chronicle written by John, Bishop of Nikiu, a small city on the western margins of the Delta.[6] John was a near-contemporary of the events he describes, so his account is a reflection of attitudes of the time. He also provides us with some clear dates, which help to anchor the swirling confusion of the Arabic narratives in a chronological framework. The chronicle is not, however, without its problems. The Coptic original is long since lost and survives only in a single manuscript translation into Ge'ez (the ancient and liturgical language of the Ethiopian Church), made in the twelfth century. The translation is clearly confused in places and it is hard to know how accurately it reflects the original. There are also gaps at crucial points, such as the surrender of the fortress at Babylon. John does, however, give a reasonably coherent narrative and provides a useful check on the Egyptian-Arabic tradition.

In modern times the history of the conquest of Egypt was covered in Alfred Butler's *The Arab Conquest of Egypt and the Last Thirty Years of Roman Domination*.[7] In his expansive and orotund late Victorian prose, Butler provides a memorable picture of the dramatic but confused events. Butler was a great enthusiast for the Copts and felt able to make sweeping moral judgements about their enemies and those who cast aspersions on them in a way modern historians are very reluctant to do. He was also a great scholar, however, and even though he wrote before the original text of Ibn Abd al-Hakam became readily available, many of his insights and conclusions have stood the test of time.

Egypt had been the land of the pharaohs, whose monuments and temples dominated much of the landscape, their pyramids as amazing and mysterious to medieval Muslims as they are to us today. No traveller or conqueror could fail to be impressed by the relics of ancient grandeur. Muslims knew of Egypt from the story of Joseph, which is retold, or rather commented on, in the Korán, and for them the pyramids were Joseph's granaries.

But by the time the Muslim armies first crossed the Egyptian frontier, it was almost a thousand years since the last of the pharaohs had been deposed by Alexander the Great (the same span of time that separates us from the Battle of Hastings and the Norman conquest of England).[8] In the intervening period, the country had been ruled by Alexander's successors, the Ptolemies, and had then become a rich and valuable province of the Roman Empire, supplying much of the grain for the capital. Nowadays Egypt is a major importer of food, as the resources of the Nile valley cannot possibly feed 70 million inhabitants. In Roman times, however, there were probably no more than 5 million people living in the area: in the later Roman period, as a result of plague, it may well have been no more than 3 million.[9] Properly managed, the rich lands along the river, irrigated and fertilized by the annual flood, could produce a regular surplus.

Despite this subservience to the interests of outsiders, many things in Egypt remained unchanged. The deified emperors were easily accommodated within the old Egyptian pantheon and, indeed, Egypt exported gods like Osiris along with corn to Rome. It was the coming of Christianity which marked the real break with the ancient past.

The fourth and fifth centuries were something of a golden age for Egyptian Christianity.[10] The patriarchs of Alexandria now became some of the greatest officials of the eastern empire, immensely wealthy and influential. At the same time St Pachomius (d. 346) led the movement to establish large communal monasteries, the first in the Christian world, and it was in Egypt more than in any other area of the early Christian world that monasticism was first developed. Hermits like St Antony (d. 356) lived in the fearsome deserts that bordered the Nile valley and set an example for Christian ascetics everywhere.

If it was a time of beginning and hope for the Christians, it was also the end of an era for ancient Egyptian paganism and the culture that went with it. In Hellenized Alexandria the famous Serapeum was sacked on the orders of the patriarch Theophilus (385–412) and was converted to a church dedicated to St John the Baptist while the temple and Serapeum at Canopus became a church dedicated to Saints Cyril and John. The last pagan intellectuals fled in fear of their lives, while monks took to squatting in the ruins of antique grandeur. The myth that the Arabs burned the library at Alexandria, and with it the great heritage of classical learning, has a long history and is still trotted out by those wishing to discredit early Islam. The sad reality is that the great library of the Ptolemies was probably destroyed in 48 BC when Julius Caesar fired the fleet in the harbour and the flames spread. The temple libraries that succeeded it were probably destroyed or dispersed by the Christians at the end of the fourth century.[11]

At the same time as the classical heritage was coming under sustained attack in Alexandria, the traditions of the more ancient Egypt of the pharaohs were finally coming to an end. The last dated hieroglyphic inscription, recording the birth festival of Osiris, was carved on 24 August 394 on the temple of Philae at Aswan.[12] Long before the Muslims conquered the country, the knowledge of the old script, which had recorded the doings of pharaohs, their priests and their ministers, had been lost beyond recall and remained so, even to Egyptians, throughout the Middle Ages.

The loss of the old pagan traditions did not mean that writing and recording disappeared from Egypt. The imperial administration operated in Greek, as it did throughout the eastern empire. Alongside it, the Church took to using a variation of the Greek alphabet to write the native Egyptian spoken language. This 'Coptic' became the vehicle through which the growing Christian literature and traditions of Egypt were preserved, and it gave its name to the local Church.

The establishment of Christianity as the sole official religion of Egypt, and the conversion of most of the population to the new religion, did not mean the end of ideological strife. The Monophysite schism that had so divided the church in Syria was, if anything, even more fiercely fought out in Egypt. The great majority of Egyptian bishops and monks adamantly rejected the decrees of the Council of Chalcedon in 451, which had established Diophisite Christianity as the state religion of the Roman Empire. From this point onwards, there was an open and often violent rift between the imperially appointed patriarchs in Alexandria and the rest of the Egyptian Church. The opposition, which can now be described as the Coptic Church, elected its own patriarchs and bishops. In the small towns and villages of the Nile valley and the numerous monasteries along the fringes of the desert, the imperial Church of Alexandria was regarded as alien, oppressive and above all heretical. Few were likely to rally to its support if it was attacked by an outside power.

As in other areas of the Middle East, Byzantine rule had been shaken by a series of catastrophes from the mid sixth century onwards. In 541 Egypt was the first country in the Mediterranean basin to be visited by the plague that caused such devastation throughout the area. The first outbreak was followed by others, and it has been suggested that the population declined to about 3 million as a result.[13] Egypt became a half-empty land. The great Persian wars, which began in 602, also had their effect in Egypt. At first the campaigns were confined to northern Syria and Anatolia, but after the fall of Jerusalem to the Persians in May 614, Egypt was in the front line. The country was flooded by refugees escaping from the invaders. In 617 a Persian army entered Egypt along the coast road from Palestine. They took Pelusium, sacked the monasteries and then headed south to the apex of the delta. There are no reports of any resistance at the Roman fort of Babylon, which guarded this important strategic point, and the Persian armies then headed north-west along the western edge of the delta to Alexandria. Here they encountered the only serious military resistance of the entire campaign. The city walls were clearly in good condition. A contemporary Syrian source tells us that the city had been 'built by Alexander in accordance with the advice of his master Aristotle, a city girt with walls, encircled with the waters of the Nile and furnished with strong gates'.[14] These walls were actively defended and the Persian army settled down to besiege the city. They also took the opportunity to sack and pillage the suburban monasteries that surrounded it. The inhabitants may have been demoralized by the cutting off of food supplies from the rest of Egypt and the lack of any prospect of relief from Constantinople, but we also have a story of treachery and betrayal by one of the inhabitants. In the end, it seems that the Persians entered the city by the harbour and the water gates, which were less strongly defended than the land walls, and in 619 they made themselves masters of Alexandria. The Persian armies then marched south, pillaging the country and sacking numerous monasteries, until the whole of the Nile valley as far south as Aswan had been subdued.

The initial Persian conquest in Egypt, as in Palestine, seems to have been very destructive of life and property, and especially of churches and their contents, but once they had established control, they seem to have ruled with a lighter touch: there are certainly no indications that they made any effort to force people to adopt Zoroastrianism, or even to encourage people to convert. The Persians must have remained a separate and alien minority without firm roots in the country.

We know little about the eleven years of Persian rule[15] other than that it came to an end quite peacefully. In July 629 the emperor Heraclius, who had by this time invaded Persia and sacked Ctesiphon, met the Persian general Shāhbarāz at Arabissos in south-east Turkey and agreed on the peaceful withdrawal of all remaining Persian troops in Egypt.

The resumption of Roman control was not marked by an outbreak of peace and harmony. As often in this period, the real cause of conflict was the enmity between different Christian sects, in this case the majority Monophysite Coptic Church and the minority Chalcedonians, who enjoyed the support of the government in Constantinople. In the case of Egypt, matters were exacerbated by a vigorous personal rivalry. The Coptic patriarch Benjamin came from a wealthy landowning family.[16] At Christmas 621, during the Persian occupation, he had entered a monastery near Alexandria and had soon distinguished himself by his piety and his learning. According to his admiring biographer, he was 'handsome and eloquent, calm and dignified in his speech'.[17] He soon moved to the city as chief assistant to the Coptic patriarch Andronicus, and before he died in about 623, Andronicus appointed Benjamin, then probably about 35 years old, as his successor. In the comparatively benign environment of Persian rule, the new patriarch set about the business of reforming his Church, going on a tour of inspection to Babylon and Hulwān, welcomed everywhere by popular acclaim.

The reimposition of Byzantine rule brought an end to this period of tolerance. As he had been in Syria, Heraclius was determined to reunite the Christian Church in Egypt under imperial authority. To achieve this, he appointed a man called Cyrus, known in the Arabic sources, for reasons that are quite unclear, as al-Muqawqis. Like many of Heraclius's supporters, he came from the Caucasus, having previously been Bishop of Phasis. Unlike Benjamin, he had no roots in Egypt and no experience of the country. He was now appointed

Patriarch of Alexandria and also civil governor of Egypt, a veritable viceroy. On Cyrus's arrival in the autumn of 631, Benjamin fled the city, warned, it was said, by an angel in a dream. Before he did, he summoned the clergy and laity, exhorting them to hold fast to their faith, and he wrote to all the bishops, advising them to flee to the mountains and the deserts to hide from the wrath to come. He then left the city by night, at first heading west to the city of St Menas (Mina) and then along the western side of the delta, finally making his way to a small monastery near Qus in upper Egypt, which remained famous for centuries as his place of refuge.[18]

Cyrus arrived armed with the full weight of imperial authority and entrusted with the task of uniting Diophysite Chalcedonians and Monophysite Copts with the emperor's ingenious Monothelite theological formula, which attempted to find a middle ground between the two. As far as we can tell, Cyrus was a determined but somewhat charmless man, to whom command came more naturally than persuasion. He held a council in Alexandria but the meeting was not a success. The Chalcedonians felt that too much had been surrendered and their support was only grudging; the Copts rejected it entirely. For them the formula was not a compromise at all, just another attempt to impose the hated doctrines of the Council of Chalcedon. Far from being smoothed over, the rift between the Greek-speaking ruling and military class in Alexandria and the majority Coptic population was as deep and unbridgeable as ever.

Roman garrisons were established throughout the country and Cyrus sought to impose imperial authority by force. The Coptic sources – the lives of saints and patriarchs – conjure up a vivid picture of ruthless and systematic persecution, with Cyrus in the role of those pagan emperors who had conducted the persecutions of the third century. The replacement of Persian by Christian rule was of no advantage to the Coptic Church. As Butler put it, 'Chastisement with whips was to be followed by chastisement with scorpions.'[19] Stories multiplied of the cruelty of Cyrus and the imperial authorities, and the heroic resistance of the Copts. Benjamin's own brother, Menas, became a martyr, and the tortures he suffered for his faith were lovingly recalled. First he was tortured by fire 'until the fat dropped down both his sides to the ground'. Next his teeth were pulled out. Then he was placed in a sack full of sand. At each stage he was offered his life if he would accept the decrees of the Council of Chalcedon; at each stage he refused. Finally he was taken seven bow-shots out to sea and drowned. Benjamin's biographer left no doubt who the real victors were. 'It was not they who were victorious over Menas, that champion of the faith, but Menas who by Christian patience overcame them.'[20]

The persecution was said to have lasted for ten years. Whether it was as cruel and unrelenting as the martyrologies claim we cannot know, but the accounts reveal a climate of fear and deeply held hostility to the imperial authorities. Many Copts must have thought that anything would be better than this.

It was against this background, that of a very recently reinstated Roman administration and the sharp divisions between Romans and Copts, that the Muslim conquest of Egypt began. As Cyrus attempted, with little success, to impose his will on Egypt, the Muslim conquests were gathering pace in Syria. By 636, when Gaza and most of the coast of Palestine were in their hands, the authorities in Alexandria must have been seriously concerned. Reactions to this new menace were mixed. Cyrus was prepared to offer tribute to the Muslims in exchange for a non-aggression pact, and even suggested that a marriage alliance should be made between the emperor's daughter Eudokia and Amr b. al-Ās, commander of Muslim forces in southern Palestine, after which Amr, like so many other barbarians in Byzantine history, would be baptized, 'for Amr and his army had confidence in Cyrus and regarded him with affection'.[21] Tribute may indeed have been paid in the period between the loss of Syria and the Muslim invasion of Egypt. In 639 or possibly 640 Heraclius's policy changed. He denounced the treaty made by Cyrus and replaced the patriarch/governor with a military man who was given instructions to organize a more robust defence. Cyrus was sent into exile in Cyprus and Constantinople, protesting in a public hearing that if his plan had gone ahead and he had raised taxes for the Arabs by a tax on trade, they would have remained at peace. The suspension of the payment of tribute seems to have been the immediate trigger of the Muslim invasion.[22]

The Egyptian–Arabic accounts of the conquest begin with a legend about Amr b. al-Ās discovering the wealth of Egypt at first hand. Before the Muslim conquests began, he had come with a group from Quraysh to trade in Jerusalem. They took it in turns to pasture their camels on the hills around the city. One day, when it was Amr's turn to do this, he came across a deacon, wandering in the hills. It was very hot and the deacon was half dead from thirst. Amr gave him a drink from his waterskin and the deacon then lay down and went to sleep. As he lay there, a huge snake emerged from a hole next to where he lay. Amr saw the snake and shot it with an arrow and killed it. When the deacon woke up, he asked what had happened. When Amr explained, the deacon was overwhelmed that his man had saved his life, not once but twice, both from dying of thirst and from the snake. He asked what Amr was doing and Amr explained that he was trading, hoping to make enough money to acquire a third camel to add to his two existing ones. The deacon asked how much blood money would be offered among Amr's people for saving another man's life, and was told that it would be one hundred camels, to which he replied that they had no camels in his country, but what would it be in dinars? One thousand was the answer.

The deacon explained that he was a stranger to the country, that he had come to pray at the church of the Holy Sepulchre and to spend a month in the wilderness in accordance with an oath he had taken. He was now going home, and he invited Amr to come with him, promising that he would be given double blood money when he got there.

So Amr left his companions and went off to Egypt, and was astonished by the size, prosperity and architecture of the city of Alexandria, where the deacon brought him. He was duly rewarded by the deacon, who then appointed a guide to lead him back to his companions in Jerusalem, now vividly aware of the wealth Egypt and Alexandria could offer.

We would be right to be very sceptical about the details of this story, but it makes the point that Amr, possibly alone among the early Muslim military leaders, knew something of Egypt and the opportunities it afforded. He seems to have consulted the caliph Umar in person, possibly when he came to Jābiya on his visit to Syria, about his plan to invade Egypt. Umar gave his consent to the project, although there are indications that he had his doubts about it. Amr set out with a force of between 3,500 and 4,000 men, chosen from tribes, notably the tribe of Akk, whose members lived in the Yemen, in the villages of the Tihāma plain along the shores of the Red Sea. These were not the tent-dwelling nomads of the Arabian and Syrian steppe, but men who lived in reed or brushwood huts by the coast, or in the stone houses of the mountain villages, and who tilled the fields. They were usually physically smaller and slighter than the Bedouin of the steppes, but just as tough and hardy. They were also used to a settled life, if not in towns at least in villages, and would not have brought flocks that needed to be pastured; in many ways they might have found the towns and villages of the delta and the Nile valley a familiar environment, though there was nothing in their native land to compare with the splendours of Alexandria.

It was an extremely bold undertaking. This tiny army would have to cross Sinai and then, in the unfamiliar territory of the delta, defeat the local Byzantine army and take a number of well-fortified cities. They would be far from help if things went wrong. According to one well-known story, the caliph changed his mind and wrote to Amr, saying that if he was already in Egypt he should go on but that if he had not already crossed the frontier he should abandon the project. Amr guessed the contents of the letter and refused to open it until he had reached al-Arīsh, which marked the beginning of Egyptian territory,[23] on 12 December 639.[24] He could then claim that he had the caliph's sanction for what he was doing.

The small army followed the ancient road along the coast to Egypt. As Butler remarks, 'It was the immemorial high road to Egypt, the road which had witnessed the passage of the first prehistoric settlers in Egypt, the passage of Abraham, of Jacob and Joseph, of Cambyses, Alexander and Cleopatra, of the Holy Family and lately of the Persian invaders.'[25]

The first town of any consequence was Farāma, ancient Pelusium, which lay near the coast just to the east of Port Said. The site is now uninhabited but it was important in pharaonic and Roman times. The fragmentary illustration in the Madaba map shows a town with colonnaded streets, surrounded by a wall with towers. The Romans in Egypt must have been aware of the earlier Arab conquest of Palestine, if only from the refugees who arrived from there, but Farāma seems not to have had a strong garrison. The Arabs besieged it for a month before taking it, but we have no real details of the conflict.

The arrival of the Muslims seems to have been seen by at least some of the Copts as an opportunity to cast off the authority of the hated Romans. Butler was shrilly dismissive of the idea that the Copts helped the Muslims at all, and says that the idea is only to be found in very late sources,[26] but his affection for the Copts and the absence of any edition of Ibn Abd al-Hakam clouded his judgement. (Ibn Abd al-Hakam, who certainly reflected eighth-century perceptions among the Arabs, makes a sharp distinction between the Copts and the 'Rūm'. While the Rūm were the chief enemies of the Muslims, men with whom no compromise was possible, the Copts played a more ambiguous role.) He says that when the Arabs arrived, the Coptic patriarch Benjamin wrote to his followers saying that Roman rule had come to an end and ordering them to go to meet Amr. As a result the Copts of Farāma were an active ($a^cw\bar{a}na$) help to Amr in the siege.[27]

The Muslims then marched up the eastern side of the delta, probably keeping to the desert rather than being delayed by the canals and villages of the settled lands. At Bilbays the Byzantines put up some resistance and it took a month to reduce the town. They then went on to Umm Dunayn, probably on the Nile to the north of modern Cairo. According to the Egyptian tradition, the Byzantines had fortified themselves in an earthwork with gates and had scattered iron caltrops (*hasak hadīd*) in the open spaces. The fighting was hard and victory was slow.[28] After the victory, Amr distributed some modest rewards to his followers: a dinar, a *jubba*, a *burnūs*, a turban and two pairs of shoes. The *jubba* and the *burnūs* were typically Egyptian garments: the Yemenis were beginning to adopt the customs of the country.[29]

What happened after the hard-won victory at Umm Dunayn is not clear. For the Muslims, the main objective must have been the great fortress of Babylon (Old Cairo), strongly held by a Byzantine garrison. But Amr may have felt that this was beyond his power until he received reinforcements from Arabia. It is at this point that the Christian source, John of Nikiu, takes up the story (the pages that may have described the first Arab incursions being lost). According to him, Amr decided to bypass the fortress until reinforcements arrived from Arabia and to move south to the fertile oasis of the Fayyum. From Umm Dunayn he crossed the River Nile and marched past the pyramids and the ruins of the ancient Egyptian capital of Memphis, through the palm groves and fields of the Nile valley to the entrance of the Fayyum. The Fayyum is a large oasis about 70 kilometres south-east of Cairo. In Roman times it was famous for its grain production, and it must have been a tempting target for Amr and his men as they waited for reinforcements.

Amr's expedition to the Fayyum is not recorded in any of the Arabic sources, but is described by John of Nikiu.[30] Access to the oasis was defended by the local garrison and the Arabs seem to have been unable to penetrate very far, contenting themselves with seizing sheep and goats from the high ground on the edge of the cultivated area. They did take the little town of Bahnasā, however, which they sacked, slaughtering all the men, women and children they came across. Amr's movements were being shadowed by the commander of the local militia, called John, with about fifty men, but Amr discovered their presence. The Byzantine forces tried to escape to their fortress at Abwit, travelling by night and hiding up in the gardens and palm groves by day. They were betrayed by a local man, however, surrounded and all killed. John was drowned in the river. It seems that Amr then heard of the arrival of the expected reinforcements and made his way back north to begin the assault on the fortress of Babylon.

The raid on the Fayyum and the death of John seem to have caused consternation among the Byzantines: raiding along the desert margins of the delta was one thing, penetrating into the Nile valley was altogether more serious. The body of the dead John was rescued from the river with a net, embalmed and sent eventually to Constantinople. The emperor Heraclius is said to have been extremely angry at what had happened and the commander of Byzantine forces in Egypt, Theodore, hurried to the Fayyum to see what he could do. Another general called Leontios was sent to the Fayyum to stabilize the defences. According to John of Nikiu, 'he was obese in person and unacquainted with warlike affairs', and after leaving half his troops in the oasis, he returned to Babylon. The Fayyum was saved for the empire, but only temporarily.

Meanwhile, Muslim reinforcements were approaching along the eastern side of the delta, just as Amr had done. When he returned from the Fayyum, he had to cross the river again to meet up with them. It was a dangerous moment, but the Byzantine commanders failed to take advantage of their opportunity and Amr successfully joined the newcomers. The new army was said to have numbered 12,000 men,[31] commanded by Zubayr b. al-Awwām. Zubayr had been one of the earliest followers of Muhammad and had great prestige as an early Muslim, but this was Amr's expedition and there was no doubt that he would remain in charge. Zubayr is described as of medium height, good looking (*ḥasan al-qāma*) with a pale complexion, a thin beard but thick hair on his body. He was brave, even rash, in battle, but Amr was the brains of the whole operation and he remained in overall command.[32]

The united Muslim armies camped at the ancient city of On (Heliopolis), now a suburb of greater Cairo but then on the fringes of the desert. The city had been of great importance in antiquity but was now largely abandoned: 'When the Arabs came, little of the ancient grandeur remained beyond some broken walls, and half-buried sphinxes, and the solitary obelisk which stands to this day as a memory of a vanished world.'[33] The site was on high ground and well provided with water. Amr made it his base. Knowing that he lacked the equipment or technical expertise for a siege, he attempted to lure the defenders out of their fortress and engage them in battle in the open country. The main Byzantine force under Theodore advanced towards Heliopolis across the flat lands between the River Nile and the Muqattam hills, where modern Cairo now stands. The two armies probably met in July 640. Amr's main force engaged the Byzantines but he also sent a small cavalry detachment of some five hundred men through the hills by night so that they could ambush the enemy from the rear. The strategem worked. As the main forces were engaged the ambush party attacked and the Byzantine army was thrown into confusion. Some succeeded in reaching the safety of the walls of Babylon, but many perished as they tried to flee by land and river.[34]

The next objective for the invaders was the fortress of Babylon itself. This fortress was a massive product of Roman military engineering,[35] probably built in around AD 100 by the emperor Trajan in response to a Jewish rebellion in Alexandria. It lay at a crucial point at the head of the delta where the Rawda island narrowed the Nile so that it could be crossed on a bridge of boats. The name Babylon, by which it always seems to have been known in ancient times, gave rise to a number of legends about its foundation by Nebuchadnezzar or later refugees or colonists from the original Babylon in Iraq. The Arabs came to know it as Qasr al-Shama, but its old name lingered on in medieval Europe, where the Sultan of Egypt was often known, confusingly, as the Soldan of Babylon. Almost triangular in plan, the great brick and stone walls, 12 metres high and almost 3 metres thick, ran along the river bank to the west and through gardens and monastic compounds to the east and north. At the south there was a massive gate flanked by D-shaped towers, known as the Iron Gate, which gave on to the Roman port. Overlooking the river bank there were two more massive towers, 30 metres in diameter. With an area of 5 hectares, it contained about ten churches or monasteries within its walls and a substantial civilian population, as well as the garrison. It may have been over six centuries old at the time of the Muslim invasion, but it had lost nothing of its military strength. Before the early twentieth century the fortifications remained virtually intact, sheltering within their walls Coptic churches and a synagogue. Since then, however, much of the fabric has been demolished, and only traces remain of its ancient grandeur.

It was around the beginning of September 640 that Amr began his investiture of the fortress. It has been suggested that there was a garrison of 5,000 or 6,000 men, well provided with supplies to withstand a siege. Against these mighty walls, the Arabs could only muster some puny siege engines and attempt to scale the ramparts using ladders. If there had been hope of relief or widespread support from the people of the surrounding countryside, it might well have held out. But no Byzantine army came to the rescue and Cyrus's oppressive policy towards the Copts had ensured that they looked on his fate with indifference or even hostility.

Meanwhile, in Babylon, the defenders still held out. There is no coherent account of the siege and we have only a few improving anecdotes, intended to show the warlike puritanism of the Muslims. In one of these Zubayr and Ubāda were surprised by the enemy when they were praying, but they leapt on their horses and drove their attackers back to the fortress. As they retreated, the Byzantines threw off their valuable belts and ornaments in the hope that the Arabs would pause to pick them up. The Muslims, however, showed their customary scorn for worldly wealth, pursuing their enemies to the city walls, where Ubāda was injured by a stone thrown from the ramparts. The two heroes then returned to their devotions, leaving the valuable spoils untouched.

In March 641 news came of the death of the emperor Heraclius and a succession crisis in the empire. This event would certainly have depressed the defenders and raised the morale of the Arabs, who still seem to have regarded the old emperor with a certain awe. With no prospect of relief in sight, the end could not be far off. On Easter Monday, 9 April 641, the Byzantines finally surrendered the great fortress to the Muslims and left, taking some of their gold but abandoning their considerable military equipment.[36]

According to one version, it was Zubayr who finally took the city. He brought ladders to climb the walls and shouted out 'God is great', on hearing which there was a mass assault and the defenders gave up hope and surrendered.[37] On the face of it, this is a classic narrative topos, suspiciously similar to the account of how Khālid b. al-Walīd stormed the walls of Damascus. On the other hand, the Muslims of Egypt certainly took the story seriously. Zubayr's ladder was kept as a relic. Balādhurī, writing in the second half of the ninth century, records that Zubayr built a house, later inherited by his son and descendants, in which the ladder was still preserved in his day.[38] A later source says that it survived until it was destroyed in a house fire in the year 1000, more than three and a half centuries later.[39]

The facts of the story are also important because the surrender of Babylon was a catastrophic blow for Byzantine power in Egypt, 'a source of great grief to the Romans', as the contemporary Coptic historian John of Nikiu put it with considerable *schadenfreude*. He had no doubts about the reasons: 'They had not honoured the redemptive passion of our Lord and Saviour Jesus Christ, who gave his life for those who believe in Him.' In particular they had persecuted the Orthodox Christians (by whom, of course, he meant his fellow Copts). Throughout the siege it seems that Coptic leaders had been kept imprisoned in the fortress. On Easter Sunday the prisoners were released but 'enemies of Christ as they were they [the Byzantines] did not let them go without first ill-using them; but they scourged them and cut off their hands'.[40]

It was probably at this time that the document known as the Treaty of Misr (Egypt) between the Muslims and the Byzantine authorities was drawn up, though the exact context of this document remains unclear.[41] It is in many ways similar to the treaty Umar had made with Jerusalem and was presumably modelled on it. It begins with a general clause safeguarding the people their religion (*millat*), their property, their crucifixes, their lands and their waterways. They would be obliged to pay the *jizya* (tribute) every year when the rise of the Nile (*ziyādat nahrihim*) was over.[42] If the river failed to rise properly, payment would be reduced in proportion. If anyone did not agree to it, he would not pay the tribute but he would not receive protection. Romans and Nubians who wanted to enjoy the same terms might do so and those who did not were free to leave. There are more clauses which specifically relate to the Nubians: they were not to be settled in people's houses and those who had accepted the treaty would contribute so many slaves and so many horses. In return, they would not be raided and their trade would not be interrupted. The treaty was witnessed by Zubayr and his sons Abd Allāh and Muhammad and was written by Wardān.

This treaty is just one of a number of slightly differing accounts which we have of the terms that were made with the people of Egypt.[43] In many of them the tax to be paid was assessed at 2 dinars per adult male except for the poor. Some also said that the Egyptians should provide the Muslims with supplies.[44] Each landowner (*dhī ard*) was to provide 210 kilos of wheat,* 4 litres of oil, 4 litres of honey and 4 litres of vinegar (but, of course, no wine).† They were also to get clothing: each Muslim was to be given a woollen *jubba*, a *burnūs* or turban, a pair of trousers (*sarāwīl*) and a pair of shoes. It may be that many of these south Arabians had arrived very ill prepared for the coolness of an Egyptian winter.

Now that Babylon was in Muslim hands, Amr hastened to make preparations for the inevitable assault on Alexandria. It was only three months before the rising of the Nile would make mobility very difficult. The walls of the fortress were repaired and put in order. Then he ordered the restoration of the bridge of boats across the Nile. According to a story lovingly preserved in the Arabic tradition, a dove made her nest in Amr's tent just before it was to be taken down for the expedition. He ordered that she be left in peace: 'She has taken refuge under our protection [*taharamat bi jawārinā*]. Let the tent stand until she has hatched her brood and they are flown away.' The story is further embellished by having a sentry stand guard so that the dove was not disturbed.[45]

---

* 3 irdabbs, an irdabb being about 70 kilos.
† 2 qists, an Egyptian qist being 2.106 litres.

According to the Egyptian tradition, the campaign was greatly helped at this stage by the Copts who went with the army and 'made the roads safe and constructed bridges and established markets. The Copts were a help to them in their fight against the Romans'.[46]

As usual the actual course of the campaign is confused. The first objective seems to have been Nikiu, home of the bishop-chronicler. It was a strong fortress on the western branch of the Nile near modern Manuf. The Roman commander Theodore had left one of his subordinates, Domentianus, in command of the garrison and the fleet of river boats, but he panicked on the approach of the Arab army and fled by boat to Alexandria. Finding their leader gone, the garrison threw down their arms and attempted to escape by boat, but the boatmen had already fled to their villages. The hapless soldiers were caught by the Arabs as they stood by the water and were all put to the sword apart from one man called Zacharia, who is said to have been spared for his bravery. The Muslims entered the city unopposed on 13 May 641 and, according to John, 'slaughtered everyone they found in the streets and churches, men women and infants and showed mercy to none'.[47]

The Muslims now followed the Roman army under Theodore as it retreated northwards towards Alexandria. It was not always plain sailing for the Arabs. At one point the commander of the Muslim vanguard, Sharīk b. Shuway, was surrounded by Roman troops and in danger of being overwhelmed. He ordered one of his men, who had a bay horse renowned for its speed, to gallop to find Amr, 26 kilometres in the rear at Tarnūt, to tell him of the danger. The Romans set off in pursuit of the messenger but were unable to catch him up. On hearing of Sharīk's plight, Amr advanced as quickly as possible and the enemy retreated, being unwilling to face him in battle. Ever after that, the place was known as Kūm Sharīk (Sharīk's Hill).

The Arab forces continued to advance. There was another fierce encounter at Karyūn in the delta. It seems that here Romans and Copts fought together and reinforcements came from all the surrounding towns and villages.[48] Theodore's forces were routed but only after a fierce struggle, and Amr 'prayed the prayer of fear'.[49] It was in this conflict that Amr's son was seriously injured fighting in the advance guard. In the end Theodore and his surviving troops were forced to retreat to Alexandria.

The Arab forces now approached the great city. Butler gives us a lyrical description of what they must have seen.[50]

Many of the soldiers in that [Arab] army must have seen beautiful cities in Palestine, like Edessa, Damascus and Jerusalem;[51] some may even have gazed on the far famed splendours of Antioch or the wonders of Palmyra; but nothing can have prepared them for the extraordinary magnificence of the city which now rose before them, as they passed among the gardens and vineyards and convents abounding in its environs. Alexandria was, even in the seventh century, the finest city in the world: with the possible exception of ancient Carthage and Rome, the art of the builder has never produced anything like it before or since. As far as the eye could reach ran that matchless line of walls and towers which for centuries later excited the enthusiasm of travellers. Beyond and above them gleamed domes and pediments, columns and obelisks, statues, temples and palaces. To the left [as the Arabs approached from the south-east] the view was bounded by the lofty Serapeum with its gilded roofs, and by the citadel on which Diocletian's Column stood conspicuous: to the right the great cathedral of St Mark was seen, and further west those great obelisks called Cleopatra's Needles,[52] which even then were over 2,000 years old, or twice as old as the city's foundation. The space in between was filled with the outlines of brilliant architecture: and in the background, stood that stupendous monument known as the Pharos, which rightly ranked as one of the wonders of the world. Even these half-barbarian warriors from the desert must have been strangely moved by the stateliness and grandeur, as well as by the size and strength, of the city they had come to conquer.

Archaeological evidence suggests, however, that some of the glory of classical Alexandria had long since departed.[53] The Pharos was still intact, lighting up the entrance to the harbour, and the main street of the city still ran along the course of the ancient Via Canopica, but much of the eastern part of the ancient city had been abandoned. Furthermore the important southern harbour on Lake Mareotis had been ruined by fighting between the supporters of the emperor Phocas and his rival Heraclius in 608–10, which had destroyed the canal systems. In the aftermath of this destruction, much of the southern part of the city was also abandoned. When the Abbasid caliph Mut-awwakil (847–61) ordered the building of a new set of city walls in the ninth century, they enclosed only about a third of the ancient city. Earthquakes, the destruction of the city by Crusader raiders from Cyprus in 1365 and the rebuilding of the city on the orders of Muham-mad Ali in the early nineteenth century have obliterated most of ancient and early medieval Alexandria. The sparse archaeological evid-ence does suggest, however, that the city the Arabs conquered had shrunk within its ancient walls and that many areas were abandoned. The fortifications, dating from the heyday of the city in Ptolemaic times, may have been much too lengthy for the diminished population to defend effectively.

Despite these problems, the city of Alexandria might have held out for months or even years, especially if it was supplied from the sea, but this was not to be. The empire as a whole and Alexandria in particular were torn apart by rivalry and jealousies. For details of this we are entirely dependent on the narrative of John of Nikiu, for the Arab authors tell us nothing of the conflicts.

The emperor Heraclius had died on 11 February 641, two months before the surrender of Babylon. He had ordained that imperial authority should be shared between his two sons, Constantine and Heraclius. It was never a workable scheme, and Constantine took effective charge. He summoned Cyrus back from exile and the military commander in Egypt to a conference, at which he agreed that he would send more troops to Egypt. Preparations for the expedition were already under way when, on 24 May, Constantine suddenly died. Power now passed to his younger half-brother Heraclius and his ambitious mother, Martina. The new government seems to have been determined to make peace with the Muslims and Cyrus was now sent back to Alexandria, not to strengthen the resistance but to see what terms could be negotiated. The new rulers in Constantinople may have felt that they needed all their military resources to maintain their position in the capital. Cyrus may have hoped that he could re-estab-lish the tribute arrangements he had put in place before 639. After all, the Byzantines had often paid subsidies to barbarians to keep out of their territory before, and this small group of marauders might be prepared to accept terms.

Meanwhile there were bitter disputes in Alexandria between two rivals for the post of military commander: Domentianus, the man who had surrendered first the Fayyum and then Nikiu, and Menas, who is said to have been more popular. The two men were each supported by one of the circus factions, Domentianus by the Blues and Menas by the Greens. Rival circus factions, named after colours, originally supported rival charioteers. They were an important focus of loyalty and strife in big cities in late antiquity but none of them survived the Muslim conquest. The two generals could and did call their supporters out on the streets. It is not clear whether this hostility was more than personal rivalry: John of Nikiu speaks of religious tensions but gives no further explanation. There may also have been a difference in policy: Domentianus agreed with Martina and Cyrus about reaching an accommodation with the Arabs.

John does not mention any serious fighting but the Egyptian-Arabic tradition describes a blockade enlivened by occasional sorties by the garrison and by single combats. There was clearly some skirmishing outside the city walls but, it would seem, no general assault. When the end came, it was through negotiation rather than military action.

Cyrus returned to Alexandria on the morning of the Feast of the Holy Cross, 14 September 641. He stopped first at the monastery of Tabensi near the port where a fragment of the True Cross, sent on the orders of the great Heraclius, was kept. Cyrus then took it in procession through the streets to the famous church of the Caesarion. John of Nikiu tells how the people covered the way with carpets and chanted hymns in his honour, and the crowds were so great that they trampled on each other.[54] It is interesting that the Coptic historian records the popular welcome given to the arch-enemy of his Church. He preached a sermon on the subject of the True Cross but at the end of the service a deacon gave out the wrong psalm, hoping to please the patriarch with a direct reference to his return. The people shook their heads at this departure from the proper order and sagely predicted that Cyrus would never see another Easter in the city; or so we are told.

In October Cyrus left the city quietly and went to negotiate with Amr in Fustāt. It was the time of the Nile flood and Amr, who had been campaigning in Middle Egypt, had returned to his base. According to John, Amr welcomed the patriarch, saying, 'You have done well to come to us', and Cyrus replied that 'God has delivered this land into your hands: let there be no enmity between you and Rome'. According to a Syriac chronicle, Cyrus explained that he was not responsible for the breaking of the treaty and the non-payment of tribute and 'he beseeched [the Muslims] eloquently to accept the gold he was offering but Amr replied to him: "Now that we have taken the country, we will not abandon it."'[55] Cyrus felt that he had no alternative but to accept the fait accompli and peace was finally agreed on 28 November 641. The people of Alexandria were to pay tribute. The Roman army was to leave the city with its possessions and treasures and return to Constantinople by sea. There was to be an armistice for eleven months until September 642 for these arrangements to be put into effect. In the meantime, the Muslims would keep 150 soldiers and fifty civilians as hostages to ensure that the terms of the agreement were implemented.

Cyrus now returned to Alexandria to sell his agreement to the military commander Theodore and to inform the emperor. All the people of the city came to pay tribute to him but he did not dare to explain what he had done. It was not until an Arab force appeared to collect the first instalment of the tribute that the population of Alexandria realized that peace had been made. When they saw the Muslim force, the Alexandrians gathered their arms to make ready for battle, but the military commanders announced that the city had been surrendered. The immediate popular reaction was very hostile and the patriarch was threatened with stoning. At this point Cyrus came clean: with tears of grief, he urged the people to accept the terms, saying that he had made the treaty to save them and their children. Finally they were won over; the money was collected and paid on 10 December 641, which was the first day of the Muslim year 21.

After the fall of Alexandria, there was little more resistance. It seems that Amr had already led an army into Middle Egypt. There had been some resistance from the local governor at Antinopolis but elsewhere the Muslim armies had been unopposed. During the period of truce that followed the surrender of Alexandria, Muslim armies visited the smaller towns of the northern delta. Again, there was sporadic resistance but no sustained opposition.

Meanwhile, Alexandria was adjusting to the new situation. Many Romans, including we must suppose the bulk of the army, set sail for

Constantinople or other areas still in Byzantine hands. Cyrus himself died peacefully of natural causes. It is a measure of the normality that reasserted itself that his successor as Chalcedonian patriarch was duly elected. Meanwhile the Coptic patriarch Benjamin reappeared from hiding and was able to return to the city. The last Byzantine troops under Theodore set sail for Cyprus on 17 September and the final act was played out when, at the end of the eleven-month truce, Amr formally entered the city without meeting any resistance on 29 September. A thousand years of Graeco-Roman rule were at an end.

In many ways Islamic rule was a continuation of what had gone before. We know from the administrative papyri that tell us so much about everyday life in Egypt that the same tax collectors collected much the same taxes under Byzantine and Muslim rule and they continued to use Greek as the language of government. It was to be another half-century before Arabic became the language of administration.

In a number of ways, however, the Muslim conquest did mean major changes. Most obviously, orders now came from Medina not Constantinople, and the governors were Arabic-speaking Muslims, not Greek-speaking Christians. Indicative of this change was the shift in the direction of grain exports. Grain from Egypt had sustained first Rome, then Constantinople. After the conquest, it sustained Medina and Mecca. One of the first projects undertaken by the new Muslim government was to reopen the ancient canal that ran from the Nile at modern Cairo to the Red Sea. Grain could now be shipped directly from the fertile fields of Egypt to the capital of the new empire.

The story goes that Amr had intended to make Alexandria his capital, which would have been the natural move, but that he was prevented from doing so by the caliph Umar, who feared the Christian and Hellenic influence of the city. Instead, the governor and the army of conquest were established just north of the fortress of Babylon, on a site that became the nucleus of old Cairo. The Egyptian-Arab tradition claims that the decision was made by the caliph Umar, who, as in Kūfa and Basra, did not want the Muslim armies to be separated from Arabia by water. It was also in a superb strategic position at the head of the delta, only a few kilometres away from the capital of the pharaohs at Memphis. Here the first mosque was built. Although most of its fabric is later, the mosque is still known as the Mosque of Amr and occupies the site on which he built it. Around it the Arabs pitched their tents and built their shelters. The names of the different tribal groups who settled there were lovingly preserved in the Egyptian-Arabic tradition, and for at least two centuries to have ancestors who had come over with the conquest meant not just social prestige but entitlement to a share of the tax revenues. The list shows that the overwhelming majority of the settlers were southern Arabs, from the settled areas of the Yemen and the Hadramawt in south Arabia. The settlement became known as Fustāt, either from one of the numerous Arabic words for tent or as a corruption of the Greek word *fossaton* or ditch. Compared with the Islamic new town at Kūfa in Iraq, which seems to have been laid out with broad streets and an open urban centre, Fustāt was much more haphazard and organic. Different tribes and families settled where they liked and the streets developed from the winding paths they walked to go down to the Nile for water or to find their way to mosque and market. The settlement was very spread out, running about 5 kilometres from north to south along the banks of the Nile and at least a kilometre from west to east. People settled in their kinship groups, each 300 to 350 men being allotted a *khitta* or plot on which to build their houses. The first Fustāt was, according to its greatest historian, 'a conglomerate of thirty or forty tribal (or multi-tribal) settlements of several hundred tents and huts made of reeds or clay, set more or less close together and separated by vast expanses of uninhabited land'.[56] More recent archaeological research has confirmed that much of the site was open and unbuilt on at the time of the Muslim conquest and that the building of permanent, brick houses was begun at a very early stage.[57]

This haphazard settlement was to have a glorious future. From the time that Amr founded it in 641 to the present day, the city at the head of the Nile delta has never ceased to be the capital of Egypt. True, the centre of power has gradually shifted north, through the ninth-century official quarter laid out on the northern boundaries of Fustāt to the walled city of Cairo (al-Qāhira, the 'Victorious'), founded by the Fatimids in 969, but despite this slow migration north, Fustāt remained a centre of population and commerce until 1171, when much of it was burned at the time of a threatened Crusader invasion. Since then much of the site has been a ruin, where low mounds of debris conceal the remains of houses, mosques and baths. But the old fortress of Babylon has remained a centre of the Coptic cult and culture, and Muslims still worship in the mosque that bears Amr's name, venerated as the oldest in Egypt.

The foundation of Fustāt put an end to the role of Alexandria as a capital. For almost a millennium, Egypt had been ruled from this Mediterranean city by a Greek-speaking elite. Contact across the Mediterranean with Rome and Constantinople was easy and frequent. In the truce between negotiation of the surrender of the city and the arrival of the Arab garrison, many of this elite left. Alexandria became a frontier town. In late 645 a Roman force under the command of a General Manuel landed in Alexandria and took the city with ease. From there they set out to ravage the delta but failed to strike home their advantage and attack Fustāt. Amr, who had by this time lost his position as governor, was hastily reappointed, and led the soldiers he had led so successfully in the first conquest. The Romans were driven back to Alexandria. In the summer of 646 the city was besieged. Some say the attacking Muslims battered down the walls with siege engines, others that it fell through the treachery of one of the gatekeepers. It is impossible to prove whether either of these versions is true. What is clear, however, is that the city was taken by force: some of the Roman soldiers escaped by ship, many more, including Manuel, were killed in the fighting. This time the arrival of the Arabs was accompanied by the burning of much of the city and widespread slaughter until Amr put an end to the killing at a place known ever since as the Mosque of Mercy.

This second conquest confirmed the status of Fustāt as the capital and sealed the fate of Alexandria, which now became a provincial city. In some ways this was a return to a much older pattern: Fustāt was the successor to the pharaonic capital at Memphis.

Arab settlement remained very limited. It is unlikely that there were more than 40,000 men[58] and their families, say a total Arab immigration of around 100,000 souls.[59] Once they had secured the country and learned how to manage its wealth to their own advantage, they had no incentive or desire to encourage further immigration: that would just have meant spreading the resources more thinly. Nor did they have any desire to encourage the conversion of the Copts, for they too would have demanded shares. For most of the first century after the conquest, Arab settlement was restricted to Fustāt, the garrison at Alexandria and another at Aswan to defend Upper Egypt from attacks from Nubia. The overwhelming majority of the population remained Coptic Christians and the lower ranks of the administration were largely drawn from the same families and groups who had served the Roman and Persian imperial administrations before. Only the military and the highest ranks of the administration were Arabs.

The main protagonists in the drama of the conquest of Egypt met very different fates. Cyrus was the first to go, dying of natural causes in the period of truce between the treaty of surrender and the final Arab occupation. Basing himself imaginatively on John of Nikiu, Butler reconstructs his last months:

> Cyrus was now a broken man in mind and body. All his dreams of ambition had dissolved: his very hopes of personal safety were gone [because of the emperor's anger at what he had done]. As he felt the shadows closing around his life, his conscience awoke to a sense of his crimes as well as his failures. Torn by unavailing remorse, he deplored his betrayal of Egypt with ceaseless tears. So plunged in gloom and despondency he fell an easy victim to a dysentery, which seized him on Palm Sunday and on the following Thursday, 21 March 642, he died.[60]

In reality, Cyrus may have been right to agree to pay tribute and play for time rather than risk military defeat at the hands of the Arabs. If his policy had been followed, the history of Egypt might have been very different.

The last years of the saintly Coptic patriarch Benjamin could hardly have been more different.[61] We have some details in the highly partisan but near-contemporary biography of the patriarch. When Amr occupied Alexandria, a Coptic nobleman (*duqs*) called Sanutius persuaded him to send out a proclamation of safe conduct for Benjamin and an invitation to return to Alexandria. When he arrived, after thirteen years in concealment, Amr treated him with love and respect and said, 'In all the lands I have conquered, I have never seen a man of God like this!' He was then instructed by the governor to resume control over the Coptic Church and he set about reconciling those Copts who had deserted the faith during the period of Cyrus's rule, including a number of bishops. He arranged for the restoration of the monasteries in the Wadi Natrun that had been ruined by the Chalcedonians, including the great house of St Macarius, which still exists as a functioning monastery in the present day. 'The good works of the orthodox [i.e. the Copts] grew and increased and the people rejoiced like young calves when their halters are unfastened and they are set free to be nourished by their mother's milk.'⁶² Now once again in Alexandria, seated in the midst of his flock, he established himself in the monastery of St Metras, because all the monks there were Egyptians (*misriyūn*) and they had not allowed it to be polluted by the hated Chalcedonians.

Benjamin also established good relations with Amr. Shortly after the fall of Alexandria, Amr prepared to set out on his expedition to Libya. He made a request of Benjamin: 'If you pray for me so that I go to the west and the Five Cities and take possession of them as I have of Egypt and return in safety and speedily, I will do everything that you ask of me.' The pious biographer then presents us with the striking image of the patriarch praying for the success of the Muslim commander against the (Christian) inhabitants of the Cyrenaica.⁶³

Benjamin survived for almost twenty years after the fall of Egypt to the Muslims, dying full of years and honour in 661. His body was laid to rest in the monastery of St Macarius, where he is still venerated as a saint. There can be no doubt that he played a major role in the survival of the Coptic Church through the transition to Arab rule.

Amr survived Benjamin by another three years, but not continuously as governor of Egypt. In 645 he was dismissed by the new caliph Uthman, who was trying to centralize the government of the caliphate, and replaced by one Abd Allah b. Saᶜd b. Abī Sarh, who would not have such close ties with the conquering army and could be relied upon to send more revenue to Medina. But Amr was not finished yet. He played an important role as adviser to his distant cousin Muᶜāwiya b. Abī Sufyān, the first Umayyad caliph, in the struggle for power that followed Uthman's death in 656. In 658 Muᶜāwiya appointed him to lead an army to take Egypt from the supporters of his rival Alī. Although it was now thirteen years since he had last governed the province, he could still attract support from the surviving conquerors and their children. In a fierce battle near Fustāt in the summer of 658 he defeated Alī's supporters and entered the capital he had founded in triumph. He remained governor until, aged about seventy, he died of natural causes early in 664. He was buried at the foot of the Muqattam hills, which rise to the east of Fustāt, but the early Muslims made little attempt to mark the burial places of their dead and the site of his tomb has never been identified.

The historical sources give Amr a good reputation. Of his competence as a military commander and politician there can be no doubt – the results speak for themselves – but he also has a reputation for straight dealing and justice. In the Egyptian-Arab tradition, he is revered not just as a conqueror but as a man who upheld the interests of the soldiers and families of the conquering army against the central government in Medina or Damascus. He is portrayed on his deathbed as wise and pious, a man whom the Prophet himself had commended in person.[64] He also has a good image in the Coptic sources. We have already seen how the biographer of Benjamin describes the good relations Amr had with his hero. Even more striking is the verdict of John of Nikiu. John was no admirer of Muslim government and was fierce in his denunciation of what he saw as oppression and abuse, but he says of Amr: 'He exacted the taxes which had been determined upon but he took none of the property of the churches, and he committed no act of spoliation or plunder, and he preserved them throughout all his days.'[65]

Of all the early Muslim conquests, that of Egypt was the swiftest and most complete. Within a space of two years the country had come entirely under Arab rule. Even more remarkably, it has remained under Muslim rule ever since. Seldom in history can so massive a political change have happened so swiftly and been so long lasting.

While the country came under Arab-Muslim rule, it did not at this stage become an Arab or a Muslim land. For centuries, Arabic speakers and Muslims were in a minority, at first a very small minority which grew very slowly. If we suggest a total Arab population of 100,000 in a total population of 3 million we can have some idea just how small, about one in thirty, this minority was.[66] Paradoxically, however, the fact that the conquerors were so few may actually have made their rule easier. They did not initially exert intolerable pressure on resources and they did not deprive local people of their lands or houses; they lived off the proceeds of taxation and they built a new town to live in. Nor did they interfere in the religious practices or buildings of the Christians. The administration continued largely unchanged. Certainly a hundred years later, taxation was beginning to seem very oppressive and we hear of violent Coptic revolts, but by that time Muslim rule was too well established to be overthrown.

The Muslims came to rule Egypt because of their military success. They defeated the Byzantine army in battle on a number of occasions and took its bases at Babylon and Alexandria. Quite why the Byzantine forces performed so badly is not clear. It was certainly not superior numbers nor superior technologies which allowed the Muslims to win. Part of the problem may have been the contrast that the Arab sources love to make between the tough, austere Muslim soldiers and the plushy and coddled Romans, and it is interesting to note John of Nikiu's comment about the overweight and unwarlike John, who failed to defend the Fayyum.

There was also a failure of leadership on the Roman side. One of the abiding mysteries attached to the Muslim conquest of Egypt is the policies of Cyrus towards the Arabs. He had spent the decade before the coming of the Muslims in a sustained and ruthless attempt to impose imperial authority over the land and the Church of Egypt. Yet the testimony of both Christian and Muslim sources makes it clear that he soon despaired of defending the land against the Muslims and set out to make terms. John of Nikiu's description of his secret surrender of Alexandria is a particularly telling example of this. It is difficult to account for this attitude. For Butler, writing with a deep sense of moral outrage, he was a treacherous schemer, working to betray the empire to build up the power of the patriarchate.[67] He played a 'dark and subtle part' in events and 'the guilt of deliberate treason to the Roman empire must remain an indelible stain on his memory'.[68] It is possible that he simply had a failure of nerve, but it is also possible that he imagined himself being viceroy for the caliphs as he had been for the emperors. Whether they were a product of incompetence or misguided realpolitik, it is clear that Cyrus's policies were a significant if not determining factor in the course of events.

Part of the explanation for the speed of the conquest lies in the political structure of Egypt. From pharaonic times the administration of the country was highly centralized. In late antiquity, defence was in the hands of the governor and his army. Most of the population had neither arms nor military training. There were no semi-independent lords with their own military following who could continue resistance on a local basis. There is a clear contrast here with Iran, where local lords and princes preserved their local cultures and a measure of independence long after the central Sasanian government had been defeated.

The attitude of the Copts, the vast bulk of the population, remains the subject of controversy. Did they, or did they not, aid the Muslim conquest? For Butler the answer was clear: they did not and he repeatedly and adamantly denounces any writer who suggests that they may have done. Butler was a great authority on Coptic culture and he was clearly determined to exculpate them from any charge of betraying Christianity. Standing back from the controversies of the late nineteenth century, the picture is less certain. The Egyptian-Arab tradition makes repeated reference to Copts aiding the Muslims, but always in a supporting role, never as fighting soldiers. The Coptic patriarch Benjamin is said to have urged his followers to make friendly contact with Amr as soon as the invasion began. This is interesting evidence. There seems to be no good reason why the tradition should make this up, particularly because it was probably first written down in the eighth century, at a time when relations between Muslims and Copts were deteriorating. It is hard to see why the tradition would give credit to the Copts for some of the Arab military achievements unless it was an ancient and integral part of the record. These references are all the more telling because they seem to have no parallel elsewhere: the accounts of the conquest of Syria, for example, give no specific examples of the Monophysite Christians, whose relationship to the Roman authorities was not very different from that of the Copts, aiding the Muslims.

John of Nikiu's testimony is even clearer. John was no apologist for Muslim rule. For him Islam was 'the faith of the beast'.[69] Nevertheless, he records that at Antinoe in Middle Egypt the inhabitants of the province, who must have been overwhelmingly Coptic, submitted to the Muslims and paid them tribute. And they put to the sword all the Roman soldiers they encountered.[70] The Copts, in fact, are said to have helped the Muslims on a number of occasions, but this was by no means a general pattern, and they suffered like the Romans from the depredations of the Muslims and the effects of heavy and arbitrary taxation. The truth seems to be that the responses of the Copts were varied and perhaps confused: some of them at some times clearly welcomed and collaborated with the conquerors. At other times they are to be found fighting alongside the Romans. Many Egyptians in the villages and small towns of the Nile valley and the delta must have felt that they had simply exchanged one group of alien and exploitative rulers for another.

5

THE CONQUEST OF IRAN

꘎

The Zagros mountains rise steeply in a series of folds from the flat plains of Mesopotamia.[1] The foothills are green and friendly in the spring, and successive rulers of the rich flat lands of Iraq have used them to find some coolness and an escape from the heat of the plains. The Sasanian kings had loved their palaces here, and later the caliphs of the Abbasid dynasty in the eighth and ninth centuries liked to come here for the hunting. The higher mountains are much more barren and there is snow in the winter, blocking most access between Iraq and Iran. There are small fertile plains within the folds of the mountains but much of the land is fit only for use by tribes of transhumant shepherds, mostly Kurdish-speaking at the time of the conquests. They are the ancestors of those Kurds who still inhabit the mountains of north-west Iran and south-eastern Turkey.

The ridges of the Zagros run parallel to the edge of the plain, one formidable obstacle after another. Apart from shepherds' paths, there are only two major routes through the mountains. The most important of these was the Great Khurasan Road, the series of valleys and passes that led from Hulwān in the Iraqi plains, past the Sasanian palaces and gardens at Qasri Shīrīn and Daskara, and the rock-cut arch at Tāqi Bustān, with its spring-filled pool and relief sculptures of the Sasanian king hunting. From here the road wound on up through narrow defiles in the plain to Bisitun. Here, a thousand years before the Arab armies passed this way, the great Darius had set up a trilingual inscription, on a vertiginous site overlooking the road in the plain far below. It was unlikely that anyone at this time could understand the ancient languages, Babylonian, Old Persian and Elamite, carved in the old cuneiform script, but they may have been able to pick out the image of the king, sitting enthroned while his vanquished opponents were paraded before him. This was a route that great kings had passed

along for centuries, leaving their mark on the main artery of the
Sasanian Empire. Beyond the plain at Bisitun, the road wound up the
steep pass above Asadabad before reaching the plateau. Here the lands
opened out, the mountains receded and the traveller reached the
ancient city of Hamadan.

The other route from plain to plateau lay far to the south. The
road passed through the flat and fertile lands of Khuzistān around
the head of the Gulf, crossing the Tāb river on the long Sasanian
bridge at Arrajān, before winding its way through the mountains to
Bishapur, the capital of Shapur I and Istakhr, the ancient capital of
Fars. The route was longer than the northern road, and fiercely hot
in the summer, but it ran through well-watered valleys and was seldom
blocked by snow. Of course, the traveller or invader from Arabia could
also cross the Gulf by boat and arrive at a little port like Jannāba on
the scorching coast, then make his way up through the mountains. It
was by all these routes that the Arab invaders penetrated the interior
of Iran.

The Iranian plateau itself provides few obstacles to the movements
of armies. The centre, to be sure, is occupied by a series of salt deserts
which are virtually impassable, but to both north and south there are
wide, flat plains between the mountain ranges. There is water to be
had and, especially in the spring, grazing for animals. The Arab armies
were able to move through these landscapes and cover large distances
with impressive speed. This enabled them to achieve overlordship of
the vast areas of the Iranian plateau in a very short period of time, the
eight years from 642 to 650. It also meant that much of the conquest
remained very superficial. They established control over most of the
main routes and the principal towns probably had Arab tax collectors
protected by a small military force. The only major Arab settlement
in the seventh century, however, was in Merv on the north-eastern
frontier. Many mountainous areas were effectively unscathed by the
conquests, their lords simply arranging to pay a tribute to the Muslim
administrators.

The final defeat of Persian forces on the plains of Iraq might have
been the end of the fighting. There would have been a certain logic
for the Muslim forces in stopping and consolidating at least for a
while, and there are hints in the sources that this option was discussed
among the Muslim leadership. Iraq was an integral part of the Sasanian

Empire, however, and no self-respecting king could simply abandon it to the enemy. The young Yazdgard III, now intent on establishing his power after the political chaos that had followed the death of Chosroes II in 628, was determined to recover his control of the rich lands of the Mesopotamian plains. He had fled far to the east to escape the invaders, but he now began to try to rally support to prevent them from reaching the Iranian plateau. Letters were sent to all the provinces of western and northern Iran and troops were told to muster at the little city of Nihāvand, on a side road off the main Zagros highway. Nihāvand itself was a small but ancient country town famous for the production of saffron and the manufacture of perfumes. The position was probably chosen because the open plains and good grazing made it a suitable place to assemble a large number of troops.

The accounts of the Nihāvand campaign[2] of 642 begin with a series of letters from the caliph Umar to Kūfa and Basra, ordering that armies should be assembled. The most enthusiastic recruits in Kūfa were drawn from those who had recently arrived from the Arabian peninsula and had not had the opportunity to distinguish themselves in the earlier fighting or acquire booty; this new campaign would give them the chance to make up for lost time.[3]

The Muslim armies gathered on the old Khurasan road and the horses were pastured at the Meadow of the Castle (Marj al-Qalʿa), where the Abbasid caliphs later kept their stud farm. They then marched on towards the Persian army at Nihāvand, about 100 kilometres away, without encountering any resistance.[4] Meanwhile another force was ordered to station itself on the borders between the provinces of Fars and Isfahan to prevent the Sasanians sending reinforcements from the south.[5]

According to the main Arabic sources, the invaders found the Persian army drawn up on the near side of a ravine, which was later to prove fatal to many of them. The Arab army is said, plausibly, to have numbered 30,000 men, the Persian army three or four times that, an exaggeration typical of the Arab chronicles.[6] Like the Arab forces, the Persian army had been swollen by volunteers from all the neighbouring areas who had missed the battle of Qādisiya and the fighting in Iraq and who now wished to prove themselves. The army was drawn up in the conventional way, with the commander, Fayzurān, in the centre and two wings on each side. As in other accounts of battles, we are told that the Persian troops were bound or chained together so that they would not flee[7] and that they scattered caltrops on the ground behind them, again to stop the cavalry escaping. The Arab historians loved to make the contrast between the Muslim troops, inspired by religious zeal, and their servile opponents, coerced into fighting. There are no Iranian sources to give their point of view.

The Arab army halted and the tent that was to serve as a command post was pitched. The Persians had fortified themselves behind trenches. The Muslim armies attempted to storm them but without much success, and the disciplined Persians emerged from their fortified posts only when it suited them. After a few days, the Muslim leaders met in a council of war. Again it is typical that the Muslims are presented as acting by consensus after calm deliberation, perhaps an implied contrast with the authoritarian command structure of their opponents. In the end it was decided that the Arab cavalry would advance and taunt their opponents and make as if to attack the trenches. They then withdrew and gradually lured them from their prepared positions in search of booty. Meanwhile the main Muslim army was kept in check. Despite protests from the more restless members of the army, the commander, Nuʿmān b. Muqarrin, kept them back until the day was well advanced and it was almost dark, claiming that this had been the Prophet's preferred time to do battle. He made his rounds of the troops on his brown, stocky horse, stopping at every banner to exhort his men. He told them that they were not fighting for the lands and booty that they saw around them but for their honour and their religion. He also reminded them of their colleagues back in Kūfa, who would suffer grievously if they were defeated. He concluded by promising them 'one of two good things, everlasting martyrdom and eternal life, or a quick conquest and an easy victory'.[8]

When they finally did attack the enemy, victory seems to have come quickly. As usual, most of the army fought on foot with drawn swords. Soon the ground was soaked in Persian blood. The horses began to slip and the Muslim commander, Nuʿmān, was thrown and killed. Despite this, the Muslims continued to advance. The Persians began to flee, and in the gathering darkness many of them lost their way and plunged to their deaths in the ravine. When the great Arab encyclopaedist Yāqūt came to compile his geographical dictionary in the early thirteenth century, 600 years after the event, the watercourse was still remembered as the place where the Persian army had been destroyed and the Iranian plateau opened up to Muslim conquest.

The surviving Persians, including Fayzurān, attempted to flee over the mountains to Hamadan but their progress along the narrow mountain paths was delayed because the road was full of a caravan of mules and donkeys carrying honey. Fayzurān himself attempted to avoid his pursuers by leaving the track and climbing over the mountains on foot, but the Muslims were soon hot on his trail and he was killed defending himself.[9]

The surrender of the towns soon followed the military victory. Immediately after the battle the invaders surrounded the little city of Nihāvand itself. They had been there only a short time when the Herbadh, the chief Zoroastrian priest in the city, came out to begin negotiations. He had a prize to offer, a large quantity of gems that the king had left there as a reserve for emergencies. He offered to hand this over in exchange for an *aman*, a guarantee of security for life and limb for the inhabitants. This was duly accepted and the city passed into Muslim rule without any further conflict.[10]

According to one story,[11] the treasure consisted of two chests of pearls of immense value. When the caliph Umar was told of this, he gave orders, following his usual policy, that the pearls should be sold for cash and the proceeds divided up among the Muslims. Accordingly the contents of the chests were sold to a speculator, a young man from the Prophet's tribe of Quraysh called Amr b. al-Hurayth, who paid for them out of the stipends that had been granted to him and his family. Having made his purchase, Amr then went to Kūfa and sold one of the chests for the same sum he had originally paid for both; the other chest he kept for himself, and 'this was the first part of the fortune Amr amassed'. We can see here the process of de-thesaurization, the converting of treasure into cash to pay the troops, and how shrewd, even unscrupulous men in the early Islamic elite could exploit the process to make fortunes.

The survivors of the Persian army had fled through the mountain to Hamadan pursued by an Arab army of some twelve thousand men. Hamadan was a much bigger prize than Nihāvand.[12] A very ancient city, it was known to the classical geographers as Ecbatana and had been the capital of Media. A bleak, upland city, it lay at the eastern end of the main road through the Zagros passes and had been an important political centre since its foundation, allegedly in the eighth century BC. At the centre of the city lay an old hilltop fortress. When the city was founded it was said to have had seven lines of walls, each of a different colour, the innermost two being plated with silver and gold.[13] There is no hint that this ostentatious opulence survived to the Muslim conquest, when the walls of the citadel seem to have been made of common clay. Hamadan was also famous as the residence of Esther, the Jewish wife of Xerxes I (486–65 BC) and eponym of one of the books of the Apocrypha: her tomb is still shown to visitors. The town may have been in decline by this time: the Arab geographer Ibn Hawqal, writing 300 years later, says it had been rebuilt since the Muslim conquest.

In the event, the fortifications proved to be of little use. The commander of the garrison was Khusrawshunūm, who had already failed to hold Hulwān against the invaders. Now he made terms for Hamadan and the city surrendered peacefully.

The collection and division of the spoils followed next. As usual the Arabic sources discuss this in great detail – the 6,000 dirhams a mounted warrior was given, the 2,000 for each foot soldier. Shares were also paid to those men who had remained behind at the Meadow of the Castle and other points along the road. The fifth was retained for the government and forwarded to the caliph Umar in Medina. As always, the sums of money must be taken with a large grain of salt, and the emphasis on fair shares for all probably reflects the enthusiasm of later commentators for finding examples of perfect practice in early Islam rather than any historical reality.

The next objective of the Arab armies was Isfahan,[14] for, as a Persian renegade is said to have explained to the caliph Umar, 'Fars and Azerbaijan are the wings and Isfahan is the head. If you cut off one of the wings the other can still work but if you cut off the head, the wings will collapse. Start with the head!'[15] Since the sixteenth century, Isfahan has been famous for its tiled mosques, palaces and gardens, but the Isfahan conquered by the Muslims was a very different place. It was essentially a well-watered plain between the eastern flanks of the Zagros mountains and the great desert of central Iran. In the plain there were a number of villages and a fire-temple on an isolated outcrop of rock. One of the villages, called Yahūdiya or Jewry, was an unfortified settlement inhabited by Jews which was later to become the nucleus of the medieval and modern city. At this time, however, the only fortified settlement was the round city of Jayy, which lay on the banks of the Ziyanda Rud river some 4 kilometres from the present city. Local legend said that Jayy had been built by Alexander the Great but the walls had been rebuilt in Sasanian times and had four gates and 104 round fortified towers. According to one local source, Jayy was not a real inhabited city but rather a fortress and place of refuge for the inhabitants of the villages of the area.[16] The fortifications must have been impressive, though nothing survives on the site except for the piers of the Sasanian bridge across the river.

Once again, the fortifications were never put to the test. The local governor led his troops out to meet the advancing Arabs. There is said to have been an inconclusive individual trial by combat between him and the commander of the Arab forces before the Persian made an agreement, in which the inhabitants were allowed to remain in their homes and keep their property in exchange for the payment of tribute. The text of the treaty is given in the sources. It takes the form of a personal agreement between the Arab commander and the governor. Tribute would be paid by all adults but it would be set at an affordable rate. The only other important provisions were that Muslims passing through should be given hospitality for a night and given a mount for the next stage of their journey.

Thirty diehard adherents of the Sasanian regime left the town to go eastwards to Kirman and join the Persian resistance, but the vast majority accepted the new dispensation.[17] The occupation seems to have been conducted with a light touch. There was no violence or pillaging. Disruption to the existing community was limited; there was no large-scale Muslim settlement and no major mosque was constructed for the next century and a half.

Sometimes the Arabs were welcomed by the local inhabitants. In the little town of Qumm, later famous as one of the great Shiite shrines of Iran, the local ruler, Yazdānfar, welcomed Arab settlers, giving them a village to settle in and supplying them with lands, beasts and seeds to begin agriculture. The reason for his generosity was that the people of Qumm had been suffering from raids by the Daylamite people of the mountains to the north and Yazdānfar hoped that the Arabs would defend the community in which they had made their homes against the depredations of these raiders. In the first generation this seems to have worked and relations were more or less harmonious. Later, as the number of Arab immigrants increased, there were tensions over landownership and above all water rights which led to violence, but the initial 'conquest' of the area was largely peaceful.[18]

The Muslim armies pressed on along the road that led to Khurasan and the east. After defeating an army of Daylamites and other mountain people attempting to block his progress at Wāj al-Rūdh,[19] he headed for Rayy. Rayy lay just south of modern Tehran, which was no more than an obscure village until it was made the capital of Iran by the Qajar dynasty in the late eighteenth century. Rayy was known to the ancient Greeks as Rhages. It was already established when Alexander the Great passed through in his pursuit of Darius III, and it was rebuilt as a Macedonian polis by Seleucus Nicator in about 300 BC. He called it Europos after his own birthplace in Macedonia but, as so often, it was the old name which stuck. In around 200 BC it was taken by the Parthians and became the summer residence of the kings. Isidore of Charax describes it as the greatest city of Media, and its strategic position meant that it continued to thrive under the Sasanians.

Rayy was of immense strategic importance. To the south lay the great desert of central Iran, waterless, encrusted with salt and virtually impassable. To the north, the mountains of the Elburz range rose with dramatic suddenness from the plains. It was the water from these mountains which gave birth to the two small rivers that watered the city before they lost themselves in the desert margin to the south. Any army wanting to pass from western Iran to Khurasan and the east had to use this narrow belt of watered, fertile land and pass the city of Rayy. Siyāvush, the governor of this important place, came from one of the most aristocratic families in Iran, the Mehrans, who had a hereditary position as lords of Rayy.[19] He was the grandson of no lesser man than the great Bahrām Chūbin, one of the most respected generals in the Sasanian army, who tried to usurp the throne from the young Chosroes II in 590. The rebellion failed as Chosroes, with Byzantine military support, regained his throne. Bahrām was killed but his family clearly maintained their control of Rayy.

The Arab armies would have found a walled city, with brick or clay houses dominated by a castle on a rocky outcrop overlooking the site.

They might have expected that an assault or even a major siege would be necessary. In the event, rivalries among the Persians gave them an opportunity. The dominance of Rayy by the Mehran family was resented by the rival Zinābi family and the leader of the Zinābis came to meet the Arab armies at a village on the main road from Qazvin to the west of the city. He made an offer to lead some horsemen inside the walls by a back way. The Muslims mounted a night attack. At first the Persians stood firm but then the horsemen within the city charged them from behind, shouting the traditional Muslim war cry, '*Allāhu Akbar*'. The resistance crumbled and the invaders soon took possession of the city. There was obviously a considerable amount of looting, and it was said that as much booty was taken from Rayy as had been from the imperial capital at Ctesiphon. The Arab conquest resulted not so much in Arab occupation as in a reshuffle among the Persian elite. The Mehran family lost their authority and their quarter of the city, later known as the 'Old Town', was devastated. Meanwhile Zinābi was named as governor, and even given the Persian rank of Marzban. He gave orders for the building of a new city centre and his family, including his two sons, Shahram and Farrūkhān, were in effective control of the city.[20]

The Arab armies continued to advance along the Khurasan road to the small piedmont city of Bistām, renowned for the fertility of its soil and the excellence of its fruit, and received the peaceful submission of the provincial capital at Qūmis.

While the Arab army was encamped at Bistām, the commander, Suwayd b. Muqarrin, began to make some diplomatic overtures to the rulers of the mountain areas to the north. From Gīlān in the west through Tabaristān and Dubavand in the centre to Gurgān in the east, the southern shores of the Caspian Sea are dominated by mountain ranges, which reach their highest point at the spectacular summit of Damavand. The mountains are very unlike most of Iran. In contrast to the open and bleak slopes and summits of the Zagros, the mountains of the Elburz range are often well wooded. The northern slopes are humid and nowadays suitable for rice- and tea-growing. The roads through the mountains are few and narrow. It was not an area that any Arab military leader would be eager to attack: they always avoided narrow mountain passes and steep valleys.

Suwayd began by making contact with the ruler of Gurgān. The lands of Gurgān lay to the south-east of the Caspian Sea. This was where the mountains met the almost limitless plains of Central Asia. It has always been a frontier area and the meeting place of the settled Iranian peoples to the south and west and the nomadic Turkish speakers to the north-east: for most of the twentieth century it was the border between Iran and the territories of the Soviet Union. Today the border between Iran and Turkmenistan runs through it. The great Sasanian monarch Chosroes I Anushirvan (531–79) built a long wall, strengthened with forts at regular intervals, from the Caspian coast 100 kilometres along the desert frontier.

Remote Gurgān had always been a semi-detached part of the Sasanian Empire, being ruled by hereditary princes with the title of Sūl. The Sūl of that time, Ruzbān, entered into negotiations with Suwayd. The two met on the frontier of the province and went around assessing what tribute was to be paid. A group of Turks were allowed to escape taxation in exchange for defending the frontier, perhaps the first time in what would become a long history of Muslims employing Turks as soldiers. The text of the treaty[21] reflects the unusual status of the province. The tribute was to be paid by all adults unless the Muslims required military assistance, which would, in that case, count instead of payment. The people were allowed to keep their possessions and their Zoroastrian religion and laws as long as they did no harm to any Muslims who chose to settle there. This was conquest in name only. The traditional ruler remained in charge, paying tax now to the Muslims rather than to the Sasanian king, but there is no indication of Muslim settlement or military occupation.

At the same time, the ruler of Tabaristān, further to the west, opened negotiations to regularize his position. Tabaristān was more inaccessible than Gurgān and was completely covered by mountains, apart from a narrow strip of land along the Caspian shore. The treaty that Suwayd made with the local ruler merely stipulated that he was to restrain robbers and bandits from attacking neighbouring areas and that he should pay 500,000 of the locally minted dirhams a year. He was not to harbour fugitives or carry out treacherous acts. Muslims would visit the territory only with the permission of the ruler.

Tabaristān was not visited by any Muslim army and, at least according to the treaty, the tribute was a global payment for the whole area, rather than a poll tax. It looks as if all aspects of government, including tax collecting and the minting of coins, remained in the hands of the local ruler. The ruler of neighbouring Gīlān to the west was granted similar terms. The 'Arab conquest' of these areas was so swift because it amounted to so little in real terms: the rulers may even have been paying less tax than they had in Sasanian times. The reality was that these areas remained outside Muslim control until the eighth century. The road east from Rayy remained insecure and Muslim troops going to Khurasan were obliged to use the route that led south of the Great Desert and then turned north through Sistan.

At the same time more Muslim armies were moving into Azerbaijan. Azerbaijan was the vast province at the north-west of the Iranian plateau. This was a land of strongly contrasting environments. In some areas down by the Caspian coast the land was warm and comparatively well watered. Further south and west were vast open uplands with high mountains. This was good territory for summer pasture, and much of it was probably inhabited by Kurdish tribesmen, who spent their winters in the plains of northern Iraq or the Mughan steppes by the Caspian and their summers in the upland pastures. There were few important cities here and population must have been sparse and scattered in these vast landscapes. Booty too must have been thin, with none of the allure of the rich cities of Iraq or Fars.

The first troops had set out from Hulwān under the command of Bukayr b. Abd Allāh al-Laythī.[22] It seems likely that they found the going difficult, and after the conquest of Hamadhan, Nuʿmān was ordered to send troops from his army to support him. Nuʿmān chose to delay until after he had secured Rayy. Once again, the Arabs were helped by the cooperation of an important figure in the Iranian elite. Isfandiyādh was the brother of the Rustam who had led the Persian armies in the disastrous defeat at Qādisiya, which had opened the door of Iraq to the Muslim armies. The family may have come from this area, and Isfandiyādh led the armies of Azerbaijan in a futile attempt to halt Nuʿmān's advance to Nihāvand. He had been taken prisoner by Bukayr at the beginning of the Azerbaijan campaign and had agreed to mediate between the Arab commander and the local population. He warned Bukayr that unless he made peace with the people, they would disperse into the Caucasus and the mountains of eastern Anatolia, where they would be almost impossible to dislodge. Once again it was diplomacy which ensured the success of the Muslim armies.

The details are very sparse but it looks as if there was little fighting and that most people agreed to pay tribute in return for being allowed to keep their property and their customs and religion. There is no mention of any sieges, nor does it seem that Arab garrisons were established.

The Arab armies moved on up the western coast of the Caspian Sea to the town the Arabs called Bāb al-Abwāb, the Gate of Gates, which is now called Derbent. It was here that the main range of the Caucasus mountains came down to the sea coast. At this point the Sasanians had established a fortified outpost. The long, strong stone walls still run from the sea to the spur of the mountains. Like Gurgān, this was frontier territory. Beyond the wall was nomad country, the vast plains of what is now southern Russia.

The commander of the Sasanian garrison was one Shahrbarāz. He was very conscious of his aristocratic origins and clearly had little sympathy with the people of the Caucasus and the Armenians who surrounded him. Knowing that the Sasanian regime elsewhere had collapsed, he sought instead to make common cause with the Arab leaders, entering into a series of negotiations in which it was agreed that he and his men should be exempt from paying a poll tax in exchange for military service in the frontier army. In this way the remaining elements of the Sasanian army were not defeated but incorporated into the armies of Islam. No doubt some of them soon came to convert to Islam. Interestingly, other reports show that while the Arab commanders were keen to attack the nomads beyond the wall at Bāb, the experienced Persians warned against it, saying effectively that they should let sleeping dogs lie.[23] The Arabs did launch raids north of the wall, but no permanent gains were made. In the long run, the frontier established at the wall in 641–2 has remained the frontier of the Muslim world in the eastern Caucasus to the present day.

Similar arrangements are said to have been made with the Christian inhabitants of upland Armenia, and Arab armies penetrated as far at Tblisi in Georgia, but details are sparse and it is not clear what the effect of this activity was.

Meanwhile, a completely separate campaign was under way in southern Iran. The conquest of Fars[24] began with a seaborne invasion. There had always been close contacts between the peoples on both shores of the Gulf, and Oman especially had an ancient seafaring tradition and lots of sailors for whom the crossing of the usually tranquil waters between the coasts of Iran and Arabia presented no problems. At the time of the earliest conquests the Gulf was virtually a Sasanian lake, the Persians maintaining a number of small outposts on the Arabian shore. In the absence of large timbers and iron, navigation was possible in boats made of palm trunks, sewn together with thread, ancestors of the dhows that can still be seen in local waters today. It was natural that when the Arabs of Oman and Bahrain saw the success of their northern cousins against Sasanian Iraq, they too would wish to join in.

As in other areas, the first conquests immediately followed on from the *ridda* wars. The governor of Bahrain appointed from Medina, Alā b. al-Hadramī, apparently acting on his own initiative, took the Persian outposts on the Arabian coast. In 634 he sent a maritime expedition under the command of one Arfaja, which took an unnamed island off the Persian coast and used it as a base for raids. It seems that the caliph Umar, always portrayed as suspicious of maritime expeditions, disapproved of this exploit and the force seems to have withdrawn without achieving any permanent gains.

The next attempt was made by Uthmān b. Abī'l-Ās, who was appointed governor in 636 and was responsible for most of the conquest of Fars. He was not a native of the Gulf coast. Like many early Muslim commanders he came from the hilltop city of Tā'if near Mecca and was no doubt drafted in to ensure the control of Medina over the area. In about 639 he sent a naval expedition across the Gulf under the command of his brother Hakam. Part of his intention must have been to engage the energies of the local tribesmen and provide them with opportunities for booty, but it is also likely that Umar could see that an attack from this quarter would distract the still-formidable Persian forces from the conflict in Iraq. In particular, it would divert the energies of the Persians of Fars so that they could not join the main armies further north. Umar also ordered that the Julandā family, hereditary rulers in Oman, should provide support for the expedition. The expeditionary force was comparatively small, 2,600 or 3,000 men are the numbers given in the sources, and they were mostly drawn from the great Umani tribe of Azd. They set off from the port of Julfar on the site of the capital of the modern emirate of Ra's al-Khayma and established themselves at the island of Abarkāwān (nowadays known as Qishm) just off the Iranian coast. It was a sea journey of some 130 kilometres and would hardly have taken more than a couple of days in favourable winds. Like their predecessors in 634, they intended to use the island as a secure base for attacking the mainland.

The local commander made peace with them without putting up any resistance, but Yazdgard III was still trying to mount a vigorous defence against the invaders. He ordered the lord of Kirman to launch an expedition from Hurmuz to retake the island, but this was defeated. The Muslims then moved across to the mainland and began raiding the surrounding areas. Not surprisingly the Sasanian Marzbān of Fars, Shahrak, set out to oppose them, but his army was defeated at Rashahr in 640 and he himself was killed. After this, in 642, when the victory at Nihāvand and the Arab conquest of Ahvaz had reduced the threat posed by the Persian army, the Muslims established a permanent base at the little town of Tawwaj, which became their *misr*, their military base. The city lay not on the coast itself but a few kilometres inland, where the Shapur river provided a water supply. The town was extremely hot, like all the settlements on the Persian side of the Gulf, but surrounded by palm trees. They built mosques there, presumably very simple structures of mud brick and palm. Tawwaj might have developed as a small-scale Basra or Kūfa but events were to turn out otherwise. The town continued to thrive as a commercial centre famous for its linens woven with gold thread, but its role as a military base ceased as the Muslim armies moved further inland.

Starting from Tawwaj, Uthmān b. Abī'l-Ās embarked on the conquest of the upland areas of Fars. Fars was one of the most important provinces of the Sasanian Empire. The great monuments of the first Persian dynasty, the Achaemenids, were to be found here, and the great columned halls of Persepolis were witnesses to this ancient grandeur. It was in Fars at the city of Istakhr that the Sasanian dynasty itself originated as guardians of the temple of Anahita. The first two monarchs had created new capitals here at Jūr and Bishapur, and though later kings seldom stayed there any more, it was still remembered as the birthplace of the dynasty. Yazdgard III, in his flight, had gone back to Istakhr, back to the cradle of his dynasty, to try to rally support. Geography too was on his side. This was a land of rugged mountains, narrow passes separated by grain-growing plains and salt lakes.

We have few details of the campaign that brought this important area under Muslim rule, but the campaigning seems to have met considerable resistance. Fars was a land of mountain-top castles[25] and easily defended passes. A first attempt against the capital Istakhr in 644 failed. In 647 Muslim forces, now bolstered by reinforcements from Basra, took the city of Bishapur. The uninhabited ruins of the city can still be seen today. It lies in a fertile plain at the foot of steep mountains where a river of clear fresh water tumbles through the limestone crags to the plains. Along the side of the gorge, Shapur I, the builder of the city, had ordered the carving of bas-reliefs, depicting his triumphs. At the heart of it lay a great stone fire-temple, said to have been constructed by Roman prisoners of war, captured when Shapur defeated the Roman emperor Valerian in 260. Beside that lay the subterranean temple of the water goddess Anahita. Around it spread the city itself, laid out on a grid plan like a Greek or Roman polis. The city survived the Muslim conquest but by the eighth century its population was already being drained away by the expanding city of Kāzirūn near by and the new Muslim metropolis of Shiraz. By the twelfth century, it was a deserted ruin.

In 648 the Muslims made peace arrangements at Arrajān on the main road between Iraq and the uplands of Fars and Darābjird in the uplands to the east. Darābjird was another round city, in this case with a fortress in the centre. According to Balādhurī, it was the fountain (shadrawān) of the science and religion of the Zoroastrians, though he did not clarify what this tantalizing reference meant. It was nonetheless a religious leader, the Herbadh, who surrendered it to the Muslims on condition that the people were given the same terms and guarantees as for other cities in the area.[26]

By 650 only the capital Istakhr and the round city of Jūr were holding out against the Muslims. In this year the command structure was completely revised. Authority in Fars was entrusted to the new governor of Basra, Abd Allāh b. Āmir. Abd Allāh was an aristocrat from the Prophet's tribe of Quraysh, a man renowned for his wealth and his easygoing generosity. He dug new irrigation canals in Basra and improved the supply of water for pilgrims in Mecca. He was also a daring military commander, prepared to lead his army far from their homes in Iraq to the farthest outposts of the Sasanian Empire. His appointment also meant that all the resources of the Muslim base at Basra could be devoted to the conquest of southern and eastern Iran. As usual the accounts of this final campaign in Fars are both sparse and confused, but it seems clear that there was considerable resistance in both Jūr and Istakhr. Jūr, we are told, had been raided for some time but only fell to Ibn Āmir's troops after a dog, which had come out of the city to scavenge in the Muslim camp, showed them a secret way back in.[27]

After this, it was the turn of the capital of Fars. The scanty remains of the city of Istakhr are still visible today. It lies on flat ground on the main road a few kilometres north of the ruins of ancient Persepolis. It is not a naturally fortified site but was clearly walled at this time. The defenders seem to have mounted a more prolonged resistance than anywhere else. As happened in several other places, the city was said to have surrendered on terms and then rebelled or broke the agreement. It was during the subsequent reconquest that the conflict took place. According to one account,[28] Ibn Āmir's men took the city after fierce fighting, which included a bombardment with siege engines. The conquest was followed by a massacre in which 40,000 Persians perished, including many members of noble and knightly families who had taken refuge there.

The scale of death and destruction at Istakhr seems to have been unparalleled in the conquest of west and central Iran. It was the only conflict in which siege engines are said to have been used to reduce a fortified enclosure and the only occasion on which a massacre on this scale took place. There also seems to have been a systematic attempt to destroy the main symbols of the old Persian religion, the fire-temples, and confiscate the properties: one Ubayd Allāh b. Abī Bakra is said to have made 40 million dirhams 'extinguishing fires, destroying their temples and collecting the gifts that had been deposited in them by Zoroastrian pilgrims'.[29] Although the details are very scanty, and we have no Persian accounts to place alongside the bare Arabic narratives, it seems that there was much more resistance to the Arab invaders in Fars and especially in Istakhr than elsewhere in Iran. The role of the province as cradle and original homeland of the Sasanian dynasty may have led the local people to fight the invaders with such vigour.

Abd Allāh b. Āmir continued to push east from Fars, following hard on the heels of Yazdgard III, who had escaped before Istakhr fell. He moved on rapidly to the province of Kirman. Here the main towns, including Bam and the then capital Sirjān, fell quickly. We are told that many of the inhabitants abandoned their houses and lands rather than live under Muslim domination. Arabs came and settled in their properties.

The province of Sistan, or Sijistan, lies to the north and east of Kirman. Nowadays this is a sparsely inhabited and often lawless area straddling the Iran–Afghan border. It suffers a fierce continental climate, the daytime temperature regularly reaching 50°C in the summer, while in the winter blizzards sweep across the desolate landscape. Much of it is desert and the landscape is studded with the shapeless mud-brick ruins of ancient buildings. It has not always been so uninviting, and the present desolation of the area probably dates from the Mongol and Timurid invasions of the thirteenth and fourteenth centuries. The province owed its prosperity to the waters of the Helmand river, which brings the meltwater of the Hindu Kush mountains of Afghanistan to the plains. Like the Murghab river at Merv and the Zarafshan in Samarqand and Bukhara, the river could be used to irrigate fertile lands before it petered out in the desert. Early Islamic travellers commented favourably on the fields and crops of areas that are now treeless wastes. Sistan took its name from the Sakas, an Indo-Iranian people who played an important role in the history of the Parthian period: mail-coated Saka cavalry were an important element in the Parthian army that famously defeated the Roman general Crassus at Carrhae in 53 BC. All memory of the Sakas had been lost by the time of the Muslim conquest, but the Sistanis retained a reputation for hardiness and military prowess, though mostly as foot soldiers.

Sistan was also important as the setting for some of the most important events in the *Shahnāmah*, the Persian national epic poem. The province was the home of the great hero Rustam, the warrior par excellence of the ancient Iranian tradition. It was this Rustam who slew his son Sohrab in ignorance in one of the most famous dramas of the entire corpus. As they have come down to us, the stories were composed by the poet Firdawsi in the early eleventh century. In fact, legends of Rustam were well known by the time of the coming of

Islam, not just in Iran but also in the Arabian peninsula. We are told that they were recited in Mecca in the Prophet's lifetime and are said to have distracted frivolous minds from his preaching. It is not clear what, if any, historical truth lay behind the legends, but the so-called stable of Rakhsh, Rustam's celebrated horse, was still shown to travellers in the early Islamic period. At the time of the conquests, the province boasted a famous Zoroastrian fire at Karkūya. It survived the Muslim conquest and was still in use in the thirteenth century when it was said to have two domes dating 'from the time of Rustam the Strong'. The fire, which was never allowed to go out, lay underneath the domes. It was served by a group of priests. The priest on duty sat well back from the flames with a veil over his mouth so as not to pollute them with his breath. He fuelled the fire with tamarisk logs, put on with silver tongs. We have no idea when the temple was destroyed but it may have been a victim of the chaos that engulfed the whole area at the time of Timur's invasions at the end of the fourteenth century.

Sistan was also the home of a small Christian community. Out here, the east of the Sasanian Empire, the Christians were all Nestorian, that is to say that they belonged to the eastern Syrian Church, regarded as heretics by the Greek 'Orthodox' of Constantinople. It is typical that most of our information about this community comes down as a result of a dispute about the election of rival bishops in 544, when the patriarch at Ctesiphon had to broker a compromise that left one bishop at the capital Zaranj and another further east at Bust, now in southern Afghanistan. A Christian text composed in about 850 also records a monastery of St Stephen in Sistan, but the history and whereabouts of this establishment are otherwise completely unknown.

The Arab invasion of Sistan[30] was the logical continuation of Abd Allāh b. Āmir's drive to the east in pursuit of Yazdgard III as he fled to escape the invaders. The route from Kirman to Sistan was always difficult, lying as it did across the corner of the great salt desert, the Dashti-Lut. The road is long and hard, and the first Muslim raid was wiped out, not by the heat, but by a fierce snowstorm. In 651–2 Abd Allāh sent an expedition into the province. As usual, many towns surrendered, content to make terms that would spare them war and destruction. The local capital, Zaranj, however, was a well-fortified city, with a powerful citadel which some said had been constructed by

Alexander the Great. Here there was some fierce fighting before the Marzban agreed to make terms. He held a council of the local notables, including the *mobadh*, a Zoroastrian religious leader, and they agreed to surrender to avoid further bloodshed. The terms were the payment of a million silver dirhams in tribute each year along with a thousand slave boys, each with a golden cup in his hand. After the capture of Zaranj, the invaders considered making an attack on Bust, the leading city of southern Afghanistan, but they encountered fierce resistance.

The last of the Sasanian kings, Yazdgard III, was still on the run, looking for a place of refuge where he could rally the fugitive remnants of his army.[31] The king was offered asylum in the mountainous principality of Tabaristān. This would probably have saved his life, but it would have been impossible to mobilize sufficient resources in Tabaristān to recover his kingdom. There is also a tradition that he appealed for support from the rulers of China. Instead he headed for Sistan, probably intending to reach Khurasan in the end. According to later tradition, he insisted on moving with a swollen and luxurious court, despite his straitened circumstances. He is said to have had 4,000 people with him: slaves, cooks, valets, grooms, secretaries, wives and other women, old people and children of the household – but not a single warrior. What made the situation worse for his reluctant hosts was that he also had no money to feed them: they would need to be generous as well as brave.[32] His appeals for assistance in Sistan fell on deaf ears: after all, he had only been king for a very short time and had no tradition of loyalty to rely on. The local lords seem to have preferred the idea of making their own peace with the invaders rather than pledging their loyalty to a king with a track record of failure.

From Sistan he moved on to Khurasan. It was here in the northeast corner of his empire, in a land he may never have visited before, that the endgame of the Sasanian Empire was played out. It was a miserable end to a great story; no heroic resistance against the odds here. The fugitive king seems to have been regarded as a liability, an unwanted guest rather than a hero, and the divisions that had undermined the Sasanian resistance to the Arab invasion continued to the very end. At Tus the local lord gave him gifts but also made it clear that the citadel was not big enough to contain his entourage; he would have to move on.

And so it was that Yazdgard came to the great frontier city of Merv.

Merv had long been the eastern outpost of the empire against the Turks of the steppes. It was an enormous and very ancient city. At its heart was the old *ark* or citadel, a huge, roughly round construction of mud brick, with the vast sloping walls characteristic of Central Asia. It dated back to the Achaemenid times if not before. To this the Seleucids had added a vast rectangular enclosure which now contained the residential quarters of the city. It was also defended by a massive rampart, crowned by fired-brick interval towers. The tops of the defences had recently been strengthened by the addition of galleried walls with arrow slits. It could have held out against the Arab invaders indefinitely. Within the walls, the city was a maze of narrow streets and one-storey mud-brick houses. Traces of a Buddhist temple have been discovered and there must have been Zoroastrian fire-temples as well. We know there was a Christian community which was to play its role in the unfolding tragedy.

The reaction of the Marzban of Merv to the arrival of his fugitive sovereign was to try to get rid of him as soon as possible. He made an alliance with the neighbouring Turkish chief, the ancient enemy, against Yazdgard. The monarch got to hear that troops were being sent to arrest him and left the city secretly at night. The exhausted king eventually took refuge in a watermill on the Murghāb river, which watered the Merv oasis, and it was here that the last of the Sasanians was done to death. What exactly happened that night can never be known,[33] but the great Iranian epic, the *Shahnāmah*, suggests what transpired, and the poet Firdawsi uses it to conclude his great epic of Persian kingship.[34]

According to the *Shahnāmah*, after the defeat and death of Rustam at Qādisiya, Yazdgard consulted the Persians. His adviser, Farrukhzād, suggested that he should flee to the forests of Narvan, at the south end of the Caspian Sea, and prepare a guerrilla resistance, but the king was not convinced. The next day he sat on his throne, put his crown on his head and asked advice from the nobility and the priests. They were not in favour of the plan and the king agreed: 'Am I to save my own head and abandon Persia's nobility, its mighty armies, the land itself, and its throne and crown? ... In the same way that the king's subjects owe him allegiance in good times and in bad, so the world's king must not abandon them to their sufferings while he flees to safety and luxury.'

The king then proposed that they go to Khurasan: 'We have many champions there ready to fight for us. There are noblemen and Turks in the Chinese emperor's service, and they will side with us.' Furthermore Mahuy, the lord of the marches there, had been a humble shepherd until Yazdgard had raised him to fortune and power. Farrukhzād, the wise counsellor, was not convinced, arguing that he should not trust men 'with a lowly nature', a typical example of the aristocratic mind-set of the Sasanian nobility. The king set out for Khurasan, accompanied by the lamentations of Persians and Chinese alike. They went stage by stage to Rayy, where 'they rested for a while, consoling themselves with wine and music', before pressing on 'like the wind'.

As they approached Merv, the king wrote to the governor, Mahuy, who came out to meet him with a great show of loyalty. At this point the faithful Farrukhzād handed over responsibility for his monarch to Mahuy and left for Rayy, full of gloomy presentiments and lamenting Rustam, 'the best knight in all the world', who had been killed by 'one of those crows in their black turbans'. Mahuy's thoughts turned to treachery. He wrote to Tarkhūn, ruler of Samarqand, and suggested a joint plot against Yazdgard. Tarkhūn agreed to send his Turkish forces against Merv. When Yazdgard was warned of their approach, he put on his armour and prepared to confront them. He soon realized, however, than none of his men was following him, that Mahuy had withdrawn from the fight and the king was left on his own. He fought furiously but was soon forced to flee, abandoning his horse with its golden saddle, his mace and his sword in its golden sheath. He took refuge in a watermill on one of the rivers of Merv.

At this low point in the king's fortunes, the poet reflects, with that world-weary pessimism that was to characterize the work of later Persian poets like Umar Khayyām, on the harshness of fate.

This is the way of the deceitful world, raising a man up and casting him down. When fortune was with him, his throne was in the heavens, and now a mill was his lot; the world's favours are many, but they are exceeded by its poison. Why should you bind your heart to this world, where the drums which signal your departure are heard continuously, together with the caravan leader's cry of 'Prepare to leave'? The only rest you find is that of the grave. So the king sat, without food, his eyes filled with tears, until the sun rose.

The miller opened the mill door, carrying a load of straw on his back. He was a humble man called Khusraw, who possessed neither a throne, nor wealth, nor a crown, nor any power. The mill was his only source of living. He saw a warrior like a tall cypress seated on the stony ground as a man sits in despair; a royal crown was on his head and his clothes were made of glittering Chinese brocade. Khusraw stared at him in astonishment and murmured the name of God. He said, 'Your majesty, your face shines like the sun: tell me, how did you come to be in this mill? How can a mill full of wheat and dust and straw be a place for you to sit? What kind of man are you with this stature and face of yours, and radiating such glory, because the heavens have never seen your like?

The king replied, 'I'm one of the Persians who fled from the army of Turan [the Turks]'. The miller said in his confusion, 'I have never known anything but poverty, but if you could eat some barley bread, and some of the common herbs which grow on the river bank, I'll bring them to you, and anything else I can find. A poor man is always aware of how little he has.' In the three days that had passed since the battle the king had had no food. He said, 'Bring whatever you have and a sacred barsom',* The man quickly brought a basket of barley bread and herbs and then hurried off to find a barsom at the river toll-house. There he met up with the headman of Zarq and asked him for a barsom. Mahuy had sent people everywhere searching for the king, and the headman said, 'Now, my man, who is it who wants a barsom?' Khusraw answered him, 'There's a warrior on the straw in my mill; he's as tall as a cypress tree, and his face is as glorious as the sun. His eyebrows are like a bow, his sad eyes like narcissi: his mouth is filled with sighs, his forehead with frowns. It's he who wants the barsom to pray.' The headman duly sent the miller on to Mahuy, who ordered him to return to his mill and kill the king, threatening that he himself would be executed if he did not, and adding that the crown,

* The barsom was a bundle of twigs of the haoma bush, which were bound together and held by anyone reciting a Zoroastrian grace before a meal. The implication of the story must be that only a member of the nobility would require this.

earrings, loyal ring and clothes should not be stained. The reluctant miller returned and did as he was told, stabbing the king with a dagger. Mahuy's henchmen soon appeared and, stripping off the insignia of royalty, threw the body into the river.

In a curious coda to the story, the poet describes how the Christian monks from a neighbouring monastery saw the corpse, stripped off their habits and pulled it out of the water. They made a tower of silence for him in a garden. They dried the dagger wound and treated the body with unguents, pitch, camphor and musk; then they dressed it in yellow brocade, laid it on muslin and placed a blue pall over it. Finally a priest anointed the king's resting place with wine, musk, camphor and rosewater.

Mahuy, of course, was furious, saying that Christians had never been friends of Iran and that all connected with the funeral rights should be killed. He himself soon came to a bad end. Macbeth-like, he regretted his regicidal actions: 'No wise man calls me king and my seal's authority is not respected by the army ... Why did I shed the blood of the king of the world? I spend my nights tormented by anxiety, and God knows the state in which I live.' His Malcolm soon arrives, in the guise of the leader of the troops of Tarkhūn of Samarqand. The treacherous Mahuy and his sons are taken and, after their hands and feet are cut off, they are burned alive.

'After that', the poet laconically concludes, 'came the era of Umar, and, when he brought the new faith [Islam], the pulpit replaced the throne.'

The death of Yazdgard III was followed by the Arab occupation of Merv, which seems to have been accomplished peacefully, but the details are entirely lacking.

The fall of Merv and the death of the last Sasanian marked the end of the first phase of the Muslim conquest of Iran. Virtually the whole of what is now the territory of modern Iran, along with some areas in the Caucasus and Turkmenistan, had now acknowledged Muslim overlordship in one form or another. The fall of the great Sasanian Empire had been swift and decisive. Despite the great reputation of the ancient monarchy, attempts to revive it were few and ineffectual. The old political order had gone for good, but much of Iranian culture survived the conquests. The Arabs had defeated the Sasanian armies. They had secured tribute from most of the major cities and had control of most, but by no means all, of the great routes, but that was about it. The only major Muslim garrison seems to have been at Merv, on the north-eastern frontier, and even here the troops were sent on rotation from Iraq for some years, rather than being permanently settled. For the first half-century of Muslim rule, there was no extensive Muslim presence, no Muslim new towns were founded, no great mosques built. 'Conquest' was often a form of cooperation with local Iranian elites, as was the case at Qumm and Rayy. Many areas, such as the mountain principalities of northern Iran, were entirely outside Muslim control, and the direct road from Rayy to Merv remained unusable because of the threat they posed.

The fall of Merv may have marked the end of the campaign against the Sasanians and the establishment of Muslim hegemony in what is now Iran, but there was much more fighting before Arab rule became a reality in many areas of the country. Throughout the late seventh and first decades of the eighth century, Arab armies were pushing into unknown territory on the fringes of the Iranian world.

An interesting example of these secondary conquests can be seen in the case of Gurgān and Tabaristān. The story is a complex one but does illustrate how many different factors could be involved in the Muslim conquest of an area, and above all the interplay between existing political powers and the Arab incomers. Tabaristān was the mountainous region on the southern shore of the Caspian Sea, Gurgān the lower area to the east where the heights of the Iranian plateau gave way to the steppe land and deserts of Central Asia. At the time of the initial conquests, the rulers of these areas, the Sūl of Gurgān and the Ispahbādh of Tabaristān, had entered into treaty arrangements with Arab commanders which effectively allowed them to remain in control of their own domains. By the beginning of the eighth century, as Muslim rule in the rest of Iran strengthened, this position began to look increasing anomalous. They posed a clear threat to communications between the Arab base in Merv and the west, and it was not until after 705 that the Arabs were able to use the direct road from Rayy to Merv, rather than the much longer southern route through Kirman and Sistan.[35] Local resistance was also weakened by the tensions between the Turks of Dihistān on the desert margins, led by the Sūl, and the settled inhabitants of Gurgān.

In 717 Yazīd b. al-Muhallab, the newly appointed governor of

Khurasan, decided to launch a major military expedition in these areas. Yazīd's predecessor as governor, Qutayba b. Muslim, had achieved great fame for his conquests in Transoxania, and there is no doubt that Yazīd wanted to emulate him and show that he could lead armies against the unbelievers and reward them with abundant booty. He is said to have gathered 100,000 men from Khurasan, and the Iraqi military towns of Kūfa and Basra.[36] The first objective seems to have been the town of Dihistān, an isolated outpost of settlement in the deserts of Turkmenistan. He blockaded the city, preventing the arrival of food supplies, and the Turks, who formed the bulk of the defenders, began to lose heart. The *dehqān* in command wrote to Yazīd asking for terms. He asked only for safety for himself and his household and animals. Yazīd accepted, entered the city and took booty and captives; 14,000 defenceless Turks, who were not included in the amnesty, were put to the sword.[37]

In another version of the story, the Sūl of Dihistān retired to his fortified stronghold on an island at the south-east corner of the Caspian. After a siege of six months, the defenders became ill with the bad drinking water and the Sūl opened negotiations and agreed terms. As usual, there are admiring descriptions of the booty, including sacks of food and clothes. Yazīd himself acquired a crown and immediately passed it on to one of his subordinates. Crowns were frequently worn by members of the Iranian aristocracy but were regarded with deep suspicion by the more pious and austere Muslims, who considered them typical of the pomp and vanity of the Persians. Perhaps because of this, the subordinate protested that he did not want it, and the officer gave it to a beggar. Yazīd heard about this and purchased the crown back from the mendicant.

After the defeat of the Sūl, Yazīd was able to occupy much of the settled land of Gurgān without major resistance, especially as some at least of the local Iranian population were happy to accept Arab support to protect them from the Turks. Yazīd then turned his attention to mountainous Tabaristān. The local ruler, the Ispahbādh, had summoned allies from the mountainous provinces of Gīlān and Daylam further to the west.

The people of Tabaristān had defeated earlier Muslim attempts to penetrate the narrow passes of their native mountains[38] and were determined to do so again. When the two armies met on the plains, the Muslims had the advantage, but as soon as they retreated to the mountains, the local people were able to make good use of the terrain to defend themselves: 'as soon as the Muslims began their ascent, the enemy soldiers, who were looking down on them, opened fire with arrows and stones. The Muslim soldiers fled without suffering great losses because the enemy was not strong enough to pursue them, but the Muslims crowded and jostled each other so that many of them fell into ravines.'[39] This success emboldened the local people, there was an uprising against the small number of Arabs left as a garrison in Gurgān[40] and for a time Yazīd's army was in serious danger of being trapped and destroyed. Only some clever diplomacy allowed him to make a peace deal, which could be portrayed as a success. In addition to some fairly large sums of money, the Ispahbādh of Tabaristān agreed to pay 400 donkeys loaded with saffron and four hundred slaves. Each slave was to be dressed in a cloak with a scarf on it, carrying a silver cup and a piece of fine white silk.

The silk and the silver cups could not disguise the fact that the massive campaign had ended in partial failure. The lowlands of Gurgān were brought under Muslim rule, but the people of Tabaristān, protected by their mountains, had fought off the challenge. According to a local history of the area, written several centuries after the events but still preserving old traditions, Yazīd set about urbanizing Gurgān, which until then had not been a real city at all. He is said to have built twenty-four small mosques, one for each Arab tribe, most of which could still be identified in the author's own day.[41] This marks the real beginning of Muslim rule in Gurgān, seventy years after the initial Arab conquest. Even then the Islamic community seems to have been confined to the newly established capital; it would take much longer for the new religion to penetrate the villages and nomad encampments.[42]

The most determined resistance the Arabs faced in the lands of the Sasanian Empire came from the area of eastern Sistan, the Helmand and Kandahār provinces of modern Afghanistan. The campaigns in this area are also interesting because the harshness of the fighting provoked the only full-scale mutiny recorded among Arab troops at this time. The desert areas of southern Afghanistan are a difficult environment for any invading army. The scorching heat is very debilitating and the rugged hills provide endless points of shelter and refuge for defenders who know the area well. This was neither Zoroastrian nor Buddhist territory but the land of the god Zun, whose golden image with ruby eyes was the object of veneration throughout the area. The kings of this land were called Zunbīls, their title proclaiming their allegiance to the god, and they moved between their winter palaces on the plains by the Helmand river and their summer residences in Zābulistān, the cooler mountains to the north.

A Muslim force had raided the area as early as 653–4, when the Arab commander had allegedly poured scorn on the image of the god, breaking off one of his arms and taking out his ruby eyes. He returned them to the local governor, saying that he had wished to show only that the idol had no power for good or evil. The god, howoever, survived this insult and was still being venerated in the eleventh century, symbolizing the fierce resistance of the people of these barren hills to outside interference. The early Muslims were well aware that this area was a potential route to India, with all its riches, but the Zunbīls and their relatives, the Kabulshāhs of Kabul and their peoples, mounted a spirited and long-lasting resistance to the Arabs, making it impossible for Muslim armies to reach northern India.

It was into this fiercely hostile environment that Ubayd Allāh b. Abī Bakra led the 'Army of Destruction' in 698.[43] Ubayd Allāh himself was a typical example of a man of humble origins who had done very well out of the Muslim conquest. His father was an Ethiopian slave in the city of Tā'if near Mecca. When the Muslims were besieging the town in 630, two years before the Prophet's death, he had proclaimed that any slave who came over to his side would be free. Abī Bakra had used a pulley to lower himself over the town walls and so acquired his nickname, the Father of the Pulley. He married a free Arab woman and their son, Ubayd Allāh, inherited his dark skin colour. His slave origins were exploited by satirists. The family moved to Basra when the town was founded and made large sums of money out of urban development by building public baths. Ubayd Allāh was able to build himself a very expensive house and to keep a herd of 800 water buffalo on his estates in the marshlands of southern Iraq. The conquest of Fars provided new opportunities for making money, and we have already seen him making vast sums from the confiscation of the assets of the fire-temples there. He was, in short, a man of obscure origins and little military experience who made a fortune out of the conquests.

Hajjāj b. Yūsuf, governor of Iraq and all the east, now appointed him to command a Muslim army against the Zunbīl, who was refusing to pay tribute, ordering him to go on attacking until he had laid waste the land, destroyed the Zunbīl's strongholds and enslaved his children. The army was assembled at the Muslim advanced base at Bust. They then marched north and east in pursuit of the Zunbīl. Their enemies withdrew before them, luring them further and further into the rugged mountains. They removed or destroyed all the food supplies and the heat was scorching. Ubayd Allāh soon found himself in a very perilous position and began to negotiate. The would-be conqueror was forced to offer a large sum of tribute, to give hostages including three of his own sons and to take a solemn oath not to invade the Zunbīl's land again. Ubayd Allāh was lavishly entertained by the monarch with women and wine.[44] Not all the Muslims were happy to accept this humiliation and some determined to fight and achieve martyrdom, arguing that Muslims should never be prevented from attacking infidels, and, much more practically, that Hajjāj would deduct the tribute from their salaries, leaving them without any rewards for the hardships they had endured during the campaign.

A few brave souls elected to fight and achieved the martyrdom they wished. Most followed their commander in a desperate retreat to Bust. Only a small number made it, the rest perishing from hunger and thirst. Of the 20,000 men 'with their mailed horses and panoply of weapons' who had set out, only 5,000 returned. It was widely believed that Ubayd Allāh himself was exploiting the situation by commandeering any grain and selling it on to his troops at vastly inflated prices. As the ragged remnants of the army approached Bust they were met by a relieving force bringing some supplies, but many of the starving wretches ate so fast that they perished and the survivors had to be fed slowly with small quantities. Ubayd Allāh himself reached safety but died very soon after. The poets were merciless in their criticism of his incompetence and, above all, of his greed and the way he had exploited his troops to make money.

You were appointed as their Amir
Yet you destroyed them while the war was still raging
You stayed with them, like a father, so they said
Yet you were breaking them with your folly

You are selling a *qafiz** of grain for a whole dirham
While we wondered who was to blame
You were keeping back their rations of milk and barley
And selling them unripe grapes.[45]

It was probably the most significant setback for Muslim arms since
the Arab conquests had begun. Hajjāj in Iraq was determined to seek
revenge and seems to have been genuinely afraid that the Zunbīl
would attack areas already under Muslim rule: if he was joined by an
uprising of local people all of Iran might be lost. He wrote to the
caliph Abd al-Malik in Damascus, explaining that 'the troops of the
Commander of the Faithful in Sistan have met disaster, and only a
few of them have escaped. The enemy has been emboldened by this
success against the people of Islam and has entered their lands and
captured all their fortresses and castles'.[46] He went on to say that he
wanted to send out a great army from Kūfa and Basra and asked the
caliph's advice. The reply gave him carte blanche to do as he saw fit.

Hajjāj set about organizing the army, 20,000 men from Kūfa and
20,000 from Basra. He paid them their salaries in full so that they
could equip themselves with horses and arms. He reviewed the army
in person, giving more money to those who were renowned for their
courage. Markets were set up around the camp so that the men could
buy supplies and a sermon encouraging everybody to do their bit for
the jihad was preached.[47] The expeditionary force became known as
the 'Peacock Army' because of the elegance of its appearance.

Despite these preparations, the expedition set in train the only
military mutiny in the history of the early conquests, the only time an
Arab army refused to go on fighting and turned on its Muslim political
masters. All was not as straightforward as it looked. Hajjāj had been
struggling for some years to force the militias of the Iraqi towns to
obey him and the caliph in Damascus. Sending them on a long, hard
campaign could be very advantageous: if they were successful they
might become rich and satisfied and even settle in the area. If they
were not, then their power would be broken. As commander, he
chose one Ibn al-Ashᶜath. Unlike the unfortunate Ubayd Allāh, Ibn
al-Ashᶜath came from the highest ranks of the south Arabian

---

* A measure of 4 litres, the implication being that this was very expensive.

aristocracy, being directly descended from the pre-Islamic kings of Kinda. He was also a proud man who did not like being ordered about, and had become one of the leaders of the Iraqi opposition to Hajjāj. Putting him in charge was really offering him a poisoned chalice.

At first all went well. The Zunbīl, who seems to have been very well informed about the Muslim preparations, wrote to Ibn al-Ashᶜath offering peace. He was given no reply and the Muslim forces began a systematic occupation of his lands, taking it over district by district, appointing tax collectors, sentry posts to guard the passes and setting up a military postal service. Then, sensibly, Ibn al-Ashᶜath decided to pause and consolidate, before advancing the next year. He wrote to Hajjāj about this perfectly reasonable course of action and received a massive blast in return. Hajjāj accused the commander of weakness and confused judgement and of not being prepared to avenge those Muslims who had been killed in the campaign. He was to continue to advance immediately. Ibn al-Ashᶜath then called for advice. Everyone agreed that Hajjāj's demands were unreasonable and designed to humiliate the army and its leader. 'He does not care', one said, 'about risking your lives by forcing you into a land of sheer cliffs and narrow passes. If you win and acquire booty he will devour the territory and take its wealth ... if you lose, he will treat you with contempt and your distress will be no concern of his.'[48] The next speaker said that Hajjāj was trying to get them out of Iraq and force them to settle in this desolate region. All agreed that the army should disavow its obedience to Hajjāj. Ibn al-Ashᶜath then decided to lead them west to challenge Umayyad control of Iraq and the wider caliphate, leaving the Zunbīl in control of his territory and the Muslim dead unavenged.

The mutiny was not a success. Ibn al-Ashᶜath and his Iraqi followers were defeated by the Syrian Umayyad army and crushed. But the story is important in the annals of the conquests: a Muslim army had decided that asserting its rights against the Muslim government was more important than expanding the lands of Islam and that preserving their salaries was more valuable than the acquisition of new booty. We can see the conquest movement beginning to run out of steam.

The failure of Muslim arms in southern Afghanistan marked the end of the conquests in Iran. Only to the north-east, across the River Oxus, did wars of conquest continue. The partial and scattered nature

This mosaic of Emperor Justinian I (527–65) and his court from San Vitale, Ravenna, shows Byzantine imperial style. Stately, almost motionless, the Emperor is in civilian clothes and surrounded by his retinue of officials, soldiers and clergy. (© San Vitale, Ravenna, Italy/The Bridgeman Art Library)

The last Sasanian shāh Yazdgard III (632–51) is depicted on this silver gilt plate. In contrast to Justinian, he is depicted as a mighty hunter and warrior pursuing his prey on a galloping horse. (Bibliotheque Nationale, Paris, France/Flammarion/The Bridgeman Art Library)

TOP Mushabbak Church (Syria). The sixth-century basilical church in northern Syria is typical of the hundreds built for congregational worship in what was a profoundly Christian country before the Muslim conquest. (Author)

ABOVE Fire-temple Konur Siyah (Fars, Iran). Zoroastrian fire-temples like this one were constructed to shelter the sacred fire under the main dome and to accommodate the priests who tended the fire. Zoroastrianism was the official religion of the Sasanian Empire. (Author)

TOP Taqi-kisrā (Iraq); photograph taken in 1901, after the collapse of much of the palace in the 1880s. The iwān (arch) of the great palace at Ctesiphon, capital of the Sasanian Empire, was probably built by the last great Sasanian shāh, Chosroes II (d. 628). The victorious Muslims used it as their first mosque and prayed surrounded by the statues of former Persian monarchs. (Royal Geographical Society/The Bridgeman Art Library)

ABOVE The ruin of the Marib dam, Yemen. The final collapse of the dam in the late sixth century was symbolic of the decay of the old kingdom of Himyar, which had dominated Yemen in the centuries before the coming of Islam. (Author)

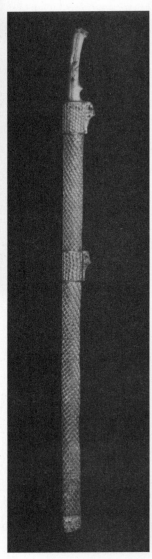

This seventh-century Sasanian helmet shows the rich military equipment typical of the Persian army. Arab writers like to contrast the ostentation of the Persians with their own simple arms. (Römisch-Germanisches Zentralmuseum, Mainz. Inv. O.38823.)

This richly decorated Sasanian sword would have been worn by the aristocrats who led the Persian armies. (British Museum, London. Inv. BM 135738)

David confronts Goliath, from the 'David Plates'. These Byzantine silver plates illustrate the triumph of David over Goliath and depict the arms and armour of Byzantine troops in about 600, a metal breastplate with protective strips or scales covering his arms and skirt. (The Metropolitan Museum of Art, Gift of J. Pierpont Morgan, 1917 (17.190.396) Photograph © 2000)

Modern sketch of an early eighth-century wall-painting, depicting a swing-beam siege engine in operation, probably being used by Muslims attacking Samarqand. The Arab conquests in Transoxania witnessed a series of hard-fought sieges. (Tile fragment from the Hermitage, St Petersburg; Drawing by Guitty Azarpay, in *Sogdian Painting*, Berkeley: University of California Press, 1981, p. 65)

TOP Wadi Duᶜān. Not all the early Arab conquerors were tent-dwelling nomads. Many were village people from settlements like this one in Yemen. They played a major but often forgotten role in the conquests of Iraq and Egypt. (Author)

ABOVE Syrian desert. For the Bedouin Arabs the desert was a place of opportunity, danger and beauty, a wild homeland celebrated in poetry and legend. (Author)

TOP Ancient Roman walls of Damascus. The city is still largely surrounded by the Roman walls to which the Muslims laid siege in c 636. (Author)

ABOVE Jerusalem seen from the Mount of Olives. The temple platform, where the Dome of the Rock now stands, seems to have been a waste land at the time of the Muslim conquests. Here the caliph Umar is said to have constructed a simple place of worship. (Author)

TOP The Zagros Mountains separate the flat plains of Iraq from the Iranian plateau. After the conquest of Iraq, the Muslim leaders decided to push on through this rugged terrain where they defeated the Persian armies once more at Nihāvand (641). (Author)

ABOVE Walls of Bishapur. The Sasanian fortifications of this town in Fars, with their stone walls and regularly spaced round towers, could not survive Muslim attack after the main Persian Imperial army had been defeated. The ruins of the citadel can be seen on the hills in the background. (Author)

TOP Sistan. The wild and remote landscapes of Sistan and Zābulistān saw some of the fiercest resistance to Muslim armies and one of the few major military set-backs Muslim forces suffered. (Author)

ABOVE Central Iranian landscape. The mountains are divided by broad plains, which allowed for the swift movement of armies across long distances. (Author)

The mighty mud-brick ramparts of old Samarqand. Under the rule of its tough and wily Prince Ghūrak, the city was the centre of fierce resistance to the invading Muslims. (Author)

LEFT Old Bukhara seen from the walls of the citadel, home of the hereditary princes, the Bukhara Khudas, who continued to rule alongside the Arab governors after the conquest. (Author)

TOP The Tashtakaracha Pass in the mountains south of Samarqand, where Arab and Turkish forces met in 730 in one of the fiercest battles the whole of the conquests. (Author)

ABOVE View from the ancient walls of Balkh, across the fertile fields of Tukhāristān the distant mountains of the Hindu Kush. (Author)

TOP Cordova (Spain). The old Roman city was taken without much difficulty and soon became the capital of al-Andalus (Muslim Spain). The great mosque was begun sixty years after the first Muslim invasions. (Author)

ABOVE Toledo (Spain). Despite its superb natural fortifications within the bend of the Tagus river, the Visigothic capital of Toledo seems to have put up little resistance of the Muslim armies. (Author)

LEFT The Ribat of Sousse (Tunisia). This ninth-century fortress guarded the harbour at Sousse on the coast of Tunisia from which Muslim raiders set out for the coasts of Sicily, Italy and the south of France. (Author)

TOP RIGHT Modern reconstruction of a Byzantine dromon. With its oars and its twin lateen sails, the dromon was the classic warship of the Byzantine navy at the time of the Arab conquests and it is likely that Muslim naval ships were very similar in design. (Drawing reproduced by the kind permission of John Pryor, from his book *The Age of the Dromon*, Leiden, 2006, frontispiece.)

ABOVE Tyre (Lebanon). The old port of Tyre was the main Muslim naval base on the eastern shores of the Mediterranean from c 730 to 861. (Author)

TOP The site of early Muslim Basra (Iraq). Little remains of the site old of Basra, founded by the Muslims immediately after their conquest of southern Iraq and no scientific excavations have ever been undertaken. (Author)

ABOVE The centre of old Kūfa (Iraq). In the foreground lie the ruins of the governor's palace, the first phases of which may date back to the time of Saʿd b. Abī Waqqās. In the background lies the much-rebuilt mosque. (Author)

THE CONQUESTS REMEMBERED

ABOVE The Prophet Muhammad (centre, on the white horse) preparing for his first battle against the Quraysh of Mecca at Badr in 634. This early fourteenth-century Persian view of the first Muslim armies, shows them without any body armour and only the simplest military equipment. (The Nasser D. Khalili Collection of Islamic Art)

LEFT A fifteenth-century Persian manuscript shows the murder of Chosroes II by his courtiers in 628, an event which caused political chaos in the Sasanian Empire and allowed to Muslims to take advantage of the confusion. (The Metropolitan Museum of Art, Gift of Arthur A. Houghton Jr, 1970.301.75)

LEFT The battle of Qādisiya as seen in a fifteenth-century Persian book painting. This personal encounter between the Arab commander Saʿd b. Abī Waqqās and the Persian general Rustam never took place but the Muslim victory at Qādisiya opened the way for the conquest of Iraq. (British Library)

BELOW Piero della Francesca, *Legend of the True Cross* in the church of S. Franceso in Arezzo (*c* 1466). This panel depicts Heraclius' defeat of Chosroes II in 627 which led to the return of the True Cross to Jerusalem in the same year in which Muhammad came to an agreement with the Quraysh of Mecca, the prelude to the Muslim conquests. (San Francesco, Arezzo, Italy/The Bridgeman Art Library)

of the Muslim conquest of Iran had an important cultural legacy. In Syria, Iraq and Egypt, the Muslim conquests also led to the triumph of the Arabic language, both as the medium of high culture and the vernacular of everyday life. This did not happen in Iran. For two centuries after the conquest, and longer in some areas, Arabic was the language of imperial administration. It was also the language of religious and philosophical discourse. But it was not the language of everyday life. When independent Iranian dynasties asserted their independence from the rule of the caliphs in the ninth and tenth centuries, the language of their courts was Persian. This 'New Persian' was written in Arabic script and contained numerous Arabic loan-words, but the grammar and the basic vocabulary were clearly Persian, an Indo-European language in contrast to the Semitic Arabic. It is worth considering how different this is to the position in Egypt. In Egypt in the year 600 nobody spoke Arabic; by the twelfth century at the latest, everybody spoke Arabic and in modern times Egypt is thought of as a prime centre of Arabic culture. In Iran in 600 nobody spoke Arabic; by the twelfth century they still did not. Arabic was established as the language of certain sorts of intellectual discourse, very much like Latin in medieval Europe. In modern times Iran is emphatically not an Arab country.

The survival of the Persian language was accompanied by the survival of aspects of Persian political culture. In the princely courts of northern and north-eastern Iran where the first wave of Arabs hardly penetrated, rulers still looked to old Iranian models and claimed descent from the Sasanian kings and noble families. These courts functioned almost like reservoirs of Iranian culture, and it was from them that the Persian renaissance, the great cultural revival of the tenth century, emerged with works such as Firdawsi's *Shahnāmah*, the Book of Kings.

This survival of the non-Arab culture of Iran was in part the result of the nature of the initial Arab conquest, the very slow pace of Arab settlement and the way in which the conquerors were happy to leave existing power structures intact. The country became firmly Muslim. Among the myriad princes and nobles there was never to be another non-Muslim but, at the same time, the Persian language and identity lived on into the twenty-first century.

6

INTO THE MAGHREB

❧

If you travel along the coast road it is over 2,000 kilometres from Alexandria to Carthage, capital of Roman Africa Proconsularis, and it is about 1,500 more from there to the Straits of Gibraltar.[1] At a good regular travelling pace of 20 kilometres a day, it would have taken almost half a year to make the journey. And that would be without days off, sick horses, obstructive officials or dangerous enemies. The expedition would have taken you through many varied landscapes and environments. On the eastern half of the journey, you would have had to have kept close to the coast, along the flat lands of the Egyptian littoral. In Cyrenaica the mountains of the Jabal Akhdar, the 'Green Mountain', came down almost to the sea and attracted enough rainfall to allow permanent settlement, not only on the coast but in the southern valleys of the range as well. A Mediterranean agriculture of wheat, vines and olives flourished.

Pushing further west, the traveller skirted the Gulf of Sirte. It was a long haul. The desert comes down to the sea and for perhaps a month the traveller passed almost nothing in the way of orchards and fields, villages and towns. Not until Tripolitania were settled lands reached once again, with farming land and pastures and the city of Tripoli, 'a large maritime city, walled in stone and lime and rich in fruits, pears, apples, dairy products and honey'.[2] West of Tripoli the route led to the settled lands of what is now Tunisia. The southern province was called Africa Byzacena, the northern, Africa Proconsularis or Zeugitania, and the whole came to be known to the Arabs as Africa, or, as they preferred to write it, Ifrīqīya. The two late Roman provinces of Byzacena and Zeugitania were the heart of Roman rule. It was here that the wheat, wine, olives and pottery that constituted the main exports were produced, and it was here that the cities and country towns were most numerous. Carthage, at the

north-east corner of Africa Proconsularis, was the real capital, not just
of Tunisia but of the whole of Roman North Africa. The capital of
Hannibal and the ancient Carthaginians had become the Roman
capital and survived as the major political centre into late antiquity.

West of Carthage the main route continues further inland along
the high plateaux, which lie between the sea and the coastal mountains
to the north and the beginnings of the Sahara to the south, making a
sort of natural east–west corridor. On the coast there were little ports
built around the mouth of wadis and sheltered anchorages. Inland,
the high plateaux were the lands of the nomads. Eventually the traveller would reach the twin cities of Ceuta and Tangier, fortified settlements which looked across the straits of Gibraltar to Spain, rich and
tempting. Beyond, south of Tangier, lay the flat, well-watered plains
of the Atlantic coast of Morocco and finally the High Atlas mountains,
which bordered the northern fringes of the Sahara.

North Africa had been one of the richest areas of the Roman
world. Something of the wealth can still be seen in the great ruins
of cities like Volubilis in Morocco, Timgad in Algeria and Leptis
Magna in Libya, which rank among the most impressive classical
sites to be found within the frontiers of the Roman Empire. The
large and elegant cities were sustained by a well-tended and vigorous
agricultural resource base. Naturally fertile lands were tilled, and
arid and inhospitable wastes, like the pre-desert valleys of Cyrenaica,
were brought into cultivation by careful irrigation and continual
nurturing. Grain was grown, but it was above all the cultivation of
olives that distinguished the agriculture of the area, and the export
of olive oil, to Rome and all round the Mediterranean basin, was a
major source of wealth. The olive oil was transported from North
Africa in long cylindrical amphorae, designed to be stacked in the
holds of ships. North African potters also mass-produced a fine
tableware, African Red Slip, which, like the amphorae, stacked neatly
in cargo holds. The shiny red bowls and plates came to be the most
common and widely distributed fine pottery of the late antique
Mediterranean.

Until the early fifth century, North Africa had been a prosperous
part of the Roman Empire, fully integrated into the imperial system,
and much of the agricultural surplus was extracted in taxes by the
imperial government. The prosperity of the land depended on its links

across the Mediterranean, where the markets for its exports were to be found. Its cities were as distinctively Roman as any in Italy, Gaul or Spain with their fora, temples, baths and theatres. There was a developed Latin high culture and Christianity spread early. By the beginning of the fifth century North Africa was as firmly Christian as any other area of the empire. Cities and countryside were adorned with graceful churches and St Augustine (d. 430), the greatest intellectual figure of the age, was bishop of the small North African city of Hippo.

In the fifth century North Africa, like most of the western empire, was lost to imperial control. Germanic tribes, called collectively the Vandals, crossed from Spain and between 429 and 440 conquered all the Roman provinces. The Vandals have given the English language one of its most commonly used words for violence and destructiveness. In reality, the Vandals do not seem to have wrought significantly more havoc than other Germanic invaders of the Roman world, and in many ways they sought to take over the Roman structures and ways of doing things and use them for their own ends. The Vandal kingdom survived until 533 when the emperor Justinian sent a military expedition that successfully put an end to their power and brought the area back under imperial rule once more. The North Africa of the second half of the sixth and the early seventh centuries was, however, different in many respects from that of the second and third centuries, when the great cities had been constructed and the agricultural area had reached its greatest extent. One important difference was that the language of newly revived Roman administration was Greek, a foreign tongue that had never been widely spoken in the area before: it must have made the imperial authorities seem more like alien invaders than restorers of past glories. There were also continuous religious tensions between the African Christians and the imperial authorities in Constantinople, and both Justininian in the sixth century and Heraclius in the seventh resorted to persecution to enforce obedience to their theological views.[3] As in the Fertile Crescent, many North African Christians must have been resentful and distrusting of the Byzantine authorities.

Most of what is now Morocco and western Algeria, with the exception of the fortified city of Ceuta, where Justinian rebuilt the walls and constructed a new church, had ceased to be part of the empire in the third century. In the areas that did remain under imperial control, town and countryside were very different. The centres of many great cities were abandoned. Timgad, a bustling city in inland Algeria with imposing classical architecture, was destroyed by the local tribesmen, 'so that the Romans would have no excuse for coming near us again'.⁴ The major monuments in any townscape were the Byzantine fort, built in general out of the ruins of the forum, and one or more fourth- or fifth-century churches, often built in suburban areas away from the old city centre. The cities had become villages, with parish churches, a small garrison, the occasional tax or rent collector but without a local hierarchy, a network of services or an administrative structure. Even in the capital, Carthage, where some new building had occurred after the Byzantine reconquest, the new quarters were filled with rubbish and huts by the early seventh century. From the mid seventh century the city suffered what has been described as 'monumental melt-down' – shacks clustered into the circus and the round harbour was abandoned.⁵

More than any other province of the empire, Africa had been dependent on the Mediterranean trading and tax system. African grain and olive oil supplied the city of Rome. Much of this was paid as tax, but it is clear that the ships that took the tax also transported African products for sale. The grain tax system was broken by the Vandal conquest of Carthage in 439, the volume of African exports began an inexorable decline and African products began to disappear from Mediterranean markets. The Byzantine reconquest of 533 did not reverse this downward trend. Western Mediterranean markets were now too poor to import much, while the eastern Mediterranean could survive without African products. By 700 African Red Slip was no longer manufactured. Africa had become marginal to the Byzantine Empire.⁶ More than anything this explains the failure of Byzantine troops in North Africa to repel the Arab forces: in the end, the imperial authorities simply did not care enough.

Byzantine North Africa may also have been weakened by political events. In 610 the governor Heraclius had used the army of the province to overthrow the emperor Phocas and claim the imperial title for himself. He then became involved in the struggle for survival against the Persian invasion. There is no sign that troops he had withdrawn from the province, probably the best troops in the area, were ever replaced.

Rural settlement suffered as much as the cities did. Archaeological surveys suggest a general abandonment of settled sites. For example, in the area surrounding the ancient city of Segermes (near modern Hammamet) there were eighty-three settled sites in the mid sixth century. In the next 150 years, half of these were abandoned. By 600 the city of Segermes itself was largely deserted and by the first part of the seventh century, just before the Arab conquest, only three sites in the area, all in high defensible positions, survived. This contraction of settlement happened not in some remote frontier area but in the heart of agricultural Africa Proconsularis, barely 50 kilometres from the capital and centre of government in Carthage.[7]

In Africa Proconsularis, settlement seems to have peaked in the mid sixth century, but in other areas the decline had begun earlier. In Tripolitania increasing insecurity led to the abandonment of many sites from the end of the fifth century, and there is evidence for the increase of semi-nomadic herding of animals at the expense of settled agriculture in Byzacena at the same period. In those settlements that did survive, there was a movement from open villages to communities dependent on gsūr (sing. gasr, a dialect form of the classical Arabic qasr/qusūr), fortified farmsteads, an architectural form that was continued with some variations from the third century until well after the Muslim conquest.[8]

We have, of course, no population statistics, no hard economic data, but the results of archaeological surveys and some excavation suggest that the first Muslim invaders found a land that was sparsely populated, at least by settled folk, and whose once vast and impressive cities had mostly been ruined or reduced to the size and appearance of fortified villages.

This land was peopled by at least three different groups. There were no doubt Greek-speaking soldiers and administrators in Carthage and other garrisons, but there is no reason to suppose that they were very numerous. Living alongside them, in what is now Tunisia, were the Afāriqa (sometimes Ufāriqa), who may have been ultimately descended from the Carthaginians and may still have spoken a Punic dialect as well as Latin. At the time of the Muslim conquest, they were a settled Christian population, with no tradition of military activity. Ibn Abd al-Hakam describes them as 'servants [khādim] of the Romans, paying taxes to whoever conquered their country'.[9]

The vast majority of the population, however, were Berbers. The name Berber derives, of course, from the term *barbari* (foreigners) by which the Romans described these people, and it passes into Arabic as *Barbar*. The range of Berber habitation stretched from the borders of the Nile valley in the east as far as Morrocco in the west. They were in no sense politically united and belonged to a bewildering number of different tribes, but they were united by a common language, or family of languages, totally distinct from both Latin and Arabic. Narrative or administrative texts were seldom written in the language before the twentieth century and Berbers who wished to take part in government or acquire an education were obliged to learn Latin or Greek during the Roman period, or Arabic after the Muslim conquest.

Berber society can be described as a tribal society, but there were many different Berber lifestyles. Some Berbers, mostly in mountain areas, lived in tribal villages, practising agriculture. Others were trans-humants, moving their flocks up the mountains in the summer and down in the winter. Still others were 'pure nomads', roaming the vast deserts of the northern Sahara. Classical sources provide the names of numerous Berber tribes in North Africa and, a few centuries later, the earliest Arabic sources do the same. Even given the differences in language and script it is difficult to detect much real continuity, and it seems that the period from the sixth to the eighth centuries saw widespread movement among the Berbers and the disappearance of some tribal groups and the emergence of others. In general, Berbers seem to have been moving from east to west in the century before the Arab conquests. This reality is perhaps reflected in the way later Arabic sources report that the main Berber groups came from the Arabian peninsula or Palestine.[10] There is no real evidence for this; indeed, the fact that Berber is not a Semitic language suggests that this is unlikely, but it may reflect a memory of these western migrations. The Laguatan (Luwāta) moved from the Barqa area west into Tripolitania during the sixth century[11] and drove the Byzantine governor out of Leptis Magna in 543.[12] They were followed by the Hawāra, another Berber group moving west from Cyrenaica. The process of *taghrība*, the drive to the west, used of the movements of Arab tribes in the eleventh century, seems to have had precedents among the Berbers of the sixth and early seventh centuries.

The conquest of North Africa seems to have begun as a natural follow-on to the conquest of Egypt. Our information about the first raids comes entirely from the Egyptian chronicler Ibn Abd al-Hakam, whose narrative is used by all later sources. It was probably in the summer of 642, very shortly after the final surrender of Alexandria to the Muslims, that Amr led his troops west.[13] The journey does not appear to have been a difficult one and the army seems to have moved fast and without encountering any real opposition until they reached Barqa. The Byzantine garrison, accompanied by some local land-owners, withdrew before them and retired to the coastal port of Tokra (ancient Tauchira), from where they later left by sea. Most of the population of the city seem to have been Luwāta Berbers,[14] and it was with them, not with any Byzantine authority, that Amr made peace in exchange for a tribute (*jizya*) of 13,000 dinars. The treaty is said to have included the somewhat bizarre provision that the people could sell their sons and daughters into slavery to raise the money. This may point to the beginning of the massive exploitation of Berbers as slaves that was characteristic of the first century of Muslim rule in North Africa. It was also agreed that no Muslim tax collectors should enter the area and that the people of Barqa themselves would take the tribute to Egypt when they had collected it.

Amr then led his men around the Gulf of Sirte, bypassing Tokra, to Tripoli. Here they encountered more serious resistance. The Byzantine garrison held out for a month. Ibn Abd al-Hakam recounts how the end came in one of those anecdotes that enliven the Arab narratives without encouraging any belief in their credibility. The story goes that one day one of the Arabs besieging the city went out hunting with seven companions. They went round to the west of the city and, becoming separated from the main bulk of the army and overcome by the heat, they decided to return along the seashore. Now the sea came up to the walls of the city and Roman ships were drawn right up to the walls of their houses in their anchorage. The Arab and his companions noticed that the sea had retreated a little from the walls and that there was a gap between the water and the walls. They made their way through it as far as the main church, where they raised the cry '*Allāhu akbar!*' The Romans panicked and fled to their ships with what they could carry, hoisted sail and fled. Amr, seeing the chaos, led his army into the city, which was then pillaged.[15] There is no evidence of Arab occupation at this stage and the city probably reverted to Byzantine control when the Muslim forces left.

Amr was soon off again, leading his men west to Sabra (Sabratha). Here the local people, imagining that Amr was far away and occupied with the siege of Tripoli, had dropped their defences. The city was taken and plundered. Soon after this Leptis Magna (*Labda*) also fell into Arab hands. Amr then returned to Egypt, no doubt well pleased with the booty he and his followers had amassed. It had been a great raid, but it was not a conquest. Only in Barqa did Amr leave any sort of presence by imposing taxes and appointing a governor, Uqba b. Nāfi, who was to become the hero of of the Muslim conquest of North Africa and whose name, like that of Khālid b. al-Walīd in Iraq and Syria, was to go down in history and legend as an example of military leadership and derring-do.

The dismissal of Amr from the governorship of Egypt in 645 (see p. 164) meant that there was a pause in Arab operations. It did not last long. In 647 the caliph Uthmān sent a new army to Egypt to help in the African campaign. A list of the composition of the army suggests that it numbered between 5,000 and 10,000, mostly recruited, like the majority of the Arabs who had originally conquered Egypt, from south Arabian tribes.[16] They were commanded by the new governor of Egypt, Abd Allāh b. Saʿd b. Abī Sarh. The expedition moved fast along the North African coast into what is now southern Tunisia. They do not seem to have wasted time trying to retake Tripoli. The Byzantine forces in the area were commanded by Gregory, the exarch of Africa. He seems to have decided to move from the traditional capital at Carthage and base himself at Sbeitla in southern Tunisia, probably so that he could meet up with Berber allies and oppose the invaders more effectively. The two armies met outside the city. The Byzantines were heavily defeated and, according to Arabic sources, Gregory was killed in the battle, though according to Theophanes and other Christian sources, he escaped and was later rewarded by the emperor.

This was the only major military encounter between the Muslims and the Byzantine forces in North Africa. It is interesting to note that Gregory made no attempt to use the Byzantine fortresses constructed in the area, but chose to encounter the enemy in an open field battle. After this defeat, what remained of the imperial army seems to have retreated to Carthage and left the Arabs and the Berbers to fight for control of the countryside.

The quantity of booty was enormous and, as often, the Arabic sources spend as much space telling us how much there was and how it was divided up as they do on the whole of the rest of the campaign. (For example, horsemen received 3,000 gold dinars, 1,500 for the horse and 1,500 for the man, and foot soldiers were given 1,500.)

For almost twenty years after this Arab forces made no extended attempt to make more permanent conquests in North Africa. It is probable that Barqa and Cyrenaica remained under Muslim rule in this period, but that seems to have been the limit of expansion. Intermittent raids by Arab-Egyptian leaders using Egyptian troops were made into Tripolitania and the Fezzan but the armies always returned to their bases after seizing as much booty as they could.

During this long period, only Uqba b. Nāfi seems to have maintained a vision of doing anything more than short-term raiding. In central Algeria, where the mountains of the north gradually flatten out and meet the fringes of the Sahara, lies the little town of Sidi Okba, built around an ancient shrine, still visited by pilgrims, hoping for the *baraka* (blessing) that can be acquired from coming close to a great saint. The term Sidi comes from the classical Arabic *sayyidī*, meaning 'my lord': it is this Arabic word which gave the title El Cid to the Castillian hero. The Okba is Uqba b. Nāfi al-Fihri, the man credited in historical record and popular imagination with bringing Islamic rule to the Maghreb. He is the only one of the great early Muslim commanders whose grave is still honoured in this way. He also had a claim to be a Companion of the Prophet, if only in the sense that he had met Muhammad when he was a small child. This gave him immense prestige in the eyes of posterity. Born in Mecca towards the end of the Prophet's life, Uqba came from Muhammad's own tribe, Quraysh, but from a different sub-group, the Fihr. His background in the urban aristocracy of Mecca was typical of that of the men who formed the elite of the early Islamic state and led its armies. He was the only Companion to have played an important role in the conquest of Algeria and Morocco, and he can be said to have brought the *baraka* of the Prophet himself to this part of North Africa. In addition, he was the only important member of Quraysh to have fought there, which also contributed to his status and reputation. To

cap it all, Uqba became a martyr when he and his small band of
warriors were confronted by a much larger Berber army in 683 and
he himself was killed.

Uqba owed his initial rise to power to the fact that his maternal
uncle was none other than Amr b. al-Ās, the conqueror of Egypt. It
was only natural that Amr should entrust his able and ambitious
young nephew with important roles. Uqba soon showed his appetite
for adventure. He joined in Amr's first campaign to Cyrenaica in
642 and distinguished himself by leading a raiding party to the oasis
of Zuwayla, to the south of Tripoli. We hear of him raiding as far
away as Ghadāmis, deep in the Libyan desert, and, perhaps more
importantly, establishing links with the Luwāta Berbers in the
Tripoli area.[17] According to the Arab geographer Yāqūt, Uqba 'had
remained in the area of Barqa and Zuwayla from the days of Amr
b. al-Ās and he gathered around him the Berbers who had converted
to Islam'.[18]

In 670 the Caliph Muᶜāwiya appointed Uqba as governor of the
land under Muslim rule in North Africa under the overall control of
the governor of Egypt.[19] He decided to launch a campaign to conquer
Ifrīqīya (that is roughly modern Tunisia) and bring it firmly under
Muslim rule. With his long experience in the area, Uqba would have
known that it was a good moment to strike. The Byzantine administration was weakening by the day. The Arabs were attacking Constantinople itself and all the resources of the empire were required to
defend it. Just as dangerous was an outbreak of that internal dissent
which had undermined the empire so often before. Emperor Constantine IV (668–88) was faced by a pretender to his throne in Sicily
and had been forced to withdraw troops to combat him. The Romans,
however, were not the real challenge: it was conquering or working
with the Berbers which was to be the crucial issue.

Uqba arrived in southern Tunisia with an army largely drawn from
the Arabs of Egypt. He is said to have had 10,000 Arab horsemen
with him and the numbers were swelled by Berbers, probably mostly
from the Luwāta tribe, who had already converted to Islam. His first
objective was to establish a military base in the heart of Ifrīqīya. The
story of the foundation of the city of Qayrawān is told by the thirteenth-century geographer Yāqūt working from older sources now
lost to us.

He went to Ifrīqīya and besieged its cities, conquering them by force and putting the people to the sword. A number of Berbers converted to Islam at his hand and Islam spread among them until it reached the lands of Sudan.* Then Uqba gathered his companions [ashāb] and addressed them saying, 'The people of this country are a worthless lot; if you lay into them with the sword, they become Muslims but the moment your back is turned, they revert to their old habits and religion. I do not think it would be a good idea for the Muslims to settle among them but I think it would be better to build a [new] city here for the Muslims to settle in.'

They thought this was a sound plan and came to the site of Qayrawān. It was on the edge of the open country and covered with scrub and thickets which even snakes could not penetrate because the trees were so thickly intertwined.

Uqba went on: 'I have only chosen this place because it is well away from the sea and Roman ships cannot reach it and destroy it. It is well inland.' Then he ordered his men to get building, but they complained that the scrub was full of lions and vagabonds and that they were afraid for their lives and refused to do it. So Uqba collected the members of his army who had been Companions of the Prophet, twelve of them, and cried out, 'O you lions and vermin, we are Companions of the Prophet of God, so leave us and if we find any of you here we will kill them!' Then the people witnessed the most extraordinary sight, for the lions carried their cubs and the wolves carried their young and the snakes carried their offspring and they left, one group after another. Many Berbers were converted to Islam as a result of this.

He then established the government house and the houses for the people around it and they lived there for forty years without ever seeing a snake or a scorpion. He laid out the mosque but was uncertain about the direction of the *qibla* and was very worried. Then he slept; and in the night heard a voice saying, 'Tomorrow, go to the mosque and you will hear a voice saying "*Allāhu akbar*". Follow the direction

---

* Meaning sub-Saharan Africa, certainly an exaggeration.

of the voice and that will be the *qibla* God has made pleasing for the Muslims in this land'. In the morning he heard the voice and established the *qibla* and all the other mosques copied it.[20]

With all its miraculous trappings, this foundation myth still reveals a good deal about the motivation for the founding of the city. It was to be a permanent garrison for the Muslims in this area. The site was chosen because there were no earlier buildings there. Different accounts also stress the importance of grazing in the area.[21] It was well away from the coast. The Romans were still considered to be a threat from the sea, if not on land. Founding the city was quite simple. It required only the laying out of the mosque, the government house and the plots on which people could build their houses. There is no evidence that the Arab authorities constructed markets, baths, *funduqs* or any other public building. Despite its modest beginnings, Qayrawān thrived. Alone of all the garrison towns erected by the Arabs in the immediate aftermath of the conquests, it has remained an inhabited city on the same site down to the present day: in Iraq, old Basra is a hardly visible ruin on the edge of the desert, old Kūfa has disappeared, Fustāt in Egypt is a deserted archaeological site and rubbish tip and Merv in Khurasan a vast desolate ruin field. Qayrawān, by contrast, is a charming old town, redolent with Muslim antiquity.

The foundation of Qayrawān was a decisive step in the establishment of a Muslim presence in Ifrīqīya but it did not mean the end of conquest. Carthage still remained in Roman hands and no Muslim army had yet penetrated west of the modern Tunisia–Algeria frontier.

Like Amr b. al-Ās in Egypt before him and Mūsā b. Nusayr in Spain after, Uqba was removed from the governorate of the country he had so recently conquered. In 675 he was arrested by his successor, who humiliated him by keeping him in chains before sending him to the caliph Muʿāwiya in Damascus. He was, however, to make a spectacular comeback.

The new governor, Abū'l-Muhājir, was not an Arab at all but a *mawlā* (freedman) of Uqba's superior, the governor of Egypt. He may have been of Coptic, Greek or even Berber origin. He brought with him new troops from Egypt who may also have been non-Arabs, and when he arrived in Ifrīqīya he established himself outside Qayrawān, perhaps because he knew that many of the inhabitants remained loyal to his predecessor.²² The new governor's first priority was to win over the most powerful Berber leader in the Maghreb. Kusayla (also Kasīla) was 'king of the Awraba Berbers' with a domain that stretched from the Aurès in western Algeria to Volubilis in the plains of Morocco. Kusayla and probably many of his followers were Christians who had had good relations with the Romans. Abū'l-Muhājir confronted him at his power base in Tlemcen and succeeded in converting him to Islam and winning him over to the Muslim cause. Kusayla came to live with the governor in his base outside Qayrawān. This brilliant strategic alliance meant that Abū'l-Muhājir was now free to attack Carthage. He set up a blockade in 678 and though the city did not fall at this time, Roman rule was now confined to Carthage and its immediate surroundings.

As often in the history of the Arab conquests, events were shaped by changes in the government of the caliphate as much as by events on the campaign. In 680 the caliph Muʿāwiya died and his son and successor Yazīd I decided to reappoint Uqba to his old command. Now it was Abū'l-Muhājir's turn to be kept in chains as Uqba returned in triumph. His reappearance marked an important change of policy. His predecessor's conciliatory attitude to the Berbers was sharply reversed. Kusayla joined his patron and ally in chains and Uqba prepared for his last great adventure.

According to one Arab chronicle, Uqba hardly paused to draw breath in Qayrawān.²³ He left his son in charge of the troops there, saying 'I have sold myself to God most high,' and, expressing his doubts that he would ever see them again, he set out west, to lands no Muslim forces had ever visited. He and his small army moved fast through the plateaux that lie to the south of the coastal mountains. His first encounter was at Bāghāya at the foot of the Aures mountains, where he defeated a contingent of Romans and captured a large number of horses. He then went west to Monastir. The defenders came out to challenge him and the fighting was fierce but 'God gave him victory'. The Muslim forces do not seem to have taken the city but collected a lot of booty before moving on to Tahert, where Berbers and Byzantines awaited him. Once more the fighting was fierce and once more the Muslims triumphed.

The expeditionary force pressed on. One has the impression of a band of men, perhaps a few thousand strong, moving quickly through a largely empty landscape. There is no record of any resistance until they reached Tangier. Tangier was one of the very few urban settlements in what is now Morocco. According to the thirteenth-century historian Ibn Idhārī it was one of the oldest cities of the Maghreb, but, he goes on, 'the ancient city, the one mentioned in accounts of Uqba's raid, has been buried by the sand and the present city stands above it on the coast: if you dig in the ruins you can find all sorts of jewels'.²⁴ Tangier was governed by the mysterious Julian, who later plays an important part in the history of the first Muslim invasion of Spain. His main concern seems to have been to get rid of Uqba as quickly as possible, and so he dissuaded him from attempting to cross the straits to Spain and instead encouraged him to go down the Atlantic coast of Morocco.

His next stop was the city of Walīla. In contrast with Tangier, we know quite a lot about Walīla at this time. Under the name of Volubilis it had been one of the most important cities of Mauretania in Roman times. Although imperial government had effectively withdrawn in the third century, 400 years before Uqba's raid, it had retained an urban aspect and at least part of the old city area was still inhabited. Although most of the population were probably Berbers, and they certainly lived in Berber-style houses, the sixth-century tombstones show that they had Roman-style names and titles.²⁵ Once again, Uqba is said to have defeated the local Berbers but moved on quickly. He was now heading south across the flat plains of Morocco towards the Atlas mountains. It would seem that he crossed the mountains to the Wadi Dra in pursuit of some fleeing Berbers and then came back to besiege the town of Aghmāt, near where Marrakesh stands today. The town was inhabited by Christian Berbers, and it seems to have been one of the few places that Uqba took by force.

He now penetrated into the Atlas again, following the passes that led down to the fertile lands of the Wadi Sūs, which runs between the High Atlas and the more barren Anti-Atlas mountains down to the sea near Agadir. This was the land the Arabs called Sūs al-Aqsā, furthest Sūs. It had never been conquered by the Romans and it was to mark the final frontier of Muslim rule for centuries to come. In contrast to many of the areas Uqba had passed through, Sūs seems to have been densely populated by Berber tribes living in mountain villages, as they do to this day. They put up some stiff resistance to this band of marauders. Uqba had some successes, and when he conquered the little town of Naffīs he is said to have founded a mosque there, probably more a votive offering for his victories rather than as the place of worship for a Muslim community. In other places he was less successful and a 'Place of Martyrs' (*mawdīʿ al-shuhadā*) and another 'Cemetery of Martyrs' (*maqbarat al-shuhadā*) recorded for posterity the places where his companions fell in combat.

It was at the end of his raid in the Sūs that Uqba reached the Atlantic. The moment has passed into legend. He is said[26] to have ridden his horse into the sea until the water came up to its belly. He shouted out, 'O Lord, if the sea did not stop me, I would go through the lands like Alexander the Great [Dhū'l-Qarnayn], defending your faith and fighting the unbelievers.' The image of the Arab warrior whose progress in conquering in the name of God was halted only by the ocean remains one of the most arresting and memorable in the whole history of the conquests.

From the western edge of the continent, he made his way back east to the Aurès mountains. Here he divided his army, allowing many of his troops to go home. He kept by him a small force with the intention of conquering Tubna in the Zāb. There he came up against a large army led by Kusayla, who had escaped from his enforced confinement in Qayrawān. He had now repudiated his earlier alliance with the Muslims and had established himself once again as leader of the Berber resistance. It seems to have been a short and unequal struggle and Uqba found the martyrdom to which he is said to have aspired.

Uqba's expedition to the west remains one of the most important foundation myths of the Muslim Maghreb. In practical terms, however, the results were fairly meagre. He is said to have been reluctant to besiege fortified strongholds, preferring to raid further and further in the deserted lands of the west.[27] When he returned, he left no garrisons in the places he had 'conquered' and no arrangements for the collecting of tribute or taxes. Apart from the mosque at Qayrawān itself, just two mosques in Sūs and the Wadi Dra are attributed to him[28] and there is no evidence that either of them was a lasting and substantial structure. There was, however, a more sinister side to his exploits. He is said to have acquired human booty in the form of young Berber girls, 'the likes of which no one in the world had ever seen'.[29] They could fetch 1,000 gold dinars in the slave markets of the Middle East and were much favoured by the elite: the mother of the great Abbasid caliph Mansūr (754–75) was one such Berber girl, captured at about this time. This slave trade was to continue through much of the first half-century of Muslim rule in North Africa and provoked bitter resentments among the newly Islamized Berbers.

The defeat and death of Uqba might have meant the end of the Arab presence in the Maghreb. His aggressive expedition had united most of the main Berber tribes to oppose the Arab invaders. They came together under the leadership of Kusayla, who decided to march on Qayrawān. In the city there was confusion and despair. Men gathered in the mosque to decide what they should do. There were those, like Zuhayr b. Qays, who were determined to hold out and spoke the language of martyrdom: 'God has bestowed martyrdom on your friends and they have entered the garden of paradise. Follow their example!' Others were unconvinced, saying that they should retreat to the safety of the east. Despite the stirring words about sacrifice, the majority decided to withdraw and Zuhayr, finding that only his own family had stayed with him, followed the rest, halting only when he reached his palace in Barqa.[30]

The victorious Kusayla now occupied the city Uqba had founded. Here he established himself as 'amir of Ifrīqīya and the Maghreb', giving guarantees of security to those Muslims who wished to remain and perhaps collecting taxes from them, a neat reversal of roles. For about four years (684–8) Kusayla ruled in Qayrawān, holding sway over the interior while the Byzantines still held out in Carthage as their fleet patrolled the coastline, seeking to sustain their remaining outposts and prevent the Muslims attacking Sicily.

In part the weakness of the Arabs can be explained by the chaos that engulfed the caliphate after the death of Yazīd I in 683. Even after the accession of Abd al-Malik as Umayyad caliph in 685, it was some years before the Muslims were in any position to try to re-establish their position in Tunisia. In 688 Abd al-Malik in Syria now ordered the appointment of Zuhayr, the idealist holy warrior, to lead an expedition from Tripoli to retake Qayrawān. One source says that his force consisted of just 4,000 Arabs and 2,000 Berbers.[31] They seem to have reached Qayrawān without meeting any opposition. As they approached the city, Kusayla received word and decided to withdraw.

The city was at this stage unwalled so it offered little protection. He was also concerned that the Muslims still resident there might form a fifth column and he wanted to be near the mountains in case things went wrong. He encamped at a place called Mims on the edge of the Aurès mountains. It was here that Zuhayr's army defeated and killed him. As so often, it is difficult to see reasons for the military success of the Muslim forces over what was probably a much larger army, well acquainted with the terrain. We can only observe that, once again, when it came to crucial battles, the Muslim forces proved superior.

While the Byzantines do not seem to have offered Kusayla any military support in his final conflict, their fleet was still a force to be reckoned with along the Mediterranean coast. They now launched an attack, which seems to have been intended to divert the attentions of the Muslims to Cyrenaica, and Zuhayr, professing an ascetic distaste for political power and governorship, was obliged to lead his men back east to counter the threat. He found that the Byzantines had now occupied Barqa, which had been in Muslim hands since the first expedition of Amr b. al-Ās half a century before. As he tried to dislodge them, he died as a martyr and his small army was defeated.

The death of Zuhayr at Barqa was the low point in the Muslims' attempt to conquer North Africa, but all that was about to change. By 694 the vigorous and effective Umayyad caliph Abd al-Malik had defeated all his numerous enemies within the lands of Islam. He now had troops to spare, troops who might appreciate the opportunities of booty and plunder to keep them loyal. There were other good reasons for reopening campaigns in North Africa. If Cyrenaica was in enemy hands, Egypt itself would be vulnerable to attack. Besides, the Muslims had never yet surrendered control over lands they had once conquered; no one who claimed to be the Commander of the Faithful could allow that to happen without putting up a strong resistance.

The caliph appointed Hassān b. al-Nuʿmān al-Ghassānī as leader. Hassān was descended from the Ghassānid family, who had led the Arabs of the Syrian desert in the century before the Muslim conquest. Some members of the family had emigrated across the frontier to the Byzantine Empire but others had remained in Syria and been incorporated into the Umayyad elite among those Syrian Arab tribesmen who were the backbone of the regime. He was given the epithet of *shaykh amīn*, the trustworthy old man. He was to prove an able general and reliable administrator and was, in many ways, the real founder of Muslim North Africa. The caliph also supplied him with an army of 40,000 men, the largest Muslim force that had ever been seen in the area. This was to be a major expedition.

When he arrived in Ifrīqīya after the long march along the North African coast, Hassān decided that his first priority was to make an assault on Carthage, the centre of what remained of the Roman admin-istration in the area. In some ways it is curious that Muslim forces had not attacked the city before. The most likely explanation for this apparent omission is that they realized that the Berbers were a much more formidable enemy and it was important to defeat them or come to some arrangement first. The Byzantines were permitted to shelter behind the walls of the city. The recent naval attack on Cyrenaica had demonstrated that they were still a threat, and Hassān decided to put an end to it once and for all.

The fall of Carthage was a major event because it meant the final, irretrievable end of Roman power in Africa. In military terms, it seems to have been more a peaceful occupation than a major siege. The city, on a wonderful seaside site overlooking the Gulf of Tunis, had been the pivot of Roman power on the North African coast for almost eight hundred years. At one stage it had been graced by numerous monumental buildings, and in late antiquity these had been sup-plemented by magnificent churches. In the second century AD it is thought to have had half a million inhabitants, and the Antonine Baths, of which fragments still remain, were the largest in the Roman world. The Arab chronicler Ibn Idhārī says that in his day (*c.* 1300) the city was still distinguished by its impressive remains, vast buildings and huge standing columns, which showed its importance to the people of the past. He adds that the inhabitants of nearby Tunis, just like modern tourists, still visited the site to contemplate the wonders and monuments that had survived the ravages of time.[32] The Carthage of 698 was a mere shadow of the great city that had existed since long before the Roman conquest. According to Ibn Abd al-Hakam there were only a few feeble inhabitants.[33] The city seems to have been largely deserted, and there had been no significant new building for at least half a century. With the collapse of Mediterranean commerce, the city had lost its *raison d'être*, with only a few inhabitants and a small garrison now living among the vast ruins.

Not surprisingly, the city seems to have put up little resistance. According to some sources, inhabitants had already packed their possessions into ships and sailed away at night so that the city was actually deserted when the Arab armies entered.[34] We have no accounts of any formal siege and no accounts of the booty seized after the conquest, a further indication that the city may have been almost abandoned before the Arab conquest. After the Muslims were firmly in control, they made no effort to establish a garrison in the city or build a mosque. In fact, the centre of population moved from seaside Carthage to inland Qayrawān, just as in Egypt it shifted from seaside Alexandria to inland Fustāt.

The fall of Carthage may have marked the end of the Byzantine presence in North Africa but many Berber tribes remained defiant. The leadership of the Berber resistance was now seized by the mysterious figure of Kāhina ('the Sorceress'). The reputation of this Berber Boudicca, with her wild, long hair and ecstatic prophecies, has survived through the centuries in history and legend as a symbol of resistance to Arab conquest and the norms of conventional Muslim life. Contemporary cultures hail her variously as champion of female emancipation and power, a heroine of Berber resistance and independence, a Jewish princess 'who never abandoned her faith' and a great African queen. She was certainly a Berber from a branch of the great Zanāta tribe, but is said to have married a Byzantine and to have been either Jewish or Christian by religion.

The traditional view of Kāhina was summed up in eighteenth-century English prose by Edward Gibbon, the breadth of whose learning never ceases to amaze. He describes how the 'disorderly' Berbers were united:

Under the standard of their queen Cahina the independent tribes acquired some degree of union and discipline; and as the Moors respected in their females the character of a prophetess, they attacked the invaders with an enthusiasm similar to their own. The veteran bands of Hassān were inadequate to the defence of Africa; the conquests of an age were lost in a single day; the Arabian chief [Hassān], overwhelmed by the torrent, retired to the confines of

Egypt, and expected, for five years, the promised succours of the
caliph.

He then goes on to tell how Kāhina was determined to discourage the
Arabs from returning:

> The victorious prophetess assembled the Moorish chiefs, and recom-
> mended a measure of strange and savage policy. 'Our cities,' she said,
> 'and the gold and silver which they contain, perpetually attract the
> arms of the Arabs. These vile metals are not the objects of our ambi-
> tion; we content ourselves with the simple productions of the earth.
> Let us destroy these cities; let us bury in their ruins those pernicious
> treasures; and when the avarice of our foes shall be destitute of temp-
> tation, perhaps they will cease to disturb the tranquillity of a warlike
> people.'
> The proposal was accepted with unanimous applause. From
> Tangier to Tripoli the buildings, or at least the fortifications, were
> demolished, the fruit trees were cut down, a fertile and populous
> garden was changed into a desert and the historians of a more recent
> age could discern the frequent traces of prosperity and the devastation
> on their ancestors. Such is the tale of the modern Arabians.[35]

The reality behind the legend is difficult to assess. Kāhina's power
was centred on the Aurès mountain area. The Aurès are a massif in
western Algeria rising to 2,300 metres at the highest point. The heart
of the mountains is no more than 100 kilometres from west to east
and 50 from north to south. To the north lies the fertile plateau; to
the south the land slopes steeply to the fringes of the Sahara. The
mountains are rugged and rocky and the deep valleys shelter isolated
villages and palm groves. They were in an important strategic position.
Although wild and inaccessible, they were only a few days' march
from the plains of Tunisia and the centres of Arab power. The massif
also commanded the route from Tunisia to the rest of Algeria and
Morocco: until the Aurès were subdued, or at least friendly, no Arab
armies could safely operate in those areas. It was a perfect stronghold
for those who wanted to resist invaders from outside, and it was always
a centre of Berber resistance; the first shots of the Algerian rebellion
against French rule were fired in the Aurès in 1954.

Our fullest account of Kāhina comes from the work of Ibn Idhārī. When Hassān entered Qayrawān he asked who was the most important king still surviving in Ifrīqīya, and he was told it was Kāhina in the Aurès mountains and that all the Romans went in fear of her and all the Berbers obeyed her. They added that if he killed her the whole Maghreb would fall into his hands. He set off to confront her. She reached the town of Bāghāya before him, driving out the Romans and destroying the city because she was afraid that Hassān wanted to go there and use it as a fortified base. He approached the mountains and set up camp in the Wadi Maskiyāna, and it was here that Kāhina came to meet him. He was encamped at the top of the wadi while her forces were lower down. The horsemen of both sides made contact one evening but Hassān refused to do battle that day and both armies spent the night in the saddle. The next day there was a long hard fight but in the end Hassān's forces were put to flight. Kāhina pursued him, killing many, taking prisoners and driving him beyond Gābis. It seems that he took refuge in Cyrenaica, whence he wrote to the caliph, asking for reinforcements and explaining that the nations of the Maghreb had no political progamme or objective but were like freely grazing flocks. The caliph replied, telling him to remain where he was. The castles he and his men settled in near Barqa were still known in Ibn Idhārī's day, six centuries later, as 'Qusūr Hassān' – Hassān's palaces.

Our author then goes on to report a speech allegedly made by Kāhina which was to form the basis of Gibbon's account. According to this she addressed the Berbers in the following words:

'The Arabs only want Ifrīqīya for its cities and gold and silver while we only want agriculture and flocks. The only solution is the destruction [kharāb] of the whole of Ifrīqīya so that the Arabs lose interest in it and they never return again!' Her audience approved, so they went away to cut down their trees and destroy their fortresses. It has been said that Africa was shaded from Tripoli to Tangier, villages were continuous and there were cities everywhere, to the extent that no area of the world was more prosperous, or favoured: no area had more cities and fortresses [husūn] than Africa and the Maghreb and it went on for two thousand miles like it. The Kāhina destroyed all of that. Many of the Christians and Africans left seeking to escape from what the Kāhina had done, going to Andalus [Spain] and the other islands in the sea.

The account is interesting. It shows a clear recognition in a medieval Arabic source of the environmental and urban degradation of the area which has struck modern archaeologists and other commentators. As such it is most unusual. Of course, as Gibbon noted, the account concertinas the changes of two or three centuries into as many years. It does, however, point to some fundamental truths. The sixth and seventh centuries certainly did see a decline in urban life and settled agriculture in the area, combined with a growth in pastoralism. The narrative also puts the Arab conquests in an unfamiliar light. Here it is the Arabs who appear as preservers of urban life and civilization, not, as often in modern literature, as its destroyers.

It seemed that Kāhina's triumph was complete, and Hassān effectively abandoned Ifrīqīya. He soon received more troops from the caliph. He also attracted large numbers of Berbers who were, presumably, unwilling to accept Kāhina's authority. It is said that 12,000 of them joined in the *jihād*. With these he marched to the region of Gābis where he defeated her forces. He then pursued her to her stronghold of the Aures. The final battle occurred north of the modern town of Tobna, probably in 698. We have very few details about the battle in which Hassān defeated and killed Kāhina, except that she is said to have foreseen the catastrophe that was to come upon her. With flowing hair, she uttered wild prophecies of disaster while, at the same time, sending her sons under safe conduct to the Arab camp.[36]

The rebellion over, Hassān established himself once more in Qayrawān. Here he began to establish the norms of Umayyad administration, establishing a *dīwān* for the troops and enforcing the payment of the *kharāj* on the Christians. According to some sources, he founded the new town of Tunis, near Carthage. This was to be a naval base to prevent any more raids by the Byzantines, and 1,000 Coptic artisans were transported from Egypt to work there.[37] This marks the beginning of a permanent Muslim administration in Ifrīqīya and another stage in the conversion and recruitment of Berbers into the Muslim army of Africa, a process that was to be fundamental to the Muslim conquest of Spain.

In 704 Hassān was dismissed from his post. The loss of his job was the result of worsening relations between the caliph Abd al-Malik in Damascus and his brother, Abd al-Azīz b. Marwān, the governor of Egypt. Abd al-Azīz wanted to assert his authority, and the authority of Egypt, over North Africa. He also wanted to appoint his own protégé to the position of governor. The man he had in mind was Mūsā b. Nusayr. His origins were humble (see above, p. 105) and he was certainly not a member of one of the great elite families of the Umayyad caliphate. He was an intelligent and forceful man who worked his way up through his own abilities and the trust of his patron. He began his career in Syria, working for the Umayyad government, and first came to Egypt in 684. It was probably while he was there that he first came to the notice of Abd al-Azīz b. Marwān who set out to promote him and advance his career. By 704 Abd al-Azīz and Mūsā had been working together for twenty years; Abd al-Azīz wanted to reward him and knew that he was the ideal man to bring the unruly but potentially lucrative province of Ifrīqīya under his control.

He arrived to find the province in some disarray. Hassān had saved Arab Africa from the Berbers and expelled the Byzantines. Arab authority stopped at what is now the Tunisia–Algeria border. The lightning raid that Uqba b. Nāfi had led to the far west more than twenty years before had not resulted in any permanent settlement. The Berbers of the Aurès mountains and points west were still in a position to resist Arab authority.

Mūsā was determined to change that. Hassān left the province and made his way back to Damascus. When he reached Egypt, Abd al-Azīz despoiled him of all his possessions, even the presents he was taking to the new caliph, Walīd I. Meanwhile, in Africa, Mūsā was planning a great push west into the Maghreb. He began with an assault on the Berber fortress of Zaghwān, only a few kilometres from Qayrawān. It was soon taken and the first prisoners brought into the capital. Prisoners were the main object of his campaigns. In accounts of the Muslim conquests of cities and lands in the Middle East, we find constant references to the amount of booty taken – goods and chattels and, above all, money. And we are told how carefully it was divided among the conquerors. In the account of Mūsā's campaigns in the Maghreb, it is the numbers of captives acquired and sent east which dominate the accounts. The numbers are exaggerated with uninhibited enthusiasm, and the Islamic *jihād* looks uncomfortably like a giant slave raid. Almost as soon as he arrived in Qayrawān, Mūsā sent two of his sons on separate raids in the Maghreb and each came back with 100,000 prisoners. When Mūsā wrote to his patron Abd al-Azīz that he was sending 30,000 captives as the government share of the booty, Abd al-Azīz assumed that there had been a mistake in the letter because the number was impossibly large. In fact the scribe had made a mistake, but in the opposite direction: the real figure should have been 60,000.[38]

Mūsā himself soon set out to the west. At Sajūma he allowed the sons of Uqba b. Nāfi to take revenge for their father's death and 600 old men of the district were put to the sword. He then went on to subdue the great Berber tribes, Huwwāra, Zanāta and Kutāma, taking prisoners and appointing new chiefs who would be loyal to the Muslim conquerors. There was very little resistance from the settled people because, as the chronicler noted, 'most of the cities of Africa were empty [*khālī*] because of the hostility of the Berbers towards them'.[39] Following in the footsteps of Uqba b. Nāfi, Mūsā pushed on to the west, pursuing Berber tribes who were fleeing before him. Unlike Uqba, however, he was not diverted from Tangier. He is said to have taken the city and installed his Berber freedman, Tāriq b. Ziyād, as governor, the first time, as far as we know, that a converted Berber enjoyed a position of command in the Muslim army. With him he left a garrison, mostly made up of newly converted Berbers with a few Arabs, 'and he ordered the Arabs to teach the Berbers the Koran and to instruct them in the faith'. The garrison at Tangier were given lots to build on (*ikhtatta li'l-muslimīn*). The establishment of this Muslim outpost, just across the Straits of Gibraltar from the rich and inviting lands of southern Spain, was the prelude to invasion, and the garrison was to be the nucleus of the first Muslim force to invade the Iberian peninsula. Mūsā carried on to the south and west until eventually he reached Sūs and the Wadi Dra, taking hostages from the Masmūda tribe of the Atlas mountains. He then returned east to Qayrawān.

The Muslim conquest and settlement of Tangier was probably complete by 708. It was less than seventy years since the first Muslim troops had crossed from Egypt into Cyrenaica. During that time the war had ebbed and flowed in the most dramatic fashion. Throughout, the key had been the Arab control of Tunisia and their new capital at

Qayrawān. By 708 there was a firmly established Arab administration in most of modern Tunisia. To the east both Cyrenaica and Tripolitania were under Muslim rule. The areas of modern Algeria and Morocco remained a real 'wild west'. The only major Muslim presence in this area seems to have been the garrison at Tangier. In other areas, Muslim control depended on maintaining good relations with the Berber tribal leaders, who may have been converted to Islam, at least nominally. Muslim rule was to be challenged again, notably by great Berber rebellion in 740–41, but it was never to be overthrown.

7

CROSSING THE OXUS

༄

The initial conquest of Iran had been completed by the year 651.
Armies in pursuit of Yazdgard III had come as far as Merv.[1]
From there it was only a few days' journey north-east to the great
River Oxus (modern Amu Darya). Beyond the river lay the lands of
Transoxania, a world very different from Iran. Although many of the
inhabitants were Persian speakers living in the towns and villages, the
Sasanian Empire had never really controlled the area in any administrative sense. In place of a central imperial government there were
numerous princely courts in city palaces and mountain castles and
there were nomad encampments where great Turkish chieftans held
sway. Far to the east lay the frontiers of China and Chinese emperors
of the Tang dynasty had won the allegiance of the inhabitants of the ֦
area. It was a rich land, full of opportunities and wealth but defended
by warlike men who valued their independence very highly. The lure
of riches and the challenge of combat proved irresistible to the Arab
warriors.

Of all the campaigns of the early Arab conquests the fighting in
Transoxania was the hardest fought and longest lasting. An entire
century passed from the conquest of Merv (650–51) and the Arabs
crossing the Oxus to the final battle of Talas, which ended the prospect
of Chinese intervention in 751. The first phase of the conquests,
lasting intermittently from the 650s to 705, saw Arab governors
leading sporadic raids across the river but almost always returning to
their base in Merv before the onset of winter and leaving no permanent
presence in the territories. The second phase was the governorate of
Qutayba b. Muslim from 705 to 715, when there were systematic
attempts at conquest of Tukhāristan, Soghdia and Khwārazm, and
Arab garrisons were established in major cities like Bukhara and Samarqand. The third phase from 716 to about 737 was marked by serious

reverses for the Arabs at the hands of the resurgent Turks and their allies among the local princes. The fourth and final phase (737–51) saw two Arab governors, Asad b. Abd Allāh and above all Nasr b. Sayyār, reaching an accommodation with the local princes which left them acknowledging Arab overlordship in all of Transoxania but retaining much of their power and status.

The history of the Arab conquests in Central Asia is important for another reason. These campaigns are by far the most fully reported of all the expeditions of the early Islamic conquests. Rather than the vague and legendary accounts we have of earlier conquests, and indeed of the contemporary conquest of Spain, the battle narratives from Transoxania in the early eighth century are full of gritty and realistic detail. It is only here that we can hope to get some feeling for the harsh reality of conquest and destruction, of defeat and victory. We owe this material to a historian called Abū'l-Hasan al-Madā'inī. He was born in Basra in 753, just at the end of the era of the great conquests, but lived most of his life in Madā'in (Ctesiphon, whence his name) and Baghdad, where he died some time after 830.[2] He is said to have collected a vast number of history books, including histories of the invasion of Khurasan and biographies of individual governors, among them Qutayba b. Muslim and Nasr b. Sayyār. In around 900 this material was edited by Tabarī and incorporated, with full acknowledgements, into his own *History*, and it is from this that the material has been passed down to us.

Compared with the accounts of the early conquests of Syria, Iraq and Iran, chronology is more secure, though the narratives are still composites with different authors having developed their narratives for very different purposes.[3] Some strands belong to tribal traditions, clearly glorifying the memory of their great chiefs and the role that they played in these stirring events. The tribe of Azd preserved the memory of the deeds and virtues of their great chief Muhallab and his son Yazīd, and the fame of the greatest of all the Muslim generals in these campaigns, Qutayba b. Muslim, was preserved by his own followers from the Bāhila tribe. In addition, we have a local, independent historical tradition preserved in Narshakhī's *History of Bukhara*, which tells us much about how the conquest affected one city and the surrounding countryside.

The Oxus is an astonishing river. If you approach it along the ancient road to the east, travelling across the flat, bleak desert wastes from Merv to the traditional crossing point at Charjui*, you come upon it quite suddenly. It flows between the Kara Kum (Black Sands) to the west and the Kizil Kum (Red Sands) to the east, banked by low cliffs. There is little irrigation and few settlements; the river carves and meanders its way through a desolate and unpeopled land: here are no palm trees, fields and villages like those that make the banks of the Nile in Egypt such a delight to the eye. The river itself, its breadth and the strength of its current, seems an alien invader in this flat desert landscape.

The Victorian poet Matthew Arnold, at the end of his 'Sohrab and Rustam', based on one of the great stories of the *Shahnāmah*, apostrophizes the river. After Rustam has killed his only son in tragic error, the Persian and Turkish armies return to their camps, light their fires and start their cooking, leaving the hero alone with the corpse. The poet imagines the whole course of the mighty river:

But the majestic river floated on,
Out of the mist and hum of that low land,
Into the frosty starlight, and there moved,
Rejoicing, through the hushed Chorasmian waste,
Under solitary moon: he flowed
Right for the polar star, past Orgunje,
Brimming, and bright, and large: then sands begin
To hem his watery march, and dam his streams,
And split his currents; that for many a league
The shorn and parcelled Oxus strains along,
Through beds of sand and matted rushy isles –
Oxus, forgetting the bright speed he had
In his high mountain-cradle in Pamere,
A foiled circuitous wanderer – till at last
The longed for dash of waves is heard, and wide
His luminous home of waters opens, bright
And tranquil, from whose floor the new bathed stars
Emerge, and shine upon the Aral Sea.

* Ancient Amul.

The Oxus marked a real frontier. The Arabs referred to what lay beyond simply as *mā warā al-nahr*, 'what is beyond the river', and the name has continued in use down to the present day, long after the people of the area stopped speaking Arabic. Western scholars and travellers have long used the term Transoxania to describe the area. In the early Muslim period, these lands were considered to be part of Khurasan, the vast province that also included north-east Iran, and were ruled from the provincial capital at Merv, where the governor normally resided.

It is a land of many different environments which determined the aims and strategies of the Arab invaders. There are fertile river valleys where towns and villages clustered together. Close by, some-times separated only by the wall around the oasis, were vast deserts, searingly hot in summer, bitterly cold in winter, where only the hardiest nomads could survive. Then there were the mountains, often rising with the abruptness of a wall from the plains, mountains that sheltered and protected ancient cultures and ways of life even centuries after the plains were dominated by alien invaders. Here lay another, different world, of remote mountain villages where people spoke incomprehensible dialects and worshipped their princes as gods.

The most basic divide between the people who lived in these contrasting landscapes was between the speakers of Iranian dialects and those who used one of the different Turkic languages. This is a distinction that persists to the present day between the Persian-speaking Tajiks and the Turkish-speaking Uzbeks. In the seventh century, when the Arabs first arrived, the linguistic differences were accom-panied by marked cultural differences, the Persian speakers being, in general, the inhabitants of the towns and villages of the settled lands and the Turkish speakers being mostly nomads.

Politically and socially, the lands along the Oxus fell into four distinct and separate zones.[4] Around the middle Oxus valley lay the land of Tukhāristan, bordered to the north by the Hissar and other mountain ranges, and to the south by the great Hindu Kush, which form the barrier with southern Afghanistan and the plains of India. Since the nineteenth century, the river has formed the border between Afghanistan to the south and the Russian-ruled land of Tajikistan to the north, but in the seventh and eighth centuries there was no such border and people on both sides of the river were part of the same community and cultures.

Tukhāristan was studded with ancient settlements. The most important of these was Balkh, whose mighty mud-brick walls still look out over the flat plain to the mountains to the south. Balkh, ruined and desolate since it was destroyed by the army of Genghis Khan in 1220, was once one of the great cities of Central Asia. It had been conquered by Alexander the Great and had become the capital of the Greek kingdom of Bactria. Here, in the heart of Asia on the banks of the Oxus, Alexander's soldiers and their descendants established an outpost of Hellenic culture. They minted coins with images of their rulers, in the Greek fashion, as fine as any produced in the Greek world. The palace of the kings overlooking the Oxus at Ai Khanum was an architectural vision directly imported from Macedonia, laid out with broad straight streets, a palace with a peristyle courtyard and a gymnasium for athletes.

The Greek kingdom had withered by the second century BC and the Mediterranean Hellenism and Greek gods had been replaced by the Buddhist culture brought in by the Kushan kings. Balkh became a great centre of Buddhist culture and pilgrims came from as far away as China to visit the great Nawbahār stupa in the fields outside the town.

At the time when the Arabs first began to invade the area after 650, Tukhāristan was divided into numerous principalities, although the prince, who held the title of Jabghū, claimed a vague overlordship over the whole area. The rulers of these principalities were of Iranian or Turkish descent, Zoroastrian or Buddhist in religion. The most remote of them, way to the east on upper Oxus, was mountainous Badakhshān, where the rubies and lapis lazuli were mined, then came Khuttal, Kubadhiyan and Saghānān. To the south, deep in the jagged Hindu Kush mountains, lay Bamiyan, where the giant Buddhas presided benignly over the vivid green fields of the valley floor, while even beyond that lay distant Kabul.

After passing the fortified town of Tirmidh (modern Termez), one of the few settlements actually on the banks of the river, the Oxus turns north. Eventually it reaches the flat lands known as Khwārazm (the 'w' is silent), known nowadays as Khorezm, split between Uzbeki-stan and Tajikistan.[5] Here it is divided into the different streams and canals that form its delta. Remote, cut off by deserts on all sides, these fertile lands were inhabited from the fourth millennium BC by settled people with their own distinctive culture. They spoke their own Iranian language, which reminded one outsider of 'the chatter of starlings and the croaking of frogs',[6] and which was written in a version of the old Aramaic script. This fertile land was ruled by a dynasty of kings, the shahs of the Afrīghid dynasty, who had held sway for three centuries before the coming of the Arab armies, building fortified palaces and defending the borders of their lands against hostile nomads.

Finally the river reaches, or used to reach, the Aral Sea. Alas, the 'dash of waves' imagined by the poet can no longer be heard, for the sea has dried out, so much water having been taken off to irrigate the cotton fields of Turkmenistan; now the fishing boats lie stranded where the shoreline used to be, surrounded by a desolate world of salt-laden dust and sand.

East of the Oxus and north of the Hissar mountains, in modern Uzbekistan, lay the land of Soghdia (Sughd), around the river nowadays known as the Zarafshan (the 'Gold Scatterer') but known more prosaically to the Arab conquerors as 'the River of Soghdia'. The river flows from east to west, rising in the Turkestan mountains and flowing through the lowlands, past Samarqand and Bukhara, losing itself in the sands of the Kizil Kum before it can join the Oxus. The river created Soghdia as the Oxus created Khwārazm or the Nile created Egypt.

We know much more about Soghdia than the other areas. It was the centre of an ancient civilization which also had its own Iranian language, written, like the language of Khwārazm, in a variation of the Aramaic script. A substantial number of Soghdian documents have survived. It was also the scene of the most prolonged and hard fought of the Arab campaigns, and the Arab narratives tell us of the deeds of local kings, such as the stubborn and wily Ghūrak of Samarqand.

Soghdia was a land of princes, the most important of whom were based in the two great urban centres of Bukhara and Samarqand. These princes maintained a chivalrous and courtly culture, images of which survive on wall paintings discovered in Soghdian palaces in Old Samarqand and Penjikent. Something of the atmosphere of one of these princely courts can be glimpsed in the account that the local historian of Bukhara, Narshakhī, gives[7] of the court of his native city shortly before the Arab conquest in the time of the lady Khātūn (c. 680–700), of whom it was said that 'in her time there was no one more capable that she. She governed wisely and the people were obedient to her'. This tribute is particularly striking in contrast to the generally hostile attitude to female rule encountered in early Muslim historical sources. Every day she used to ride out of the gate of the great citadel of Bukhara to the sandy open ground known as the Registan. Here she would hold court, seated on a throne, surrounded by her courtiers and eunuchs. She had obliged the local landowners and princes (dehqānān ve malikzādegān) to send 200 youths every day, girded with gold belts and carrying swords on their shoulders. When she came out, they would stand in two rows while she enquired into affairs of state and issued orders, giving robes of honour to some and punishing others. At lunchtime she returned to the citadel and sent out trays of food to her retinue. In the evening she came out again and sat on her throne while the landowners and princes waited on her in two lines. Then she mounted her horse again, and returned to the palace while the guests returned to their villages. The next day another group would attend, and it was expected that each group would take their turn at court four times a year.

Soghdia was also a land of merchants. The period from the fifth to the eighth centuries saw the first great flowering of the overland 'Silk Road' between China and the west. The 'Silk Road' is a term loved by romantic historians and travel agents, conjuring a world of luxury goods, azure-tiled cities fragrant with spices and long photogenic caravan journeys through some of the bleakest landscapes on earth. The reality is rather more prosaic. The overland routes between China and the west were only intermittently used for trade, and for much of the Middle Ages the sea route from the Middle East through the Indian Ocean to China was a much more important highway of commerce. There were two main historical periods when the overland route came into its own and when the Silk Road became a major focus for world trade. The first of these was the period just before and during the Muslim conquests; the second was the period in the thirteenth century when the Mongol Empire provided a measure of security along the route, encouraging merchants like Marco Polo.

The emphasis on silk, however, is not just an empty cliché: it reflects an important reality. Though imperial China used a lot of bronze coinage, it had very little high-value coined money, silver or gold. Instead, silk, along with bushels of wheat, was used as an alternative currency. Much of this 'money' found its way to Central Asia. In the seventh century the Chinese authorities were attempting to consolidate their control in Sinkiang by expending massive resources in paying officials and soldiers. Some indication of how this worked can be gleaned from ancient documents recovered from the Gobi Desert near the great Buddhist shrine at Dunhuang. One example describes an army officer in 745 who was owed 160 kilograms of bronze coins by the central government for half a year's salary.[8] Only by paying him in light, easily transportable silk, instead of coins, could this system be practicable. The official would then be able to sell the silk to Soghdian merchants in exchange for silver or goods from the west. The Soghdians in turn would carry the silk to the markets of Iran and Byzantium. Control of this lucrative commerce was certainly one of the reasons why the Arabs were so determined to expand their power in this remote area.

The fourth, and most remote, part of Transoxania was the lands around the Jaxartes (modern Syr Darya) river, now part of Uzbekistan and Kazakhstan. These lay 160 kilometres north of Soghdia across the plains grimly known as the Hungry Steppe, where the trail across the desert was marked by the whitening bones of men and animals that had perished along the way. Smaller than the Oxus and fordable in many places, the Jaxartes watered the lands of the principality of Shāsh (modern Tashkent) and, further east, the open plains of the vast Farghāna valley. Beyond that, over the mountains, lay Kashgar and the lands of the Chinese Empire.

The nomads of Inner Asia are generally described in the Arab sources as Turks, and it was during their invasions that the Arabs first encountered these people, who were to have such a profound effect on the development of Muslim culture.[9] The relationship between these Turks and the inhabitants of modern Turkey is not straightforward. At the time of the Muslim conquest, what is now Turkey was part of the Byzantine Empire, and was to remain so for the next four centuries. As far as we know, not a single Turk lived there. The origins of the Turks are to be found far to the east. In the mid sixth century, Chinese chronicles begin to refer to a people called the T'u-chüeh, who were establishing an empire in the vast grassy steppe lands north of the Great Wall which were later to be the home of the Mongols. The founder of this empire, according to the Chinese sources, seems to have been Bumin, who died in 553, with his brother Ishtemi. We have confirmation of this in a series of remarkable inscriptions in old Turkish, carved on stones found in the grassy valley of the Orkhon river in Mongolia. A later king recorded in stone the glory days of the founders of the dynasty:

> When high above the blue sky and down below the brown earth had been created, betwixt the two were created the sons of men. And above all the sons of men stood my ancestors, the kaghans* Bumin and Ishtemi. Having become masters of the Turk people, they installed and ruled its empire and fixed the law of the country. Many were their enemies, but, leading campaigns against them, they subjugated and pacified many nations in the four corners of the world. They caused them to bow their heads and bend their knees. These were wise kaghans, they were valiant kaghans: all their officers were wise and valiant; the nobles, all of them, the entire people were just. This was the reason why they were able to rule an empire so great, why, governing the empire, they could uphold the law.[10]

The power of the Turks was based on more than justice and individual valour. It was based on the skills of these hardy nomads as mounted warriors and, above all, as mounted archers. The early Turks were horse nomads; they lived on their horses, they drank the milk of the mares, they ate their horses and, *in extremis*, they would open their veins and drink the blood of the living animals. A young Turk could often ride before he could walk. In addition to being great riders, they were also unbelievably hardy. Brought up in the blistering heat and painful cold of Inner Asia, they were able to endure hardships that would destroy other people.

The fighting techniques of the Turks were described at the beginning of the seventh century by the author of the *Strategikon*, ascribed to the Byzantine emperor Maurice. He writes:

* Khagan, and the alternative khan, were traditional Turkish titles meaning ruler or chief.

The nation of the Turks is very numerous and independent. They are not versatile or skilled in most human endeavours, nor have they trained themselves for anything else except to conduct themselves bravely against their enemies ... They have a monarchical form of government and their rulers subject them to cruel punishments for their mistakes. Governed not by love but by fear, they steadfastly bear labours and hardships. They endure heat and cold and the want of many necessities, since they are nomadic peoples. They are very superstitious, treacherous, foul, faithless, possessed by an insatiate desire for riches. They scorn their oath, do not observe agreements, and are not satisfied by gifts. Even before they accept the gift, they are making plans for treachery and the betrayal of their agreements. They are clever at estimating suitable opportunities to do this and taking prompt advantage of them. They prefer to prevail over their enemies not so much by force as by deceit, surprise attacks and cutting off of supplies.

They are armed with mail, swords, bows and lances; lances slung over their shoulders and holding bows in their hands, they make use of both as need requires. Not only do they wear armour themselves but in addition the horses of their leaders are covered in front with iron or felt. They give special attention to training in archery on horseback.

A vast herd of male and female horses follows them, both to provide nourishment and give the impression of a huge army. They do not encamp inside earthworks, as the Persians and Romans do, but until the day of battle, spread about according to tribes and clans, they continuously graze their horses both summer and winter. They then take the horses they think necessary, hobbling them next to their tents, and guard them until it is time to form their battle line, which they begin to do under cover of night. They station their sentries at some distance, keeping them in contact with one another, so that it is not easy to catch them by surprise attack.

In combat they do not, as do the Romans and Persians, form their battle line in three parts, but in several units of irregular size, all closely joined together to give the appearance of one long battle line. Separate from their main force, they have an additional force which they can send out to ambush a careless adversary or hold in reserve to aid a hard-pressed section. They keep their spare horses close behind their main line and their baggage train to the right or left of the line about a mile or two away under a moderately sized guard. Frequently they tie the extra horses together to the rear of their battle line as a form of protection.

They prefer battles fought at long range, ambushes, encircling their adversaries, simulated retreats and sudden returns, and wedge shaped formations, that is, in scattered groups. When they make their enemies take to flight, they put everything else aside, and are not content, as the Persians, the Romans and other people are, with pursuing them a reasonable distance and plundering their goods, but they do not let up until they have achieved the complete destruction of their enemies, and they employ every means to this send. If some of the enemy they are pursuing take refuge in a fortress, they make continual and thorough efforts to discover any shortage of necessities for horses or men. They then wear their enemies down by such shortages and get them to accept terms favourable to themselves. Their first demands are fairly light, and when the enemy has agreed to these, they impose stricter terms.

They are vulnerable to shortages of fodder which can result from the huge number of horses they bring with them. Also in the event of battle, when opposed by an infantry force in close formation, they stay on their horses and do not dismount, for they do not last long fighting on foot. They have been brought up on horseback, and, owing to their lack of practice, they simply cannot walk about on their own feet.[11]

It was these formidable warriors that the Arabs encountered when they crossed the great River Oxus, and they were impressed.

Between 557 and 561 the Turks, led by Bumin's brother and successor Ishtemi, made an alliance with the Sasanian shah Chosroes I (531–79) to destroy a nomad people known to history as the Hepthalites, who had dominated the steppes of Transoxania for a century. This brought Turkish power right up to the borders of the Persian Empire. There was even a marriage alliance between the Sasanian shah and the daughter of the khagan Ishtemi. At the same time, direct diplomatic links were established between the Turks and the Byzantine authorities, with a view to establishing a trade in Central Asian silks through the steppe lands to the north of the Black Sea.

This first great Turkish empire was not destined to last. Disputes among the ruling family led to civil war and by 583 the western

Turks had separated from their eastern cousins and a separate Turkish khaganate had been established in Transoxania. The Turkish khagan T'ung Yabghu was still a great ruler in 630 when a Chinese Buddhist pilgrim called Hsüng-tsang came through his territories and met him in person, but shortly after that he was murdered and the western khaganate began to fall apart. By the time the Arab armies arrived at the beginning of the eighth century the leader of the Turks, Türgesh Khagan, was a nomad chief acknowledging the overlordship of the Chinese emperor. Despite the break-up of their empire, when the nomad Turks of Transoxania allied with the local Iranian princes, they provided what was perhaps the fiercest opposition the early Muslim armies ever encountered.

It was into this mosaic of warlike peoples and cultures settled in a vast and variegated landscape that the first Arab military prospectors arrived in the early 650s.

The earliest Arab incursions across the river were simple raiding expeditions, designed to extort tribute. The Arabic sources often present such raids as real conquests and the subsequent resistance to more systematic attacks are presented as rebellions against Muslim authority. These first raids reached as far as Samarqand, but they encountered stiff resistance and the Arab armies withdrew before the onset of winter. This withdrawal allowed the local people some respite, and we are told that the 'Kings of Khurasan' met and joined forces, agreeing not to attack each other, but to exchange information and cooperate against the invaders.[12] Such cooperation was to prove rare in the years to come.

One Arab death in these early years of Arab incursions across the river had unexpected but lasting consequences. It is said that among the Muslims killed at Samarqand in the first raids was Quthm, son of al-Abbās, the Prophet Muhammad's uncle.[13] Quthm not only had the coveted status of Companion of the Prophet but he was also his first cousin. Despite his lineage and exalted connections, he was remembered for his humility and his refusal to accept more than a normal share of the spoils for himself and his horse. His memory has been revered among the Muslims of Central Asia and, however modest his real achievements, he is seen as having brought something of the charisma of the Prophet's immediate circle to these far-off lands, a direct link between Muhammad and the Muslims of Transoxania. The legend arose that he had not died but lived on in his tomb, deep in the ancient mud-brick walls of Samarqand. He was called the Shāhi Zinda, the 'Living King', and in the Timurid period (late fourteenth and early fifteenth century) his grave became the centre of a complex of tombs where the princes and above all the princesses of Tamerlane's court were buried. Their mausoleums with their turquoise and blue-tiled domes remain among the most refined and exquisite examples of Persian architecture and decoration to be found anywhere.

In 671 Ziyād b. Abī Sufyān, governor of Iraq and all the East, arranged that 50,000 men from Iraq, mostly from Basra, should move to Merv to relieve pressure on resources. Until this time, Arab armies had come to Khurasan on an annual basis, returning to Iraq each winter, leaving only a small force to defend the city. The arrival of this large number of Arabs as permanent residents transformed the Muslim presence in the area. There may well have been more Arabs settled in Merv and the surrounding small towns and villages than in the whole of the rest of Iran. They were hungry and ambitious for wealth and adventure: these men were to form the core of the Muslim armies invading Transoxania.

The appointment of Salm b. Ziyād as governor of Khurasan in 681 meant the incursions across the Oxus became more frequent and deliberate. He set about his preparations in a methodical fashion, raising an army of several thousand men from the Arab settlers. Many of these were volunteers who wanted to take part in the *jihād* but not all were overwhelmed by enthusiasm: one man[14] told later of how he went to the *dīwān* (register of troops) to enlist for a forthcoming expedition but when the clerk asked whether he wanted his name put down, 'for it is a mission in which there will be holy war and spiritual merit', he lost his nerve and replied that he would seek the decision of God and wait. He was still waiting when the list closed and his wife asked him whether he was going. Once more he replied that he was waiting for God to decide, but that night he had a dream in which a man came to him and said that he should join up for he would be prosperous and successful, which proved more enticing than the spiritual benefits. The next morning he went to the clerk and found a way to enlist.

We have few details about the expedition apart from the fact that Salm was the first man to winter across the river, probably in

Samarqand, with his men. The army attacked Khwārazm and extracted tribute before crossing into Soghdia, where they made peace. According to the Bukhara tradition, Salm attacked the city and obliged the queen, Khātūn, to sue for peace, but the details are very confused.[15] Salm had taken his wife with him and in Samarqand she gave birth to a son whom she called Sughdī (Soghdian) in memory of his birthplace. She sent to the wife of the lord (*sāhib*) of Soghdia asking to borrow some trinkets for the baby and she sent her her crown. When the Muslim army retreated, Salm's wife took the crown with her.[16] This shows that relations between the Arab and Iranian upper classes were not always hostile and that the wives of the enemies saw themselves as equals, though history does not preserve the Soghdian queen's reaction to the permanent loss of her crown.

Any plans Salm may have had to continue the conquest were brought to an abrupt halt by the chaos that engulfed the caliphate after the death of Yazīd I in 683. Salm's family had been leading supporters of the dead caliph, and he now abandoned Khurasan to make his way back west, wanting to join in the discussions about the succession. The Arabs in Khurasan were left with no official leader and the tribal rivalries, which had been contained by the governors, flared up with astonishing ferocity. Three main tribal groups were represented in Khurasan – Mudar, Rabīᶜa and Bakr b. Wā'il – and they now began a fierce struggle for control of the province. Abd Allāh b. Khāzim of Mudar took power in Merv. He ordered the death of two of the leaders of Rabīᶜa. Now there was blood between the groups and war was inevitable. All the rivalries of tribal Arabia during the *jāhiliya* reappeared in this distant outpost of the Muslim world, given added intensity by the competition for the wealth of the conquered lands. These seventh-century conquistadors began to slug it out among themselves.

Rabīᶜa and Bakr fled from Merv south to Herat and established themselves in this ancient city, pursued by Abd Allāh. The fugitive tribesmen swore there was no place in Khurasan for Mudar. For a full year they confronted Abd Allāh's forces. When Abd Allāh finally broke through their lines, there was a massacre. He swore that he would execute all prisoners brought to him before sunset, and he was as good as his word. It was said that 8,000 Rabīᶜa and Bakr were slain. Things in Khurasan would never be the same[17] and feuds between Arab tribes were fought out with unremitting ferocity, even as Muslim armies were conquering new areas. When news of the massacre reached distant Basra, the original home of many of these men, it provoked a new round of inter-tribal violence in the city.[18]

Abd Allāh was now master of Khurasan, responsible to no one but himself, but trouble was brewing. He felt he could dispense with the support of the powerful tribe of Tamīm: members of the tribe and their allies were humiliated, and two were flogged to death. In revenge they captured Abd Allāh's son Muhammad, who had been put in charge in Herat. As he lay bound in their camp that night, they sat about drinking, and whenever one of them wanted to urinate, they did it over their prisoner. They killed him before dawn.[19]

Humiliated and vengeful, Abd Allāh struck back and the inter-Arab war was renewed with added intensity. There was still room, however, for some of the old chivalry. Abd Allāh was a man around whom stories grew. In one of these he agreed to single combat with one of the opposition leaders called Harīsh.[20] 'They skirmished with each other like a pair of stallions' until Abd Allāh was butted by his enemy's head. It was only the fact that his opponent's stirrup snapped and he dropped his sword, which enabled Abd Allāh to escape, galloping back to his own lines, clinging on to the neck of his horse.[21] In the general fighting that followed, Abd Allāh's men were victorious and he caught up with his opponent, now deserted by all but twelve of his men, holed up in a ruined fortress, determined to defend themselves. Abd Allāh offered peace. His enemy was to leave Khurasan, and was to be given 40,000 dirhams and have his debts paid. As they discussed the terms, the bandage around Abd Allāh's head, which protected the wound inflicted on him in the single combat, blew off. Harīsh bent down to pick it up and replace it. 'Your touch is much more gentle than your touch yesterday,' joked Abd Allāh, to which Harīsh retorted that if only his stirrup had not broken, his sword would have made a fine mess of Abd Allāh's teeth. So, laughing, they parted and, like any good Bedouin, Harīsh composed a poem about his lonely struggle.

> Carrying a spear all night and all day
> Has kept the bone of my right hand out of joint.
> For two years my eyes have not closed at any resting place,
> Unless my fist made a pillow for me upon a stone.

My coat is of iron, and when night brings sleep,
My covering is the saddle of a full-grown stallion.[22]

That is how the Bedouin liked to remember their heroes: tough, solitary, self-reliant, brave. It was this spirit which was to take Arab armies to the frontiers of China.

There could be no joking, however, with the men who had killed his son, and Abd Allāh pursued them with relentless ferocity. They took refuge in a mud-brick fortress in the little town of Mervrūd, on the banks of the Murghab river. The defence was led by one Zuhayr, who was bold and adventurous, leading sorties along dried-up river beds to launch surprise attacks on Abd Allāh's men, swearing that he would divorce his wife if he did not break Abd Allāh's lines. On one occasion Abd Allāh had ordered his men to put hooks on their spears to catch in Zuhayr's chain mail and pull him down. Four spears duly hooked on to his armour but he was too strong for them; pulling away, he wrenched the spears from their grasp and returned to his fortress, the captured spears dangling from his armour as trophies.[23]

The year-long siege took its toll and the fugitives were on the point of surrender. Zuhayr urged them to come out fighting and break through Abd Allāh's siege lines, then, he said, their way would be as clear as the Mirbad, the great open square in the centre of their home town of Basra, a thousand kilometres away. But he could not drum up enough support among the defenders, who chose rather to surrender and put their trust in Abd Allāh's mercy. They opened the gates and came down. Their hands were bound and they were brought before Abd Allāh. The story goes that even now he was prepared to be merciful, but his surviving son Mūsā, standing beside him, was relentless: 'if you pardon them,' he told his father, 'I will fall on my sword so that it comes out of my back!' So one by one the prisoners were killed in the traditional Arab form of execution; a swift, hard sword-blow on the back of the neck was all it took. Only three were spared when some of Abd Allāh's men interceded for them.

When it was Zuhayr's turn, Abd Allāh wanted to spare him and even give him an estate to live on. 'How can we kill a man like Zuhayr? Who will there be to fight the enemies of the Muslims? Who to protect the women of the Arabs?' But again Mūsā showed his ruthlessness, asking how his father could kill the female hyena and leave the male, kill the lioness and leave the lion. The demands of vengeance were more important than the safety of the Arabs in this remote, hostile land; he would even kill his own father if he had participated in his brother's death. So once again, Abd Allāh was swayed by his implacable son. Zuhayr had one last request, that he should be killed separately from the rest of the defenders. 'I commanded them to die as honourable men and come out against you with drawn swords. By God, had they done so they would have given this little son of yours a fright and made him too worried about his own life to seek vengeance.' So he was taken aside and executed separately.

As long as civil war raged in Syria and Iraq, the heart of the caliphate, Abd Allāh ruled Khurasan as his private dominion, but by 691 the Umayyad caliph, Abd al-Malik (685–705), was firmly in control in Damascus and determined to restore the power of the central government. Part of his plan was to establish effective rule over Khurasan and its unruly Arab warriors. He began to negotiate, writing to Abd Allāh, offering very reasonable terms: for seven years he would enjoy the revenues of the province as his 'food' (tuʿma). But Abd Allāh was too proud to accept terms, ordering the messenger to eat the caliph's letter as a gesture of contempt. At the same time, the caliph began to make contact with possible rivals in the province. They were encouraged to rise up against the tyrant. Abd Allāh began to panic and left the capital at Merv to try to join his son Mūsā in Tirmidh. On the way he was intercepted by his enemies. The battle was over by midday. Abd Allāh was pinned to the ground by a spear point while a man sat on his chest and prepared to kill him, in revenge for the death of his brother. Abd Allāh was not quite finished yet. He spat at his assailant, hissing that the man's brother had been a mere peasant, not worth a handful of date stones, while he, Abd Allāh, was the leader of the tribe of Mudar. Defiant to the last, he was killed and his head cut off. A local man reported seeing his body, tied on to the side of a mule, with a stone on the other side to balance it. The head was sent to the caliph. Many certainly rejoiced in his death but his own tribesmen mourned him sadly as a brave and generous chief. 'Now only barking dogs remain,' one of their poets said. 'After you, there is no lion's roar on earth.'[24]

By 696 there was a new governor, Umayya, appointed by Abd al-Malik. He was a member of the ruling Umayyad family, easygoing,

generous, peace-loving and, his enemies alleged, pompous and effeminate. He was to have a hard struggle keeping the unruly Arabs of
Khurasan in order. The most effective way of doing this was to lead
them in campaign across the river, to fill their minds with thoughts
of Holy War and booty rather than tribal feuding and vengeance.
Preparations were made for a major campaign against Bukhara.
Umayya spent a vast amount of money on horses and weapons, money
that he is said to have borrowed from Soghdian merchants.²⁵ The
process reveals how complex relations were between the Arabs and
the local people. Bukhara was situated in Soghdia, yet at least some
Soghdian merchants were prepared to lend money to the Arabs who
were trying to conquer their Soghdian homeland! For many Arabs
too, the expedition was a speculative venture: we know of one man
who borrowed money to equip himself to join the expedition but,
when he decided not to go, was put in prison by his creditors and had
to be bailed out by a rich friend.²⁶ Many of the Arabs in fact seem to
have found themselves in financial difficulties, and they complained
that the local landowners were left in charge of the tax-collecting,
giving the conquered a certain authority over the conquerors.²⁷ For
impoverished and discontented Arabs, a raid across the river with the
prospect of serious booty was a very attractive proposition.

   In the event, Umayya does not seem to have commanded the
respect and confidence of his troops and the expedition was a fiasco.
After he and his men had crossed the bridge of boats over the Oxus
at Amul, his second-in-command refused to follow him any further,
crossing back over the river with some of his men, burning the boats
and heading back to take over Merv and establish himself as governor.
Appeals to Muslim solidarity failed to move him and he shrugged off
concerns about the fate of the Muslim forces under Umayya's
command, now cut off beyond the river, saying that they had numbers,
weapons and courage and that they could go as far as China if they
wished.²⁸ Umayya's forces were surrounded and in desperate straits
and he was obliged to make peace with the Bukharans 'for a small
payment'²⁹ and return to take control. Power politics and rivalries
among the Arabs had clearly become more important than Holy War
and the spread of Islam. And events showed clearly that the north-
east frontier was no place for easygoing and peace-loving leaders:
Umayya was soon withdrawn from the province.

Khurasan, and with it the command of the north-east frontier, was now given to the caliph's right-hand man, the ruthless and effective Hajjāj b. Yūsuf, governor of Iraq and all the east and one of the architects of the early Islamic state. He in turn appointed a man called Muhallab to take command in Khurasan. Muhallab was a figure of almost legendary prowess on the battlefield and a man with a great reputation as a commander. His tribe of Azd, one of the most import-ant and numerous in the east, revered him and his family as their greatest leaders and took care to keep his memory alive in myth and song. He had made his reputation fighting an Arab guerrilla insur-gency in southern Iran, hard, unrewarding campaigning in difficult country. He was also credited with the introduction of metal stirrups into the Muslim armies.

Muhallab brought with him his son Yazīd. It was of course expected that the new governor would launch an expedition to Transoxania to provide an opportunity for plunder: neither the Azdi tribesmen he had brought with him from Iraq nor the longer-established Arabs in the province would expect anything less. He chose Kish as his object-ive. Kish, known since the fifteenth century as Shāhri Sabz, 'the Green City', was later famous as the birthplace of Tamerlane, the great conqueror. It lies in a fertile plain at the foot of the mountains that rise to the north and east. It was not one of the most important cities of Transoxania, but it was still a significant prize. Muhallab seems to have acted very cautiously. For two years he blockaded the city, refus-ing advice to bypass it and push further into Soghdia. In the end, he withdrew in exchange for a payment of tribute.[30] The cities of Soghdia were not going to be taken over easily.

The confusion and lack of direction left open opportunities to the more adventurous and unscrupulous and none was more adventurous or more unscrupulous than Mūsā, son of the old governor Abd Allāh b. Khāzim. He carved out a position for himself on the frontiers of the Muslim world, in the borderlands between the two worlds of the Arab conquerors and the old princes of the area. In some ways he resembles El Cid in eleventh-century Spain, operating on the margins, happy to make alliances with anyone who could help him, greedy for money and generous to his followers. Like El Cid as well, Mūsā inspired a biography, or rather a record of heroic deeds, and so his reputation has come down to us.

The saga of Mūsā b. Abd Allāh b. Khāzim was edited in the form
we have it now by the great Madā'inī more than a century after the
events. He obviously used earlier sources but he does not give the
names of his authorities.[31] The story clearly has a basis in fact but
there are many elements which seem to be fanciful, even mythical,
but even these give us an insight into the frontier mentalities of the
time and place. Unlike many early Arabic historical texts, the story is
a linear narrative, uninterrupted by *isnād*s or alternative versions. It
tells the tale of the adventures of Mūsā, his rule of the city of Tirmidh,
his relations with Arabs and non-Arabs alike and his eventual downfall.
Mūsā's faults, especially the way in which he bowed to pressure from
his Arab followers against his own better judgement, are not glossed
over, but he clearly emerges as the roguish hero of the whole narrative.
The saga makes it clear that Mūsā was supported by Arabs and non-
Arabs, Muslims and non-Muslims alike and, at the same time, that
many of his fiercest opponents were Arabs. The politics of his meteoric
career are explained in terms of ethnic identities (Arabs, non-Arabs,
Turks) and tribal rivalries. Religion is never mentioned. This was no
jihād and Mūsā never claimed it as such. He may have built a mosque
in Tirmidh and he may have worshipped in it, but, if so, it is never
mentioned in the sources. In contrast to many narratives of the early
conquests, enthusiasm for Islam and the rewards of the afterlife never
figure. The values extolled are those of bravery in battle, of loyalty to
kin and companions, of endurance and of cunning. This frontier world
was a complex environment where alliances and allegiances shifted
rapidly, where Muslims and non-Muslims made alliances against other
Muslims and non-Muslims and where the *jihād* took second place to
personal ambition and the desire for wealth and power.

Mūsā had taken over the fortress town of Tirmidh during his
father's lifetime. Tirmidh, where the swift-flowing Oxus swirls around
the low cliffs and tawny mud-brick walls of the fortress, lay opposite
an island in the river which made it an easy crossing place. Along with
the impressive rectangular citadel[32] there was a walled town (*rabad*)
outside. The Greeks had called it Alexandria on the Oxus and later
under the Kushans a number of Buddhist stupas had been constructed
around it. The site of the old town has been deserted since the Mongol
invasions of the 1220s.

It was probably the strength of the citadel and the strategic position at the Oxus crossing which attracted Mūsā to the site. Here he established himself and defied all comers. He is portrayed as a flamboyant, larger-than-life figure who went into battle with a red silk bandana around his helmet, topped by a blue sapphire.[33]

He had originally come to Tirmidh almost by accident. When his father's fortunes were on the wane and he was losing support among the Arabs of Merv, his father had told Mūsā to take all his baggage and find a safe place for them. He was to cross the Oxus and take refuge with one of the local princes or find a suitable fortress and occupy it. He set off with 200 horsemen, but as he went on his party grew. By the time he reached the river crossing at Āmul he had been joined by a group of bandits (sa'ālīk: it is not clear whether these were Arabs or Iranians) and some men of his own tribe. The band was now over four hundred. He now needed a base where he could settle with his men.

The first place he tried was Bukhara, but the prince of the city was, rightly, very suspicious of him and his intentions. 'He is a murderer,' he said, 'and his companions are like him, people given to war and evil; I do not feel safe with him around.' So he gave him some money, riding animals and a robe and sent him on his way. Next Mūsā tried the lord (dehqān) of a small town near Bukhara. Again he got a frosty reception, the lord saying that the local people were frightened of him and would not accept him. Nevertheless, he stayed for a few months before setting off once more to find a suitable prince or fortress.

He had more luck in Samarqand, where the local king, Tarkhūn, honoured him and allowed him to stay, presumably hoping to use his military abilities against his enemies. It was too good to last long. The story goes that in Soghdia there was a local custom according to which, on one particular day of the year, a table was set with a meat dish, bread and a jug of something to drink. This was the food of the 'Knight of Soghdia', and he was the only person who was allowed to eat it. If anyone else dared to take any of the food, he would have to fight the knight, and the table, and thereby the title, would belong to whichever of them killed the other. Needless to say, this was an invitation these tough and reckless Arabs could not resist, and one of Mūsā's companions came and sat at the table, saying that he would fight the knight and himself become the new 'Knight of Soghdia'. When the knight came he challenged him, 'O Arab, fight a duel with me.' The Arab readily agreed and slew the knight. At this point, however, the rules changed; it seems there could not be an Arab Knight of Soghdia. The king was furious and told Mūsā and his men to get out, adding that if he had not previously granted them safe conduct, he would have had them all killed.[34]

Mūsā and his men were now complete outlaws and every man's hand was against them. They crossed the mountains south to Kish. Here the local king took up arms against them and appealed to Tarkhūn of Samarqand for help. Mūsā and his 700 companions fought the kings for a whole day and many of his men were wounded. In the evening they began negotiations. One of Mūsā's followers argued with Tarkhūn that killing Mūsā would be of no advantage to him; he would inevitably lose many of his own best men in the fighting and, besides, Mūsā was a man of high standing among the Arabs (a debatable point by this stage) and that if he killed him, the Arabs would certainly try to avenge him. For his part Tarkhūn said he was not prepared to allow Mūsā to remain in Kish, which was too close for comfort. So it was agreed that Mūsā and his men should set off on their travels once more.[35]

In 689 they marched south to Tirmidh on the Oxus, which was to be Mūsā's base for the rest of his life. Here he met one of the *dehqāns* of the Tirmidh shāh, who was on bad terms with his master and was prepared to give Mūsā advice on how to approach him. He told him that the shāh was a generous and extremely shy monarch and if he was treated kindly and given presents, he would let Mūsā into his citadel, 'for', he added, 'he is weak'. At first, when Mūsā arrived at the citadel, he ignored the advice and simply demanded to be let in, but when this was refused he resorted to guile. He invited the unsuspecting shāh to come out hunting with him and went to great lengths to treat him kindly. When they got back to the city the shāh prepared a banquet and invited Mūsā and a hundred of his followers to have lunch (*ghadā*). When Mūsā and his men rode into the city, their horses started to neigh to each other and the people of the city saw this as an evil omen. Worried, they told Mūsā and his men to dismount. Then they entered the palace and had their meal. When they had finished, Mūsā reclined and settled in but the shāh and his men, now increasingly anxious, asked them to leave. Mūsā simply refused, saying that he would never find another palace (*manzil*) as nice as this and it would either be his home or his grave. Fighting broke out in the city. A number of the inhabitants were killed and others fled. Mūsā took control of the city and told the shāh that he could leave and he would not stand in his way. So the shāh left and went to seek support from the Turkish nomads. They dismissed him with contempt, mocking him for allowing a hundred men to expel him from his homeland. 'Besides,' they said, 'we have already fought these men at Kish and we don't want to fight them again.' History does not record the fate of the shāh, now an exile, but Transoxania in the eighth century was clearly no place for a naive and trusting ruler like him.

Mūsā was now established as ruler of the fortress and the city, owing allegiance to no one. He already had 700 men with him and when his father, Abd Allāh, was ignominiously killed in battle as he attempted to come to join him there, 400 of his followers survived to join Mūsā. With this small band, he set out to acquire more followers and wealth and defend himself against his enemies.

There were plenty of those. Against the Turks he is said to have used a mixture of wit and bluff to avoid conflict. Some of the stories seem to belong to a genre of folklore in which one ethnic group is terribly clever and another terribly stupid, in this case 'smart Arabs, dim Turks'. They may reflect jokes that were in circulation at the time. In one improbable anecdote a deputation of Turks arrives in the height of summer (when temperatures in Tirmidh can reach 50 degrees Celsius), to find Mūsā and his companions sitting round a fire in all their winter clothes. When asked what they were doing they explained that they found it cold in the summer and hot in the winter. The Turks concluded that they must be *jinn*, spirits, not ordinary men, and so they left the Arabs without fighting them.[36] In another tale the Turkish chiefs sent Mūsā a gift of arrows (to signify war) or the valuable perfume musk (to signify peace) and asked him to choose. Typically, Mūsā responded by breaking the arrows and throwing the musk away. At this the Turks concluded that they would not take on a man who was so clearly out of his mind.

When Umayya became governor of Khurasan in 691, he decided to send an expedition to root Mūsā out. The people of Tirmidh, too, had had enough of Mūsā and his gang and approached the Turks proposing that they ally together against him. Mūsā found himself besieged by an Arab army on one side and a Turkish one on the other.

We are told of one of those advice-giving sessions that the Arab narrators employ when they want to discuss military strategy. In the end it was decided that Mūsā should launch a night attack on the Turks as the Arabs were better at night fighting. The raid was a success and they fell upon the unsuspecting Turks and took possession of their camp and weapons and money. Against the Arabs, Mūsā and his men decided to use a stratagem. One of Mūsā's officers volunteered to be beaten by his master so that he could go to the Arab commander as a defector. When Mūsā remonstrated that he would certainly be flogged and probably killed, the man replied that he risked being killed every day anyhow and that being beaten was much easier than the rest of his plan. The stripes on his back must have made his case plausible for he was accepted as a defector and admitted into the Arab commander's inner circle. One day he found the commander alone and unarmed. He remonstrated that he thought it unwise to be so defenceless but the commander pulled back his bedding (*farāsh*) to reveal an unsheathed sword – whereupon Mūsā's man seized it and killed him. He galloped back to Mūsā's lines before anyone knew what had happened. After the death of their commander, the attacking Arab army broke up, some fleeing across the river, others appealing to Mūsā for safe conduct, which he readily granted.[37]

After this triumph against Turks and Arabs allied together, Mūsā's position became much stronger. The Arab governors who succeeded Umayya made no attempt to dislodge him from his riverside domain. On the contrary, he became a focus for all those who resented the Arab presence in Transoxania.

Among these were two brothers, Hurayth and Thābit b. Qutba. They were local men, probably of upper-class Iranian stock, who had converted to Islam and attached themselves as *mawāli* (clients) to the Arab tribe of Khuzāʿa. This connection brought them Arab allies from the tribe. They had made themselves useful to the Arab governors and tax collectors and intermediaries, since they knew the local languages and conditions. Thābit was especially popular among the non-Arabs (*ajam*), enjoying great reputation and honour. It was said that if someone wished to swear a binding oath, they would do so on the life of Thābit and would never break their word.[38] They were rich and powerful but were still not fully accepted as equals by the Arabs. At one point Hurayth did a favour to the king of Kish, allowing the return of hostages taken in exchange for tribute. This was against the express orders of the governor of Khurasan, Yazīd b. al-Muhallab, who clearly suspected that Hurayth's sympathies lay with the king. Hurayth compounded the offence by appearing to cast doubt on Yazīd's ancestry. A band of Turks intercepted him and demanded a ransom, boasting that they had already extracted one from Yazīd. Hurayth defied them and defeated them saying, 'Do you imagine that Yazīd's mother gave birth to me?' If there was one sure way of incurring an Arab's wrath it was to insult his mother, and Hurayth's incautious words reached Yazīd, who arrested him, had him stripped naked and given thirty lashes. The beating was bad enough, but the shame of being stripped naked in public was worse: Hurayth said he would rather have had 300 lashes and kept his modesty intact.[39]

After this Hurayth and his brother decided to get away from the governor while they could. They left with 300 of their *shākiriya** and some Arabs. They rode first to Tarkhūn, the king of Samarqand, who had let Mūsā go free some time before. He took up their cause and gathered support from the people of Bukhara and Saghanian and two other princes, Nayzak and the Sabal of Khuttal. Together they set out to join Mūsā in Tirmidh.

At the same time Mūsā was joined by a large number of fugitive Arab tribesmen. Further south in Sistan, the Arab army had mutinied, fed up with long and difficult campaigns in harsh and unrewarding country. Under the leadership of Abd al-Rahmān b. al-Ash'ath they had marched west to Iraq to challenge Umayyad rule. The caliph Abd al-Malik and his right-hand man Hajjāj were too powerful for them, the rebels were defeated and the survivors now fled to the east. Eight thousand of them now came to Tirmidh to join Mūsā.

Mūsā's forces were now much larger, but they were united only in their hatred of the Umayyad regime. Relations between the Arabs and non-Arabs were likely to be strained, and Mūsā seems to have realized that he had to act very carefully and diplomatically in the handling of his troops. Hurayth and the Iranian princes were ambitious. They suggested that Mūsā should cross the Oxus, drive out the Umayyad

---

* The *shākiriya* were the military and domestic following of Central Asian aristocrats at the time. They were a group of young men who undertook domestic and household tasks in times of peace but could become a band of warriors in times of war.

governor and take over the whole province of Khurasan. They thought that Mūsā would essentially become their puppet and half a century of Arab-Muslim conquest would have been reversed. The Arabs in Mūsā's army were suspicious, seeing nothing in it for them: either the Umayyads would counter-attack, for they could not simply let all of Khurasan go, or the Iranians would rule the province in their own interests. They were able to persuade Mūsā to adopt a more limited objective, the expulsion of Umayyad governors from all of Transoxania so that, as they put it, 'the region will be ours to devour'.[40]

This seems to have been achieved without any great difficulty and the Transoxanian princes now went home, hoping, no doubt, that they had finally put an end to the Arab threat to their homelands. Mūsā ruled Tirmidh with Hurayth and Thābit as his chief ministers. Revenues flowed in and Mūsā became powerful. Many of his Arab supporters, however, resented the influence of the Iranian administrators, telling Mūsā that they were treacherous and urging him to kill them. At first he refused these blandishments, saying that he would not betray men who had done so much for him, but gradually they managed to convince him.

Meanwhile Mūsā faced a more pressing threat. The Iranian princes may have seen him as an ally but the nomad Turks did not. They now assembled an army which the Arab sources said, no doubt with some exaggeration, numbered 70,000 'men with tapering helmets [bayda dhāt qunis]',[41] the characteristic pointed helmets of Central Asia as distinct from the more rounded helmets favoured by the Arabs. This massive Turkish attack, if indeed it ever happened, gave the author of the saga another opportunity to show Mūsā's military skill and cunning. Mūsā, like many of his contemporaries, commanded the battle seated on a chair (kursī), with an escort of 300 heavily armoured horsemen. He allowed the Turks to breach the walls of the suburb of Tirmidh and sat there calmly, playing with the axe in his hand until he saw the moment to fall upon them and drive them out. He joined the battle and then returned to his chair. The intimidated Turks, according to our narrator, compared him to the great Iranian hero (and legendary opponent of the Turks) Rustam and withdrew.

In the next episode the Turks captured some of Mūsā's grazing livestock. Mūsā was very depressed by the insult to his prestige; he refused to eat and 'played with his beard', contemplating his revenge.

Then he decided on another night attack. With 700 men he followed a dry river bed, hidden by the vegetation on each side, until he reached the earthwork of the Turkish encampment. Here they waited until the livestock were driven out to pasture in the morning. Then they rounded them up, killing anyone who objected, and led the beasts home.

The next morning the Turks renewed the fighting. Their king stood on a hill surrounded by 10,000 of his best-equipped soldiers (again the numbers must be taken with a grain of salt). Mūsā encouraged his followers, saying that if they defeated this group, the rest would be easy. Hurayth led the attack but was wounded by an arrow in the head. He died two days later and was buried in his yurt (*qubba*). Meanwhile, in yet another night attack, Mūsā's brother wounded the king and his horse, which galloped off to the river. Here the king, weighed down by his heavy chain mail, was drowned.[42] The heads of the slain enemy were taken back to Tirmidh and made into two pyramids.*

After this victory, the tensions between the Arabs and Hurayth's surviving brother Thābit intensified. Mūsā was under constant pressure to get rid of him but he steadfastly refused, so the Arabs decided to take matters into their own hands. Thābit, however, was aware that something was up. He found a young Arab from the tribe of Khuzāʿa, the tribe he was affiliated to, and prevailed upon him to act as an informer. The youth was to play the role of a humble servant who was a captive from distant Bamyan in the heart of the Hindu Kush mountains. He was to pretend he knew no Arabic. Thābit remained on the alert, with his *shākiriya* guarding him every night. Meanwhile Mūsā still refused to allow the killing of Thābit because there was no justification for it and it would lead to disaster for all of them. In the end, one of his brothers, with some Arab friends, decided to take the initiative. They wore Mūsā down so that he weakly accepted their suggestion that they should waylay Thābit as he came in the next day, take him to a nearby house and execute him. Mūsā was very reluctant and warned them again that it would be the end of them.

Thābit's young agent, of course, heard all this and immediately

* The Arabic word used is *jawsaqayn*.

informed his master, who gathered twenty horsemen and slipped away that night. When morning came and Thābit had disappeared the group of Arabs did not at first realize how they had been out-manoeuvred, but when they noticed that the young man was no longer with them, they understood the ruse.

Thābit and his men fortified themselves in a nearby town,[43] where he was joined by Tarkhūn and the people of Kish, Nasaf and Bukhara, who had supported him when he originally came to Tirmidh. It had become a straight conflict between the Arabs and the locals. Now that open conflict was inevitable, Mūsā wanted to finish it off as quickly as possible, and he led his men to attack Thābit. He and his men soon found themselves surrounded and in dire straits. Once more treachery would have to be used where force was failing. Yazīd, one of Mūsā's Arab supporters, decided that being killed was better than death by hunger and came to Thābit pretending to be a defector. Unfortunately for him, he had a cousin called Zuhayr, who was a close adviser to Thābit and knew Yazīd only too well: political allegiances in Trans-oxania often cut across racial and even kinship boundaries. He warned Thābit against Yazīd. Yazīd in turn said that he was a man who had already suffered enough, having been forced by the Umayyad author-ities to leave Iraq and come to Khurasan with his family and, anyhow, Zuhayr was only acting out of spite. So he was allowed to stay as long as he left his two young sons as hostages.

Yazīd bided his time and waited for his opportunity. One day news came from Merv that the son of one of Thābit's Arab supporters had died, and so with a small entourage he went to offer his condolences. By the time they were returning it was dark, and in a moment when Thābit was separated from his other companions, Yazīd seized his chance and gave Thābit a mighty blow to the head with his sword. He lingered for a couple of weeks before dying. With his two accom-plices Yazīd fled, but his unfortunate children were left to pay the price of their father's crime. Zuhayr brought them to Tarkhūn, who seems to have taken command after Thābit's death. One was executed immediately, his corpse and his head being thrown into the river. The second turned aside at the moment when the blow was being struck and was injured in the chest. Severely wounded, he was thrown into the river, where he drowned.

With the death of Thābit, his followers and allies lost heart.

Leadership of the army was assumed by Tarkhūn. When warned that Mūsā was about to attempt a night attack on his camp, he was full of scorn: 'Mūsā couldn't even enter his own privy without help,' he told his followers. It was never a wise move to underestimate Mūsā. The night attack duly came and there was fierce fighting in and around the camp. At one stage one of Mūsā's Arab followers reached Tarkhūn's own tent, finding him sitting on a chair in front of the fire his *shākiriya* had lit. His *shākiriya*, who should have been protecting him, fled, but he fought off the attacker himself and in the counter-attack he succeeded in killing one of Mūsā's own brothers. He sent a message to Mūsā, who, of course, he knew quite well, asking him to call off his men if he agreed to withdraw. The next day, the non-Arabs packed up and went home to their own lands.[44]

On the surface, this seemed like a famous victory for Mūsā, but in fact it marked the beginning of the end. He had been able to maintain his independence because he enjoyed the support of his Arab followers and the non-Arabs led by Hurayth and then by Thābit. When Mūsā had only a thousand or so Arab followers, they seem to have been able to cooperate, but with the arrival of many more Arabs from the defeated rebel armies, the pressures proved too great. Without the support of the non-Arabs of Transoxania, Mūsā's dream of independence perished. To his credit, he himself seems to have understood this and made considerable efforts to keep his coalition together. But in the end blood was thicker than water and he sided with the Arabs against the rest.

The end came in 704 when the new Umayyad governor of Khurasan[45] allied with the Iranian princes sent an army against him in Tirmidh and Mūsā was killed when his horse stumbled as he tried to escape. He had enjoyed fifteen years of effective independence, king of his riverside stronghold and magnet for the restless and disaffected, Arab and Iranian alike. He was a man whose reputation had spread far and wide. In the little provincial town of Qūmis in northern Iran, 800 kilometres from Tirmidh, there was a man called Abd Allāh, at whose house the young men of the district would gather, no doubt telling stories and generally shooting the breeze. His hospitality cost Abd Allāh dear, and when his debts mounted up it was all the way to Mūsā that he went for help. He was not disappointed and was rewarded with a gift of 4,000 silver dirhams. It was among men like Abd Allāh that Mūsā's memory was kept green, celebrated in poetry, and it must have been they who remembered the stories that form the basis of his saga as it has come down to us.

8

THE ROAD TO SAMARQAND

❧

By the beginning of the year 705 Arab armies had conquered almost all of Khurasan up to the Oxus river. Only outlying mountainous areas still resisted. This is not to say that the whole province was peacefully ruled by Arab governors collecting taxes from a docile and obedient population, but the Arab authorities were in control. From their bases at Merv and Balkh, they could mount expeditions to crush any insurgents and pillage their lands and properties. Across the river, things were very different. Apart from Mūsā's outpost at Tirmidh, there was no Arab Muslim settlement at all and, as far as we know, not a single mosque had been constructed. The local kings and the Turkish nomads remained firmly in control.

All this was about to change. In this year Hajjāj, viceroy of Iraq and all the East, appointed a new governor of Khurasan. Qutayba b. Muslim came from the small tribe of Bāhila, which was not attached to any of the great tribes whose quarrels were tearing the Arabs of Khurasan apart. This made him an attractive candidate for this most difficult job. Not only could he be neutral in these feuds, but he would not be subject to the relentless pressure for favours which leaders of large tribes had to endure from their followers. He also enjoyed the support of the shrewd and determined Hajjāj. The fact that he lacked a major tribal following of his own meant that he was dependent on Hajjāj for his authority, and this in turn meant that Hajjāj could trust him not to lead a rebellion. Qutayba comes across as a man more respected than loved. The sources emphasize his competence as an organizer and leader of armies, but there are no tales of his generosity or of his patronage of poets. He could be a ferocious opponent and had no compunction about executing prisoners, even ones he had granted safe conduct to, if he thought it was necessary. On the other hand, he was willing to work with local kings and chiefs if he felt it would help the Muslim cause. He also enjoyed the support of an extensive and competent immediate family, especially his brother, Abd al-Rahmān, who was his ever-reliable second-in-command and right-hand man.

Qutayba arrived with a clear policy, to unite the Arabs of Khurasan in the cause of Islam and the *jihād* and lead them to conquer the rich lands across the river which his predecessors had not managed to secure. Every spring he would assemble the Muslim army in Merv and set out, returning to the capital in the autumn, when the troops would disperse to their towns and villages in Khurasan until the next year's campaigning season. The campaigns that were about to begin were to prove the toughest, bloodiest and probably the most destructive of all the campaigns of the great Arab conquests.

According to what claims to have been an eyewitness account, Qutayba arrived from Iraq in the capital Merv just as his predecessor was reviewing the troops before leading a raid across the river. He immediately took command and addressed the soldiers, urging them to the *jihād*. 'God has brought you here so that he may make His religion strong, protect sacred things through you and through you to increase the abundance of wealth and mete out harsh treatment to the enemy.' He stressed that those who fell in the *jihād* would be still be alive, quoting the Koran:[1] 'Count not those who are slain on God's path as dead but rather as living with their Lord, by Him provided.' He ended with a brisk exhortation: 'Fulfil the promise of your Lord, get yourselves used to travelling the greatest distances and enduring the greatest hardships, and beware of looking for easy ways out.' The nature of the appeal was clear; there was no mention here of tribal or ethnic solidarity: this was going to be a campaign for all Muslims, Arab and non-Arab alike. He promised the classic combination of serving God and getting rich. We will never know how many of his listeners responded with lively excitement to the new opportunities for wealth and spiritual rewards, and how many of them heard his words with sinking hearts, dreading the hardships and dangers that lay ahead.[2]

We have a detailed picture of his army in the year 715 at the end of his period in office.[3] At this time Qutayba is said to have commanded 40,000 troops originating from Basra in southern Iraq. They were organized in their main tribal groups and brought with them the sense of tribal solidarity that served them well on the battlefield, but also the tribal rivalries that could easily erupt into violence. In addition there were 7,000 troops newly arrived from Kūfa in central Iraq and 7,000 who are described as *mawāli*, non-Arab converts, who had enrolled in the Muslim forces. They were led by a man called Hayyān al-Nabatī. One of the reasons for Qutayba's eventual success was that he attracted the loyalty of these local troops, who, if the figures are to be believed, comprised around 12 per cent of his forces. They seem to have fought as hard as any of the Arabs, and their local knowledge must have made them especially useful, but not all Arabs were prepared to accept them as equals and this tension lay just below the surface. Perhaps the most important reason for Qutayba's success was that, until things went wrong, leading to his tragic end, he was able to manage these disparate groups and give them a common purpose, expanding the lands of Islam into Transoxania and perhaps eventually as far as China.

Qutayba began campaigning immediately, leading his men up the Oxus to Tukhāristan. Here his main objective was pacification rather than conquest. He paid a state visit to Balkh, where he was welcomed by the local landowners. He then crossed the river and was met by the king of Saghāniyān, with gifts and a golden key as a symbol of his submission. In return he was offered protection against the next-door king of Shūmān, which was Qutayba's next stop. Here again the king hastened to make peace and hand over tribute. Having secured his southern flank with this show of force and diplomacy, Qutayba returned to Merv for the winter.

He began the next year, 706, by settling some unfinished business in the south. The most powerful of the local princes, the Buddhist Nayzak, maintained his independence in the mountainous area of Badhghīs, north-west of Herat. He had captured some Muslims and kept them prisoner. Qutayba sent a messenger to him, who warned him about provoking the new governor. Nayzak was induced to free the prisoners and go in person to see the governor at Merv. The people of Badhghīs made peace on the understanding that Qutayba would not enter their lands.[4] This sort of live-and-let-live arrangement characterized much of the nature of the Arab conquest in the remoter areas of Transoxania.

· Then he turned his attention to his real objective, the rich cities of Soghdia in the Zarafshan valley. At the beginning of spring he crossed the river to Paykand, the nearest of them and the first on the road from the river crossing at Amul. The site of the city now lies wasted and deserted about 60 kilometres west of Bukhara, but in the early eighth century it was a great trading centre, whose merchants regularly visited China along the overland Silk Road. It lay at the very end of the fertile lands of the Zarafshan valley, surrounded by desert. It was a very tempting prize, but the city was well protected by great mud-brick walls and an inner citadel with only one gate.[5] It was so strong that it was known simply as 'the Fortress' or 'the Bronze Fortress', and the inhabitants had no desire to submit to the financial demands of the Arabs. The initial conquest seems to have been fairly quick, the defenders being forced back behind the walls and then asking to make peace. This was granted in exchange for tribute, and Qutayba was on his way back to the Oxus when he heard that the citizens had risen in revolt and killed the governor he had left in charge; there was, as so often, a story about how an Arab had tried to take advantage of the daughters of a powerful local man and had been stabbed as a result,[6] but it is just as likely that the inhabitants felt that now the Muslim forces had withdrawn, they no longer needed to pay the tribute they had been forced to promise.

Qutayba was determined to teach them a lesson that would be learned by all the people of Soghdia. After a month of blockade, he set workmen to dig a mine under the walls of the city and prop up the roof with wood. He had intended that they should burn the props and that the wall should then collapse. Things did not work out quite as planned; the wall fell down when they were still propping it up and forty of the unfortunate workmen were killed. The technique of digging a siege mine is well attested in western European warfare from the time of the Crusades on, but this seems to be the only recorded example of its use in the early Islamic conquests, and it is possible that it was a technique Qutayba had learned from the local troops recruited into his army in Central Asia. Though things clearly turned out very badly for the unlucky workmen, the mine achieved the desired result – the Muslims forced their way in, not without great difficulty, through the collapsed portion of the wall. Once the city had been taken by force, its inhabitants and their wealth were at the mercy of the conquerors. All the fighting men were systematically killed, the women and children taken into captivity, the town deserted. Many of the merchants were said to have been off on a trading expedition to China. When they returned they searched for their women and children, ransomed them from the Arabs and set about rebuilding the city.[7] In reality, it seems that Paykand never really recovered from the sack, and it was soon completely overshadowed by the growth of neighbouring Bukhara.

The Arab sources remember the conquest not for the human misery it caused but for the wealth of the booty acquired. One captive attempted to ransom himself with 5,000 pieces of Chinese silk, the equivalent of a million dirhams.[8] They found a silver statue in a Buddhist shrine (*butkhāna*) weighing 4,000 dirhams and other treasures, including two pearls the size of pigeons' eggs. When Qutayba asked where the pearls had come from, he was told that two birds had come and placed them in the temple with their beaks. For Muslim writers, this charming tale was simply evidence of the obvious wrongheadedness of Buddhism.[9] The pearls were sent, with other choice items, to Hajjāj in Iraq, who wrote back, full of praise for Qutayba's generosity. The rest of the silver was melted down and made into coin to pay the Muslim soldiers: in so doing much of the ancient art of Central Asia was lost for ever. There was so much new money that the Muslims were able to equip themselves with the most splendid armour and weapons, soldiers, as usual, being expected to pay for their own gear. In this case, however, captured weapons were handed out to the troops as well. After the triumph at Paykand, the army moved on to the Bukhara oasis, where some villages were attacked and obliged to make peace.

The next year, 707, Qutayba was on the march again. Once again, the objective was the Bukhara oasis. This year he was accompanied by Nayzak, who now appears as a member of his army, part soldier and part hostage. The campaign did not achieve very much. The Soghdians were now well aware of the threat the Arab armies posed and they had made alliances with the Turks and the people of distant Farghāna. The allies hovered in the steppe, waiting for an opportunity to attack. As the Arab army moved along the road towards Bukhara it was very spread out, with more than a kilometre and a half between Qutayba, who was leading, and his brother and right-hand man Abd al-Rahmān, who was in command of the rearguard. The Turks saw their chance and attacked the tail of the column. Abd al-Rahmān sent a messenger to his brother, appealing for help. By the time Qutayba, accompanied by Nayzak, had reached the rear of the army, the Muslim forces were facing defeat, but his appearance turned the tables, the Turks were seen off and disaster averted. Qutayba decided not to press on, however, but turned south, crossing the river at Tirmidh and returning via Balkh to Merv for the winter.

The campaigning season of 708 was also a failure. Qutayba came up against the forces of a local ruler in the Bukhara area called Wardān-Khudā, and was unable either to make conquests or extract tribute. He won a stinging rebuke from Hajjāj for his pains.[10]

The next year, 709, Qutayba decided to move against Bukhara again. He may well have been aided by the death of his opponent of the previous year, Wardān-Khudā. The accounts of this campaign are quite unclear, but it seems that when the Muslims approached the city, the inhabitants appealed for help to the other Soghdians and the Turks and the main fighting was against this relieving army. The fullest narrative we have comes from the tribe of Tamīm and reads like an account from the earliest phases of the conquests, full of heroic speeches and individual deeds of valour but leaving the wider picture quite obscure. Qutayba is portrayed as sitting on a chair to command, wearing a yellow tunic over his weapons. At one point we are told the infidels entered Qutayba's camp and rampaged through it until the women started beating them back by hitting the faces of their horses and weeping. This spurred the men into action and the attack was repelled. This is the only mention of women in Qutayba's armies, and whereas it may be a complete fabrication, it might suggest that women did play a significant role in the campaigns and particularly in the organization of the camps.

According to the Tamīmis the real victory was achieved, unsurprisingly, by their own tribe. The Turks were on a hill on the other side of a river and the Muslim forces were very reluctant to cross and engage them. Qutayba appealed directly to tribal pride, telling them that they were like 'a coat of mail on which swords break', and he harked back to the traditions of the tribe in pre-Islamic times, saying that he needed them to fight today as they had fought of old.[11] The chief of the tribe, Wakī,* a tough, uncouth, foul-mouthed Bedouin who was later to be Qutayba's nemesis, took the standard and began to advance on foot towards the enemy. He urged the cavalry to go on in advance, but when the commander of the cavalry reached the river he refused to continue; when Wakī urged him to go over 'he gave him the look of a fierce camel' and refused to budge. Wakī, who had a well-deserved reputation for violence and brutality, started to abuse him and belabour him with his iron mace and the cavalry commander, shamed into action, led his men up the hill. At first Wakī followed with the infantry and, while the cavalry distracted the Turks by attacking them from the wings, the infantry were able to drive them from the hill.

In the aftermath of the battle, the Muslims occupied Bukhara for the first time. It seems most likely that once the relieving force had been defeated, the people of the city made their peace with the Muslims, possibly allowing a Muslim garrison in the citadel. The conquest of Bukhara lasted at least four campaigning seasons, the inhabitants being forced to submit and pay tribute each year. It was only after the fourth time this had happened that Qutayba took steps to establish a firm Muslim presence in the city.

Bukhara at this time was made up of three distinct zones. The oldest was the citadel, the Ark, on the ancient tell where the king, with the title of Bukhara-khudā (Lord of Bukhara), lived. Slightly to the east, and separated by open ground, was the walled city, the Shahristān, where the merchants and other citizens lived. Finally there were numerous fortified dwellings, called *kushk*s in the local language, scattered in the fields and orchards of the oasis. Qutayba was determined to establish a Muslim presence in the heart of the Shahristān, by persuasion, bribery or force if necessary. He destroyed fire-temples, built mosques and enforced the laws of Islam. He obliged the inhabitants to give half of their houses and fields to the Arabs so that they could live with them and provide them with fodder for their horses and firewood. Many of the richer inhabitants chose to leave the city proper and retire to their country houses. The walled city was divided into different zones and assigned to different tribal groups to settle. Soon neighbourhood mosques were set up by the different groups,

---

* Abū Mutarrif Wakīʿ b. Hassān al-Tamīmi.

one of them on the site of a Christian church. Within a generation the walled city seems to have been predominantly inhabited by Muslims of Arab descent while Iranians lived in the suburbs and villages.[12] The Arab amirs lived in the walled city and the kings, the Bukhara-khudās, continued to live, as they had always done, in the citadel. Relations between the Arab governors and the kings were usually, but not always, friendly, and Tughshāda, the king who accepted Muslim rule over the city, called his son Qutayba, in honour of the conqueror.

In 713 Qutayba built a great mosque in the citadel on the site of a fire-temple. The new religion was now publicly established in the old centre of power and prestige. Finding a congregation to fill it was not so simple. Local people were paid 2 dirhams for coming to Friday prayers as a way of encouraging them. Since they did not know how to perform the rituals of prayer, Persian-speaking instructors were appointed who would tell them when to bow and when to prostrate themselves. The Koran was read in Persian because the people did not know Arabic. Not all the people of the city were impressed by the new religion. The poor, we are told, were attracted by the 2 dirhams on offer but many of the rich obstinately stayed in their country houses. One Friday the Muslims went out to these country houses and called on the inhabitants to come to the mosque. They were met with showers of stones. The Muslims then attacked the houses. By way of humiliating the inhabitants, they removed the doors of the houses and carried them off to be used in the new mosque. These doors had images of household gods on them, and when the doors were brought to the mosque these images were defaced, either as a result of the Islamic prohibition of images or, more simply, to humiliate the old religion and its devotees. Many years later Narshakhī, the local historian of Bukhara, noticed the erased images on the doors and made enquiries about what had happened, which is how the story has come down to us.[13] Qutayba also laid out a place for festival prayers at the foot of the citadel in the Registan (square). When they first came to pray there, the Muslims were ordered to bring their arms, 'because Islam was still new and the Muslims were not safe from the infidels'.[14]

Despite the changes in rituals, religion and ceremony, the kings of Bukhara continued to wield very considerable power in the city and the surrounding oasis, and the old line survived through the rule of the Umayyad and Abbasid caliphs until the coming of the Samanids at the end of the ninth century. So, as in many other areas of Transoxania, Muslim government was really a protectorate and the Arab authorities ruled with and through the local aristocracy. In the aftermath of this success, the king of Soghdia, Tarkhūn, came from his capital Samarqand seeking peace. He approached Qutayba's camp with two men, keeping the Bukhara river between them, and opened negotiations. He agreed to pay tribute in exchange for an agreement that the Arabs would not invade.

Any sense of satisfaction Qutayba may have felt as he returned to Merv after the first conquest of Bukhara in the autumn of 709 was soon rudely interrupted. The prince Nayzak, who had been brought to Merv and had joined Qutayba's expedition to Bukhara, now seems to have felt that if he ever wanted to regain his independence, he had to act before it was too late. 'I am with this man,' he is said to have told his retinue, 'and I don't feel safe with him. The Arab is like a dog: if you beat him he barks and if you feed him he wags his tail. If you fight against him and then give him something, he is pleased and forgets what you have done to him. Tarkhūn fought him several times and when he gave him tribute, he accepted it and was pleased. He is violent and full of himself.' Presumably the implication of this was that Nayzak felt he could attempt a rebellion and, if it failed, could make his peace again with Qutayba. When the army reached Āmul on the west bank of the Oxus, Nayzak asked permission to return to his homeland, and this was granted.

He headed as quickly as possible to Balkh. He had clearly formulated a plan to rouse all the princes of Tukhāristan, the middle valley of the Oxus, against Arab rule. When he reached the city the first thing he did was to pray at the great Buddhist Nawbahār shrine for success in the forthcoming struggle. He was aware that Qutayba would soon regret giving him permission to depart and would order the local Arab governor to detain him so he kept on the move. He wrote to a whole list of local princes encouraging them to join him, to the Ispahbādh of Balkh, to Bādhām, king of Mervrūd, Suhrak, the king of Tāliqān, Tūsik, the king of Faryāb, and the king of Jūzjān. All responded positively and he arranged that they should come and join him in the spring of 710. He also made preparations in case things went wrong. He wrote to the shāh of distant Kabul, securely beyond the range of Arab armies, requesting his help. Nayzak sent much of his baggage to Kabul for safe keeping and was given an assurance that the shāh would give him refuge if he needed it.[15] Then he expelled Qutayba's governor and prepared to wait until his allies gathered in the spring. He had taken every precaution but had underestimated his adversary.

Qutayba was now in his winter quarters in Merv and his troops had mostly dispersed to their homes, but he immediately sent 12,000 men under the command of his brother to Balkh with orders to hold out there until spring. Very early the next year (710), before the rebels had mobilized, he assembled an army from Merv and the Arab settlements in the western parts of Khurasan and marched on Tukhāristan. His first stop was Mervrūd, a small town on the upper Murghāb river, whose ruler had pledged his support to Nayzak. The ruler himself fled but Qutayba caught his two sons and crucified them. Next was Tāliqān, where, according to some reports, he killed and crucified a large number of people to intimidate the inhabitants of the area.[16] Then the king of Faryāb humbly made his submission and he and his people were spared. The king of Jūzjān soon followed suit and Qutayba went on to receive the submission of the people of Balkh.

Nayzak could now see that his plan was in ruins. Qutayba's swift and decisive action had wrong-footed him and almost all his princely allies had now reconciled themselves with Qutayba. There were Arab governors in all the towns of Tukhāristan. He now fled south to the Hindu Kush, hoping to reach Kabul. He left a detachment of his supporters at Khulm (modern Tashkurgan), where the road south leaves the Oxus plains and enters a narrow defile, probably in the citadel whose ruins can still be seen in the town.[17] Qutayba could find no way to get round this obstacle until a local landowner approached him and offered to show him a path round behind the castle in exchange for safe conduct. Once more, divisions and rivalries among the local people allowed the Arabs to take advantage of them. Qutayba's men fell on the garrison at night and took the fortress. Nayzak, meanwhile, had fled along the route of the modern road that leads from the Oxus valley to the Salang Pass and Kabul. He holed up in a mountain refuge at a site that cannot now be identified in Baghlān province. Qutayba was hard on his heels. He soon caught up with him and laid siege to his refuge for two months. Nayzak's supplies began to run low but Qutayba too had his problems; winter would soon be upon them and he did not want to be trapped in the mountains.

Negotiations began. Qutayba sent an adviser of his called Sulaym, who took with him loads of food, including a dish called *khabīs* made of dates and clarified butter. The starving fugitives fell on the food and Nayzak could see that he had to try to make terms or perish, especially when Sulaym stressed that Qutayba was prepared to spend the winter there if necessary. Sulaym offered safe conduct. Nayzak was very suspicious: 'My feeling is that he is going to kill me even if he gives me safe conduct but safe conduct makes my decision [to give myself up] more excusable and gives me some hope.'[18]

So they made their way down the steps from Nayzak's refuge to the plain where his riding animals were, Sulaym trying to reassure him all the way. When they reached the pass, Sulaym's escort slipped round behind Nayzak in case he changed his mind and attempted to escape back to the mountains. Nayzak took that as a bad sign. When he was brought to Qutayba, his worst fears were realized. Questioned by the governor, he said that he had been granted safe conduct by Sulaym but Qutayba retorted that he was lying. Qutayba was in a quandary as to whether to execute him or not. He was the ringleader of the rebels and a very dangerous man, who could easily try to foment another insurgency. On the other hand, safe conducts were taken very seriously and to breach one might make negotiations with other rebels and defectors much more difficult in the future. Opinion among the governor's advisers was very divided. Finally one of them said that he had heard the governor promise God that if Nayzak fell into his hands he would kill him and that if he did not do so, he could never ask for God's help again. The governor sat for some time thinking about this before giving his orders: the prisoner was to die. This brutal and treacherous murder was a stain on Qutayba's reputation for ever but it terrified the rest of the princes into submission. Nayzak's death meant the end of the insurrection and most of the princes of Tukhāristan were, at least for the moment, firmly under Arab control.

Qutayba still faced a smaller but nonetheless significant challenge to his authority. The little kingdom of Shūmān lay on the north bank of the Oxus. Its capital was a fortified city at or near the site of Dushanbe, the modern capital of Tajikistan. The king of Shūmān had

made peace with Qutayba and is said to have become a friend of
the governor's brother Sālih, another example of the ties that were
developing between Arab and local elites. An Arab political agent had
been installed. The king now repudiated the treaty and expelled the
political agent. The ease with which this was done suggests that the
kingdom had been 'conquered' in a very superficial way and that there
was no Arab garrison there. Qutayba's reaction was to try diplomacy.
He selected a man who is described as a 'Khurasani ascetic', presumably a preacher of Islam, a sort of proto-dervish, and a man
called Ayyāsh al-Ghanawī. When they arrived they received a hostile
reception from the local people who shot arrows at them. The ascetic
turned back but Ayyāsh was made of sterner stuff and called out,
asking whether there were any Muslims in the city. One man replied.
He came out to ask what Ayyāsh wanted, to which he replied that he
wanted help in waging *jihād* against the people. The man accepted,
and despite the fact that there were only two of them, they engaged
the enemy with some success. Then the local Muslim, clearly feeling
that his loyalties to his fellow citizens were stronger than his commitment to his new faith, came up behind Ayyāsh and killed him.
They found sixty wounds on him and the Shūmānis immediately
regretted what they had done, saying that they had killed a brave
man.

But the damage was done. After the recent rebellion of Nayzak,
Qutayba could not afford to let any of the local kings defy his authority
and was determined to extract obedience and tribute, by force if
necessary. The king, however, was in a defiant mood. He was not
frightened of Qutayba because he had the strongest castle of any of
the kings. 'When I shoot at the top of it – I, the strongest of men
with the bow and the strongest of them in archery – my arrow does
not get even halfway up the walls of my fortress. I am not afraid of
Qutayba.'[19]

Qutayba was likewise undeterred. He marched to Balkh, crossed
the river and soon reached the fortress of Shūmān. Here he set up
catapults and began to batter the walls. One of these siege engines
was called 'the Pigeon-Toed', and it discharged stones that landed
right inside the city and killed a man in the king's court.[20] From that
point, it all seems to have been over quite quickly. When it became
clear that he could hold out no longer, the king collected all his

treasure and jewels and threw them into the deepest well in the castle, from which they were never retrieved. Then he went out to meet his death fighting. Qutayba had taken the fortress by force and the defenders had to pay the price; the fighting men were all killed and the non-combatants taken prisoner. Shūmān was taken, and the king killed, but the principality seems to have survived and retained its identity, for we hear of a later prince of Shūmān fighting as an ally of the Muslims.

On his way back to Merv, Qutayba sent his brother Abd al-Rahmān to pay a visit to Tarkhūn, the king of Samarqand, just to make sure that he was not planning any mischief and to collect the tribute. He met up with Tarkhūn's army in a meadow in the afternoon. The Soghdian soldiers dispersed into groups and began to drink wine 'until they became silly and made mischief', as the Arab chronicler sniffily remarks. Firm measures were taken to prevent the Muslims following their bad example. The tribute was duly collected and Abd al-Rahmān returned to his brother in Merv.

Qutayba's heavy-handed behaviour was resented in many quarters. At Samarqand there was mounting unrest and dissatisfaction at Tarkhūn's supine attitude; he was called an old man, eager to be humiliated, and they resented the fact that he had agreed to pay taxes. He was deposed in favour of a man called Ghūrak, said by some to have been his brother.[21] Tarkhūn took his deposition very badly and, saying that he would rather die by his own hand than be killed by someone else, he fell on his sword until it came out of his back.[22] Political suicides like this were completely unknown in the Arab world, though they were, of course, common in imperial Rome, and they also seem to have been a Central Asian custom. His death was to have dangerous consequences for Samarqand, since it allowed Qutayba to pose as Tarkhūn's avenger when he next led his army into Soghdia, but Ghūrak proved an able and wily ruler, constantly intriguing to preserve his independence from his powerful neighbours.

The next campaigning season, 711, saw Qutayba going further south to confront the Zunbīl of Sistan, perhaps the most formidable of all the princely foes the Muslims encountered. This time, however, there was no serious fighting and the Zunbīl agreed to a peace treaty. It would be interesting to know whether Qutayba heard that in the same year, but 6,000 kilometres to the west, another Muslim military commander, Tāriq b. Ziyād, had crossed the Straits of Gibraltar and begun the conquest of Spain.[23]

The next year, 712, before campaigning began, Qutayba was warned that many of his troops were exhausted after the long march from Sistan and wanted a year's respite from military expeditions,[24] but an unexpected situation forced them to resume campaigning. The king of Khwārazm appealed to Qutayba for help against his over-bearing brother, Khurrazādh. Khurrazādh had been in the habit of taking for himself any slaves, riding animals or fine goods he fancied; courtiers' daughters and sisters had even been seized. The king professed himself powerless to act but he sent messengers in secret to Qutayba, inviting him to his land to arrest his brother and hand him over for judgement. As a token of his good faith he sent three golden keys to the cities of Khwārazm. It was too good an opportunity to miss and Qutayba, who had been planning another expedition to Soghdia, decided to make a detour.

The king of Khwārazm told his nobles that Qutayba was heading for Soghdia and that they would be spared military action that year, so, we are told, they began drinking and relaxing. The next thing they knew Qutayba and his army appeared at Hazārasp (the name means Thousand Horses in Persian), the city that lay on the west bank of the Oxus, at the head of the delta. The king and his court gathered at the capital, Kāth, on the other bank of the river. He persuaded his men that they should not fight Qutayba, and negotiations began: they agreed to make peace in exchange for 10,000 prisoners and some gold. During the negotiations, Qutayba's brother and right-hand man, Abd al-Rahmān, fought and killed the king's brother, executing many of his supporters in cold blood. It was another stage in the Muslim domination of the ancient delta kingdom, but the Afrīghid dynasty continued to rule as shāhs of Khwārazm for another two hundred years and the area retained its distinctive individual culture and identity.

The real objective of the 712 expedition, however, was Samarqand. Samarqand was the largest and most powerful city in the area, the effective capital of Soghdia. The city as it exists today was built after the Mongol sack of 1220 and beautified by Tamerlane and his family in the late fourteenth and fifteenth centuries with the blue-tiled domes and minarets that have made it famous. Later Uzbek rulers added more madrasas and completed the square known as the Registan, and, after the conquest of 1880, the Russians developed the Tsarist-period town with its elegant tree-lined streets. The early medieval town lay behind massive mud-brick ramparts between the Timurid city and the river. The site is now lonely and deserted.²⁵ It is easy to pick out the lines of the wall and the remains of the citadel behind its deep moats, overlooking the river. Among these ruins is an old palace, the walls of which are painted with processions of elegant Soghdian princes and their guests, giving a vivid picture of the world the Arabs destroyed.

Samarqand was ruled by its new king, Ghūrak, who was determined to put up a stiff resistance to the Arabs. Qutayba's army is said to have consisted of 20,000 men, one of the largest forces the Muslims ever fielded in Transoxania. A considerable proportion of them were local recruits from Khwārazm and Bukhara, but it is not clear whether they were converts to Islam joining in the *jihād*, mercenaries or men pressed into fighting against their will.

At first Qutayba seems to have made an attempt to surprise the defenders by sending his brother back to Merv, giving the impression that the campaigns were over for that year, but the defenders were not deceived. The Samarqandis, meanwhile, had appealed to the king of Shāsh (Tashkent) and the Ikhshīd of Farghāna to come to their aid, persuading them to assist with the warning that if the Arabs conquered Samarqand, their turn would be next. A force of horsemen, recruited from all the aristocracy of Transoxania, set out to launch a surprise night attack on the Arab camp. Unfortunately for them, Qutayba knew of their plans: he always seems to have had very good intelligence. He sent one of his brothers, Sālih, with a small force to ambush them. The night fighting was extremely fierce. The nobility of Transoxania gave a good account of themselves, but in the end they were defeated; many were killed, few prisoners were taken and many famous families lost their sons and their horses. The Muslims acquired rich equipment and excellent riding animals and Qutayba allowed the small band of victors to keep the spoils of the night ambush, rather than dividing them up among the whole army in the customary way.

The defeat of this force seems to have discouraged the defenders. Qutayba blockaded the city for a month, setting up siege engines outside the walls, creating a breach which the defenders blocked up with sacks of millet. The Muslims pressed on into the breach, holding their shields over their faces to protect them from the showers of arrows the Soghdians shot at them. Once they had established themselves on the walls, Ghūrak sent messengers to sue for peace. Qutayba agreed.[26] The Samarqandis were to pay a substantial annual tribute and a large number of high-quality slaves with no old men or young boys among them. Qutayba's domination also had a conspicuously religious aspect to it. He insisted that a mosque with a pulpit be set up and he ordered the destruction of the old fire-temples and their 'idols'. All the sculptures of Samarqand were stripped of their silver, gold and silk adornments and piled up in a huge heap. Qutayba ordered that they be burned. Ghūrak and the Soghdians urged him not to do this, warning that anyone who destroyed them would suffer for it, but Qutayba was undaunted, and lit the fire himself. A vast sum was made from the gold and silver nails that were collected. This deliberate purging of the old religion was unusual in the Muslim conquests. Qutayba had always made it clear that his campaigns were a *jihād*, though he was rarely as destructive as this. It may also have been that he wanted to break the Soghdian resistance once and for all, and his triumph was emphatically apparent as he lit the bonfire of the accoutrements of the old religions.

He did not, however, destroy the previous order entirely. Ghūrak remained king of Soghdia, establishing himself at Ishtīkhān, some 40 kilometres from Samarqand, and Qutayba contented himself with leaving an Arab garrison of some four thousand men in the city under the command of his brother Abd al-Rahmān. The old walled city became a Muslim-only stronghold. Local non-Muslims were allowed within the city walls only if they had permits in the form of clay seals on their hands: if the seals had dried before they left, they were to be killed because it showed that they had been in the city too long. If any of them brought knives or weapons in they were to be killed, and none of them was allowed to spend the night inside the walls.[27]

The conquest of Samarqand was decisive but it was also precarious. Ghūrak and many of the Soghdians were still settled in the area[28] while the Arab garrison remained isolated in a largely hostile environment. There could be no doubt in the minds of the soldiers stationed there that Ghūrak would try to expel them if any opportunity presented itself.

Qutayba responded to the situation, not by strengthening the Arab hold over Soghdia, but by leading his armies to further and even more distant conquests. In 713 he crossed the river as usual. In addition to his Arab troops, he imposed a levy (farada ʿalā) of 20,000 troops on the people of Bukhara, Kish, Nasaf and Khwārazm. They marched through Soghdia without apparently encountering any resistance. The local levies were then directed north to Shāsh while Qutayba led his own men east to Farghāna. There is little reliable information about what these raids achieved – a few poems and inconsequential stories. We can be reasonably certain that they were not a disaster, but no new lands were conquered.[29]

The next year Qutayba was back in the Jaxartes provinces again, perhaps trying to establish control over the Silk Road. There is even some suggestion that he reached Kashgar, which was in the territory of the Tang emperors.[30] China was certainly featuring in the wilder hopes of the Arabs at this time. Hajjāj, in distant Kūfa, is said to have offered the governorship of Sīn (China) to whichever of his commanders in the East reached it first.[31] Arab troops were now coming ever closer to the borders of the Chinese Empire and both the Arabs and the Soghdians began to send envoys to try to win Chinese support. In 713 an Arab delegation reached the imperial court. We know from Chinese sources that a delegation arrived and that they caused a diplomatic scandal by refusing to kowtow to the emperor in the traditional way, but that the mission was still deemed to be a success. No doubt both military and commercial matters were discussed.[32] At the same time, the ruler of Shāsh, under increasing threat from Qutayba's power, appealed to China for military support, but none was forthcoming.

These diplomatic exchanges are remembered both in Chinese sources and in an unusual narrative in the Arabic sources. As the Arabic source has come down to us, it has many fantastical elements and has been dismissed as worthless by modern commentators. The Chinese 'king' has no name and no geographical location is given. It is quite unclear whether the Arabs are supposed to have visited the imperial capital at Ch'ang-an or simply negotiated with a Chinese commander or governor in Sinkiang. Yet it almost certainly dates from the eighth century and tells us much about the self-image of the Arabs and their attitudes to other peoples.

The story goes that the 'king' of China requested Qutayba to send him some envoys so that he could find out more about the Arabs and their religion. Ten or twelve strong, good-looking men were chosen and they set off. When they arrived at the Chinese court they went to the bath house and emerged dressed in white robes and adorned with perfume. They entered the court. No one from either side spoke, and eventually they withdrew. When they had gone, the Chinese king asked his attendants what they thought, to which they replied, 'We think that they are a people who are nothing but women, there was not one of us who on seeing them and smelling their perfume, did not have an erection.'[33] On the second day they appeared in richly embroidered robes and turbans and when they had gone the courtiers conceded that they were after all men. On the third day they went to see the king in full military gear, with their aventails and helmets – 'they girded themselves with their swords, took up their spears, shouldered their bows and mounted their horses', and the courtiers were duly impressed.

That evening the king interviewed the leader of the delegation. He explained that they had dressed the first day as they did among their families, the second as they did when they attended a prince's court and the third as they did when they faced their enemies. The king then said that he was prepared to be magnanimous since he knew how needy the leader of the Muslims was and how few companions he had; if that had not been the case he would have sent someone against them to destroy them. The Muslim envoy retorted with indignation that his master's army was so large that while its leaders were in China the rearguard was 'in the places where the olive trees grow', and as for being needy, he had left a whole world behind him under his control. He then said that Qutayba had sworn an oath that he would not give up until 'he treads your lands, seals your kings [that is, puts a seal on their necks to show that they had paid the humiliating poll tax] and is given tribute'. The king of China then said that he could see a way out of this: he sent some golden dishes of soil, four young noblemen and some gifts. Qutayba was able to stand on the soil, put seals on the necks of the young men and accept the gifts as tax. Honour was satisfied all round and, once again, the Muslim leaders can be seen to be accepted as peers by old-established rulers.

The year 715 was to prove to be Qutayba's last of campaigning. His career of conquest was brought to an end, not by Chinese military power but by internal Muslim politics. Qutayba's conquests had been so successful because of his personal drive and because he enjoyed the unstinting support of the Umayyad authorities, Hajjāj, the governor of Iraq and all the east in his new capital at Wasit, and ultimately the caliph, al-Walīd b. Abd al-Malik. Now both these supports disappeared, Hajjāj died in the summer of 714, al-Walīd in early spring 715. The new caliph, Sulaymān, was known to be close to the Muhallabi family, whom Qutayba had ousted from Khurasan. Qutayba was wary of the new monarch, fearing that he would lose his position or worse. At first all seemed to be going well and the new caliph sent an encouraging letter to Qutayba, urging him to carry on the good work of conquest, but Qutayba remained anxious and took the precaution of moving his family from Merv to Samarqand, where it would be very difficult for his enemies to reach them. He posted a guard on the Oxus river crossing with orders not to let anyone cross from the west if they did not have a pass.[34] Interestingly, the man he relied on for this important security role was not an Arab at all, but a *mawlā* of his from Khwārazm, a new convert to Islam. It was a measure of the bitterness caused by inter-Arab feuds that he felt more secure in recently conquered Samarqand, surrounded by resentful Soghdians, than he did in the old provincial capital, where Muslim rule had been securely established for sixty-five years.

Qutayba seems to have decided that he would certainly lose his job under the new administration and he decided to reject Sulaymān's authority, trusting in the loyalty of his men to give him military support. He may have imagined leading the battle-hardened army of Khurasan west to Iraq and eventually to Syria, installing a compliant caliph of his own choosing, much as Abū Muslim and the supporters of the Abbasids were to do thirty-five years later.

He made a speech to his troops[35] in which he laid out his achievements as he saw them and demanded their support. He pointed out how he had brought them from Iraq, had distributed booty among them and paid their salaries in full and without delay. They only had to compare him with previous governors to see how superior he was. Today they lived in safety and prosperity. God had given them opportunities for conquest and the roads were so safe that a woman could travel in a camel litter from Merv to Balkh without fear of molestation.[36]

His speech was greeted with stony silence. Perhaps he had not prepared the ground or consulted enough. Everyone knew he had been a great commander but there was a strong groundswell of opinion against opening the doors of civil strife. Qutayba may have been a great leader of the Muslims against the non-Muslims, but he could not count on a strong tribal following to push his cause against fellow Muslims. He had taken considerable pains to cultivate the support of the non-Arab Muslim converts in Khurasan and incorporate them in his army, but they too were reluctant to get involved in an Arab civil war. Their leader, Hayyān al-Nabatī, told his followers that 'those Arabs are not fighting in the cause of Islam, so let them kill one another'.[37]

There was now no going back. Qutayba had staked everything on a public appeal to the loyalty of his troops and they had not responded. He now seems to have lost his cool completely and began abusing the Arab tribesmen with all the scorn of traditional Arab rhetoric. He called them the refuse of Kūfa and Basra; he had collected them from the desert, 'the places where wormwood, southernwood and wild senna grow', where they were riding cows and donkeys. They were Iraqis and had allowed the Syrian army to lie in their courtyards and under the roofs of their houses. Each major tribe was singled out: Bakr were a people of deceit, lying and, worst of all, meanness, Abd al-Qays were farters who had taken up the pollination of palm trees rather than the reins of horses, Azd had taken ship's ropes in the place of the reins of stallions. The implication was clear; they were farmers and fishermen, not proud Arab warriors. Within a few minutes he had succeeded in alienating anyone who might have been persuaded to support him. When he retired to his house, he explained to his household what he had done, 'When I spoke and not a single man responded, I became angry and did not know what I was saying,' and he went on to abuse the tribes again: Bakr were like slave girls who never rejected any sexual advances, Tamīm were like mangy camels, Abd al-Qays were the backside of a wild ass and Azd were wild asses, 'the worst God created'.

His position was now hopeless. The opposition coalesced around Wakī al-Tamīmī, the tough old Bedouin. The Arab sources give a vivid picture of this man in terms that go beyond the usual forms of abuse. Among other things, he was accused by his enemies of being a drunkard who sat around boozing with his friends until he shat in his own underclothes.[38] His supporters claimed that he could take charge of the business, 'enduring its heat, shedding his blood', for he was 'a brave man who neither cares what he mounts or what the consequences will be'.[39] He was prepared to risk launching an attack on Qutayba. He made an agreement with the leader of the non-Arabs, Ḥayyān al-Nabaṭī, that they would divide up the tax revenues of Khurasan between them. Qutayba was now deserted by all but his immediate family. He called for the turban his mother had sent him, which he always wore in time of difficulty, and a well-trained horse he considered lucky in war. When the horse came, it was restless and he could not mount it. The omen convinced him that the game was over and he abandoned himself to despair, lying down on his bed, saying, 'Let it be for this is God's will.'[40]

The mayhem continued. Qutayba sent his brother Sālih, the one who had been friends with the king of Shūmān, to try to negotiate with the rebels, but they shot arrows at him and wounded him in the head. He was carried to Qutayba's prayer room and Qutayba came and sat with him for a while before returning to his couch (sarīr). His brother Abd al-Rahmān, who had so often led the Muslim troops in the most difficult situations, was set upon by the market people (ahl al-sūq) and the rabble (ghawghā) and stoned to death. As the rebels closed in on Qutayba himself they set fire to the stables where he kept his camels and riding animals. Soon the ropes of the great tent were cut and the rebels rushed in and Qutayba was killed. As so often there were disputes about who actually killed him and about who had the honour of taking his head to Wakī. Wakī ordered the killing of all the members of his immediate family and that the bodies be crucified.

The fury and vindictiveness of the attack on the man who had led the Muslim armies in Transoxania so successfully astonished contemporaries. Persians in the Muslim army were amazed that the Arabs could have treated a man who had achieved so much so badly; 'if he had been one of us, and died among us,' one of them said, 'we would have put him in a coffin [tābūt] and taken him with us on our military expeditions. No one ever achieved as much in Khurasan as Qutayba did.'[41] Needless to say, numerous poems were written about the subject, many glorifying the deeds of the tribesmen who killed him. But others lamented the death of a great warrior for Islam, such as the poet[42] who addressed his words to the new caliph in Damascus,

capturing something of the sense of excitement and adventure in the
unknown that many of Qutayba's followers must have felt:

> Sulaymān, many are the soldiers we rounded up for you
> By our spears on our galloping horses.
> Many are the strongholds that we ravaged
> And many are the plains and rocky mountains
> And towns which no one had raided before
> Which we raided, driving our horses month after month
> So that they got used to endless raids and were calm
> In the face of a charging enemy
> Even if the fire was lit and they were urged towards it
> They charged towards the din and the blaze.
> With them we have ravaged all the cities of the infidels
> Until they passed beyond the place where the dawn breaks.
> If Fate had allowed, they would have carried us
> Beyond Alexander's wall of rock and molten brass.

THE TURKISH COUNTER-STROKE, 715–37

The death of Qutayba marked the end of an era in the Muslim
conquests of Central Asia. Up to this point, the Arab forces, with an
increasing number of local allies, had made general progress. True,
there had been setbacks, but the overall pattern had been one of
expanding Muslim power and influence. All this was now to change.
Part of the reason for this was political events in the Muslim world.
After the death of al-Walīd I in 715 three caliphs, Sulaymān (715–17),
Umar II (717–20) and Yazīd II (720–24), followed each other in quick
succession. Each caliph had different advisers with different ideas
about policy on the north-eastern frontier. Constant changes of governor meant that tribal rivalries among the Arabs and resentments
between Arab and non-Arab Muslims became much more open and
frequently violent. It was not until the accession of Hishām (724–43)
that Muslim policy again enjoyed a period of stability and consistency.

But there were other pressures from much further east. We know
from Chinese sources that the princes of Soghdia were sending regular
embassies to the Chinese court, trying to persuade the Chinese to

intervene to help them against the Muslims. In 718, for example, Tughshāda, king of Bukhara, Ghūrak of Samarqand, and Narayāna, king of Kumādh, all presented petitions asking for help against the Arabs, even though both Bukhara and Samarqand had been 'conquered' by the Arabs and their kings had entered into treaty arrangements with the Muslim authorities. In the event, the Chinese were not prepared to intervene directly in this area so remote from the centres of their power, but they gave some encouragement to the Türgesh Turks to invade Soghdia in support of the local princes.

The Arab sources talk of two Turkish leaders.[43] The chief is the Khagan and the Khagan referred to by the Arabic historians of this period was the Turkish chief known to the Chinese sources as Su-Lu. He sometimes appears in Transoxania as overall leader of the Turks. He had a subordinate who is called Kūrsūl in the Arabic sources and whose Turkish name was Köl-chur.

These are almost the only named Turks in the Arabic narratives of the conquest. When describing the Arab armies, and the heroic (and unheroic) deeds they performed, the protagonists are often named: preserving the identity of the individuals was a key concern of the authors. The Turks, by contrast, are very much 'the other', a mass of warriors without any apparent religion or morals or any motivation apart from total hostility to the Muslims and an insatiable desire for booty. The leaders, the Khagan and Kūrsūl, join the ranks of the worthy opponents of the Muslims, rather like the Byzantine emperor Heraclius and Rustam, the Sasanian general defeated at Qādisiya. They are brave and honourable, in their way, but they do not have the self-doubt and that deep inner knowledge that the Muslims are going to prevail because God is on their side which are described in the cases of the Byzantine and Sasanian generals.

The warfare of the period between the death of Qutayba in 715 and the death of Su-Lu and the collapse of the Türgesh in 739 is confusing and we will not try to follow every encounter in detail but rather give an impression of this hard-fought and bitter conflict. The Turks and the Arabs were implacable enemies, fighting for overlordship of this potentially rich area. Caught in between were the local princes, the most prominent being Ghūrak of Samarqand, who struggled to maintain their independence and their culture. They originally hoped that the Turks and Chinese would free them from the Muslim yoke but as time went on they found that the Turks too were hard and demanding masters.

Wakī, who had been the instrument of Qutayba's downfall, had none of his predecessor's gifts for holding the Muslims together. The armies dispersed, and governors followed each other in quick succession. In the spring of 721 the Turkish leader Kūrsūl led his men into Soghdia. It was a good moment to strike. A new governor, Saʿīd, was known by his troops as Khudhayna, a word that might be translated as 'the Flirt': the name was not intended as a compliment. The poets were scathing about his lack of martial qualities:

> You advanced on the enemy at night as if you were playing with your
>   girl-friend
> Your cock was drawn and your sword sheathed.
> For your enemies you are like an affectionate bride
> Against us you are like a sharpened sword.[44]

He arrived in Khurasan without any previous first-hand knowledge of the province and immediately became embroiled in a complicated dispute about financial irregularities which led to him dismissing a number of experienced officials. The administration was in disarray when the Turkish army surrounded a little Muslim outpost called Qasr al-Bāhilī, the exact location of which is not known. There were only a hundred Muslim families in the fortress and they began to negotiate their surrender. Meanwhile the Muslim governor of Samarqand called for volunteers to raise the siege. At first 4,000 men volunteered, but as they marched towards the enemy many of them drifted away, leaving their commander Musayyab* with only a thousand or so men as they approached the besieged castle. Musayyab sent two scouts on a dark night to try to make contact with the defending garrison. It was not easy, because the Turks had flooded the surrounding area. Eventually they found a sentry, who brought the commander to them. The messengers said that the relieving force was only about 12 kilometres (2 *farsakhs*) away and asked the defenders whether they could hold out for the night. The commander replied that they had sworn to protect their women and they were all prepared to die together the next day.

---

* Al-Musayyab b. Bishr al-Riyāhī.

When the messengers returned to Musayyab he told his men that he was going to march immediately. The Muslims fell upon the Turkish camp at dawn. There was a hard struggle and a number of prominent Muslims fell as martyrs, but eventually the Turks were put to flight. The relieving force entered the fortress and gathered up the Muslim survivors. One of the party later recalled meeting a woman who implored him in the name of God to help her. He told her to get up behind him on his horse and he grabbed her son and took him in his arms. Then they galloped off and the rescuer commented admiringly that the woman 'was more skilful on the horse than a man'. Eventually rescuers and rescued made their way to the safety of the walls of Samarqand, but the fort was lost. When the Turks returned the next day, they found nothing but the corpses of their comrades.[45]

The rescue of the defenders of Qasr al-Bāhilī was a stirring story of Muslims protecting their own, retold many times and celebrated in poetry and song, and it shows the solidarity felt by these settlers in a hostile land, but it could not disguise the fact that the Muslims were in trouble. The governor Saʿīd led a campaign to Transoxania, but to the disgust of his more militant supporters he did not go beyond Samarqand. What was probably worse as far as they were concerned was that he allowed them to pillage the Soghdians, saying that Soghdia 'was the garden of the caliphs'. By this he meant that Soghdia was an asset which should be taxed rather than destroyed in conflict.[46]

By the spring of 722 the situation in Transoxania was described as 'disastrous' for the Arabs. Khudayna was replaced by a new governor, another Saʿīd known as Saʿīd al-Harashī. In contrast to his predecessor, he was aggressive and brutal and determined to reassert Muslim control in Soghdia. The events that followed are especially interesting because, almost uniquely in the annals of the Muslim conquests, we have a series of absolutely contemporary documents to supplement the Arabic narrative sources. In 1933 a shepherd discovered a basket of Soghdian documents on Mount Mugh in what is now Tajikistan but was then part of Soviet Central Asia. Mount Mugh was a Soghdian fortress which had been the stronghold and last refuge of the last independent Soghdian prince of Penjikent, Dīwashtīch.[47] The documents had presumably been abandoned when the fortress was taken by the Arabs in 722 and consisted of political correspondence and administrative and legal documents. Dīwashtīch was clearly an

ambitious man who was challenging Ghūrak of Samarqand for leadership of the Soghdian princes, trying to assemble a coalition of local
nobles to oppose the Arab advance. Unfortunately for him, many of
the Soghdians had chosen to flee to the north-east, to Farghāna, to
take refuge rather than join his alliance and fight. Furthermore Kūrsūl,
the leader of the Türgesh Turks from whom he had hoped for support,
was proving elusive and failed to come to his aid. The letters are
interesting because they provide some insight into the rivalries among
the local princes as they tried to work out a response to the Muslim
invasions, but also because they substantially back up the version of
events that we find in Madā'inī's account of the Arab invasions as used
by Tabarī.[48] It is unusual and, for the historian, comforting to have
this immediate confirmation that the narratives on which we base our
understanding of these events do indeed reflect a historical reality.

The Arabs conquered Penjikent in 722. The site is the most fully
excavated of all Soghdian sites. The ancient city stood on a plateau
overlooking the fertile lands of the upper Zarafshan valley. Looking
north, across the flat plain of the river, the arid peaks of the Turkestan
range are clearly visible. The city itself was built of brick and mud-
brick and by 722 it had become a place of refuge and exile for many
Soghdian nobles.[49] Large houses decorated with frescoes showing
Soghdian lords fighting, hunting and feasting were constructed. All
this magnificence came to an end with the Arab conquest and much
of the town was destroyed. Some quarters were rebuilt, on a more
modest scale, after 740, when Arab administration was more secure in
this area and trade started to pick up again, but the town never
recovered its earlier prosperity.

Despite such occasional success for Arab arms, none of the governors in this period was able to emulate Qutayba's achievements and
re-establish the Muslim position in Transoxania. The combined forces
of the Soghdians and the Turks meant that the Arab hold over the
lands beyond the river was as precarious as ever. By 728 the only
places in the Zarafshan valley that remained in Muslim hands were
the great fortress city at Samarqand and the smaller fortified towns of
Dabūsiya and Kamarja, both defended by Muslim garrisons, on the
main road there. Even Bukhara was effectively lost. The struggle
to hold these remaining outposts was the key to the campaign in
Transoxania, and the siege of Kamarja by the Turks that year is one

of the most vividly described set pieces of the war. The conflict began almost by accident. The Khagan, the leader of the Turks, was marching along the main road from Samarqand heading for Bukhara. The Muslims in the small roadside city of Kamarja were unaware of what he was doing until they took their animals out to water, came over a hill and saw 'a mountain of steel', made up of the Turkish forces and their Iranian allies. The Arabs had to move fast if they were going to be able to take shelter behind the walls of the town. They sent some of their beasts down to the river to drink as a decoy to lure the Turks away, and then made for the fortifications as quickly as they could, with the Turks, who had now caught sight of them, hard on their heels. Because the Arabs knew the terrain better, they got there first and began to barricade themselves behind the earthworks, lighting brushwood fires to destroy the wooden bridge across the moat.

In the evening, when the Turks temporarily abandoned the assault, the defenders were approached with two offers of aid. One of them was from none other than the grandson of the last Sasanian king, Yazdgard III, who had joined the Turks, hoping to regain the empire of his ancestors. He offered to intercede on their behalf with the Khagan and acquire safe conducts for them. It would certainly have suited him to gain the friendship of a group of Arab warriors. But they were scornful, and his proposal was rejected with abuse.[50]

The next offer was more plausible. It came from a man called Bāzagharī. He was a local man whom the Khagan seems to have trusted as an intermediary. He brought with him to the city walls some Arab prisoners captured earlier in the campaign. He called up to the defenders to send someone down to negotiate with him. The first man they sent did not understand any Turkish so they had to find another man, an Arab from Qutayba's tribe of Bāhila, who did. Bāzagharī brought a financial offer from the Khagan: he would take the Arab defenders into his own army with enhanced rates of pay; those who had recived 600 dirhams would now have 1,000 and those who were on 300 would get 600. The Arab emissary greeted this with scorn. 'It won't work,' he said. 'How can the Arabs, who are wolves, work with the Turks, who are sheep? There will not be peace between you and us.' Some of the Turks were furious and wanted to execute the ambassador there and then but Bāzagharī refused. The messenger was increasingly anxious for his own safety, so he made an offer that

half the Arabs would go free and half would serve the Khagan. Then
he went to the wall, held on to the rope and was pulled up. When he
reached safety, his tone changed completely. He asked the people of
Kamarja what they felt about going to unbelief after faith with predictable results. He egged the Muslims on: 'They will call on you to
fight with the infidels,' to which they replied, 'We will die together
sooner than that.'

'Then let them know.'

So the people shouted down their refusal.

Meanwhile the Khagan ordered his men to throw green wood
(which would not burn) into the moat surrounding the city while the
defenders threw in dry wood (which did). When the moat was full,
the Muslims set it ablaze and God supported their cause by sending a
strong wind. In one hour the work that had taken the Turks six days
was destroyed. The archers on the walls also did their work: many of
the attackers were injured or killed, including Bāzagharī, who was
wounded and died that night. Things now began to turn nasty. The
Turks executed the Arab captives they had already seized, about a
hundred in number, in cold blood, throwing the heads of the best
known of them to the defenders. In return, the Arabs slew 200 of the
sons of the infidels, 'though they fought desperately'. The Turks now
attacked the gate of the earthwork and five of them managed to reach
the top of the wall before being dislodged.

Individual incidents were remembered with great clarity in the
later narratives. In one of these the prince of Shāsh (Tashkent), who
was an ally of the Khagan, asked permission to attack. The Khagan
refused, saying that it was too difficult, but the prince responded that
if he were to be rewarded with two Arab slave girls he would go ahead
and permission was granted. He and his companions came across a
breach in the wall beside which there was a house with a hole that
opened on the breach. There was a man lying sick in the house, but
despite his illness he had the strength and wit to throw a hook, which
caught the prince's chain mail. Then he called the women and boys
in the house to help him pull his victim in. The prince was then felled
by a stone and stabbed to death. A young Turk came up and slew the
killer, taking his sword, but the defenders managed to keep hold of
his body.[51]

In another incident, the Muslims took the wooden boards used to line irrigation ditches and set them up on top of the earthwork, making doors that could be used as a shelter and arrow slits for archers. One day they had a great chance when the Khagan himself came to inspect. One archer shot him in the face but he was wearing a Tibetan helmet that had a nose-piece (perhaps like the Norman helmets seen in the Bayeux tapestry) and no harm was done. He also suffered a superficial chest wound but escaped without serious injury.

As the siege dragged on, the Khagan became weary and irritable. He accused his allies the Soghdian princes of claiming that there were only fifty donkeys in the town and that it could be taken in five days, but two months had passed and the resistance was as strong as ever. Negotiations began. The Khagan said it was not the custom of the Turks to abandon a siege without conquering the city or the defenders leaving it, while the Muslims replied that they would not abandon their religion. So it was suggested that they should depart to Samarqand or Dabūsiya, the only towns in the area still in Muslim hands. The Muslims sent a messenger to get advice from Samarqand. He went off and met a Persian nobleman who was a friend of his (another of these inter-ethnic friendships we can see emerging in this area). He arranged for him to borrow a couple of the Khagan's own horses, which were grazing in a meadow near by. He reached Samarqand the same day. There the people advised that the garrison of Kamarja should evacuate to Dabūsiya, which was closer. The siege had lasted for fifty-eight days and the Muslims had not watered their camels for the last thirty-five of these.

The surrender was agreed, but in the atmosphere of mutual suspicion engendered by the siege and the execution of hostages, it was not easy to arrange things. Both sides gave five hostages to the other. The Muslims refused to leave until the Khagan and the bulk of his army had departed, and even then they kept a close eye on the hostages: each Turk was wearing only a robe, with no armour, and seated behind him on his horse was an Arab with a dagger in his hand. Meanwhile the Iranians travelling with the group were frightened that the garrison of Dabūsiya, said to have been 10,000 in number, would come out and attack them. In the event the Dabūsiya garrison, seeing horsemen, standards and a large military force approaching, thought that Kamarja had fallen and that this was the Khagan's army approaching them. They prepared for war. Then the mood changed completely when a messenger from the army told them the true story, and horsemen galloped out to help the weak and injured through the city walls. One by one the hostages were allowed to go, but only when the Arab hostages with the Turks were released. When there was only one hostage left on each side, neither side wanted to release their man first. Finally the Arab hostage[52] with the Turks told the Turkish officer, Kūrsūl, that he was happy for the other hostage to be released first. Later Kūrsūl asked him why he had taken this risk, to which the Arab replied, 'I trusted your view of me and that your spirit would be above treachery.' He was generously rewarded, given a horse and armour and returned to his companions. As in so much medieval warfare, savage cruelty was mingled with individual acts of chivalry, and some Turks, at least, were recognized as honourable and worthy opponents.

Samarqand, behind its great mud-brick ramparts, thus became the major Arab stronghold beyond the Oxus and its conquest had been one of Qutayba's most enduring achievements. It was under constant military pressure from the Soghdians and their Turkish allies and the fall of Kamarja had left it even more isolated: the Arab garrison there could not be expected to hold out for much longer. At the beginning of 730 yet another new governor, Junayd,[53] was appointed to Khurasan. According to court gossip in Damascus, he had got the job only because he had given the caliph's wife a particularly valuable necklace. He was young and inexperienced, never having visited the province before. As soon as he arrived in Khurasan, he crossed the river and began campaigning.

His first objective was Tukhāristan, so he went to Balkh, which had remained in Arab hands. He had divided his army and sent detachments in different directions when a message came from Sawra b. al-Hurr, the commander at Samarqand, saying that he was under attack and had been unable to defend the outer wall. He needed help fast. The experienced staff officers warned Junayd that he should wait until he had gathered all his troops; the Turks were a formidable army and 'no governor ought to cross the Oxus with fewer than fifty thousand men'. Junayd, however, was very conscious of the danger that faced the Muslims in Samarqand and of the damage it would do to his reputation if he failed to help them and the city fell. He announced that he would cross the river and head for Samarqand, even if he only had the few men of his own tribe who had come with him from Syria.

His first stop was Kish. Here he found that the Turks had already poisoned many of the wells and were advancing towards him. He had to defeat or bypass them if he were to relieve Samarqand. There are two routes from Kish to Samarqand. One is a circuitous route through the plains to the west, then cutting back, around the end of the mountains, to the Zarafshan valley. The other was more direct but involved going up the steep and rugged Tashtakaracha Pass. When Junayd asked his advisers which one they thought he should take, most of them were in favour of the flat route, but one of his most senior officers, the one who had advised him not to cross the river without a large army, said that it would be better to go over the pass: 'Being killed by the sword is better than being killed by fire,' he argued. 'The road through the plains has trees and tall grass by it. The area has not been cultivated for years. If we meet the Khagan there, he will set fire to it all and we will be killed by fire and smoke.'

The next day the army set out to climb the pass. Morale was low: many of the troops were openly distrustful of Junayd's military abilities and, as usual, claimed that he was favouring some tribes over others. They met the enemy some 24 kilometres (6 *farsakhs*) from the city. The enemy appeared while the men had stopped to eat and Junayd hurriedly arranged his battle lines between the sides of the pass, each tribal group fighting as a unit under its own commanders, gathered round its own banners. He ordered the commanders to dig earthworks in front of their positions.[54] Junayd started by commanding at the centre of the line but soon moved to the right wing, where the tribe of Azd were under fierce attack. Junayd now came and stood right by their banner to show his support. His action was not appreciated. The standard-bearer was blunt: 'If we win, it will be for your benefit, if we perish, you will not weep over us. By my life, if we win and I survive, I will never speak another word to you!' It was tribal solidarity around the banner which kept these units together, not loyalty to the commander, still less to the caliph in far-off Damascus. The fighting was hand to hand and very fierce; swords became blunt from too much use and slaves of the Azdis cut wooden staves to fight with. The struggle continued until both sides parted, exhausted. The standard-bearer's resolve was not put to the test, for he was soon slain, fighting bravely, with about eighty of his fellow Azdis.

As usual with accounts of battles in the early Islamic conquests, we have a number of vignettes, rather than an overall picture. Some of these vignettes are martyrdom stories, no doubt preserved to inspire the faithful in later campaigns. They all use the classical (and modern) Arabic word for martyr, *shahīd*, and show different ways in which men could attain this distinction.

One of them concerns a very rich man[55] who had just returned from a pilgrimage to Mecca, on which he had spent the enormous sum of 180,000 dirhams, much of it presumably given in alms. He now accompanied the army with a private supply train of a hundred camels loaded with *sawīq*, a sort of barley porridge, for the troops. Before he set out he asked his mother to pray that God would grant him martyrdom and her prayers were answered. With him when he died were two slaves. He had ordered them to flee and save their lives but they had refused and fought with him until they were all killed, so they too became martyrs.

In another story, the hero[56] is splendidly caparisoned, on a sorrel horse in gilded armour. He charged into the enemy ranks seven times, killing a man on each occasion so that everyone in that part of the battle was impressed by him, including the enemy. An interpreter (*tarjumān*) shouted out that if he would come over to their side, they would abandon the worship of their idols and worship him instead! Needless to say, pious Muslim that he was, he scornfully rejected any such idea, for, he said, 'I am fighting so that you will abandon the worship of idols and worship God alone.' He fought on until he was slaughtered and achieved martyrdom. In yet another such story, the martyr-to-be[57] asked his wife how she would react if he were brought in from the battle on a saddle-blanket, stained with blood. Naturally the poor woman was distraught and started to tear her clothes and wail. The martyr, however, was made of sterner, if somewhat ungallant, stuff: 'Enough from you!' he said. 'If any woman on earth wailed for me, I would still reject her out of longing for the black-eyed houris of paradise!' With that he returned to the fray and was martyred.

The climax of the battle seems to have been a determined charge on the Arab lines by the Turks. Junayd responded with a tactic that was typical of Umayyad armies. He ordered his men to dismount and get down on the ground. They would have knelt with their spears pointing upwards towards the enemy, creating a sort of wall of spear points. Protected by the trenches they had dug, they could face the enemy with some confidence.

Junayd's position, however, remained very weak. His forces had clearly suffered significant casualties and he had failed to break through to Samarqand, stuck as he was in the inhospitable mountain pass. There is some indication that the Turks had come round to his rear and interrupted his supply lines near Kish.[58] In this dangerous situation he accepted the advice of one of his officers and sent to Sawra, the governor of Samarqand, ordering him to leave the safety of the city and come to his aid. It was not a very courageous decision. He was told by his officers that he had a choice between perishing himself or having Sawra perish, to which he replied that it was 'easier' for him that Sawra should die.[59] When Sawra received the order to join Junayd, he initially refused to obey and his own officers pointed out that he was walking into a death trap, but Junayd sent another abusive message, calling him the son of a foul woman and threatening to send one of his enemies to take over the governorate in his place. In the end, Sawra felt that he had no choice but to obey. Again his officers urged caution, suggesting that he went by way of the river, but Sawra replied that that would take two days; instead he would order a night march to reach Junayd in the morning. The Turks were immediately aware of his movements and intercepted him at dawn. There was some fierce fighting and the Turks set fire to the grass and prevented the Muslims reaching water. Once again Sawra asked his officers for their opinion. One pointed out that the Turks were after only animals and booty: if they slaughtered their beasts, burned their baggage and drew their swords, the Turks would leave them alone. Another suggested that they should all dismount and walk ahead with the spears held out in front of them, a sort of mobile spear wall. Sawra rejected all this advice and decided on a direct attack. Conditions were terrible, Turks and Muslims alike obscured by the smoke and dust and falling into the flames. Sawra fell, his thigh smashed. In the heat and the dust, the Muslim forces were scattered and the Turks hunted them down, picking them off one by one. Of 12,000 men who had set out from Samarqand with Sawra, only 1,000 survived.

Meanwhile Junayd took advantage of the diversion to head for Samarqand, but he was not out of trouble yet. On the advice of one of his most experienced officers[60] he pitched camp rather than pressing on to the city. It was just as well that he did, because if the Turks had caught him in open country, they would probably have annihilated him. As it was there was a fierce battle the next morning. Junayd gave the order that any slave who fought for the Muslims would receive his freedom. The regular troops were amazed by the fierceness with which the slaves fought, cutting holes in saddle-blankets and putting them over their heads as a sort of makeshift armour. Finally the Turks withdrew and Junayd was able to go on to the city, saving himself behind its massive walls. The Turkish army, denied a complete victory, now began to withdraw and the Muslim presence in Soghdia survived, but only just.

The verdict of popular opinion was hard on Junayd and the poets were savage in their criticism:

> You weep because of the battle
> You should be carved up as a leader
> You abandoned us like pieces of a slaughtered beast
> Cut up for a round-breasted girl.
> Drawn swords rose
> Arms were cut off at the elbows
> While you were like an infant girl in the women's tent
> With no understanding what was going on.
> If only you had landed in a pit on the day of the Battle
> And been covered with hard, dry mud!
> War and its sons play with you
> Like hawks play with quails.
> Your heart flew out of fear of battle
> Your flying heart will not return
> I hate the wide beauty of your eye
> And the face in a corrupt body
> Junayd, you do not come from real Arab stock
> And your ancestors were ignoble
> Fifty thousand were slain having gone astray
> While you cried out for them like lost sheep.

Nobody's reputation could survive an onslaught like that. Junayd lost all credibility as a military leader and was shamed for ever. Meanwhile the air of martyrdom hung over the battlefield where Sawra and his men had died. Some claimed to have seen tents pitched between earth and sky for those about to be martyred, others averred that the land where they had fallen smelled of musk.[61]

After Junayd died in office in 734 open dissent broke out among the Arabs in Khurasan and the authority of the Umayyad governors was threatened by a rebel army led by one Hārith b. Surayj. Resentments over pay and the hardships of campaigning were exacerbated by the effects of famine and constant warfare. The years of Hārith's revolt, 734–6, marked the nadir of Arab fortunes in Transoxania. It seems that all the lands beyond the river were lost except Kish. The Soghdian king, Ghūrak, seems to have been able to recover control of his ancient capital at Samarqand.[62] It was the most significant reverse Arab conquerors had suffered in any theatre of operations, and it is noticeable that it came very shortly after the defeat of Arab armies in Europe at the battle of Poitiers in 732. But there was an important difference. In the west, Poitiers really did represent the end of the Arab advance. In the east, the reverses that followed the battle of the Tashtakaracha Pass represented a serious but only temporary setback.

ASAD B. ABD ALLĀH, NASR B. SAYYĀR AND THE TRIUMPH OF ISLAM, 737–51

The tide began to turn for the Arabs in 737. Ghūrak, king of Samarqand, the crafty old survivor, died of natural causes and his kingdom was divided among his heirs. In the autumn of that year, the Khagan, in league with the Arab rebel Hārith b. Surayj, invaded Tukhāristan. The Arab governor at the time (Asad (the Lion) b. Abd Allāh) had moved his capital from Merv to Balkh. He probably wanted to escape from the feuding Arab groups in the old capital but Merv had always been the capital of the western invaders, whether Sasanian or Arab, and he may have also have hoped that by moving to the ancient capital at Balkh he would be able to send a different signal to the local princes. Asad had good relations with many of them and important individuals converted to Islam at his hands, including, it is said, Barmak, founder of the famous Barmakid dynasty of viziers, and Sāmān-khudā, ancestor of the Samanids who were to rule much of Khurasan and Transoxania in the tenth century. Asad's diplomacy and conciliatory policy may have made a crucial difference and laid the foundations of future Muslim dominance in the area.

In December 737 the Khagan began raiding in the neighbourhood of Balkh. He made the fatal mistake of dispersing his troops to raid the towns and villages of Tukhāristan, perhaps trying to find supplies at this bleak and desolate time of year. Whether they had been won over by Asad's gestures or alienated by the rapacity of the Khagan's followers, some of the local princes threw in their lot with Asad and the Muslims. It seems that Asad, with 30,000 soldiers, went out to meet the Khagan and surprised him at a place called Khāristān at a moment when he only had 4,000 men with him. The struggle was fierce but was decided by the king of Jūzjān, one of Asad's local allies, who attacked the Khagan from the rear. The Turks fled with Asad in hot pursuit and it was only a snowstorm allowing them to escape which prevented a total massacre.

The battle of Khāristān was little more than a skirmish, but it marked the end of the power of the Khagan and the Türgesh empire. He retreated far to the east to his base in the Ili valley. Defeated, with his reputation in tatters, he was assassinated by his subordinate, Kūrsūl. Kūrsūl in turn was unable to hold the Turks together in the face of Chinese intrigue, and by 739 the Türgesh Empire had dissolved. It was to be another two centuries before a Turkish state was to appear again in Central Asia.

Asad died of natural causes the next year, 738. After a brief interval the caliph Hishām appointed Nasr b. Sayyār as the new governor. In some ways it was an unusual choice. Almost all the men who had governed Khurasan before came from the west. Many of them had never previously visited the province. Some were able, some seem to have been appointed to grant political or personal favours in Damascus rather than because they were suitable for this most demanding of provincial governorates. Nasr, by contrast, had spent thirty years in the province, virtually his whole adult life. He belonged to a small group of professional officers who had formed the staff of previous governors, but he was the first of these to be given the top appointment. It was also helpful in some ways that, like Qutayba before him, he belonged to the small tribe of Kināna. He was not involved in the fierce and deep-rooted tribal rivalries that had taken hold among many of the Arabs of Khurasan. But, as with Qutayba, this position had its downside: Nasr was dependent on support from Damascus, and if this were to fail for any reason he could not call on tribal support to sustain him.

He came to office at a good moment. His predecessor, the lamented Asad, had established good relations with many of the local princes. At the same time, the Türgesh Turks were no longer a power to be reckoned with. Some princes still hoped that the Chinese might intervene. In 741 the Chinese court received an ambassador from Shāsh complaining that 'now the Turks have become subject to China, it is only the Arabs who are a curse to the Kingdoms', but, while the distant Chinese might grant high-sounding titles, it became apparent that they would not intervene militarily to provide effective support. Most of the princes must have been aware that the Muslims were now the only show in town: they had to come to terms with them or perish.

Nasr, like Qutayba before him, worked with a twin-track policy. As Gibb says, 'He had seen the futility of trying to hold the country together by mere brute force, and the equal futility of trying to dispense with force.'[63] Shortly after his appointment, he gave a sermon in the mosque in the provincial capital at Merv,* which was essentially a political manifesto.[64] At first glance, it was mostly about money. He made it clear that he was the protector of the Muslims and that henceforth Muslims (not, it should be noted, Arabs) would get preferential tax status. All land would be liable for the *kharāj* tax but Muslims would be exempt from the *jizya*, by which he meant the poll tax. The implication was clear: all Muslims, whether Arab immigrants or local converts, would have the same privileged fiscal status; all infidels, whatever their class or ethnic background, would have to pay. It was said that 30,000 Muslims who had been paying the poll tax now no longer had to do so, while 80,000 infidels had to start paying up. Of course, the effect of Nasr's decree, or rather his regulation of a previously chaotic situation, had wider implications; conversion to Islam meant that you became an equal member of the ruling community. It was a clear and attractive incentive and played a part in the

---

* The Friday sermon was the one occasion on which the governor could address the leading Muslims of the city and make public pronouncements about current political issues.

creation of a ruling class in Khurasan and Transoxania which was defined by religion, Islam, rather than by ethnic identity, Arab. It was this body of Khurasani Muslims who were to rise in revolt against Nasr and the Umayyad government in 747 and install the Abbasids as rulers of the Muslim world in 750.

In the short term, Nasr's policy seems to have been successful. The fact that we hear virtually nothing about Tukhāristān and Khwārazm at this time, and little about Soghdia, suggests that these areas were largely peaceful under Muslim rule. It is probable that by this time most of the princes in this area had converted to Islam, and this is certainly true of the ones we know about, notably the rulers of Bukhara and the Barmakids of Balkh. Contingents from Transoxania served in Nasr's armies: when he was raiding Shāsh in 739, he had 20,000 men from Bukhara, Samarqand, Kish and even from wild and remote Ushrūsanā in his forces. A few of these may have been of Arab origin, but it is likely that most were locals who joined the Muslim armies in the hope of pay and booty.

He also set about encouraging Soghdian merchants, who had fled east to Farghāna during the wars of the 720s, to return. This was not a simple matter. The Soghdians demanded conditions. The first of these was that those who had converted to Islam and had then apostasized should not be punished. This was a difficult one; the penalty for apostasy from Islam was (and still is) death, and it was not easy to get around this. It is interesting that Nasr did not feel obliged to ask any religious scholars before making his decision. These were the days before the crystallization of Islamic law, and he simply decided on his own initiative that this concession should be made. Even half a century later, the idea that such a clear principle of Islam could be disregarded on the authority of a provincial governor would have been unthinkable, but in these rough-and-ready frontier conditions Nasr could get away with it in the wider cause of Islam. Then there was the question of the tax arrears that many of the merchants owed; these were written off. Finally there was the question of Muslim prisoners held by the Soghdians. Perhaps surprisingly, Nasr agreed that these needed to be returned only after their bona fides had been checked by a Muslim judge. Nasr received a good deal of criticism in some quarters and the caliph, Hishām, himself initially repudiated the agreement, but in the end it was agreed that the most important thing was to win over these prosperous and powerful men. The treaty was made and the merchants returned to Soghdia.[65]

The only major offensive operation that Nasr launched was the 739 expedition to Shāsh and Farghāna. The accounts of these campaigns are picturesque but confused and the course of events is not entirely clear. When Nasr's army reached distant Farghāna they besieged the city of Qubā, eventually coming to terms with the son of the ruler. Negotiations were carried out by the young prince's mother through an interpreter; she is said to have taken the opportunity to deliver a short homily on kingship, which gives us another glimpse into the mentality of these eastern Iranian rulers.

'A king is not a true king,' she began,

> unless he has six things: a vizier to whom he may tell his secret intentions and who will give him reliable advice; a cook who, whenever the king does not feel like food, will find something that will tempt him to eat; a wife who, if he goes in with a troubled mind to see her and he looks at her face, causes his anxieties to disappear; a fortress in which he can take refuge, a sword which will not fail him when he fights the enemy and a treasury which he can live off anywhere in the world.[66]

She was also shocked to see the treatment of one of the sons of the old governor Qutayba, who occupied a fairly modest place in the governor's camp. 'You Arabs', she complained, 'don't keep faith nor do you behave properly with one another. It was Qutayba who laid the foundations of your power, as I myself saw. This is his son, yet you make him sit below you. You should change places with him!' This is a strong affirmation both of the reputation Qutayba still enjoyed twenty years after his ignominious death and of the importance of inherited status.

This campaign seems to have marked the end of major offensive expeditions. Nasr may have spent time pacifying Soghdia but from 745 onwards he was entirely preoccupied in Merv and Khurasan with the rebel movement that later would become the Abbasid revolution. Embassies were sent to China to regulate relations now that the Turks no longer formed a barrier between the two great powers. An embassy in 744 seems to have been intended to develop commercial contacts and contained representatives from the Soghdian cities Tukhāristan, Shāsh and even Zābulistān (in southern Afghanistan). Further embassies were sent in 745 and 747.[67]

By 750 the conquest of Transoxania was essentially complete and the north-eastern frontier of the Muslim world established along lines that were to remain more or less unchanged until the coming of the Seljuk Turks three centuries later. It was also the frontier of settlement. Islamic rule was established in areas where there were ancient cities and settled villages. Further to the east, in the vast grasslands of Kazakhstan and Kirghistan, the ancient beliefs and ways of life continued largely unaltered. The conquest of Transoxania was the hardest that Muslim armies ever undertook. Their opponents were determined and resilient, and the armies of Islam endured repeated setbacks. In the end, it was only when governors like Asad b. Abd Allāh and Nasr b. Sayyār cooperated with and incorporated local elites that it was possible. Islam certainly triumphed over native religions in this area, but the princely values of Transoxanian rulers were to have a profound effect on the culture of the whole eastern Islamic world and the survival of Iranian culture within it.

There was, however, to be one final, decisive act in the struggle for Central Asia. We know virtually nothing about it from Arab sources, but the Chinese annals fill in some of the gaps.[68] In 747 and 749 the Prince of Tukhāristan appealed for Chinese help against bandits in Gilgit, near the headwaters of the Indus, an area where Muslim armies never penetrated, along a route to China sometimes used by Soghdian traders. The Chinese governor of Kucha sent a Korean officer to deal with the problem. In a series of amazing campaigns, he crossed the mountains along the precipitous route of what is now the Karakorum highway and defeated the rebels. He was then called in by the king of Farghāna to help in a local dispute with the neighbouring king of Shāsh. The Chinese forces ended up by taking Shāsh and the king fled to seek help from the Abbasid governor Abū Muslim, who had established himself at Samarqand. He sent a force under one of his lieutenants, Ziyād b. Sālih. The Chinese with their Farghāna allies and some Turks met the Muslim armies near Taraz in July 751. It was the first and last time that Arab and Chinese armies came into direct confrontation. The Arabs were victorious but sadly we have no more details of this conflict.

This encounter marked the end of an era. Arab forces were never to penetrate east of Farghāna or north-east of Shāsh, never to follow the Silk Road into Sinkiang and across the Gobi Desert. It was also the last time that Chinese armies ever reached so far west. They would probably have returned in force to avenge their defeat, but four years later, in 755, Central Asia and then China itself were torn apart by the revolt of An Lushan, and it was to be a millennium before Chinese forces once again appeared in Kashgar. Any hope the Soghdian princes may have entertained that the Chinese would support them against the Arabs were ended for ever. The battle of Taraz or Talas, like the battle of Poitiers in 732 in the west, was little reported in the contemporary Arab sources. Although Poitiers was a defeat and Talas a victory for Arab arms, both were to mark the furthest limits of Arab expansion in their areas.

The battle of Talas was also remembered in the Arab tradition for a completely different reason. It was widely believed that the artisans captured by the Arabs in the course of the campaign had brought the technology of paper-making to the Arab world. It is certainly the case that paper had been known in China before this, but it appears in Islamic society only in the second half of the eighth century, replacing both parchment and papyrus as the main writing material. Exactly what historical reality lies behind the accounts of the prisoners of Talas we cannot tell. What is likely, however, is that contacts with the Chinese in Central Asia led to the import of this new writing material. Cheap, easy to produce and use, paper was to have a major impact on the literacy and culture of the Muslim and later the European world.

9

FURTHEST EAST AND FURTHEST WEST

⁕

B y the end of the seventh century, Muslim armies had achieved some sort of control over the whole of North Africa in the west and Khurasan and much of Transoxania in the east. In many ways the frontiers they had created had a geographical logic that made them a suitable place to call an end to expansion – the Straits of Gibraltar in the west and the wild mountains of eastern Afghanistan and Makrān in the east. In the event, neither of these formed a permanent obstacle, and in the final push of the early Arab conquests Muslim armies conquered most of the Iberian peninsula and Sind, the southern part of modern Pakistan.

Sind was very remote from Arabia and the heartlands of the early Muslim state.[1] The overland route led through the pitiless deserts of Makrān, where the track led from one parched oasis to another and where supplies were almost impossible to obtain. Alexander the Great had been one of the few men to try to lead an army through this land, and it proved one of the toughest struggles he had had to face. The alternative route was by sea, along the barren southern coast of Iran and Makrān to the ports around the mouth of the Indus river. In either case, the distances and the nature of the terrain made the journey very difficult.

Our knowledge of the Arab conquest of Sind in the early eighth century is very limited. The area is largely neglected by the classical Arab authorities. Only Balādhurī gives a systematic account and that occupies only about a dozen pages of the text.[2] There is no indication that he, or any of the other Iraq-based chroniclers, had ever visited this remote outpost of the Muslim empire, and the few details they give shed little light on the country or its conquest. Nor are local sources much more forthcoming. The only Sindi chronicle to deal with the conquests is the Chāchnāmah[3] of 1216 by Alī b. Hāmid al-

Kūfī, a translation of a lost Arabic original, said to have been collected
by written by a *qāḍī* of Al-Rūr who claimed descent from the Thaqafīs,
the tribe of the leader of the original conqueror, Muhammad b. Qāsim.
The second half of this work is essentially an account of the first phase
of the conquest.[4] The Chāchnāmah has not been held in high regard
by historians and it contains many legendary accretions, but much of
the core narrative seems to be derived from early Arabic sources: the
author names the historian Madā'inī, and the outline of the narrative,
and some specific incidents, are closely based on Balādhurī's texts.
Two themes are stressed in the text. One is the powerful role played
by Hajjāj in distant Iraq. He is described as having absolute day-to-
day control of the campaigning. Muhammad b. Qāsim scarcely moved
without writing to his master and waiting for the reply, which always
came with improbable speed by return of post. On one occasion the
text describes Hajjāj ordering Muhammad to draw a sketch map of
the River Indus so that he can give advice on the proper place to cross
it.[5] What is meant to be conveyed, clearly, is the authority Hajjāj had
over his commanders in the field. A second theme is the role of
soothsayers and wise men, who are constantly telling the Sindi princes
that the Arab conquests had been predicted and that there is nothing
that can be done to prevent them. The Chāchnāmah contains some
material said to have been conserved among the descendants of the
original Arab conquerors which may be genuine, and some Arabic
poetry that was not translated into Persian along with the rest of the
book. This too may be of eighth-century origin.

Archaeology has not provided much more evidence, and even the
location of some key sites, such as Daybul, which was still flourishing
in the thirteenth century, remains doubtful. With the exception of
Multān and Nīrūn, none of the cities mentioned in the early texts has
kept its name down to modern times, so identifications are often
doubtful.

Arabs had had contact with Sind, before the coming of Islam. In
late Sasanian times there was a growing trade by sea between the Gulf
and Sind and one group of Arabs was especially important in the
development of this trade. The Azd tribe of Uman may have been
remote from the centres of early Muslim power in the Hijaz but they
were well placed to play a role in the maritime trade in the Indian
Ocean. They converted to Islam and played an important part in the

conquest of Fars and other areas in Iran. They formed a powerful lobby, wanting to invade Sind to further their commercial aspirations.

Sind at this stage has been described as 'the wild frontier of Indian civilisation',[6] but for the early Muslims it was 'the land of gold and of commerce, of medicaments and simples, of sweetmeats and resources, of rice, bananas and wondrous things'.[7] It derived its name from the Sanskrit Sindhu, the name of the river known in the west as the Indus and to the Arabs as the Mihrān. Sind is created by the Indus river system in the same way as Egypt is created by the Nile. Arab geographers of the tenth century recognized the resemblance: 'It is a very great river of sweet water,' Ibn Hawqal wrote. 'One finds crocodiles in it, like the Nile. It also resembles the Nile by its size and by the fact that its water level is determined by summer rains. Its floods spread over the land, then withdraw after having fertilized the soil, just like the river in Egypt.'[8]

At the time of the Muslim invasion, the settled parts of the country were ruled by a dynasty of kings of Brahmin origin. This had been founded by Chāch (c. 632–71) and was led in the early eighth century by Dāhir (c. 679–712), who led the resistance to the Muslims.[9] The king seems to have lived in the city that the Arabs called al-Rūr, and the main port was the city of Daybul. The shifting course of the Indus delta has made the identification of this site very difficult, but it is probably to be identified with the ruins at Banbhore which now lies in desolate salt flats about 40 kilometres from the sea east of Karachi. The city first appears in the historical record in the fifth century, when it was a distant outpost of the Sasanian Empire. In the time of King Chāch and his son Dāhir it seems to have been a base for pirates, attacking trade between the Gulf and India, and suppression of this was one of the reasons for the Muslim attack.[10]

Much of the country was occupied by semi-nomadic tribes like the Mīds and the Jats, known to the Muslim sources as the Zutt. The Mīds supplemented the meagre livelihood they could scrape from their barren homelands with piracy against merchant shipping. The Zutt were agriculturalists who used water buffalo to cultivate the swampy lands by the Indus and grow sugar cane. According to Muslim sources, some Zutt were transported to southern Iraq by the Sasanian shāh Bahrām Gūr (420–38) to cheer his people up with their music-making![11]

According to the Arab tradition, there had been proposals to invade Sind from as early as 644, when the Muslims first attacked the neighbouring province of Makrān, and there may also have been naval expeditions to India at this time. There is also a tradition, however, that the early caliphs Umar and Uthmān refused to allow raids in this distant and dangerous area, and the accounts of campaigns in the seventh century are probably largely mythical.

We are on firmer historical ground with the campaign of 710–12. According to Balādhurī, the immediate reason for the expedition was that the 'king of the Island of Rubies' (Sri Lanka) sent Hajjāj, governor of Iraq and all the east, some women who were daughters of Muslim merchants who had died in his country. The author adds the note that it was called the Island of Rubies 'because of the beauty of the faces of its women'.[12] On the journey, the ship was attacked by some Mīd pirates sailing out of Daybul and was captured with all its passengers. One of the women, in her distress, was said to have called on the name of Hajjāj, and when he heard of the attack, he determined to take action.

He first wrote to Dāhir, the king, ordering him to set them free, but the king replied that he had no control over the pirates who had taken them and was unable to help. Hajjāj then sent two small expeditions, but in both cases they were defeated and the leaders killed. He then decided on a larger-scale campaign. He chose as its leader a young cousin of his called Muhammad b. al-Qāsim al-Thaqafī (from the tribe of Thaqīf, originally from Tā'if). Muhammad was something of a golden boy and was described as 'the noblest Thaqafī of his time'.[13] He is said to have been given high command at the age of seventeen but he proved an efficient commander and a wise and tolerant governor. His brief, meteoric career and tragic end left a lasting memory in both Sind and the central Islamic lands. Hajjāj ordered him to gather an army in the newly founded city of Shiraz in south-western Iran; 6,000 professional soldiers from Syria were dispatched to form the core of the army and he sent all the equipment he needed, 'even including needles and threads'. When all was ready, they set out on the long land route through southern Iran and then into Makrān, taking the city of Fannazbūr en route. Meanwhile ships were sent with men, weapons and supplies.

The forces met up outside Daybul. Muhammad immediately began to invest the city, digging siege works. He ordered that lances be set up with tribal banners flying from them and that the troops encamp by their own flags. He also set up a catapult (*manjanīq*) served by 500 men, which was known as the Bride. This suggests a large, hand-pulled swing-beam siege engine, and is one of the very few examples we have of the Muslim forces using siege artillery during the conquests. One of the main features of the city was a temple described as a *budd*, like a great minaret in the middle of the city; this was probably a Buddhist stupa. On top of the temple there was a mast (*daqal*) from which a great red banner flapped and twisted in the wind. This mast now became the target of the siege engine and when it was brought down morale in the city collapsed. Muhammad ordered up ladders and his men soon began to scale the walls, so taking the city by force.[14] Dāhir's governor fled and there were three days of slaughter in which all the priests of the temple, among others, were killed. Muhammad then ordered the building of a mosque and laid out plots for the settlement of 4,000 Muslims.

Muhammad now made his way inland to the fortified city of Nīrūn near the banks of the Indus. Here he was met by two Buddhist (Samani) monks[15] who began negotiations. They made peace and welcomed him into their city, giving him supplies.[16] As he pressed on up the river, the pattern was repeated, with Buddhist monks frequently acting as peacemakers. According to the Chāchnāmah[17] the city of Sīwīstān fell because of divisions among the local population. On one side was the Buddhist party, on the other the Hindu governor of the fort. The Buddhists told the commander of the fort that they would not fight: 'Our religion is peace and our creed is good will to all. According to our faith, fighting and slaughtering are not allowed. We will never be in favour of shedding blood.' They added that they were afraid that the Arabs would take them to be supporters of the governor and would attack them. They urged him to make a treaty with the Arabs because 'they are said to be faithful to their word. What they say they do'. When the governor refused to listen to their advice, they sent a message to the Arabs saying that all the farmers, artisans and common people had deserted the governor and that he was now unable to put up a prolonged resistance. The fort held out for a week before the commander made his escape by night. The Muslims entered the city, which was looted in the customary way, except that the possessions of the Buddhist party were respected. As always with the Chāchnāmah, it is difficult to separate fact from fiction, but the narrative does suggest that Buddhist pacifism may have been a factor in the success of Arab arms and that division between the ordinary people and the Hindu military caste allowed the Muslims to take some towns with comparative ease.

It was during this march that Muhammad was joined by some 4,000 Zutt tribesmen, substantially increasing his forces.

Dāhir still remained as the leader of the resistance. Muhammad, on the west bank of the Indus, confronted him across the river.[18] The Chāchnāmah gives a detailed account of how Muhammad crossed the river to attack Dāhir.[19] He decided to build a bridge of boats and collected boats filled with ballast of sand and stones linked together with connecting planks. Meanwhile, Dāhir's supporters gathered on the east bank of the river to oppose their landing. Muhammad ordered that all the boats should be brought together along the west bank until the row of boats was as long as the river was wide. Then brave armed soldiers gathered on the boats and the whole row was swung round in the stream until it reached the other bank. Immediately the Arabs drove the infidels back with volleys of arrows and the horsemen and foot soldiers landed.

The final confrontation between Muhammad b. Qāsim and Dāhir is given a few terse lines in Balādhurī but is described in dramatic terms in the Chāchnāmah. The Sindi army was composed of 5,000 veteran warriors (or 20,000 foot soldiers) and sixty elephants. Dāhir was mounted on a white elephant, armed with a tightly strung bow, with two female servants with him in the litter, one to hand him betel leaf to chew, the other to keep him supplied with arrows. There were speeches made on both sides and the names of numerous Arab warriors are given, a sure sign that this part of the Chāchnāmah at least is based on an Arab original. We are also told how Arabs who had previously joined Dāhir's forces, for reasons that are not explained, now came to give Muhammad b. Qāsim vital information about his opponents' movements. In the fierce fighting that followed, the Muslims used flaming arrows to set fire to the litter in which Dāhir was fighting and the elephant threw himself into the water. Dāhir was seized and decapitated, his body being identified by the two slave girls who were with him in the litter. The historian Madā'inī preserves a short poem of triumph said to have been uttered by the Arab who killed him:

> The horses at the battle of Dāhir and the spears
> And Muhammad b. Qāsim b. Muhammad
> Bear witness that I fearlessly scattered the host of them
> Until I came upon their chief with my sword.
> And left him rolled in the dirt.
> Dust on his unpillowed cheek.[20]

The defeat and death of Dāhir meant the end of organized resist-ance. Many of Dāhir's women committed suicide, burning themselves, their attendants and all their possessions, rather than be captured. The Chāchnāmah puts a little speech into the mouth of the dead king's sister: 'Our glory has gone and the term of our life has come to its close. As there is no hope of safety and liberty, let us collect firewood and cotton and oil. The best thing for us, I think, is to burn ourselves to ashes and so quickly meet our husbands in the other world.'[21] They all entered a house, set fire to it and were burned alive. Despite this self-sacrifice, the chronicle says that many high-caste women of great beauty were sent to Hajjāj in Iraq. He in turn passed them on to the court of the caliph, where they were sold or given away to favoured relatives and supporters. The remnants of Dāhir's forces were pursued to Brahmanābādh, near where the Muslim city of Mansūra was later founded, where they were again defeated. The Chāchnāmah preserves an account of the dealings of Muhammad b. Qāsim with the inhabitants of Brahmanābādh which probably reflects many of the issues raised by the Muslim conquest. His immediate response was to spare all the artisans, traders and common folk and execute all the military classes.[22] He soon became aware of the need to recruit local officials for the administration. His first move was to conduct a census of the merchants and artisans, who were obliged to convert to Islam or pay the poll tax. He next appointed village chiefs to collect the taxes. Meanwhile the Brahmins sought to secure their status under the new regime. They came to Muhammad b. Qāsim with their heads and beards shaved, as a sign of humility, and peti-tioned him. First they secured a safe conduct for all surviving members of Dāhir's family, including his wife Lādī, who was brought out from her inner chamber. She is said to have been purchased by Muhammad

b. Qāsim and to have become his wife.[23] It is interesting to compare this with the contemporary marriage of the son of Mūsā b. Nusayr, conqueror of al-Andalus, with the daughter of the Visigothic king Rodrigo. In both cases the Arab conquerors were seeking to ally themselves with the old ruling house, perhaps in the hope that their descendants would become hereditary rulers. In both cases, however, they were thwarted by the robust action of the government in Damascus.

The Brahmins then explained how they had been much honoured and revered in the old kingdom. Muhammad said that they should be allowed the same privileges and status as they had enjoyed under King Chāch, Dāhir's father. This status was to be inherited by their children. The Brahmins then spread out as revenue collectors. They were allowed to keep their customary dues from the merchants and artisans.

More complaints were raised by the keepers of Buddhist temples.[24] They had previously survived on charitable donations but these had dried up because the people were afraid of the Muslim soldiers. 'Now', they lamented, 'our temples are lying desolate and in ruins and we have no opportunity to worship our idols. We beseech that our just governor will allow us to repair and construct our Buddhist temples and carry on worship as before.' Muhammad wrote to Hajjāj, who replied that, as long as they paid their tribute, the Muslims had no further rights over them, so they should be allowed to maintain their temples as before. In a meeting held just outside the town, Muhammad gathered all the chiefs, headmen and Brahmins and permitted them to build their temples and carry on commerce with the Muslims. He also told them to show kindness to the Brahmins and to celebrate their holy days as their fathers and grandfathers had before and, perhaps most importantly, to pay three out of every hundred dirhams collected in revenues to the Brahmins and send the rest to the treasury. It was also settled that the Brahmins (presumably those who did not benefit from the tax revenues) would be allowed to go around begging from door to door with copper bowls, collecting corn and using it as they wished.

A further problem was the status of the Jats.[25] Muhammad's advisers described their low status and how they had been discriminated against in the reign of King Chāch: they had to wear rough clothing; if they rode horses they were not allowed to use saddles or reins but only blankets; they had to take dogs with them so that they could be distinguished; they were obliged to help as guides for travellers day and night; and if any of them committed theft, his children and other members of his family were to be thrown into the fire and burnt. In short, 'they are all of the wild nature of brutes. They have always been refractory and disobedient to rulers and are always committing highway robberies'. Muhammad was easily convinced that these were 'a villainous set of people' and that they should be treated accordingly.

These discussions are very interesting, not because they are necessarily an accurate record of what happened but because of what they tell us of the Muslim settlement and how people viewed it. At the most obvious level, it shows how the Muslims took over the existing administrative personnel and left prevailing social structures largely intact. The accounts serve a twin purpose, of explaining to a Muslim audience how it was that Brahmins continued to be so influential under an ostensibly Muslim government, and why temples should be tolerated. They also showed how the Buddhists were to be tolerated and allowed to practise their religion. For all the non-Muslims, they showed how their status had been accepted by the founding father of Sindi Islam, Muhammad b. Qāsim, and his great adviser, Hajjāj himself. To the unfortunate Jats, they simply showed that the coming of Islam was to bring them no benefits at all.

Muhammad b. Qāsim's march now became something of a triumphal progress, and at one point the Muslims were greeted by the people dancing to the music of pipes and drums. When he enquired, Muhammad was told that they always greeted their new rulers in this way.[26] The next main objective was al-Rūr, described as the biggest town in Sind. Dāhir's son Fofi had fortified himself in the city and intended to resist. According to the Chāchnāmah,[27] Fofi and the people of al-Rūr believed that Dāhir was still alive and that he would soon come to rescue them. Even when Muhammad produced his widow Lādī and assured them that he was dead, the defenders accused her of conspiring with the 'cow-eaters' and reaffirmed their faith that he would come with a mighty army to save them. According to this imaginative account, they were convinced only by the testimony of a local sorceress. When consulted, she retired to her chambers and emerged after a few hours saying that she had travelled the whole world looking for Dāhir, producing a nutmeg from Ceylon as proof

of her voyages, and had seen no sign of him. This intelligence persuaded many of the inhabitants that they should open negotiations
with Muhammad, whose reputation for virtue and justice was well
known. That night Fofi and his entourage slipped away, and when the
Arabs began to assault the city the next day, the merchants and artisans
opened negotiations, saying that they had given up their allegiance to
the Brahmins and were convinced that the forces of Islam would
triumph. Muhammad accepted their overtures, after receiving assur-
ances that they would abandon all military operations. The population
gathered at a shrine called the Nawbahār (the same name as the great
Buddhist shrine at Balkh) and prostrated themselves before the marble
and alabaster image. Muhammad asked the keeper of the temple whose
image it was. He also took one of the bracelets from the arms of the
statue. When the keeper noticed that it had disappeared, Muhammad
teased him, asking how it could be that the god did not know who
had taken the bracelet. Then, laughing, he produced it and it went
back on the arm.

     After the surrender, Muhammad ordered a number of executions
of fighting men, but Lādī interceded, saying that the people of the
town were 'good builders and merchants, who cultivated their lands
well and always kept the treasury full', so Muhammad spared them.
Once again the narrative points to the compromises and working
relationships that accompanied the conquests: the temple was undis-
turbed and the livelihoods of most of the inhabitants continued
uninterrupted. The Muslim conqueror was celebrated, not for his zeal
in the rigid enforcement of Islamic norms, but for his tolerance and
easygoing humour. This is also in marked contrast with the destruction
of temples and religious figures during the Arab conquest of Transoxania at exactly the same time. It is difficult to know whether this
was the result of the pacific approach of the Buddhists or simply
because the Muslims were too few in number to challenge existing
customs. When the town had submitted completely, Muhammad left
two of his Arab followers in charge, exhorting them to deal kindly
with the people and look after them.

     The other main city, Multān, fell soon after. The conquest, called
'the opening of the house of gold' by the victorious Arabs, marked
the furthest point of the Muslim advance in Sind at this stage. The
town was rich and the temple (*budd*) was a major pilgrimage centre.

The inhabitants put up a stout resistance and the besieging Muslims ran very short of supplies, being obliged to eat their own donkeys. The end came when they were shown how drinking water entered the city and were able to cut off the supply. The people surrendered unconditionally. The men of fighting age and the priests were all put to death and the women and children enslaved. The Muslims acquired vast amounts of gold.[28] Curiously, there is an old tradition that Khālid b. al-Walīd, known to history as the conqueror of Syria, is buried in Multān and his supposed tomb is the oldest Muslim building in the city.

The conquests in India posed a new sort of problem for the victors. In most of the lands that the early Muslims conquered, the majority of the population could be considered 'people of the Book', which meant that they could be allowed to keep their lives, property and religious practices as long as they accepted Muslim rule and their status as *dhimmi*s. After the conquest of Iran, it had been gradually accepted that the Zoroastrians could be considered as 'people of the Book' too. The problem in Sind was that the population were mostly either Buddhists or Hindus. As far as most Muslims were concerned, Buddhists and Hindus, with their elaborate images and statues, were no more than idolators plain and simple, who could be exterminated at will if they did not convert to Islam. The Arab conquerors of Sind soon tempered their religious enthusiasm with pragmatism. After he had taken al-Rūr, Muhammad is said to have reasoned that 'the *budd* are like the churches of the Christians, the synagogues of the Jews and the fire-temples of the Magians' and that they should be respected in the same way. In practice this meant that both Buddhists and Hindus should, in effect, be accepted as *dhimmi*s. In many cases local Brahmins and Buddhist monks continued to run the local administration for their new Muslim masters.

The initial conquests were brought to an abrupt end by events in the Muslim heartlands. In 715, when Muhammad had been in Sind for three and a half years, there was a major change of government. Hajjāj, his relative and patron, had died in 714 and the caliph Walīd I followed him the next year. The accession of Sulaymān to the Umayyad throne saw a violent reaction against Hajjāj and his officials. Muhammad was unceremoniously ordered back to Iraq, where he was imprisoned and tortured by the new governor and soon died in captivity. He deserved better. Like his contemporaries, Qutayba b. Muslim in Khurasan and Mūsā b. Nusayr in Spain, he found that his achievements in the service of Islam were no protection against vengeful political rivals.

Muhammad's dismissal marked the virtual end of active campaigning. In the short period of his rule, Muhammad had laid the foundations for Muslim penetration of the subcontinent. He had established the legal framework and precedents that would allow Muslims to live at peace with Buddhists and Hindus. Compared with later Muslim invaders of the Indian subcontinent like Mahmūd of Ghazna in the early eleventh century, he left a reputation for mildness, humanity and tolerance, and the natives wept over his disgrace.[29] He had also made a vast amount of money. Hajjāj is reported to have made a simple balance sheet for the whole campaign. He reckoned he had spent 60 million dirhams on equipping and paying Muhammad's forces, but his share of the booty had amounted to 120 million, a tidy profit by anyone's standards.[30] As usual, the figures may well be exaggerated, but this is the only record we have of someone attempting such a clear calculation in the whole history of the early Muslim conquests. The sums make it clear that such expeditions could be a very useful way of generating revenue.

The Muslims were now in possession of most of the lower Indus valley. The area from Multān south to the mouth of the river was to be the limits of Muslim settlement on the Indian subcontinent. It was separated from the rest of India (Hind) by the deserts that now divide Pakistan from India to the east of the Indus. To the north of Multān, the Punjab was outside Muslim control until the early eleventh century, when the Ghaznevids from eastern Afghanistan extended Muslim rule further to the north and east.

There is an interesting footnote to the Arab conquest of Sind. As we have seen, some of the Zutt were already settled in Iraq before the coming of Islam. Many more seem to have arrived as a result of the Muslim involvement in their native lands in the Indus valley. Soon the Umayyad caliphs moved some of them to the hot plains around Antioch in northern Syria, along with their water buffalo. Some of those in northern Syria were later captured in a Byzantine raid on Ain Zarba and taken away with their women, children and their precious water buffalo. Gypsies under the Greek name of Atsinganoi appear in the neighbourhood of Constantinople in the eleventh century. The Zutt of Iraq remained as a restless element in the local population, but they disappear from history after the year 1000. In 1903 M. J. de Goeje, the great Dutch orientalist, published a monograph in which he suggested that these Zutt were the origin of at least some of the Gypsies of modern Europe.[31] The Gypsy language clearly originates from north-west India, and they may have emigrated from Syria through the Byzantine Empire to the Balkans, where they first appear in the fifteenth century. There is, however, no direct evidence for this, and the theory remains no more than an intriguing speculation.

SPAIN AND PORTUGAL

The conquest of Spain and Portugal, known in the Arabic texts as al-Andalus, a word whose origins remain quite unclear, was extremely swift. Substantial Muslim forces first crossed the Straits of Gibraltar in 711, and by 716 most of the peninsula had come under Muslim rule in one form or another. Events in the Iberian peninsula are hardly noted in the great chronicles that form the basis of our understanding of the formation of the Muslim state in the Middle East. The Andalusi-Arab historical tradition was slow to get going. There is some patchy material, notably the work of the Egyptian Ibn Abd al-Hakam, from the ninth century, but it was not until the tenth century, 200 years after the original conquest, that an attempt was made, by a Persian immigrant called Rāzī, to collect the traditions, memories and legends of the conquest and to arrange them in chronicle form. It is not surprising that the accounts are short of specific detail and replete with legend and confusion. The Arabic sources can be compared to, and to some extent checked against, a so-called *Chronicle of 754*, named after the year of the last entry. This short Latin work provides a skeleton outline narrative. It was probably composed in Cordoba, possibly by a Christian working as a functionary in the local Muslim administration. The account of the Muslim conquest is curiously matter-of-fact and is concerned almost entirely with secular matters. At no stage does it mention that the invaders were Muslims or that they were of a different religion from the people of Spain.

In the same year that Muhammad b. al-Qāsim was taking Daybul and pressing on up the Indus valley, the Berber commander of the

Muslim outpost at Tangier, Tāriq b. Ziyād, was making plans to lead his men across the Straits of Gibraltar to southern Spain. It is not surprising that he was looking in that direction – the Rock of Gibraltar[32] and the hills behind Tarifa are clearly visible from the African coast. The prospect of conquest and booty must have been very tempting, and there were many Berbers newly converted to Islam who would hope to benefit from their new status as conquerors rather than conquered.

Tāriq may have been aware that there had recently been a major political upheaval in the Visigothic kingdom of Hispania. The Visigoths had conquered the Iberian peninsula in the fifth century. From their capital at Toledo they had ruled one of the most successful of the Germanic kingdoms, which had taken over the lands of the western Roman Empire. Though the kingdom had been in existence for almost three centuries, there is no indication that it was feeble or decadent. It is true that the cities were small and comparatively undeveloped and that much of the countryside seems to have been very sparsely populated, but the monarchy was strong and successful and there was no tradition of internal rebellion or separatist movements. The church was well established and a long series of councils held in Toledo testified to the vitality of its organization and activities.

On the face of it, the idea that a small group of Berbers with a few Arab officers could attack and destroy this formidable state was most implausible. The kingdom was undergoing a short-term crisis, however. In 710 King Witiza had died. He had left adult sons, but for reasons that we do not fully understand the throne had been seized by Rodrigo, a noble who may or may not have been related to the royal house. The sons of Witiza, and their friends and allies, were powerful and resentful. Rodrigo had had no time to establish his authority before the Muslims invaded. Tāriq also had more immediate reasons for planning his invasion. The men he commanded were mostly Berbers who had joined the Muslim army in the previous few years. It is most unlikely that any regular system of payment had been introduced to reward them for their allegiance to the new faith. If he was to retain their loyalty, he needed to find a source of revenue quickly. Spain was the obvious area where this could be done.

In the earliest Arabic work to describe the conquest, the history of Ibn Abd al-Hakam,[33] considerable prominence is given to the story of

'Julian'. This mysterious figure is said to have been lord of Ceuta, a port city just to the east of Tangier which may still have been under Byzantine overlordship. According to the chronicler, 'Tàriq wrote to Julian, paying him compliments and exchanging presents. Now Julian had sent his daughter to Rodrigo [the Visigothic king of Spain], for her education and instruction, and Rodrigo had made her pregnant. When this news reached Julian, he said, "I do not see how I can punish him or pay him back except by sending the Arabs against him".' He then goes on to describe how Julian transported some of the men one evening and sent his ships back to the African coast to bring more the next. The people on the Spanish side did not pay them any attention because they were just like the merchant ships that were often going to and fro. Tàriq came in the last boat and the fleet remained at Algeciras while the Muslim army marched north, just in case anything went wrong and they had to be rescued. It is impossible to know whether there is any truth in the story or indeed whether 'Julian' ever existed. It does not come from the usual repertoire of Arabic conquest narratives, however, and it may reflect the reality of a widespread discontent with Rodrigo's kingship.

It was probably in April or May 711 that Tàriq embarked his small force in boats to take them across the straits. The force was unlikely to have been more than seven thousand men, of whom only a small minority were Arabs. The intention may have been simply to launch a large-scale plundering raid. Once across, the Muslims were able to take the 'Green Island', where the port of Algeciras stands today. This was to be a base but also allow them to retreat to the African coast if events turned out badly.

Rodrigo was campaigning against a Basque rebellion in the far north of his kingdom. When he heard of the Muslim raid, he hurried south, pausing at his residence at Cordova to gather more men. Like Harold of England and the Anglo-Saxons at the battle of Hastings in 1066, his army must have been exhausted by long marches to confront the invaders. Tàriq pursued a cautious policy. Rather than pushing on to attack Seville or the Guadalquivir valley, he kept close to his base and requested reinforcements from Africa; 5,000 more Berbers arrived, giving him a total of perhaps 12,000 men. He is also said to have been joined by some of the partisans of the sons of Witiza, opposed to the new king. The role of the Visigothic 'opposition' is controversial. From a modern Spanish point of view, it is easy to see that, if they did indeed aid the Muslim invasion, they were traitors. On the other hand, they, like most of their contemporaries, probably saw the Muslim invasion as no more than a raid, which would last a summer season at most. They could not have known that Muslims were to rule parts of the Iberian peninsula for the next 800 years.

The Muslim invaders may have enjoyed some support among the Jewish communities of the Iberian peninsula. This too is a very controversial issue with obvious contemporary resonances. The reality is that we have no hard evidence for this at all. We know that the Visigothic kings had introduced increasingly harsh anti-Jewish legislation, ending with the edict that they should all be converted to Christianity. It would be natural, therefore, for the Jews to welcome the Muslim invaders as potential liberators. There is no indication that this legislation was ever enforced, however, and there is absolutely no evidence that any Jews gave the Muslims active support.

The decisive battle was fought near the little town of Medina Sidonia. The exact site of the conflict is not known but it is generally believed to have been on the little river Guadalete.[34] Accounts of the battle are very sparse. The Latin Chronicle of 754 simply observes that 'Roderick [Rodrigo] headed for the Transductine mountains [location unknown] to fight them and in that battle the entire army of the Goths, which had come to him fraudulently and in rivalry out of ambition for the kingship, fled and he was killed. Thus Roderick wretchedly lost not only his rule but his homeland, his rivals also being killed'.[35] The Arabic sources say that the battle took place on 19 July 711 and, like the Chronicle of 754, suggest that divisions within the ranks of the Visigothic army allowed the Muslims to triumph when the partisans of Witiza's son Akhila turned and fled.[36]

The details will never be certain but the main point is clear: Tāriq and his men inflicted a massive defeat on the Visigothic army, the king was killed and the rest of the army dispersed in disarray.

Tāriq then led his men to the east along the Guadalquivir valley, heading for Cordova. At Ecija, where the Roman road crossed the River Genil, he encountered the first resistance and he took the city by storm. In the interests of speed, he then divided his forces.

Seven hundred men, all of them mounted, were sent to Cordova under the command of the *mawlā* Mughīth. The fall of Cordova, soon to be the capital of Andalus, is recorded with some circumstantial, and probably fictitious, details in the Arabic sources.[37] When Mughīth was approaching the city along the south bank of the Guadalquivir river, his men captured a shepherd who was looking after his flocks. They brought him to the camp and began to interrogate him. He said that the city had been deserted by all the leading citizens and only the governor (*bitrīq*) with 400 guards and some non-combatants (*duʿafa*) remained. On being questioned about the defences, he said that they were in good order except for a breach above the gate that led to the Roman bridge across the river. That night Mughīth led his men across the river and attempted to scale the walls with the aid of hooks, but it proved impossible. They returned to the shepherd, who guided them to the breach. One of the Muslims scaled the wall and Mughīth took off his turban and used it to pull others up. Soon there were a considerable number of Muslims on the wall. Then Mughīth came to the Gate of the Bridge, which was then in ruins, and ordered his men to surround the guards on the walls. Then they broke the locks and Mughīth and his men were soon inside.

When the governor (called *al-malik* in this account) heard that they had entered the city he fled with 400 of his men east to a church in which they fortified themselves. Mughīth laid siege to it. The resistance went on for three months until one day Mughīth was told that the governor had fled on his own, intending to establish a stronghold in the mountains behind the city. Mughīth set off in single-handed pursuit and caught up with him when his horse fell into a ditch and threw him. Mughīth found him sitting on his shield, waiting to be taken prisoner. 'He was', the chronicler goes on to explain, 'the only one of the kings of al-Andalus to be taken prisoner. All the others either made terms for themselves or escaped to distant regions like Galicia.' Mughīth then returned to the church. The defenders were all executed but the governor's life was saved so that he could be sent to the caliph in Damascus.

Tāriq himself headed for the capital, Toledo. This seems to have been largely abandoned by its inhabitants: according to the Chronicle of 754 the archbishop, Sindered, 'lost his nerve and like a hireling rather than a shepherd, and contrary to the precepts of the ancients, he deserted Christ's flock and headed for his Roman homeland'.[38] Ibn Abd al-Hakam's only contribution to the history of the taking of the

Visigothic capital is the story of the sealed room which, like the story of Julian, has been passed down in history and legend. According to this there was a room (presumably in Toledo) with many locks. Every king added another lock on accession and none opened the room. Rodrigo, on becoming king, insisted on opening the room. On the wall they found pictures of Arabs and there was an inscription which said that, when the room was opened, these people would conquer the country.[39]

Tāriq may have pushed on along the road that led to the Ebro valley, perhaps taking Guadalajara before returning to winter in Toledo. Meanwhile his superior, the governor of Ifrīqīya, Mūsā b. Nusayr, decided to join in what was looking like a very profitable venture. The next spring, of 712, he gathered an army of 18,000 on the coast opposite Gibraltar. This was a very different force from the one Tāriq had led the year before. The majority of them were Arabs. It included some *tābi'ūn* (followers, that is men who became Muslims in the generation after the Companions of the Prophet) and leaders of the main Arab tribes. In June 712 the army crossed to Algeciras. Rather than hasten to meet up with Tāriq in Toledo, Mūsā seems to have decided to consolidate the area of Muslim rule in the south. He began with some smaller towns, Medina Sidonia and Carmona, before turning his attention to Seville, one of the largest cities on the peninsula. Resistance does not seem to have been very prolonged and the Visigothic garrison evacuated the city and withdrew to the west.

Mūsā then went north along the Roman road to the city of Merida. Merida, now a medium-sized provincial town, had been one of the main capitals of Roman Spain and the impressive classical ruins still testify to its wealth and status. In early Christian times it had become the centre of the thriving cult of St Eulalia. Here the Muslims encountered much more serious resistance than they had in Seville or Toledo. It seems that Mūsā was obliged to lay siege to the town through the winter of 712–13 and that the city did not finally surrender until 30 June 713. Mūsā then set out to meet up with Tāriq, but before he did so he sent his son Abd al-Azīz back to Seville, where resistance had broken out. Mūsā advanced east along the Tagus to the Visigothic capital at Toledo, now held by Tāriq. Here he forced his subordinate to hand over the treasury and the riches he had confiscated from the churches. The Arab sources are, as often, very interested in the booty and its distribution. In this case, they report the rivalry between Tāriq and Mūsā. The focus of conflict was the 'Table of Solomon', kept in a castle outside Toledo. This was immensely valuable, made as it was of gold and jewels. It had been taken by Tāriq but Mūsā insisted that he should have it. Tāriq reluctantly agreed to hand it over but took off one of the legs and fixed an imitation in its place. Mūsā installed himself as a veritable sovereign in the ancient city while Tāriq retired to Cordova in high dudgeon.[40] As with the story of Julian, this clearly legendary material may point to wider political tensions, in this case the rivalry between Tāriq and his Berber followers and Mūsā and his largely Arab army.

The next spring (714) Mūsā set out again, heading for the Ebro valley. At some point during that year he took Zaragoza, where a garrison was established and a mosque founded. In the course of that summer, he also took Lerida and headed off up the Roman road that led to Barcelona and Narbonne.

The caliphs in Damascus were often very suspicious of successful conquerors, fearing, perhaps rightly, that they might escape from government control. The death of Walīd I in 715 meant that Mūsā b. Nusayr, like Muhammad b. Qāsim in Sind, was removed from office and brought back to Iraq to be punished. Both Mūsā and Tāriq were ordered to come to Damascus. Before they left, the two generals made an attempt to subdue the areas around the northern mountains. Tāriq took Leon and Astorga and then moved on over the Cantabrian mountains to Oviedo and Gijon. Many of the inhabitants abandoned the cities and fled to the mountains of the Picos de Europa.

Only then did the two conquerors decide to obey the caliph's orders. Mūsā appointed his son Abd al-Azīz as governor of al-Andalus; other sons were appointed to Sūs and Qayrawān. This had the makings of a dynastic state and in other circumstances, in late Merovingian France, for example, the Muslim west might have developed as an independent lordship ruled by the family of Mūsā b. Nusayr. In the early Islamic empire, the ties that linked the most distant provinces to the centre were too strong. Muhammad b. al-Qāsim in Sind and Mūsā b. Nusayr in al-Andalus both accepted their fate, obeyed their orders and returned to the central Islamic lands. In both cases the conquering heroes were humiliated, dispossessed of their gains and imprisoned. Mūsā died in 716–17, probably still in confinement. Of the fate of Tāriq we know nothing at all, but he must have died in the Middle East in complete obscurity.

The work of consolidating the conquest of al-Andalus was continued by Mūsā's son, Abd al-Azīz. It was probably during his tenure of office (714–16) that most of modern Portugal and Catalonia were brought under Muslim rule, but information about the nature and circumstances of this occupation is very scarce.

We are better informed about the conquest of the area around Murcia in south-east Spain. This was ruled by a Visigothic noble called Theodemir (Tudmīr). He negotiated a treaty with Abd al-Azīz, of which the text, dated April 713, is recorded in several Arabic sources.[41]

In the name of God, the Merciful, the Compassionate. This text was written by Abd al-Azīz b. Mūsā b. Nusayr for Tudmīr b. Ghabdush, establishing a treaty of peace and the promise and protection of God and His Prophet (may God bless him and grant him His peace). We [Abd al-Azīz] will not set any special conditions for him or for any among his men, nor harass him, nor remove him from power. His followers will not be killed or taken prisoner, nor will they be separated from their women and children. They will not be coerced in matters of religion, their churches will not be burned, nor will sacred objects be taken from the realm as long as Theodemir remains sincere and fulfils the following conditions we have set for him:

He has reached a settlement concerning seven towns: Orihuela, Valentilla, Alicante, Mula, Bigastro, Ello and Lorca.

He will not give shelter to fugitives, nor to our enemies, nor encourage any protected person to fear us, nor conceal news of our enemies.

He and each of his men shall also pay one dinar every year, together with four measures of wheat, four measures of barley, four liquid measures of concentrated fruit juice, four liquid measures of vinegar, four of honey and four of olive oil. Slaves much each pay half of this.

The treaty is a classic example of the sort of local agreements that were the reality of Arab 'conquest' in many areas of the caliphate. It is clear that rather than embark on a difficult and costly campaign, the Muslims preferred to make an agreement that would grant them security from hostile activities and some tribute. It is a pattern we can observe in many areas of Iran and Transoxania. It is interesting to note that much of this tribute was taken in kind (wheat, barley vinegar, oil, but of course no wine). In exchange for this, the local people were allowed almost complete autonomy. Theodemir was clearly expected to continue to rule his seven towns and the rural areas attached to them. There is no indication that any Muslim garrison was established, nor that any mosques were built. Theodemir and many of his followers may have imagined that the Muslim conquest would be fairly short lived and that it was worth paying up to preserve their possessions until such time as the Visigothic kingdom was restored. In fact it was to be five centuries before Christian powers re-established control over this area. We do not know how long the agreement was in force: Theodemir himself died, full of years and distinction, in 744. It is likely that it was never formally abolished but rather that as Muslim immigration and the conversion of local people to Islam increased in the late eighth and ninth centuries, its provisions became increasingly irrelevant.

The governorate of Abd al-Azīz was brought to an abrupt and unfortunate end. According to Ibn Abd al-Hakam,[42] he had married the daughter of Rodrigo, the last Visigothic king, who brought him vast wealth and an exalted idea of royal prestige. She was dismayed by the modest state he kept and the informality with which his Arab followers approached him, not prostrating themselves before him. According to the story, she persuaded him to have a low door constructed in his audience hall so that they all had to bow before him as they came in. The Arabs resented this strongly and some even alleged that she had converted him to Christianity. A murder plot was hatched and the governor put to the sword. Clearly the story belongs to the genre that contrasts the simple, even democratic nature of Arab government with the hierarchy and pomp of the empires and kingdoms it replaced. It may also reflect a tension between those Arabs who had married rich heiresses from among the local people and the rank and file of the invading army.

The new rulers of Spain began to make their mark on the administration almost immediately. We can see this most clearly in the case of the coinage. The arrival of Mūsā b. Nusayr was marked by the minting of a new gold coinage, based not on Visigothic but on North

African models. The earliest of these coins have the Latin legend '*In Nomine Domini non Deus nisi Deus Solus*', a direct translation of the Muslim formula 'There is no god but God', an unusual mingling of Muslim and Latin traditions. This was probably produced in mobile mints that accompanied the army to recycle booty, perhaps valuables taken from churches, into cash money which could be more easily divided among and spent by the military.

The Muslim conquerors of Spain were not settled in military towns: there was no Iberian equivalent of Fustāt or Qayrawān. It seems rather that there was a much more dispersed pattern of settlement, in some ways more similar to the ways in which the Germanic invaders of the western Roman Empire in the fifth century settled in Gaul and Hispania. It looks as if the Arabs, who must mostly have come from urban backgrounds in Fustāt or Qayrawān, chose to settle in the cities and villages of the Guadalquivir and Ebro valleys, around Cordoba, Seville and Zaragoza, while the Berbers, who came from more pastoral backgrounds, established themselves on the high plains of the Meseta in the centre and the southern mountains.

The conquest had been astonishingly successful. Within five years of the initial invasion, almost the whole of the Iberian peninsula had been brought under the control of the Muslim armies. There was, however, an important and, as it turned out, fatal exception to this rule. In the north of Spain, as in some areas of the Middle East, the 1,000-metre contour line represented the limit of the territory held by the Muslims. This meant that in the high southern valleys of the Pyrenees and the Picos de Europa further west in the Asturias, small groups of refugees and indigenous inhabitants gathered to protect their independence from Arab rule. In the Picos de Europa, the movement is said to have been led by one Pelayo, who may have been a Visigothic noble and member of Rodrigo's court. We know nothing about the history of this rebellion from the Arabic sources, but for the Christians of the Kingdom of the Asturias, the story of the rebellion was the foundation myth of their realm. As recounted in the Chronicle of Alfonso III,[43] probably composed soon after 900, Pelayo was about to be arrested by the Arabs but was warned by a friend and fled in the Picos de Europa. The landscape of the Picos is rugged, with steep gorges and rocky outcrops. Frequent rains mean that it is astonishingly green, with well-watered fields and forests and swift-flowing rivers. It was a very different landscape from the open plains of the Meseta to the south and a world away from the deserts of North Africa and Egypt. It had never been really part of Roman Spain, no big cities were established there and no Roman roads led through it.

Pelayo, according to the Chronicle, was able to escape when he came to the bank of a swiftly flowing river and swam across on his horse; his enemies were unable to follow. He fled into the mountains and established a headquarters at a cave which became the centre of resistance for people from all over the Asturias. The Arab governor was furious and sent an army of 187,000 men, a wholly fantastical figure, to put down the rebellion. They were led by an Arab commander, whom the source calls Alqama, and a mysterious bishop called Oppa, who is presented as a collaborator. The Muslims confronted Pelayo at a place called Covadonga, high in the mountains. The bishop addressed Pelayo and asked him how he thought he could withstand the Arabs (Ishmaelites) when they had defeated the entire Gothic army shortly before. Pelayo responded with a pious little homily, saying that 'Christ is our hope and through this little mountain which you see, the well-being of Spain and the army of the Gothic people will be restored'.

After the breakdown of negotiations, the Muslim army attacked. Huge numbers of them were slain and the rest fled. The battle of Covadonga, usually dated to 717, has acquired mythical status as the beginning of Christian resistance. The failure of the Muslim forces to suppress the revolt led immediately to the loss of control of northern settlements like Gijon and the foundation of a small, independent Christian kingdom. It was this kingdom, and similar small entities in the Pyrenean valleys and the Basque country, which was the foundation of the later Christian reconquest.

There were other areas of the early Muslim world where independent principalities coexisted with the Muslim authorities, moderately peacefully – in the mountains of northern Iran, for example. The Christian principalities of mountainous Armenia were in a position not entirely dissimilar from that of the Christians of northern Spain. None of these, however, seriously threatened Muslim rule in the areas to the south. When Daylamite mountaineers from northern Iran conquered much of Iran and Iraq in the tenth century, they did so as Muslims, and they soon lost their identity among the wider

Muslim populations. The Armenians maintained their independence but they never sought to make conquests beyond their traditional homelands. What distinguished the principalities of northern Spain was that they maintained, if only just, their Latin Christian high culture. At the same time they kept alive the memory of the Visigothic kingdom and the idea that the whole peninsula had once belonged to the Christians and should do so again. They also had access to and links with a much wider Christian polity to the north. These factors meant that, unlike the northern Iranian or Armenian principalities, the Christians of Spain came to be a serious long-term threat to Muslim control, until eventually, 800 years later, they finally drove them out.

The ambitions of the Arabs did not end with the Pyrenees. Muslim forces were soon raiding up the Rhône valley and through the fertile lands of Aquitaine. Unfortunately we have only the briefest accounts of these adventurous campaigns. The course of the raids is often quite unclear. The Arabic sources are frequently just one-line reports and we have brief notes in some Latin monastic chronicles. This first encounter between the peoples of north-west Europe and the Muslims is shrouded in obscurity. The first raids are said to have been directed by Tāriq b. Ziyād and to have reached Avignon and Lyon before being defeated by Charles Martel.[44] The Muslim raiding parties always went around the eastern end of the Pyrenees: Barcelona, Girona and Narbonne all came under their control, though Muslim rule in Narbonne was shortlived and ephemeral. Later Arabic sources allege that Mūsā b. Nusayr had conceived the massively daring and ambitious plan of marching his armies through the whole of Europe and the Byzantine Empire back to Syria.[45] Sometimes they must have felt that they were unstoppable.

They were not always successful. In the summer of 721 the governor* of Andalus led a raid into Aquitaine but the duke, Eudes, fortified himself in Toulouse. In a sharp conflict on 9 June, the Arabs were driven back and the governor himself killed. In 725 the Arabs launched the most ambitious raid so far. They began with the Roman and Visigothic fortress of Carcassonne, which they took by storm. They then moved east through the Midi. Nimes surrendered

---

* Samh b. Mālik al-Khawlānī.

peacefully, giving up hostages who were sent behind the lines to Barcelona. The governor* then led his men on a lightning raid up the Rhône valley, encountering little serious resistance. The army reached deep into the heart of Burgundy, taking Autun, which they pillaged thoroughly before returning to the south.

The climax of the Arab invasions of France came with the conflict generally known as the battle of Poitiers.[46] Since the late eighth century this battle has acquired a symbolic fame, marking the point when the Arab advance into western Europe was finally brought to an end by the Carolingian warlord Charles Martel. Within a couple of years Bede, in distant Northumbria, had heard of it and felt able to say with confidence that 'the Saracens who had devastated Gaul were punished for their perfidy'. Gibbon, in one of his more elegant flights of fantasy, allowed himself to speculate about what might have happened if the fortunes of battle had been different.[47]

> A victorious line of march had been prolonged above a thousand miles from the rock of Gibraltar to the banks of the Loire; the repetition of an equal space would have carried the Saracens to the confines of Poland and the Highlands of Scotland: the Rhine is not more impassable than the Nile or the Euphrates, and the Arabian fleet might have sailed without a naval combat into the mouth of the Thames. Perhaps the interpretation of the Koran would now be taught in the schools of Oxford, and her pulpits might demonstrate to a circumcised people the sanctity and truth of the revelation of Mahomet.

And he goes on to explain how Christendom was delivered from 'such calamities' by the genius and fortune of one man, Charles Martel.

In 1915 Edward Creasy, in an influential work of popular history, included it as one of his 'Fifteen Decisive Battles of the World'. In reality it does mark something of a watershed. Until this point the Muslim armies had raided far and wide in France, even if they had not made any permanent conquests. As the people of Central Asia were finding out at exactly this time, Arab raids could be the prelude to more lasting conquest. After this point, Arab military activity was largely confined to the area around Narbonne, and al-Andalus began

---

* Anbasa b. Sulaym al-Kalbī.

the transformation from a jihadist state to a more settled government. For Western military historians the battle of Poitiers has acquired a further significance. It has been argued that Charles Martel was successful because, for the first time, he used the heavily armoured mounted warriors, the knights, in a coordinated charge that destroyed the enemy. According to these theories, this marked the beginning of the dominance of the battlefield by the heavily armoured horsemen which became characteristic of western Europe in the Middle Ages. With the rise of the knight there came the emergence of feudalism as the characteristic form of fiscal and social control.

It is all the more frustrating therefore that our information on what actually happened is short and confused, and even the date of the conflict is uncertain, though the traditional date of Saturday, 25 October 732 is as likely to be as right as any other.[48] The earliest important account is given in the Christian Chronicle of 754. Writing no more than twenty years after the events, the chronicler seems to have been fairly well informed, probably by Muslim survivors of the expedition who had returned to Cordova. He describes how the governor, Abd al-Rahmān al-Ghāfiqī, first defeated a Muslim rebel, Munnuza, in the mountains of the eastern Pyrenees. Munnuza had sought support from Duke Eudes of Aquitaine and Abd al-Rahmān now went in pursuit of him. He caught up with the duke and defeated him on the banks of the Garonne.

Abd al-Rahmān then determined to continue the pursuit. He sacked Bordeaux and burned the famous church of St Hilary at Poitiers. He then decided to go on north along the Roman road to despoil the great church of St Martin at Tours on the Loire. While he was on the road from Poitiers to Tours he was confronted by Charles Martel, 'a man who had proved himself a warrior from his youth and an expert in things military, who had been summoned by Eudes'. The two armies probably met at a small town still known as Moussais la Bataille.

After each side had tormented the other for almost seven days with raids, they finally prepared their battle lines and fought fiercely. The northern peoples remained immobile like a wall, holding together like a glacier in the cold regions, and in the blink of an eye, annihilated the Arabs with the sword. The people of Austrasia [that is, the followers of Charles Martel], greater in number of soldiers and formidably armed, killed the king Abd al-Rahmān, when they found him, striking him on the chest. But suddenly, within sight of the countless tents of the Arabs, the Franks despicably put up their swords, saving themselves to fight the next day since night had fallen during the battle. Rising from their own camp at dawn, the Europeans saw the tents of the Arabs all arranged according to their canopies, just as the camp had been set up before. Not knowing that they were all empty and thinking that inside them were phalanxes of Saracens ready for battle, they sent scouts to reconnoitre and discovered that all the troops of the Ishmaelites had left. They had all fled silently by night in tight formation, returning to their own country. But the Europeans, worried lest the Saracens deceitfully attempt to ambush them in hidden paths were slow to react and searched in vain everywhere around. Having no intention of pursuing the Saracens, they took the spoils and the booty, which they divided up fairly, back to their country and were overjoyed.

The main Frankish source, the Continuator of Fredegar, is altogether briefer. 'Prince Charles', he recounts, 'boldly drew up his battle line against them [the Arabs]. With Christ's help he overturned their tents, and hastened to grind them small in slaughter. The King Abdirama having been killed, he destroyed them, driving forth the army he fought and he won.'[49]

The accounts are not nearly as detailed as we would like, but certain things do emerge clearly. The first is that this was no cavalry battle. The author of the Chronicle of 754, with his image of the glacier, suggests strongly that the Franks fought on foot as a sort of phalanx. He also makes it clear that they were very disciplined. The failure to follow up victory by pursuing the enemy that night is evidence not of cowardice but of the need for discipline and the dangers of chasing an enemy in the dark through unknown country. Most of the Arabs may have saved their lives, but they certainly abandoned their tents and much of their military equipment.

The defeat of the Muslims at Poitiers effectively marked the end of large-scale raiding in France. It became clear that they were not going to the able to conquer the country, or even to continue raiding with any degree of success. The military prowess of the Franks, like the 'northern glacier', was only one of the reasons for the end of expansion. The Muslims were probably short of manpower. The

North African conquests had been made possible because large numbers of Berbers had joined the Muslim armies; these same Berbers had formed a major contingent in the armies that invaded al-Andalus. There are no reliable reports of Franks or other inhabitants of France joining the invading armies. Perhaps they were too alien to allow easy cooperation, perhaps their presence was always too transitory to inspire confidence, but whatever the reason, the lack of local support left the Muslim armies very isolated and vulnerable.

The Muslim presence in al-Andalus was also changing. By 732 many of the original conquerors were ageing or dead. Administrative structures had been set up to collect taxes and, at least according to one Arabic source, the local Muslims 'lived like kings', a small minority in a rich land. They no longer needed the plunder from raids to maintain their lifestyles and perhaps they did not even desire the adrenalin rush that raiding must have created.

But perhaps the most important reason for the change was the great Berber rebellion in North Africa in 741. The brutalities of the slave trade had caused massive resentment throughout the Maghreb and the Berbers almost succeeded in driving the Arabs out altogether. Only the sending of a massive army from Syria restored Muslim control in the area. This great conflict meant that neither Berbers nor Arabs were able to spare manpower for extending the conquests further in the cold and unfriendly fields and forests of the north.

10

THE WAR AT SEA

⚓

In the summer of 626, the ancient world was in turmoil. The
Byzantine Empire seemed to be in its death throes. The nomad
Avars were besieging Constantinople from the west while Persian
troops looked greedily at the great city from Chalcedon, just across
the Bosporus. Within the walls the emperor Heraclius was directing
the defence, which saved the city, and may already have been planning
the great campaigns of 624–8 which were to take him and his army
far behind the Persian lines to strike at the heart of the Sasanian
Empire. Meanwhile, in distant Arabia, the Prophet Muhammad was
struggling to defend his base at Medina against the forces of Mecca,
and it is unlikely that anyone in the Byzantine or Persian military
knew anything of his new movement or his claims to be the prophet
of God.

In the same summer a small merchant ship was making its way up
the west coast of Asia Minor. As it passed through the narrow and
often stormy channel that nowadays separates the Greek islands of
Kos and Kalymnos from the Turkish mainland, it struck an underwater
reef by the little outcrop known as Yassi Adi ('Flat Island').[1] Whether
because the crew did not know of the reef or because the small boat
was trying to shelter from the fierce Meltemi winds, the ship sank in
30 metres of water. She must have gone down quickly because they
did not have time to remove the gold and copper coins they had put
in a locker for safe-keeping or the kitchen utensils from the galley.
Unless they were strong swimmers who could make the 50 metres to
the shore, they perished with their vessel.

The Yassi Adi wreck is of key importance in our understanding of
Mediterranean shipping at the end of antiquity. From 1961 to 1964 it
was the subject of a major underwater excavation which recovered a
vast amount of information about the ship and its cargo. It was not a

large boat, just under 21 metres long with a capacity of about 60 tons. It was a cargo ship, laden with some 900 large amphorae, which were probably filled with wine. The sailors intended to travel in some comfort, for there was an elaborate, tiled galley towards the stern, well equipped with cooking utensils and fine tableware.

It has been speculated that the ill-fated vessel belonged to a church and was being used to transport supplies to the Byzantine army, but the truth is that we do not know who was sailing it or why. The ship, dating as it does from the years immediately before the beginning of the Muslim conquests, tells us much about the coastal trade of the eastern Mediterranean in the last years of antiquity. The waters through which it sailed were stormy and dangerous, to be sure, but they were largely free from piracy and hostile attack, as they had been for the long centuries when the waters of the Mediterranean were the Byzantine 'Mare Nostrum'. Within two decades all that was to change and the peaceful waters of the Levant were to become the theatre for a fierce and destructive naval confrontation.[2]

There was a tradition of seafaring among the Arabs. In pre-Islamic times, Arabs did put to sea and the Koran (30: 46) tells the faithful that God sent the winds 'so that the ship may sail at His command and so that you many seek of His bounty', and that 'It is He who makes the ship sail on the sea so that you may seek of His bounty' (17: 66). These and other references make it clear that some Arabs at least were used to making trading voyages.[3] There was also a tradition of distrust of the sea among the early Muslims. The caliph Umar in particular is said to have been deeply suspicious of the sea, holding it to be a danger for the Muslims. This caution was short lived. One of the most astonishing aspects of the early Muslim conquests was the speed with which the Muslims, or more exactly fleets under Muslim command, were able to challenge the well-established naval power of the Byzantine Empire. In part this was forced on them by the need to defend the coasts of Syria and Egypt against raids by the Byzantine navy, which retained its capacity to mount seaborne assaults on the coastal towns throughout the first three Islamic centuries. If the Byzantines were allowed unchallenged command of the sea, no one along the coasts of Syria, Palestine or Egypt could be considered safe.

The Muslims soon began to see the possibility of using ships for offensive purposes as well. The island of Cyprus, lying as it does only

100 kilometres from the coast of Syria, was an obvious target.[4] In 649 the governor of Syria, Muʿāwiya, later to be the first Umayyad caliph, sent a naval expedition against the island. Interestingly the date of the invasion is confirmed by a Greek inscription commemorating the restoration of a basilica at Soli, which had been damaged by the raid, by Bishop John in 655.[5] This is an almost unique contemporary reference to destruction and rebuilding at the time of the first Muslim conquests.

According to the tradition preserved in the Muslim sources,[6] Umar had refused to allow Muʿāwiya to venture on the sea, but his successor, Uthmān, gave his permission with the curious provision that Muʿāwiya should take his wife with him, presumably to encourage him not to take unnecessary risks. He, and a number of other prominent Muslims, were duly accompanied by their women. After this first successful raid, the people of Cyprus were obliged to pay an annual tribute to the Muslims. They already paid a tribute to the Byzantines, so the island came under a sort of joint rule, both sides receiving some money but neither maintaining a permanent garrison. In 654 Muʿāwiya invaded again because, the Muslims claimed, the Cypriots had offered ships to help the Byzantines against them, so breaking the terms of the treaty. The Muslim fleet is said to have consisted of 500 ships and carried a force of 12,000 regular soldiers (that is, men whose names were entered in the dīwān). At that time Muʿāwiya is reported to have erected mosques and built a new city on the island in which he settled men from Baʿalbak as a garrison and gave them salaries. This Muslim outpost lasted until Muʿāwiya's son Yazīd withdrew the men and demolished the city, presumably because he did not consider that it was worth the expense of paying the garrison.

Throughout the late seventh, eighth and ninth centuries, Cyprus enjoyed a unique position between the Muslim and Christian worlds. It was not always easy. The Muslim jurists were unhappy about a treaty that seemed not to conform to Islamic law in many ways. From a military point of view, too, there was always suspicion that the Cypriots were aiding the Byzantines. The Umayyad caliph Walīd II deported many of the Cypriots to Syria because he suspected them of aiding the Byzantines, but they were allowed to return by his successor Yazīd III. Problems continued under the Abbasids, and in 806, during the reign of Hārūn al-Rashīd, the people of the island are said to have caused disturbances and an expedition was launched to bring them into line; 16,000 prisoners are said to have been taken to Raqqa, Hārūn's base in northern Syria, where they were ransomed or sold as slaves – one Cypriot bishop fetched 2,000 dinars.[7] Despite these setbacks, Greek Christian culture survived in Cyprus when it had effectively disappeared from the nearby mainland. In the second Council of Nicaea (in the Byzantine Empire) held in 787, the bishops of the churches under Muslim rule were unable to attend, but no less than five bishops came from Cyprus, showing that contacts with the Byzantine world were still close.

The first raid on Cyprus was followed by other attacks on Mediterranean islands, Rhodes and Kos being pillaged, probably in 654.[8] Up to this point the Muslims had not directly engaged the Byzantine navy, which still commanded the seas of the eastern Mediterranean. The first real naval engagement between the Muslims and the Byzantines was the so-called Battle of the Masts (*Dhāt al-sawārī*) or battle of Phoenix off the Lycian coast in 655.[9] Descriptions in Ibn Abd al-Hakam, the Greek Chronicle of Theophanes and the later Arabic chronicle of Ibn al-Athīr[10] mean that we have more information about this encounter than any other naval engagement of the period. According to the Arabic sources, the campaign began when Emperor Constans II (641–68) assembled a naval expedition to oppose the Muslim conquest of North Africa. He set out with a fleet of 500 or 600 ships, 'and more men than the Byzantines had ever collected since the coming of Islam'. Muʿāwiya sent Ibn Abī Sarh, governor of Egypt, who was also 'in charge of the sea'* to intercept them. The two navies met off the Lycian coast. The wind was against the Muslims when they first saw the Byzantines, but then it dropped and the two fleets anchored. The two sides agreed to a truce for the night; the Muslims read the Koran and prayed and the Byzantines rang their bells (*nawāqīs*). The next morning the two fleets closed together and the Muslims grappled with the Byzantines. The fighting was with swords and daggers and many men on both sides were killed. In the end God favoured the Muslims, the emperor was wounded and fled the scene and only a few Byzantines escaped with their lives. Ibn Abī Sarh remained at the site for a few days and then returned to Syria.

* *ʿalā al-baḥr.*

The longest account of the battle we have is given by Ibn Abd al-Hakam, who used sources from Egypt, presumably collected there because many of the men in the Arab fleet came from Egypt and returned there. The account is largely formulaic, however, and a disappointingly large amount of space is given to discussion of who married whose daughter after the event and other matters of little use to the naval historian. According to what can be gleaned from this account, the sea battle was part of a combined operation and half the ships' crews (*shihna*) were on land at the time. The Byzantines had 1,000 ships compared with the Muslims' 200. The commander, Ibn Abī Sarh, held a council of war at which one of the speakers said in an encouraging way that a small group could win over a much larger one if God supported them. With Muslim morale thus bolstered, the two fleets approached each other and the fighting began with bows and arrows (*nabl wa nushāb*). The emperor[11] sent messages to find out how the fighting was going. When he heard that they were fighting with bows and arrows, he said that the Byzantines would win; when he next heard that they were hurling stones, he again said that the Byzantines were winning; but when he heard that the boats had been tied together and the men were fighting with swords, he predicted that the Arabs would be victorious.

Theophanes' Greek account gives a somewhat different background. According to him, Muʿāwiya was preparing a fleet for an attack on Constantinople. While the fleet was being prepared in Tripoli (Lebanon) two 'Christ-loving brothers, the sons of Bucinator [the Trumpeter]', broke into the prison in Tripoli and released a large number of Byzantine captives there. They then sacked the town and killed the governor, before escaping to Byzantine territory. Muʿāwiya, however, was not deterred and the fleet, commanded by one Abū'l-Awar, duly set out. The emperor Constans joined battle at Phoenix in Lycia woefully ill prepared. The sea was soon full of Byzantine blood and the emperor threw off his imperial robes to make his escape undetected. He was saved only by one of the sons of Bucinator, who rescued him from the water and was killed in his place.

All accounts agree that the Battle of the Masts was a major victory for the Muslims and marked the end of unchallenged Byzantine naval supremacy in the eastern Mediterranean. It is unfortunate that we do

not have a clearer picture of what happened. The most recent historian
of the battle has a very low opinion of both sides:

> The most rudimentary rules of naval warfare were grossly neglected
> by both parties, partly because of the Byzantines' underestimation of
> their enemy. The two fleets faced each other the whole night before
> their engagement without any plan. No projectiles were thrown
> between each other, either with arrows or stones launched from special
> machines. No ram was used by any ships of either party. Since boarding
> practice required great skill, the Arabs found an easier solution; they
> managed to tie the ships to those of the enemy and thus they changed
> naval warfare into land warfare ... None of the parties took into
> consideration the wind.[12]

The sources are really too thin to know whether this castigation is
justified. It is clear, however, that the Muslim navy remained generally
inferior to the Byzantine forces. This was especially apparent during
the attack on Constantinople, which began in 674.[13] The Muslims
understood from the beginning that it was impossible to take the city
without first dominating the waters around it. A large Arab fleet,
commanded by the caliph Muʿāwiya's son and eventual successor
Yazīd, entered the Sea of Marmara. For four years it blockaded the
city all summer and then retired to Cyzicus, on the south side of the
sea, for the winter. Despite this relentless pressure, the defence held
firm. The Byzantines were helped by the deployment, apparently for
the first time, of the celebrated 'Greek fire', invented by one Cal-
linicus, a refugee from Arab-held Baʿalbak in Syria. Greek fire was a
combination of crude oil and other substances to make it adhere to
wood. It was lit and propelled from a siphon at enemy ships. Given
that the Byzantines received the formula from a native of Baʿalbak,
however, it is certainly not impossible that the technology originated
in the Middle East. There is indeed some evidence (see poem below)
that the Muslims had the fire during this first siege of the city.

The victory was celebrated in a contemporary Greek poem written
by one Theodosius Grammaticus. Most of the poem is a conventional
praise of God for granting the Christians this victory, but there are
some lines that seem to shed light on a contemporary reality.

For behold just as you, Lord of All, saved your city from the crashing waves of the filthy and most evil Arabs, you stole away fear of them and the trembling and their returning shadows ...

Where now, O cursed ones are your shining bright ranks of arrows? Where now the melodious chords of the bow strings? Where is the glitter of your swords and spears, your breast plates and head-borne helmets, scimitars and darkened shields?

Where are the twin decked, fire throwing ships, and again, the single decked ships, also swift in the battle step?

What do you say, miserable and voracious Ishmael? Christ was mighty in the work of salvation and He rules as God and Lord. He gives strength and supports the battle. He shatters the bow and grinds down human power ... Therefore, Ocean, you who displayed the murderers broken to pieces, applaud the Lord! And Earth who has shown forth and applauded the God of all, raise a chorus of hymns to whom honour and glory and power are proper through the unceasing aeons of aeons and long years.[14]

The Muslim navy was finally defeated and dispersed in 678 and the land army forced to withdraw. On the way back to Syria, much of the Arab fleet was destroyed in a storm off the Pamphylian coast. The success of the Byzantine navy had, in the end, saved Constantinople.

The second major naval expedition against Constantinople took place in the years 716–18. Once again the Greek chronicler Theophanes is our main witness since the Arabic sources are very brief. According to the Greek monk, the conflict began with a struggle over the timber resources so vital to shipbuilding. The Byzantines became aware that the Arabs of Egypt were going on an expedition to Lebanon to collect timber. The emperor Artemios decided to intercept them and collected swift sailing ships to do so. The Byzantine fleet assembled at Rhodes under the command of a deacon of the great church of Hagia Sofia called John, who was also minister of finance. Their orders were to raid Lebanon and burn the timber. The expedition did not work out as planned. As so often in the Byzantine Empire in this period, there was a mutiny, the imperial commander was murdered and the troops set out for the capital to overthrow Artemios, leaving the Arabs free to carry on their shipbuilding.

In 716 a massive land army commanded by Maslama b. Abd al-Malik set out to march to Constantinople. At the same time a fleet was collected. Its main function seems to have been to support and supply the land army with which Maslama was attacking the city. The winter of 716–17 was spent on the Cilician coast. In the spring the ships sailed west, then north. They anchored at Abydos on the Hellespont before entering the Sea of Marmara. On 15 August Maslama began to lay siege to the city and on 1 September a huge fleet, said to have comprised 1,800 ships, dropped anchor below the walls of the city, some by the suburbs on the Asian side of the Bosporus, others on the European coast north of the Golden Horn. Theophanes says that the Arab ships were useless because they were weighed down by their cargo. The weather was fine and they pushed on up the Bosporus. This was a big mistake. The emperor Leo III, observing and directing operations from the Acropolis, sent fire ships among Arab vessels, which turned them into blazing wrecks: 'Some of them still burning smashed into the sea wall, while others sank in the deep, men and all and others still, flaming furiously, went as far as the islands of Oxeia and Plateia [the modern Princes' Islands in the Sea of Marmara].' The citizens were greatly cheered by this while the attackers shivered in terror, 'recognising how strong the liquid fire was'. Some Arab ships survived the conflagration and the emperor tried to lure them into the Golden Horn by lowering the chain that stretched across between the city and Galata. The Arab commanders feared that if they went in, the chain would be raised and they would be completely trapped. Instead they went on up the Bosporus, where they wintered in a bay on the European coast where the great Ottoman fortress of Rumeli Hissar now stands.

The winter was very hard. Snow lay on the ground for a hundred days, and the Muslim forces on land suffered terribly from hunger and cold. The next spring reinforcements arrived, 400 food-carrying merchantmen from Egypt commanded by Sufyān, followed by 260 merchantmen from North Africa with both arms and supplies. Both commanders had now heard of the dangers of Greek fire and, rather than approaching close to the city walls, they kept their ships well hidden out of harm's way on the Asiatic shore of the Sea of Marmara.

Many of the sailors in both the Muslim fleets were Coptic

Christians from Egypt and at least some of them decided that their real loyalties lay with their fellow Christians in the Byzantine Empire. One night they took the light boats from the merchant ships and went to the city, proclaiming their allegiance to the emperor. They told the emperor about the fleets hidden along the southern shores of the sea and he prepared the fire-carrying siphons and put them on board warships and 'two-storeyed ships'. 'Thanks to the help of God,' wrote the pious chronicler, 'through His wholly immaculate Mother's intercession, the enemy was sunk on the spot. The goods and supplies from the Arab fleets were seized.'

The end came on 15 August 718 when a message arrived from the pious Caliph Umar II, who was always cautious about ambitious military expeditions, ordering Maslama to retire. Once more divine intervention came to the aid of the Byzantines:

> while their expedition was on the way back, a furious storm fell on them: it came from God at the intercession of His Mother. God drowned some of them by Prokonessos [an island in the Sea of Marmara famous in antiquity for its marble quarries] and others on Apostrophoi and other promontories. Those who were left had got through the Aegean Sea when God's fearful wrath attacked them; a fiery shower descended on them, making the sea's water foam up [this may have been connected with the earthquake in Syria at this time]. Once their caulking pitch was gone, the ships went to the bottom, men and all. Only ten survived to tell us and the Arabs the magnitude of what God had done to them.[16]

The failure of Muslim sea power before the walls and navies of Constantinople marked a major change in the balance of power between the Arabs and the Byzantines. It was the last time Muslim ships were to reach the Sea of Marmara before the late eleventh century. Sea power saved Constantinople and prevented the Muslims from achieving this ultimate triumph.

The other area of naval activity during the early Muslim conquests was the North African coast and Sicily. The first Muslim naval expedition to Sicily had been launched in 652, long before North Africa had been effectively conquered. A Muslim force of 200 ships plundered the coasts of the island for a month, taking booty from churches and monasteries before returning to Syria.[17]

With the foundation of Tunis, the Arabs began to develop a naval base in North Africa. The foundation of the city was probably begun by the governor Hassān in about 700 in the immediate aftermath of the fall of Carthage. The reason for choosing the new site, rather than simply using the Byzantine harbour of Carthage, is not clear. It may be that the earlier harbour had silted up or was becoming unusable for other reasons, but it is most likely that the attraction of Tunis was that it was not on the open sea, vulnerable to Byzantine naval attacks, but on a lagoon that was then connected to the sea by a short canal. This made it much easier to fortify. The city throve as the main naval base in Africa, though the centre of government remained at inland Qayrawān.

It was shortly after this that the Muslims made their first conquests in the Mediterranean islands with the taking of Pantelleria, probably in 700. A few years later, probably in 703, a large Egyptian fleet under the command of Atā b. Rāfi arrived in North Africa.[18] It was already autumn and storms were to be expected. The governor, Mūsā b. Nusayr, warned against undertaking a campaign that year but Atā had his eye on the potential booty that the islands could offer and was not prepared to wait. They decided to raid Sardinia. All went well until the return journey. When they had almost reached their home port of Tunis, a sudden storm struck and most of the fleet was wrecked. On the nearby shore the governor's son Abd al-Azīz collected the corpses of the drowned and the remains of their ships and cargoes. The surviving ships and their crews took shelter in Tunis where Mūsā looked after them. Perhaps as a result of the charity he showed these men, they were to form the basis of the naval force with which Mūsā invaded Spain nine years later.

This maritime disaster has left an interesting echo in the Egyptian papyri. Among a number of letters from the Arab governor to the pagarch (local landowner and official) of Aphrodito in Upper Egypt is one in which the governor enquired what had happened to the sailors, probably all Copts, from the town who had joined the fleet. With a fairly heavy-handed bureaucratic inquisitiveness, he wants to know how many have returned home and how many have stayed in the Maghreb.[19] He also wants more details of those who have not returned, of who has died and why some have remained in Africa. We have only the governor's letter, not the pagarch's reply, but the papyrus letter shows two points very clearly: how closely the fleet was supervised by the governor and how even Aphrodito, some 500 kilometres from the sea, was obliged to send men for the expedition.

After the foundation of the arsenal at Tunis, the fleet of North Africa was essentially independent of the Muslim fleets in the eastern Mediterranean and was under the command of the local governor. It was essentially a band of corsairs, independent sailors operating in effect as pirates, raiding the islands and vulnerable coastlines of the central Mediterranean for booty and slaves. As we have seen, the North African fleet could provide 360 armed ships to aid the Muslims in the attack on Constantinople in 718. Sometimes the corsairs encountered naval opposition. In 733 they were caught off Sicily by a Byzantine flotilla which used Greek fire to burn many of the Arab ships[20] and the next year another group encountered Byzantine ships and lost its stock of prisoners. In 740 a much larger-scale campaign was undertaken. This time the objective was the capital of Byzantine Sicily at Syracuse, and the Arabs brought horses with them on campaign. This might have marked the real beginning of the Arab conquest of Sicily, except that the next year, 741, saw the massive Berber revolt in North Africa against Arab tax gatherers and slavers. The Arabs were temporarily driven out of much of North Africa and were certainly in no position to launch any offensive raids.

NAVAL ORGANIZATION

Fleets are difficult and expensive to maintain and they require dedicated resources devoted to them for maintenance and upkeep of ships, even when they are not making any money. At a pinch a land army of volunteers could be assembled quite cheaply. The men would serve in the expectation of booty and they would provide their own equipment and pay for their own food. It is true that by the eighth century regular soldiers were being paid salaries, but when it came to the *jihād* against the unbelievers many of the troops were still volunteers.

Naval warfare was very different. Ships need to be built well in advance of a campaign. Even if some already exist they need to be fitted out and refurbished. Fighting men might serve as volunteers in the hope of booty but skilled sailors and oarsmen needed either compulsion or payment to induce them to serve. This means that naval organization left traces, even in the very patchy administrative records that we have from early Islamic times.

Naval organization was centred on arsenals. The English word, which comes from the Italian, is ultimately derived from the Arabic *Dar al-Sināʿa* or House of Manufacturing. It is a term that was already in use in the ninth century, if not before, to describe the naval bases used by the Muslim fleets. The first naval bases were in Syria and Egypt. The earliest one in Syria seems to have been at Acre, but it was moved to Tyre by the caliph Hishām (723–41) because the local landowner in Acre refused to sell the required property to the caliph: no question of compulsory purchase here. In Tyre he built a hotel (*funduq*) presumably to house the workers, and a granary[21] (*mustaghal*). At about this time the Anglo-Saxon St Willibald visited Tyre twice in the course of the pilgrimage to the Holy Land in 724–6, and it was from Tyre that he took ship on his way home. He recorded with glee how he was able to take some of the precious and holy balsam of Jericho through the Arab customs by disguising it in a flagon of mineral oil. He also noted that the port was in a security zone and anyone visiting without permission would be arrested.[22] We have several descriptions of Tyre from Arab geographers in the ninth and tenth centuries. One geographer describes it as 'the chief of the coastal cities, housing the arsenal. From here the government ships sail on expeditions against the Greeks. It is beautiful and well-fortified'.[23] Another writes: 'Tyre is a fortified city on the sea and one enters through one gate only, over a bridge, and the sea lies all around, the rest of it is enclosed by three walls which rise straight out of the sea. The ships enter every night and then a chain is drawn across ... there are workmen there, each with his own speciality.'[24]

In 861 the caliph Mutawwakil moved the naval base back to Acre and later, probably in the 870s, the semi-independent governor of Egypt, Ibn Tūlūn, undertook major improvement to the harbour and its defences. We have a description of the work from the Arab geographer Muqaddasī which provides the fullest account we have of the construction of an early Muslim port.[25] He recounts with considerable pride his grandfather's contribution to the work:

Acre is a fortified city on the sea-coast ... the defences of which were greatly strengthened after Ibn Ṭūlūn visited it. He had already seen the fortifications of Tyre where the harbour was protected by an encircling wall and he wanted to fortify Acre on similar lines. Engineers [sunāᶜ] were brought from all over the province but when the plan was described to them they all responded that no one could lay foundations under water. Then someone mentioned my grandfather Abu Bakr the architect [binā'] and said that if it were possible to do such a thing, he was the man who could undertake it. So Ibn Ṭūlūn ordered his governor of Jerusalem to send my grandfather to him. When he arrived they asked his opinion 'No problem,' he replied. 'Bring big strong sycamore beams!' They were floated on the surface of the water as you would for a castle built on the land and tied together. A big gate was left on the west [sea] side. He then raised a structure of stone and cement [shayyid] on them strengthening it by inserting great columns every five courses [dawāmis]. The beams began to sink under the weight. As soon as they rested on the sandy bottom of the harbour, he stopped building for a year to allow the structure to settle. Finally he connected these defences to the old walls of the city and built a bridge across the entrance to the port. Whenever there were ships in the harbour, a chain was stretched across the entrance as at Tyre. Before this was done, the enemy [the Byzantines] used to do serious damage to the ships collected there. My grandfather is said to have been given one thousand dinars besides robes of honour, horses and other gifts as his reward and his name was inscribed over the work.

Nothing of the work survives above water now but we can imagine it quite clearly. The reuse of classical columns, laid horizontally through the fabric to strengthen it, is very typical of Crusader architecture on the Levantine coast and it is interesting to see it in use at this early date.

In about 780 another naval base was established at Tarsus in Cilicia. Tarsus had been an important Byzantine city and the original home of St Paul. It seems to have been ruined and deserted in the immediate aftermath of the Muslim conquests when it was in the no man's land between Byzantine and Arab territory. The caliph Hārūn al-Rashīd ordered that it should be fortified and it became a centre for volunteers from all over the Muslim world who came to join in the *jihād* against the Byzantines. The ships were probably moored in the estuary of the river which connected Tarsus to the sea, and there is no record of any built harbour. In 900 the then caliph ordered that all the ships should be burned, apparently because he was told that the inhabitants were of doubtful loyalty. 'About fifty ships, on which large sums of money had been spent and which could never be replaced at that time, were destroyed. The loss endangered the Muslims, lessened their power and increased that of the Greeks who were now safe from attack by sea.'[26] Despite this pessimistic assessment, Tarsus soon recovered its role because in 904 the Muslim ships raided along the Mediterranean coast of Anatolia to Antalya. The city was taken by force, about five thousand prisoners were taken and four thousand Muslim prisoners of war released. Sixty Byzantine ships were taken and loaded with booty, including gold, silver, goods and slaves. Every Muslim who took part in this raid received about a thousand dinars. The Muslims rejoiced at the news.[27] At a time when the Byzantine army was increasingly effective against Muslim overland raids, this sort of booty must have made naval warfare look very attractive.

Naval bases were established in Egypt very soon after the Muslim conquest and, as we have already seen, Coptic sailors were in action in the Sea of Marmara and in North Africa at the beginning of the eighth century. As on the Syrian coast, the naval bases in Egypt were developed in Byzantine ports. The most famous of these was of course Alexandria. This certainly remained a port in the years after the Muslim conquest. The pilgrim Arculf arrived there after a voyage of forty days from Jaffa in Palestine. He found a city so large that it took a day to walk across, surrounded by walls and towers. He also describes the ancient lighthouse, the Pharos, as still being in operation.[28] Unfortunately Arabic sources tell us almost nothing about the city and its port. We know that an Arab garrison was maintained there but there is no mention of naval forces.[29] The other important base on the Mediterranean coast was Faramā. But again the sources have little to say about it. There were also bases at Rosetta and Damietta. A letter written on papyrus and dated to 710 contains orders for supplies to be sent to Damietta 'for the raiding fleet', but our fullest information about the city comes from an account of a Byzantine raid in the early summer of 853. It was the time of the feast that marked the end of

Ramadan and the governor of Egypt had incautiously ordered the local garrison to go to the capital at Fustāt to join the celebrations. While they were gone a Byzantine fleet of a hundred *shalandiya* vessels, each carrying between fifty and a hundred men, attacked. They burned the Friday mosque and the churches. They took furnishings, candy (*qand*) and flax, which were waiting to be transported to Iraq. They also found military and naval equipment, 1,000 lances on their way to the Arab forces fighting in Crete, and they burned the storehouse containing ships' sails. Some six hundred women, both Muslim and Copt, were taken captive and many more women and children drowned as they tried to escape across the shallow lake. The marauders then moved on towards the island city of Tinnis but found the lake was too shallow for their heavily laden ships. They had to content themselves with sacking the little town of Ushtum, which had recently been fortified with a wall and iron gates on the caliph's orders. Here they found and burned an arsenal of siege engines, both *manjanīq* and *arrādat*. Then, unmolested by any Muslim forces on land or sea, they returned home. We hear of fortified towns and military and naval equipment but there do not seem to have been any Muslim ships in the area to defend it.

The island of Roda in the Nile at Fustāt was a major centre of shipbuilding and in the early Arab sources the island is simply called 'Jazirat al-Sinaᶜa' or the Island of the Arsenal. This seems to have been established after a Byzantine raid on the Egyptian coastal town of Burullus in 673, presumably because the site, well upriver from the coast, would allow ships to be built and repaired safe from any raider. Papyrus documents of 709 shows the governor demanding that carpenters and other tradesmen be sent to the superintendent of the arsenal at Fustāt to help in the construction of ships.[30]

Further indications of what went on in an early Muslim arsenal can be found in a form letter of appointment from the caliph (unnamed) to the (also unnamed) governor of a frontier area, recorded in a tenth-century source.[31] Like most such documents, much of it is taken up with general exhortations and common sense. It begins with a whole series of pious commands to obey God, favour good people over bad and so on, but it does give some orders directly connected with ports and ships. The governor is urged to spend money to keep the ships and their equipment in good order and to bring the ships up out of the water in the winter. He should send out spies and keep himself well informed. He should not allow any Greek fire experts (*naffātīn*), sailors, throwers of projectiles (*qadhdhāfīn*) or any other tradesmen into the ships unless they are properly qualified and capable of working well. Only the best troops were to be employed. He is to inspect the shipbuilding yards and make sure that there are adequate supplies of wood, iron, flax, pitch (*zift*) and other things so that the ships are properly built and well caulked and supplied with oars and sails (*qulūᶜ*). Reliable and experienced sailors are to be selected. Merchants are to be watched in case they are spies. He should also keep an eye on the harbours to make sure that no ships go in or out without his know-ledge. Everything in the dockyards should be kept clean and well maintained, ready for action. He should check that there are adequate supplies of oil (*naft*), balsam and ropes, all in good order.

There is nothing in this that any sailor could disagree with. No doubt Muslim arsenals, like military installations everywhere, often fell below the highest standards, but the administration clearly had a good idea about what was required and was prepared, at least in principle, to spend money on it.

WARSHIPS[32]

Both the Arabs and their Byzantine opponents drew on a common legacy of ship design. The great triremes and quinquiremes of the Hellenistic and early Roman period had long since disappeared from the waters of the Mediterranean to be replaced by small, lighter galleys. No wrecks of warships from this period have been identified so we are dependent on scanty references in literary sources and a small number of inadequate drawings and graffiti to reconstruct what the warships of the period may have looked like. A great deal remains uncertain. The nature of the source material, both textual and in visual representations, means that we know slightly more about Byzantine ships in the early Middle Ages than about Arab ones, but there is little evidence that the warships used by each side differed in any significant way.

The standard Byzantine warship of the period was called the *dromon* or *chelandion* and the Arabs adopted the same types, calling them *shīnī* or *shalandi*. Merchant ships in this period relied exclusively on wind power but warships were propelled by oars, using sails only when cruising in suitable weather or as a supplementary power source. Oars were essential to provide speed and manoeuvrability during combat. It has been estimated that an average *dromon* would have been about 30 metres in length and, given a 1:8 ratio of beam to length, a breadth of between 3 and 4 metres. Muslim ships were probably similar. The largest *dromon* crew known from Byzantine sources was 230 oarsman and 70 marines on one ship, but most probably carried between one and two hundred men.

The early Middle Ages saw a number of important changes in the way in which warships were designed and built.[33] The first was the change in hull construction. In the ancient world, hulls had been built using planks laid edge to edge and held together by pegged mortise-and-tenon joints. As reconstructed from the preserved wood, the Yassa Adi ship of 626 was built in the modern way, using a frame of ribs to which the planks are then attached; it made for a lighter, more economical but less robust style of vessel. We do not know whether the navies took advantage of the new techniques of hull construction that we find in the Yassa Adi ship, but they probably did, because these were cheaper and lighter. The second was the change from underwater rams to above-water spurs at the bows of the ships. Classical ships had used underwater rams as an important weapon in naval warfare, but these had been phased out by late antiquity and the lighter hull constructions would have been strained by a direct impact.[34] The third innovation was a change in the shape and rigging of sails. Late Roman ships had used square sails rigged across the beam of the ship, but at some unknown time in the early Middle Ages these came to be replaced by triangular lateen sails, which made tacking close to the wind easier. Arab ships seem to have used lateen sails from the start. Another characteristic development of the period was the use of wooden, deck-top 'castles' to give a height advantage to the marines when fighting at close quarters. In late antiquity ships had been steered with two large oars at the stern, and this seems to have continued until the tenth or eleventh century, when such steering oars were replaced by a single stern rudder.

In many ways naval warfare was little more than land warfare fought on ships. Byzantine treatises on naval warfare do suggest arranging the fleet in crescent formations with the commander and the strongest ships in the centre. One of them also suggests that if battle is joined off the enemy coast, it is better to be near the shore so that their sailors will be tempted to abandon ship and swim for it! Beyond these there seem to have been few guides for the tactical deployment of ships. Battle was usually begun with the throwing of projectiles, arrows, stones and inflammable materials. In addition to siphons for the Greek fire, usually mounted in the bows, ships would carry catapults for propelling stones and pots of Greek fire. One of the more fanciful ideas was to hurl containers of scorpions or vipers on to the decks of enemy ships, an idea that may seem more attractive in theory than it does in the practical circumstances of fighting from ship to ship.[35] The main weapons were bows and cross-bows and in the end naval battles, like the Battle of the Masts, were probably decided by hand-to-hand fighting between soldiers, much as on land.

The crews were made up of two elements, the oarsmen and sailors on one hand and the soldiers or marines on the other. The evidence suggests that in Byzantine ships the two groups were not entirely separate and that sailors could also become fighters if required. In early Muslim navies, by contrast, there seems to have been a fairly strict distinction between the soldiers, who were Arab Muslims, and the seamen, who were Coptic or Syrian Christians. Such distinctions must have become irrelevant by the ninth and tenth centuries, especially in corsair ships.

THE EVIDENCE OF THE EGYPTIAN PAPYRI

The administrative papyri from seventh- and eighth-century Egypt give us a unique insight into the recruitment of sailors and the supplying of the fleet. The most important of these is the series of letters from Qurra b. Sharīk, the Arab governor of Egypt from 709 to 714, to the administrator of the small upper Egyptian town of Aphrodito, now Kūm Ishqaw, one of which has already been quoted in the discussion of the 703 raid on Sardinia. The documents are in Greek, Coptic and Arabic, but the most important from our point of view are the Greek ones, for Greek was still the main administrative language in provincial Egypt, even though the central government in Fustāt operated in Arabic.

Aphrodito is a long way from the sea, and while the local people may have had experience of river boats on the Nile, it is hard to imagine that many of them had any direct experience of sailing on the high seas. In spite of this, they were still expected to contribute to the Egyptian fleet. Each area was expected to supply a certain number of sailors. We are told that these might be recruited from bath-keepers, fullers or shepherds, that is men engaged in fairly low-status manual jobs, and each village was supposed to have a register of eligible men. The local landowners were obliged to produce these men and provide sureties so that if they did not appear, the government could hire substitutes. In one letter from the local landowners to the governor they guarantee what they will do:

> We declare we are willing, we guarantee, we are responsible and we go surety and we are reliable for the persons of these sailors, being those of our fields, whose names we shall display for you at the bottom of this guarantee-declaration We are sending them northwards as sailors of ships in the 7th year of the indiction for the cursus [raid] of the 8th indiction.* In this way they will fulfil their duty as sailors in the census of Egypt without turning aside. But if any of them turn aside, we are ready to pay any fine that our lord the all-famous governor may impose on us.[36]

The document ends with the names and addresses of three sailors and the signatures of the guarantors.

In another letter, the local people are ordered to send two and a half (!) sailors to join the fleet being organized by Abd Allāh b. Mūsa b. Nusayr in Africa. They are to be paid wages of 1⅙ solidi and travel expenses of 11⅙ from 'the state treasury', presumably meaning the money the district owed in taxes.

Rowing in galleys, especially war galleys belonging to an alien ruling class, can never have been a popular career option, but the letters suggest that, although service was in theory compulsory if you were on the list, you did at least get paid for it. These were not galley slaves as had been used in ancient Rome. Furthermore, it is clear that sometimes, but by no means always, it was possible to make a money payment instead of doing the service in person. One papyrus even

* That is, using the old late Byzantine style of dating by the fifteen-year indiction.

contains a requisition for cushions and it has been suggested, perhaps over-optimistically, that these were for the rowers' benches.[37] We have already noted how Qurra wrote to find out the fate of those men from Aphrodito who had joined the unsuccessful raiding fleet of Ātā b. Rāfi. Some had died, others had returned home but some had remained in Africa, and the governor wanted to know why. Was it possible that service in the navy offered at least some men an opportunity to escape from the restrictions of village life and make a new start for themselves?

If the navy needed people, it also needed materials for shipbuilding. Again the landowners of Aphrodito were called upon to help out. Timber was clearly the most important of these. Some timber came from the ancient forests in the Lebanese mountains but Egypt itself produced some good wood. There was the lebbek tree, of which it was said that 'if two pieces were firmly joined together and left in the water for a year, they would become as one', the acacia tree, whose wood was hard as iron, and the palm tree. One letter from Qurra requires that the pagarch of Aphrodito send beams of palm and fig-tree wood for building ships 'on the island of Babylon [Fustāt]' to be delivered this year for building ships for next year's raid.

As well as wood, iron for nails was required and, again, the people of Aphrodito were required to take scrap or rough iron from the government store, make it into nails and send them to the chief of shipbuilding operations in Fustāt. Egypt itself produces no iron so these must have been imports, perhaps from Spain, or perhaps reused iron from Byzantine buildings. Finally there were ropes, and it is interesting to note that the English word cable is ultimately derived from the Arabic *habl*, meaning rope. Egypt was well supplied with hemp for this purpose.

Alongside this official government naval activity, there were irregular Arab corsairs, unpaid and joining up in the hope of booty. It was such corsairs, not the navies of the caliphs, which were responsible for the conquest of Crete in 824 and the establishment of pirate nests in southern Italy on the Garigliano river and in the south of France at Fraxinetum (Fréjus) in the late ninth and early tenth centuries. But these lie beyond the scope of this book.

11

VOICES OF THE CONQUERED

❧

The maxim 'to the victors the spoils' applies not just to the physical reality of military success but often to the historiography of the events as well. The voices of the conquered are all too often swamped by the triumphalist histories of the conquerors. In the case of the Muslim conquests, however, we have a number of works, histories, apocalypses and poems, which give some insight as to how the people in the aftermath of the conquests regarded their new masters and what they considered to be the losses, and sometimes the benefits, that the conquests had brought them.

In this chapter, I have selected a range of responses with the aim of showing at first hand a wide range of different responses to the Muslim conquests.[1] Geographically, they extend from Spain in the west to the account of a Chinese prisoner of war in Kūfa. In tone they range from Sophronius's denunciation of the Muslims as complete barbarians to Mar Gabriel's conviction that they were much better masters than his co-religionists, the Byzantines. Christian, Jewish and Zoroastrian voices are all heard and the languages include Greek, Latin Syriac and Chinese.

The earliest and most hostile reaction to the coming of the Arabs can be found in the Greek letters and sermons of Sophronius, patriarch of Jerusalem, already discussed briefly in Chapter 4.[2] Sophronius was a native of Damascus, which, when he was growing up in the late sixth century, could still offer an excellent education in Greek philosophy and rhetoric. From about 578 to 583 he studied in Alexandria during the final flowering of classical education in the city. His studies completed, he returned to Palestine to become a monk at the monastery of St Theodosius near Jerusalem. In 614 his peace was brutally disturbed by the Persian invasions in which the extra-mural churches around Jerusalem suffered especially badly. In his anger and grief he composed a lament on the fate of the city:

Deceitfully the Mede
Came from terrible Persia
Pillaging cities and villages
Waging war against the ruler of Edom [Rome]
Advancing on the Holy Land
The malevolent one came
To destroy the city of God, Jerusalem.
Cry out in grief you tribes of blessed Christians
Holy Jerusalem is laid waste
With fearful wrath a demon has arisen
With the terrible envy of a warrior
To sack God-blessed cities and towns
With murderous daggers.

Sophronius certainly had experience of barbarians long before the Muslim conquests. He was obliged to flee to Rome in 615. He also spent some time in North Africa, where he met another of the great churchmen of his age, Maximus Confessor, with whom he became firm friends, and he also visited Constantinople on at least one occasion. He returned to Jerusalem after it had been reconquered by Heraclius, and in 633 he was persuaded by popular pressure to accept the office of patriarch.

It was as patriarch and effective political leader in Jerusalem that Sophronius confronted the Muslims. His first reference comes in a pastoral letter, probably written in 634 in the earliest phases of the Arab conquest of Syria, in which he hopes that the emperor Heraclius will be given strength 'to break the pride of all the barbarians and especially of the Saracens who, on account of our sins, have now risen up against us unexpectedly and ravage all with cruel and feral design, with impious and godless audacity'. At Christmas that year the clergy of Jerusalem were unable to process to Bethlehem, as was their custom, because of their fear of the Saracens. 'As once that of the Philistine, so now the army of the godless Saracens has captured the divine Bethlehem and bars our passage there, threatening slaughter and destruction if we leave this holy city and dare to approach our beloved and sacred Bethlehem.' In the end he remained optimistic: 'If we repent of our sins we will laugh at the demise of our enemies the Saracens and in a short time we will see their destruction and complete ruin. For their bloody swords will pierce their own hearts, their bows will be splintered, their arrows will be left sticking in them and they will open the way to Bethlehem for us.'

In many ways, Sophronius was one of the last churchmen of antiquity, brought up in a world that was slipping into oblivion even as he spoke. He had been able to travel the eastern Mediterranean in search of education, friendship and true religion: Jerusalem, Constantinople, Alexandria, Carthage and Rome were all familiar to him. In the late sixth and early seventh centuries, this was quite a normal pattern. By the time Sophronius died in 639 such wide-ranging travels were out of the question and the world he had grown up in was broken beyond repair. He wrote in the high-flown, mannered Greek of late antique rhetoric, a highly educated man talking to a highly educated audience. Sophronius took a very dim view of the Arabs. They were godless or God-hating barbarians. At no point in his writing and preaching does he give any indication that they were preaching a new religion. Their function was as instruments of God's wrath against the Christians because of their dabbling in heresy, and the way to combat them was not to raise armies or man the walls of the cities with fighting men, but to return one and all to true orthodox belief.

Many of the earliest responses to the Arab conquest found in the eastern Christian tradition took the form of apocalypses, that is predictions of the last days and the end of the world.[3] In these, the coming of the Arabs is sometimes seen as one of the signs of the end. They rarely contain hard and fast historical information but, as a recent authority has observed, 'apocalypses are extremely effective and sensitive indicators of a people's hopes, fears and frustrations'.[4] One of the most eloquent and developed of these texts is the apocalypse of the pseudo-Methodius,[5] so called because it is ascribed (wrongly) to Bishop Methodius of Olympus, martyred in 312, more than three centuries before the actual composition of the text. In fact it probably dates from the first two generations after the Muslim conquest. The second Arab civil war (683–92) was a period of violence and unrest, compounded by plague and famine in 686–7, and it was against this background that the apocalypse was written. Originally composed in Syriac, it was translated into both Greek and Latin, showing its widespread appeal among different Christian communities. The author offers his readers, presumably the Christian community of northern Syria, an elaborate wish fulfilment, shot through with biblical references and allusion. The final days begin with the arrival of the Ishmaelites (the Arabs) who will defeat the kingdom of the Greeks at Gabitha (a reference to the battle of the Yarmūk). There then follows an account of the effects of the Muslim invasions as perceived by a late-seventh-century Christian, though because it is apocalypse, it is told in the future tense.

This chastisement is not being sent only upon human but also upon everything which is on the face of the entire earth – on men, women, children, animals, cattle and birds. People will be tormented by that punishment – men, their wives, sons, daughters and possessions; the old who are weak, the sick and the strong, the poor with the rich. For God called their [the Arabs] forefather Ishmael, 'the wild ass of the wilderness' and the gazelles, along with all the animals, both of the wilderness and the cultivated land will be oppressed by them. People will be persecuted, wild animals and cattle will die, forest trees will be cut down, the most beautiful mountain plants will be destroyed and prosperous cities will be laid waste. Regions will lie desolate without anyone passing through: the land will be defiled by blood and deprived of its produce.

For these barbarian tyrants are not men, but children of desolation. They set their face towards desolation and they are destroyers ... they are destruction and they will issue forth for the destruction of everything. They are defiled and they love defilement. At the time of issuing forth from the wilderness, they will snatch babies from their mothers' arms dashing them against stones, as though they were unclean beasts.

They will make sacrifice of those who minister in the sanctuary and they will even sleep with their wives and with captive women inside the sanctuary. They will appropriate the sacred vestments as clothing for themselves and their children. They will tether their cattle to the sarcophagi of martyrs and to the graves of holy men. They are insolent murderers, destructive shedders of blood: they are a furnace of testing for all Christians.

The author then goes on to talk of the hardships that will be inflicted by plague and by taxation. 'A person will sleep in the evening and rise up in the morning to find outside his door two or three men who use force as they demand tribute and money. All accounting of what is given and received will disappear from the earth. At that time people will sell their bronze, their iron and their burial clothes.'

Then, just when things are as bad as they can be, a miraculous deliverance occurs, the King of the Greeks will attack them: 'He will be awakened against them "like a man who has shaken off his wine."' Now it is the turn of the Arabs to suffer: 'They, their wives, their children, all their encampments, all the land of the wilderness which belonged to their forefathers shall be delivered into the hands of the king of the Greeks: they shall be given over to the sword and devastation, to captivity and slaughter. The yoke of their servitude will be seven times more oppressive than their own yoke,' and he goes on to describe the hardships that will be inflicted on them. Then a universal peace will be established: 'churches will be renovated, towns will be rebuilt, priests will be free from tax. Priests and people will have rest at that time from toil, fatigue and oppression'.

But it is not over yet. The 'people of the north' will invade, causing great devastation and slaughter, but God will send one of his angels, who will destroy them in a single moment. Then the King of the Greeks will go to live in Jerusalem before standing on Golgotha, putting his crown on the holy cross as a symbol that he is resigning his sovereignty, and cross and crown will be taken up into heaven. There is then an account of the appearance of an Antichrist figure in Palestine, the 'son of Perdition' and more mayhem before the coming of our Lord finally puts an end to him and the vision fades.

The apocalypse is both faintly absurd and curiously moving. In it we can hear the voice of the subject population. A solitary priest, probably writing in a northern Syrian monastery, is dreaming of the day when a miraculous intervention will put the hated Arabs in their place. The Arabs are accused of murder and mayhem, destroying cities and the rural environment, of disrespecting churches, of sexual licentiousness and oppressive taxation. It is an eloquent indictment, all the more so because it dates from the period when Muslim rule was being consolidated. At no point, however, does he envision the Christian people taking matters into their own hands and fighting back against their oppressors. For him, the Arabs are an evil and malevolent presence. Like Sophronius, he never mentions that they brought a new religion; they are simply godless but, at the same time, the instruments by which God punishes his people for their wickedness. Many of the people conquered by the Arabs in the seventh century must have shared these very negative perceptions.

But not all Christians shared such black views. Both Sophronius and the author of the apocalypse of the pseudo-Methodius were men for whom the restoration of Byzantine rule was something to be hoped for. The Nestorian John bar Penkāyē, writing in the 690s, agreed that the Arabs were the instruments of God, sent to punish the Christians for moral laxity and, above all, for heresy; but for him both the Chalcedonian Church supported by the Byzantine authorities and their Monophysites were the real enemy. 'We should not think', he wrote,

> of the advent of the Arabs as something ordinary, but as due to divine working. Before calling them, God had prepared them beforehand to hold Christians in honour; thus they also had a special commandment from God concerning our monastic station, that they should hold it in honour. Now when these people came at God's command, and took over both kingdoms [the Byzantine and Sasanian empires], not with any war or battle, but in a menial fashion, such as when a brand is rescued out of the fire; not using weapons of war or human means, God put victory into their hands.

God was punishing the Church for flirting with the heresy and the Arabs were his instruments of punishment. But the Arabs, too, were subject to divine wrath for the sins they committed during the con-quests, and their empire was divided into two hostile powers, a ref-erence to the civil war between Alī and Muᶜāwiya that followed the assassination of the caliph Uthmān in 656. John has nothing but praise for the first Umayyad caliph, Muᶜāwiya (661–80), of whose reign he says 'the peace throughout the world was such that we have never heard, either from our fathers or from our grandparents, or seen that there had ever been any like it'. Needless to say this happy state of affairs could not last. In this atmosphere of peace and prosperity, the Church turned again to moral laxity and heresy. God again used the

Arabs to punish their behaviour, causing the destructive civil war that broke out in 683 after the death of Yazīd I (the same civil war that forms the background to the apocalypse of the pseudo-Methodius), with which his history ends. Famine and plague were everywhere, further signs of God's displeasure. For John the Arabs were God's instruments; their rule might be either good or bad depending on the behaviour of the Christians.

John does not mention any personal contacts with the Arabs but other Christians in the area were more purposeful in establishing good relations. The saintly Mar Gabriel (d. 667) was abbot of the monastery at Qartmin.[6] Qartmin stands in the mountains of the Tur Abdin in south-east Turkey, close to the plains of the Jazira. By Gabriel's time it was already an ancient establishment and, remarkably, it still survives as one of the most venerable centres of eastern Christian monasticism down to the present day. Qartmin was the stronghold of those who rejected Byzantine Orthodox Christianity, and he regarded the coming of Muslim rule as an opportunity rather than a calamity.

His biographer tells the story:

> Mar Gabriel preferred the advent of the Arabs to the oppression of the Byzantines, so he gave assistance and helped them. Subsequently he went to Jazira to their amir who received him with great joy and honoured him greatly for his action on their behalf; he gave him a *prostagma* signed in his own hand with ordinances on all the points he had asked for; in it he granted all the Syrian Orthodox freedom to use their church customs – the semantra [the wooden board that is struck in the eastern churches to summon the people to prayer], festival celebrations and funeral processions and the building of churches and monasteries; he freed from tribute priests, deacons and monks. While he fixed the tribute for other people at 4 [dirhams – a modest sum]. He also instructed the pagan Arabs to take great care to preserve the lives of the Syrian Orthodox.[7]

The life of Mar Gabriel provides almost the only indication that Syrian Orthodox Christians actually aided the Muslim conquest as opposed to being helpless and uncommitted onlookers, but we have no means of knowing how common this attitude was.

The Coptic sources have forceful opinions about of the coming of the Muslims. Among these sources is the life of the patriarch Benjamin (622–61), whose period of office coincides with the Muslim conquest. It has come down to us in an Arabic translation made by Sawīrus b. al-Muqaffa, Bishop of Ashminayn in Middle Egypt in the late tenth century. As he makes clear in his preface, however, he compiled his biographies from Greek and Coptic sources and the life of Benjamin and the opinions it contains are probably much older and may indeed date back to the seventh century.

Benjamin became patriarch during the period of the Persian occupation of Egypt, but the author has little to say about their rule except that Heraclius killed Chosroes, the unbelieving king. When Heraclius became emperor he appointed Cyrus as governor. Faced by the appointment of this staunchly Chalcedonian figure, Benjamin was warned by an angel of the Lord to flee. He put the affairs of the Church in order, wrote to all the other bishops ordering them to go into hiding and took himself to an obscure monastery in Upper Egypt to weather the storm, no doubt sustained by the prophecy of the angel that Cyrus's rule would last only ten years.

Cyrus emerges as the real villain of the story; several bishops who had not heeded the patriarch's advice to go into hiding were 'caught with the fishing-line of his error' and Benjamin's own brother was martyred because he refused to accept the decrees of the Council of Chalcedon. Heraclius's appointees acted like ravening wolves, devouring the faithful in Egypt. In contrast to this invective, our author provides a low-key account of the preaching of Muhammad who 'brought back the worshippers of idols to the knowledge of the One God [*Allah wahdu*] and they said that Muhammad was his messenger [*rasūl*]. His *umma* were circumcised and prayed to the south to the place which they called the Kaaba'.[8]

The Lord then abandoned the army of the Romans because of their corruption and their adherence to the decrees of the Council of Chalcedon. The Arab invasion is described in brief, matter-of-fact language. The author describes the treaty between the Muslims and the Egyptians, which was the kind of treaty that Muhammad, the *ra'īs* of the Arabs, had instructed them to make, by which any city that agrees to pay tax will be spared but those that do not will be plundered and its men taken as prisoners; 'for this reason', the author continues, 'the Muslims kept their hand off the province and its inhabitants [i.e. the Copts] but destroyed the nation of the Romans'.[9]

When the Muslims took Alexandria, they destroyed the walls and 'burnt many churches with fire', including the church of St Mark. The author is curiously dispassionate about this destruction, perhaps because most of the churches in the city were in the hands of the Chalcedonians. Much more important from his point of view was the triumphant return of Benjamin. This was negotiated by a Coptic *dux* (*dūqs*) called Sanutius, who told Amr about him. Amr then issued a letter giving Benjamin safe conduct and he returned to the city. He was met with great rejoicing, and Sanutius presented him to the governor, who was duly impressed, saying that in all the land he had conquered he had never seen a man of God like this man. Cyrus, meanwhile, had committed suicide, drinking poison from his ring. Benjamin was ordered to resume the government of his church and people. Amr then requested his prayers for a speedy success and quick return from the expedition he was planning to the Pentapolis in Cyrenaica. Finally, the patriarch preached a sermon, which impressed everybody, and gave Amr some secret advice, all of which turned out to be true, before leaving, 'honoured and revered'. The whole land of Egypt rejoiced over him. Amr duly set out, accompanied by Sanutius and his ship. Sanutius was also able to give the patriarch money to rebuild the church of St Mark. Even after Amr had left the province and was replaced by Ibn Abī Sarh, 'a lover of money' who set up the administration in Fustāt, the biographer refrains from open criticism of the Muslim administration.

For the biographer of Benjamin, the coming of the Arabs was a new dawn for his hero. He never actually says in unequivocal terms that it was a good thing, but it was clearly a great relief after the rule of Cyrus. The stress on the good relations between Benjamin and Amr and the role of the *dux* Sanutius point to some close links between Coptic and Muslim elites.

Our other main Coptic source, the chronicler John of Nikiu, takes an altogether less rosy view of the Arab conquerors. As with the biographer of Benjamin, the main villain of his account is Cyrus and the Chalcedonian Romans, and he explicitly says that the Muslims were helped by the fact that the persecutions of Heraclius's reign had meant that the local people were hostile to the Romans.[10] The sins of the

Chalcedonians were the reason why God allowed the Arabs to conquer Egypt, for 'He had no mercy of those who had dealt treacherously against Him but He delivered them into the hands of the Ishmaelites'.[11]

The Arabs are portrayed as brutal barbarians. In their early raids on the Fayyum they killed indiscriminately; in one town 'they put to the sword all who surrendered and spared none, whether old men, babies or women',[12] and in Nakiu 'they proceeded to put to the sword all those who they found in the streets and in the churches, men, women and infants and they showed mercy to none'.[13] Amr arrests the Roman magistrates, and has their hands and feet confined in iron and wooden boards while he takes their possessions. Things are not much better for the peasants because the taxes are doubled and they are forced to carry fodder for the horses.[14] After the final conquest of Alexandria, Amr confined himself to taking the taxes that had been agreed on but he did not take the property of the churches and preserved them throughout his days. Taxation for other people, however, seems to have been oppressive, and people hid themselves away because they could not find the money to pay.

He has harsh words for the Arabs and for those local men who cooperated with them. The Egyptians were forced to carry fodder and provide milk, honey and fruit. They were compelled to dig out the canal from Babylon to the Red Sea and 'the yoke they [the Arabs] laid on the Egyptians was heavier than the yoke which had been laid on Israel by Pharaoh, whom god judged with a righteous judgment, by drowning him in the Red Sea with all his army after many plagues wherewith he had plagued both men and cattle. When God's judgment lights on these Ishmaelites, may he do unto them as He did unto Pharaoh!' John then goes on to say that this is punishment for the people's sins but he trusts that God will destroy the enemies of the cross as the Bible promises.[15]

Despite this brutality, there was an undercurrent of cooperation. We hear early on of 'Egyptians who had apostatized from the Christian faith and embraced the faith of the beast'[16] and of local officials who were, willingly or unwillingly, working for the Muslims.[17]

A different but equally mixed Christian response can be seen in the anonymous Latin Chronicle of 754.[18] The author probably lived in Cordova and may well have been old enough to have personal memories of the fall of the Visigothic kingdom. His familiarity with the history and politics of al-Andalus suggest that he may have been employed by the Muslims in the administration. He set out to write a universal chronicle, so he deals with the rise of the Arabs in the Middle East, eighty years before the time when he was writing. He makes no mention anywhere in his work of the fact that the Muslims were the adherents of a new religion. He simply says that the Saracens rebelled and conquered Syria, Arabia and Mesopotamia 'more through trickery than the power of their leader Muhammad, and devastated the neighbouring provinces, proceeding not so much by means of open attacks as by secret incursions'. Despite his contempt for the fighting abilities of the Arabs, the author gives a matter-of-fact account of the early caliphs interwoven with the history of the Byzantine empire. Some caliphs are good men: Yazīd I (680–83), whom John bar Penkāyē dismissed as being 'fond of childish games and empty delights' and ruling 'with empty-headed tyranny',[19] is praised by the author of the Chronicle of 754 as 'the most pleasant son of Muʿāwiya' who was 'very well liked by all the peoples of the land that were subject to his rule. He never, as is the habit of men, sought any glory because he was a king, but lived like a private citizen together with everyone else'.[20]

This even-tempered attitude changes sharply when the chronicler comes to discuss the Muslim conquest of Spain. Mūsā b. Nusayr is denounced as a violent barbarian:

He ruined beautiful cities, burning them with fire; condemned lords and powerful men to the cross and butchered youths and infants with the sword. While he terrorized everyone in this way, some of the cities that remained sued for peace under duress and, after persuading and mocking them with a certain craftiness, the Saracens granted their requests without delay. When the citizens subsequently rejected what they had accepted out of fear and terror, they tried to flee to the mountains where they risked hunger and various sorts of death.

After this violent rhetorical denunciation, the chronicle reverts to its previous matter-of-fact tone. There are good Muslim rulers and bad ones just as there are good Christians and bad ones. The account of the battle of Poitiers (732), where Christian forces decisively defeated the Muslims, is given in some very useful detail but without any sense of Christian triumphalism.²¹ The worst villains in the chronicle are those Syrian Arabs who crossed into the peninsula after their defeat by the Berber rebels in 742 and began to dispute control with the descendants of the original Arab and Berber conquerors.²² Right to the end of the chronicle, he is very well informed about events in the Muslim east as well as Spain. By contrast, France and Italy, both Latin-writing, Christian areas, are almost completely unknown to him. The chronicler of 754 lived and worked in a world where Christian–Muslim interactions were everyday and businesslike and, in some ways, he clearly identifies with the ruling Muslim circles in Cordova while maintaining his clearly Christian identity. There were men in his position in the Arab administration in the east: we have no direct testimony about their attitudes but they must have been similar.

Like the Christians, the Jews of the Middle East developed an apocalyptic literature, although in their case the objective was to predict the time of the coming of the Messiah rather than the end of the world. For the Jews, the last years of Byzantine rule in Syria had been a time of distress and persecution. The Persian invasion had led to some respite but the reimposition of Byzantine rule from 628 onwards had led to renewed oppression. For the Jews, the coming of the Arabs, though attended by much violence and cruelty, promised some alleviation of their condition. The fullest exposition of Jewish views is to be found in the *Nistarot* or Secrets attributed to a second-century rabbi, Simon ben Yohai, but clearly written or rewritten after the coming of the Muslims.²³

In one passage, Simon is said to have taken refuge from the Byzantine emperor (referred to as the King of Edom throughout) in a cave. After fasting and praying he asks God for enlightenment:

Since Simon saw the kingdom of Ishmael [the Arabs] coming he began to say, 'Was it not enough what the wicked kingdom of Edom done to us, but we deserve the kingdom of Ishmael too?' At once Metatron, the foremost angel, answered him and said, 'Do not fear, son of man, for the Almighty only brings the Kingdom of Ishmael in order to deliver you from this wicked one [Edom/Byzantium]. He raises up over the Ishmaelites a prophet according to his will and he will conquer the land for them, and they will come and restore it to greatness and a great dread will come between them and the sons of Esau [the Byzantines].'

A later passage provides a favourable verdict on the second caliph, Umar (634–44): 'the second king who arises from Ishmael will be a lover of Israel. He restores their breaches and the breaches of the Temple, he hews Mount Moriah, makes it level and builds a mosque there on the Temple rock.' It was not all good news, however, and the author, like many Christian sources of the period, complains about Muslim surveying of the land for the purpose of taxation. 'They will measure the land with ropes as it is said, and he shall divide the land for a price.'²⁴ The author was also scandalized by Muslim burial practices and their treatment of cemeteries: 'And they will make cemeteries into a pasturing place for flocks; and when one of them dies, they will bury him whatever place they find and later plough the grave and sow thereon,' an observation that tallies with what we know of the casual attitude of the early Muslims to the disposal of their dead.

The Jews probably looked on the coming of the Muslims with more favour than any other group among the conquered people, but it is clear that they also suffered from the grim effects of warfare and disorder.

Iranian views of the Muslim conquests are much less well preserved because Zoroastrianism perished much more completely than Christianity and there were no monasteries to preserve ancient works. We have one surviving Pahlavi poem, probably dating from the ninth century, in which we can see something of the attitudes of supporters of the old religion at a time when conversion to Islam was gathering pace and fire-temples were being closed. Like the pseudo-Methodius, this is an apocalyptic work, prophesying that deliverance will come when a descendant of the ancient monarchs of Iran will appear from India.

When will it be that a courier will come from India to say that the Shāh Vahrām from the family of Kays [the ancient, largely mythical ruling dynasty of Iran] has come, having a thousand elephants, with an elephant keeper on each of their heads, who bears the raised standard? In the manner of the Chosroes they bear it before the army. To the generals a messenger is needed, a skilled interpreter. When he

comes he will tell in India what we have seen from the hands of the
Tajiks [Arabs] in one multitude. The Dēn [Zoroastrian religion] was
ruined and the King of Kings slain like a dog. They eat the bread.
They have taken away sovereignty from the Chosroes. Not by skill
and valour but in mockery and scorn they have taken it. By force they
take from men wives and sweet possessions, parks and gardens. Taxes
they have imposed, they have distributed them upon the heads. They
have demanded again the principal, a heavy impost. Consider how
much evil those wicked ones [the Arabs] have cast upon this world,
than which ill there is none worse. The world passes from us. We
shall bring that Shāh Vahrām worker of mighty deeds to wreak vengeance on the Arabs ... their mosques we will cast down, we will set
up fires, their idol-temples we will dig down and purify away from the
world so that the spawn of the wicked one will vanish from this world.
Finished in peace and joy. [25]

Another view of the Arab conquests can be found in Firdawsi's
Shahnāmah. Firdawsi (d. *c.* 1020)[26] came from Tus in Khurasan. He
came from a family of *dehqān*s, gentlemen-landowners. It was in these
circles that devotion to the ancient traditions of Iran were kept alive
and the achievements of the pre-Islamic kings were celebrated. Firdawsi was devoted to Iran, its language and its culture. In contrast to
the author of the anonymous Pahlavi poem, who was clearly hoping
for a revival of Zoroastrianism, Firdawsi was certainly a Muslim, but
he rarely lets his faith appear in his writing. He seems to have had no
difficulty in accepting the Zoroastrian faith of his heroes and a continuity between their God and Allāh.

Mention has already been made of the verse letter that the Persian
general Rustam is alleged to have written to his brother on the eve of
the fatal battle of Qādisiya, when Persian rule in Iraq was destroyed
and he himself killed. From internal evidence it is clear that the letter
is not an authentic document inserted into the text but was composed
when the poet was writing this section of his great work, probably in
the first decade of the eleventh century. One part of the letter[27] is
essentially a prophecy expressing Rustam's vision of the consequences
of the Muslim conquest, and it is extremely interesting in showing
how an aristocratic Persian of the period saw the coming of the
Muslims. He does not explicitly condemn Islam or the Arabs, but

he paints a sorrowful view of the consequences of the conquest for traditional Iranian culture and values. The disruption of the old social order caused by the coming of Islam leads to the decay of public and personal morality.

He begins the section with a general lament:

> But when the pulpit's equal to the throne
> And Abū Bakr and Umar's names are known
> Our long travails will be as naught, and all
> The glory we have known will fade and fall.

He then comments on the general drabness of Muslim rulers compared with the splendour of the old courts of the King of Kings. It is interesting to see how his comments on the austerity of Muslim dress are the mirror image of those Arabic narratives of the conquests which glory in their virtuous poverty and contrast it with Persian luxury.

> They'll dress in black,* their headdresses will be made
> Of twisted lengths of silk or black brocade
> There'll be no golden boots or banners then
> Our crowns and thrones will not be seen again.

It will be an era of injustice and oppression and the collapse of the old social order:

> Some will rejoice while others live in fear
> Justice and charity will disappear
> Strangers will rule us then and with their might
> They'll plunder us and turn our days to night
> They will not care for just or righteous men
> Deceit and fraudulence will flourish then.
> Warriors will go on foot, while puffed-up pride
> And empty boasts will arm themselves and ride;
> The peasantry will suffer from neglect
> Lineage and skill will garner no respect
> Men will be mutual thieves and have no shame

---

* Black was the court colour of the Abbasid caliphs from 750 onwards.

What's hidden will be worse than what is known
And stony-hearted kings will seize the throne.
No man will trust his son and equally
No son will trust his father's honesty.

The traditional Persian ruling class will be replaced by men of low
social status and different nationalities:

A misbegotten slave will rule the earth
Greatness and lineage will have no worth,
No one will keep his word, and men will find
The tongue as filled with evil as the mind.
Then Persians, Turks and Arabs, side by side,
Will live together mingled far and wide –
The three will blur as it they were the same
Their languages will be a trivial game.

Moral standards will decay and this will go along with the decay of
court culture.

Men will conceal their wealth, but when they've died,
Their foes will pillage everything they hide.
Men will pretend they're holy or they're wise,
To make a livelihood by telling lies.
Sorrow and anguish, bitterness and pain
Will be as happiness was in the reign
Of Bahrām Gūr* – mankind's accustomed fate:
There'll be no feasts, no festivals of state,
No pleasures, no musicians, none of these:
But there'll be lies, and traps and treacheries.
Sour milk will be our food, coarse cloth our dress,
And greed for money will breed bitterness
Between generations: men will cheat
Each other as they calmly counterfeit
Religious faith. The winter and the spring

---

* Sasanian shāh who ruled 420–38 and who was considered the epitome of the courtly
warrior, a great hunter and patron of musicians.

Will pass mankind unmarked,* no one will bring
The wine to celebrate such moments then;
Instead they'll spill the blood of fellow men.

It is a powerful picture of political and moral decay and the loss of old aristocratic values. The breaking down of class distinctions and the mixing of different races are all part of this destruction of traditional values. In contrast with the views of the Christians, there is no indication that the disasters of the Muslim conquest were part of God's punishment of sin. It was rather a disaster decreed by fate. It is, of course, put in the mouth of the general who knows that he will be defeated and killed and that the order he is supporting will disappear, but it is hard to imagine that his bleak view of the effects of the coming of Muslim rule does not reflect the opinions of many of the Iranian aristocrats of the centuries that followed the conquests.

The Arabs, of course, never conquered China but they did capture a number of Chinese prisoners of war in the campaign that led to the battle of Talas between the Chinese and Muslim armies in 751. Among these was one Tu Huan, who was taken to Iraq and remained there as a prisoner before being allowed to return home in 762. His account of the Muslims is short but extremely interesting, showing how the Muslim world at the end of the period of the great conquests, appeared to someone from a completely different culture.[28]

The capital is called Kūfa [Ya-chü-lo]. The Arab king is called *mumen* [that is, Amīr al-Mu'minīn, Commander of the Faithful]. Both men and women are handsome and tall, their clothing is bright and clean, and their manners are elegant. When a woman goes out in public, she must cover her face irrespective of her lofty or lowly social position. They perform ritual prayers five times a day. They eat meat, fast and regard the butchering of animals as meritorious. They wear silver belts around the waist from which they suspend silver daggers. They prohibit the drinking of wine and forbid music. When people squabble among themselves, they do not come to blows. There is also a ceremonial hall [the mosque] which accommodates tens of thousands of

---

* A reference to the great traditional Iranian feast of Nawruz, the New Year, which is celebrated in March as the crops are beginning to sprout.

people. Every seven days the king comes out to perform religious services; he mounts a high pulpit and preaches law to the multitudes. He says, 'Human life is very difficult, the path of righteousness is not easy, and adultery is wrong. To rob or steal, in the slightest way to deceive people with words, to make oneself secure by endangering others, to cheat the poor or oppress the lowly – there is no greater sin than one of these. All who are killed in battle against the enemies of Islam will achieve paradise. Kill the enemies and you will receive happiness beyond measure.'

The entire land has been transformed; the people follow the tenets of Islam like a river its channel, the law is applied only with leniency and the dead are interred only with frugality. Whether inside the walls of a great city or only inside a village gate, the people lack nothing of what the earth produces. Their country is the hub of the universe where myriad goods are abundant and inexpensive, where rich brocades, pearls and money fill the shops while camels, horses, donkeys and mules fill the streets and alleys. They cut sugar cane to build cottages resembling Chinese carriages. Whenever there is a holiday the nobility are presented with more vessels of glass and bowls of brass than can be counted. The white rice and white flour are not different from those of China. Their fruits include the peach and also thousand-year dates. Their rape turnips, as big as a peck, are round and their taste is very delicious, while their other vegetables are like those of other countries. Their grapes are as large as hen's eggs. The most highly esteemed of their fragrant oils are two, one called jasmine and the other called myrrh. Chinese artisans have made the first looms for weaving silk fabrics and are the first gold and silversmiths and painters.

The account shows a mature Muslim society, which accords with the picture we know from other sources. The picture dates from the early years of the Abbasid caliphate immediately before the foundation of Baghdad, which was begun in 762, the year Tu Huan was allowed to return home. We know from Arabic sources that the caliph Mansūr was famous for his eloquent sermons in the mosques, and it is interesting to see the emphasis our Chinese observer puts on condemning oppression and injustice on one hand and stressing *jihād* and the rewards of paradise on the other. We are shown a puritanical society where the veiling of women and the prohibition, at least in public, of alcohol and music are clearly evident. It is also a prosperous society, and one in which the prosperity is widely shared across the different social classes and in both town and village. It is understandable that many of the people conquered by the Arabs would have wanted to be part of this thriving community. Kūfa was, of course, a Muslim new town and a place where one would expect to find Muslim norms strongly adhered to. At the same time it is striking that there is no mention of non-Muslims, who must still have been in a majority, even in Iraq, an area where conversion to Islam was fairly rapid.

The voices of the conquered are scattered and in many cases the impact of the Muslims is of secondary interest to the author. There are no discussions of the new religion of Islam and its doctrines. There is a general agreement on the destructive nature of the actual conquest but views are varied about the merits of Muslim government. The burden of Muslim taxation is a frequent theme. For the Christians of the Fertile Crescent, the coming of the Arabs, and their apparently inexplicable victory, must be the result of God's wrath and the cause of that wrath was, above all, heresy. In general, the writers saw rival Christian sects and, of course, the Jews as the real enemy to be challenged and defeated. The Arabs, by contrast, could be tolerated and even manipulated to serve sectarian ends. No one even came near to proposing a Christian resistance movement or making concerted efforts to restore Christian rule. These attitudes were an important factor in explaining how the Muslims achieved and maintained their control. The Persian views show a very different reaction, the lament for the loss of old greatness and the old social order, the regrets, in fact, of a dispossessed ruling class. Overall, the most striking feature of these voices is the variety of responses to the coming of Islamic rule. Many people may have been dissatisfied with it but few turned their dissatisfation into active resistance. The fragmented nature of the response of the conquered was an important reason for the success of the Muslims, both in the initial conquest and in the consolidation of their rule.

12

CONCLUSION

❧

THE DEFINING OF THE FRONTIERS

B y the year 750 the Muslim Empire had reached frontiers that were to remain more or less stable for the next 300 years. The only significant conquests made in this later period were in the Mediterranean, Sicily and Crete. In size and population it was broadly similar to the Roman Empire at its height in the eighth century; only Tang China could rival it. About half the territories ruled by the caliphs from Damascus had been ruled from Rome in the first three centuries AD. These included Syria, Palestine, Egypt, North Africa and Spain. The Romans had, of course, also ruled France, Britain, Italy, the Balkans and Turkey and, while France, Italy and Turkey all suffered Muslim raids and some temporary, limited occupation, they never came under Arab rule. On the other hand, the caliphate included Iraq, Iran, Transoxania and Sind, areas that were always outside the frontiers of the Roman Empire.

The confines of the Roman Empire were defined with firm frontiers, the *limes*. Sometimes, as with Hadrian's Wall in north Britain, these were really a continuous line of masonry with forts placed at regular intervals. On many other frontiers, in the Syrian and Jordanian deserts, for example, there was no fortified line but a network of small castles and fortifications to shelter garrisons and so police the desert margins. The early Muslim Empire did not develop *limes* in the same way. In many areas the frontier was only very hazily defined, in others it was lost in the desert. Only in a few districts, along the Anatolian frontier with the Byzantine Empire, for example, or the places where Muslim and Christian outposts faced each other in the upper Ebro Valley in Spain, was there a fortified boundary that divided Muslims and non-Muslims.

The Mediterranean separated the Muslims from many potential enemies to the north and west. In the two centuries after the initial conquests, the Mediterranean coasts of the Muslim world were almost completely immune from attack. Only occasionally did Byzantine fleets manage to raid ports in the Levant and Egypt and, while they might pillage and burn, they were never able to establish a permanent presence.

The northern frontiers of al-Andalus, Muslim Spain, lay along the foothills of the Pyrenees in the east and the Cantabrian mountains to the west, following the 1,000-metre contour line almost exactly. The Muslims were defended by a series of fortified towns – Huesca, Zaragoza, Tudela, Calatayud, Madrid, Talavera – often protected by Roman walls. In Portugal and the west of Spain there seems to have been a wide belt of no man's land between the northern outposts of Islam and the small Christian kingdoms sheltered by the Cantabrian mountains, and further east in the Ebro Valley, Christian and Muslim outposts were only a few kilometres apart.

In North Africa, from Morocco in the far west to Egypt in the east, the frontier of the Muslim state lay along the northern fringes of the Sahara desert. In Egypt, too, the desert was the frontier. In the Nile Valley Muslim rule ended at Aswan. Here diplomacy with the Nubians secured the narrow and easily defended border. Around Arabia, along the Gulf and Indian Ocean shores of Iran, the sea coast formed the frontier and, despite occasional outbreaks of piracy, the Muslim world was never threatened from that direction.

In Sind the position was more complex. Muslim rule disappeared north of Multān but the frontier seems to have been comparatively peaceful; certainly there is no indication of major fortifications or the establishment of garrisons to defend the Muslim lands. The position in modern Afghanistan was, as ever, much more complex. The Muslims held a number of positions in the lowlands, to the north and south of the Hindu Kush. Bust, Herat, Balkh were all more or less frontier towns, but the unconquered people of the mountains were more an occasional nuisance than a serious challenge to Muslim rule.

In Transoxania the frontier was defined not so much by lines on the map as by points of control, the Muslims holding the cities and settled areas while the Turks roamed the deserts. In many areas the

Muslims established *ribāts*, fortresses inhabited and defended by *ghāzis*, warriors who devoted themselves to the service of Islam.

In the Caucasus, it was again the 1,000-metre contour line which marked the limits of Muslim control. They dominated the plains and river valleys as far as Tblisi in the heart of the mountains, but the snowy peaks of the high ranges prevented them from going further and the plains of what is now southern Russia remained beyond their power. Only at the eastern end of the Caucasus, where the mountains come down to the Caspian Sea, was there a fortified border. The great stone fortress now known as Derbent but called Bāb al-Abwāb (Gate of Gates) by the Arabs had been established by the Sasanians to guard the border, and it was taken over by the Muslims, an Arab garrison being established there at a very early date. Beyond the gate lay the steppe lands of southern Russia, dominated by a Turkic people, the Khazars, who periodically made raids into the Muslim areas to the south.

The frontier with the Byzantine Empire in south-eastern Anatolia was the most heavily fortified of all the borders of the Islamic world and it occupied a unique place in the Muslim consciousness.[1] By the year 700 this frontier was almost static. Again the Muslims controlled the lowlands while the mountains above 1,000 metres were in the hands of the Byzantines. The Byzantines, despite their defeat at the time of the first conquests, remained the enemy par excellence, the only power with whom the Muslims felt they competed on equal terms. Alone among the peoples who lived along their borders, the Byzantines had a highly developed state apparatus, a regular army, a state religion and an emperor who could correspond on equal terms with the caliphs. The Muslims knew that they were the possessors of the only true religion, but some of them at least also knew they had much to learn from the culture, philosophy and science of the Greeks.

In the years immediately after the conquest of Syria, and the Jazira, the Muslim provinces that bordered on the Byzantine Empire, the frontier was fluid and marked more by a no man's land than by a firm line. The low-lying and potentially rich area of Cilicia, at the north-eastern corner of the Mediterranean, was effectively deserted. Gradually, during the eighth century, the Muslims established frontier fortresses, defended by men paid from government funds. There was no wall but a series of fortified towns from Tarsus in the west to Malatya in the east, in which Muslim garrisons were established.

These Muslim outposts were always in the plains or river valleys: the mountains of the Taurus and anti-Taurus belonged to the Byzantines. It was from these fortresses that the Muslims launched their summer, and occasionally winter, raids into Byzantine territory. Often these amounted to little more than cattle rustling, but sometimes there were major campaigns. These were the only wars in which the caliphs and their heirs actively participated, and many of the campaigns had an almost ritual character, the caliph leading the Muslims against their hereditary enemies.

In general, the Muslim Empire did not suffer the external pressures that threatened the Roman Empire on the Rhine, Danube and Euphrates frontiers. Christians from the north of Spain, Khazars from the plains of southern Russia and Turks in Transoxania might make occasional raids into Muslim territory, but their impact was limited and could be shrugged off by the inhabitants of Baghdad and Cairo. The empire established by the great Arab conquests was economically self-sufficient and militarily self-confident. In the ninth and tenth centuries, this Muslim society survived the collapse of central government in a way in which the western Roman Empire, of the fifth century, threatened by barbarian invaders, had been unable to do.

THE SUCCESS OF THE ARAB CONQUESTS

Now is the time to return to the question asked by John bar Penkāyē with which this book began: why were the Arab conquests so swift and far reaching and why did they turn out to be so permanent?

Let us start off by looking at the lands they conquered to see how and in what ways they may have been vulnerable. There were long-term factors at work, difficult to pinpoint or quantify, but certainly important. Demographic decline may have been significant here. Of course, we have few useful figures for population in this period, but the impression given by a variety of sources is that many of the areas conquered had suffered from a declining population in the century after the first appearance of the bubonic plague in the Mediterranean world in 540, and that this loss of population was most severe in cities and villages. The Arab armies sometimes seem to have moved through an empty landscape. The rapid conquest of vast areas of Iran and the Iberian peninsula, with minimal resistance from the people, suggests this. The fact that so much of the booty taken in war was in the form of human captives again suggests that people were at a premium. When the Persians conquered Antioch in 540 or Apamea in 573, they deported large numbers of citizens to settle new or expanding towns in the Sasanian Empire, a policy that makes sense only if there is a population shortage. The large numbers of slaves taken in North Africa and imported to the Middle East show that people were a valuable and perhaps scarce resource. Towns of great antiquity and fame were apparently taken without any serious resistance. The fate of three of the most important cities of the late Roman world illustrates this clearly. Antioch surrendered with minimum resistance, probably in 636; Carthage seems to have been largely uninhabited when the Muslims eventually occupied it in 698; Toledo, despite its position as the Visigothic capital and its superb natural fortifications, failed to delay the Muslim armies for any length of time in 712. The evidence of demographic decline is scattered and often indirect, but it does, in the end, seem convincing. This decline did not, of course, cause the Arab conquests, but it may have meant that resistance was less fierce, that the way of the Arab armies was not barred by numerous populous cities whose inhabitants manned the walls, determined to resist. It was perhaps only in Transoxania that we find this sort of spirited defence mounted by a highly motivated local population.

Along with these long-term factors, there were the short-term effects of war and the dislocation it caused. There had been many conflicts between the Roman and Iranian empires since Crassus and his forces were defeated by the Parthians in 53 BC, but the war that broke out after the assassination of Emperor Maurice in 602 was the most far reaching and destructive. The effects of the Persian sweep through the lands of the Byzantine Empire affected society at many levels. It destroyed Byzantine imperial control over the lands of the Near East, it severed the links with Constantinople; governors were no longer appointed, armies were no longer dispatched and taxes were no longer paid. The Chalcedonian Orthodox Church lost its imperial patronage and became one Christian sect among many others. Many churchmen and other members of the elite fled to the comparative safety of North Africa or Italy. Archaeological work has suggested that, in Anatolia at least, the advance of the Persian armies did enormous damage to urban life and that people abandoned the spacious cities of the plains to take refuge in mountain-top fortresses.[2] The restoration of Byzantine imperial control came only a year or two before the Arab armies marched from Medina, and in many areas there may have been no Byzantine military and political structures in place at all.

A distinguishing feature of this 'last great war of antiquity' was that it devastated both of the great empires with even-handed brutality. Heraclius's invasion of the Persian Empire was as destructive as the Persian invasions of the Byzantine Empire had been; the great fire-temple at Shiz, where the Sasanian shahs had been inaugurated, was destroyed and the royal palace at Dastgard sacked. More crucially, the great king Chosroes II (591–628) was killed by his own generals. The Sasanian Empire, unlike the Byzantine, was formally a dynastic state; Heraclius's assault undermined the prestige of the dynasty and the confidence of the Persian ruling elite. Infighting among the members of the royal family caused a period of great instability. By the time that Yazdgard III (632–51) was widely accepted as shāh, the Arab armies were already attacking the Iraqi frontier.

The success of the conquest was also aided by the succession disputes that paralysed the Byzantine state after the death of Heraclius in February 641. The power struggle at the Byzantine court seems to have been directly responsible for the otherwise inexplicable failure to mount an effective operation to defend Egypt. If Heraclius had been succeeded by a strong and energetic new emperor, the Byzantines might well have been able to mount a counter-attack in Syria or along the Mediterranean coasts, especially during the very disturbed period that followed the assassination of the caliph Uthmān in 656. The Muslims had a generation in which to consolidate their power and their hold over the lands won from the Byzantines.

Both great empires shared a common strength that was also, paradoxically, a weakness when things went wrong. In the Byzantine and Sasanian states, military power was heavily centralized, both depending on a professional army supported by state taxation. This was a comparatively new development. In the Byzantine Empire there had been *limitanei*, troops settled along the frontiers and given land and salaries to defend the borders of the empire. During the first half of the sixth century these were disbanded and replaced by the Ghassānid nomad allies of the Byzantines. After 582 these too were dispensed with and the empire relied on a standing field army for its defence. It seems that the Byzantines were completely unprepared for an attack from the desert. The *Strategikon*, the military manual of *c.* 600, gives instructions on how to fight Persians, Turks and Avars but never mentions the Arabs; clearly they were not considered to be a significant threat. Apart from the Arab allies, it looks as if few of the Byzantine soldiers who tried to defend the empire against the Muslim invaders were local to the area. They were either Greek speakers from other parts of the empire or Armenians. A similar evolution had taken place in the Sasanian Empire. In the first half of the sixth century the administration had been centralized by Chosroes I (531–79), who had established an imperial army paid from the receipts of taxation. Like the Byzantines in the same period, the Sasanians had decided that they no longer needed the services of the Lakhmid kings who had defended the desert frontier. Now it was only the army of the shahs which defended the state.

In many ways these developments can be seen as a sign of the increasing power and sophistication of government, but it paradoxically resulted in these apparently powerful states being unexpectedly vulnerable. If the imperial government was in disarray, if the imperial army was defeated in one major encounter, there were no forces of local resistance to take on the burden of defence. There were no town armies raised from local citizens, no peasant militia that could be called upon. It is significant that the areas where the Arabs encountered the most sustained resistance were areas like Transoxania, Armenia, the Elburz mountains and the Cantabrian mountains of northern Spain, places that had always been outside the direct rule of the empires and monarchies of the lowland areas. Here local people actively defended their homelands against the invaders.

There are indications from many areas conquered by the Muslims that the invaders benefited from internal tensions in the ancient empires, which meant that, in some cases, they were seen as liberators or at least as a tolerable alternative. Sometimes these tensions were religious: the Monophysite Christians of Egypt and northern Syria certainly had little reason to love the Byzantine authorities, although there is little evidence that they actually helped the invaders. The peasants of the Sawād of Iraq may well have felt relieved by the destruction of the Persian ruling class; the merchants and craftsmen of Sind are said to have cooperated willingly with the Muslims against the Brahmin military ruling class. In North Africa, the Berbers fought their battles against the invaders, made alliances with them, took service with them and left the Byzantines to their fate.

The subject communities did not develop a culture of resistance after the initial conquests. They complained about harsh and unjust governors but, as far as we can tell, no preachers or writers emerged to encourage active opposition to the new regime. The anti-Muslim propaganda from Christian sources resorts to apocalyptic literature in which a great emperor or hero figure from outside will come and deliver the Christian people. Meanwhile, all they can do is pray and keep steadfast in their faith. Their hostility to other Christians from different sects, and above all to the Jews, was always fiercer and more pressing than their hostility to the Arabs. None of the voices of the conquered was an incitement to take action to overthrow the new regime.

These internal events in the Byzantine and Sasanian empires were fundamental to the success of the Arab conquests. If Muhammad had been born a generation earlier and he and his successors had attempted to send armies against the great empires in, say, 600, it is hard to imagine that they would have made any progress at all.

The weakness of the existing political structures did not, by itself, guarantee the success of Arab arms. There were potent forces at work which made the Muslim forces much more powerful and effective than any Bedouin force had ever been before or was ever to be again.

Enough has already been said about the religious motivation of the invaders, the power of the idea of martyrdom and paradise as incentives in battle. This was combined with the traditional, pre-Islamic ideals of loyalty to tribe and kin, and admiration of the lone warrior hero. The mixture of the cultural values of the nomad society with the ideology of the new religion was formidable.

It must be remembered that the armies of the early Islamic conquests were exactly that – armies. They were not a mass migration of nomad tribesmen. They left their women and their flocks, their babies and their old people, at home, in tent or house. They were organized into groups and their commanders were appointed, usually after consultation, by the caliphs or governors. Only after victory had been achieved did their households join the warriors.

As we have seen, the Arab armies did not have access to new technologies that their enemies did not possess, nor did they overwhelm by sheer weight of numbers, but they did have some purely military advantages. The most important of these was mobility. The distances covered by Muslim armies in the conquests are truly astonishing. It is more than 7,000 kilometres from the furthest reaches of Morocco in the west to the eastern frontiers of the Muslim world in Central Asia. By contrast, the Roman Empire from Hadrian's Wall to the Euphrates frontier was less than 5,000. All these areas were traversed and subdued by fast-moving Muslim armies. Much of the country in which they operated was barren and inhospitable, to be crossed only by hardy and resourceful people. Their armies moved without a supply train. It seems that the warriors carried their food with them and bought, stole or otherwise extracted supplies when these were exhausted. Both men and beasts were used to living off very little, the meagre diet of the Bedouin existence, and had experience of sleeping rough. Travelling by night, when the air was cooler and the desert stars bright enough to use for navigation, was an important part of desert life, and there are a number of conflicts recorded in the annals of the conquests in which the Arab armies showed their superiority at night fighting. This mobility meant that they could retreat into the desert, to take refuge, to regroup after a defeat or to take the enemy unawares.

The quality of leadership in the Muslim armies was clearly very high. The small elite of Hijazi city dwellers, mostly from the Quraysh and associated tribes, who provided the majority of the senior commanders, produced some extremely able men. Khālid b. al-Walīd in Syria, Amr b. al-Ās in Egypt and Saʿd b. Abī Waqqās in Iraq were all military leaders of distinction. In the next generation we can point to Uqba b. Nāfi in North Africa, Tāriq b. Ziyād and Mūsā b. Nusayr in Spain, Qutayba b. Muslim in Transoxania and Muhammad b. Ishāq al-Thaqafī in Sind as great commanders. The Arabic sources also talk a great deal about councils of war and commanders taking advice before deciding on a course of action. This is partly a literary fiction, designed to outline the possible military activity and emphasize the 'democratic' nature of early Muslim society, but it may be a genuine reflection of practice, whereby decisions were made after a process of consultation and discussion.

The effectiveness of the leadership may be in part a product of the political traditions of Arabian society. Leadership was passed down from generation to generation within certain families and kins, but within those groups any aspiring leader had to prove himself, showing his followers that he was brave, intelligent and diplomatic. If he failed, they would look for someone else. He also had to take account of the views and opinions of those he hoped to lead. Being someone's son was never qualification enough. The astonishment of the Iranian queen mother that the sons of the great Qutayba b. Muslim did not inherit his position are an indication of the difference in culture between Iranian and Arab in this respect. Incompetent or dictatorial commanders were unlikely to survive for long. Ubayd Allāh b. Abī Bakra in Afghanistan and Junayd b. Abd al-Rahmān in Transoxania are among the few examples of failure in command; they lasted only a short time and were savagely excoriated by the poets, the political commentators of their time.

There were other features of the Muslim command structure which led to success. The sources lay continuous stress on the roles of caliphs and governors, particularly the caliph Umar I (634–44), in organizing and directing the conquests. It is quite impossible that Umar could have written all the letters about the minutiae of military operations that are ascribed to him, but these narratives may reflect the fact that there was a strong degree of organization and control from Medina and later from Damascus. There are very few examples of commanders disobeying orders, equally few of rebellions against the centre by commanders in distant fields and provinces. This is all the more striking because it contrasts with events in the contemporary Byzantine Empire, where the military effectiveness of the state was constantly undermined by rebellions of military commanders hoping to take the imperial crown. The way in which successful generals like Khālid b. al-Walīd, Amr b. al-Ās, Mūsā b. Nusayr and Muhammad b. Ishāq accepted their dismissal and quietly made their way back to the centre, often to face punishment and disgrace, is very striking.

A key element in the success of the conquests was the comparatively easy terms usually imposed on the conquered. Arab commanders were normally content to make agreements that protected the lives and properties of the conquered, including rights to their places of worship, in exchange for the payment of tribute and the promise that they would not help the enemies of the Muslims. Defeated defenders of cities that were conquered by force were sometimes executed, but there were few examples of wholesale massacres of entire populations. Demands for houses for Muslims to settle in, as at Homs, or any other demands for property, are rare. Equally rare was deliberate damaging or destruction of existing cities and villages. There is a major contrast here with, for example, the Mongols in the thirteenth century, with their well-deserved reputation for slaughter and destruction. Although we cannot be clear about this, it is possible that the Arabs were, initially at least, less demanding of the resources and services of the ordinary people than their Byzantine and Sasanian predecessors, and the taxes they imposed may actually have been lower. It is not until the end of the seventh century that we get complaints about oppressive tax gathering. It must also have been the case that for many of the conquered the Arabs seemed a one-season wonder, a massive raid that could be bought off this year and would probably never happen again: better to pay up and sign the necessary documents than risk having your city stormed, your men killed and your women and children sold into slavery.

The Arab Muslim troops began to settle in the newly conquered areas very soon after the conquests. When they did so, they were almost always separate from the local population. In Iraq they were concentrated in the three Islamic new towns, Kūfa, Basra and Mosul. Arab settlement in Egypt was initially confined to Fustāt, much of it built on open land; in Africa the main early Muslim settlement took place in the new town of Qayrawān, while in Khurasan the largest Arab settlement was in Merv, where a whole new quarter was developed outside the walls of the old Sasanian city. In Syria, the Arabs tended to settle in extra-mural suburbs of existing cities like Chalkis and Aleppo, rather than taking possession of properties in the centre. To a great extent this prevented the inevitable friction that would have arisen between the conquering army and local inhabitants if they had shared the same narrow streets and courtyards.

The Arab conquest was also dispersed geographically. The Arabs rode along the main routes, and they stormed or accepted the surrender of the main towns. But away from the highways, in the mountains and more remote valleys, there must have been many communities that never saw an Arab, who heard only weeks, months or even years later that they were no longer ruled by the emperor or the shāh. The mountains of Azerbaijan, the ranges at the south of the Caspian Sea, the hills of Kurdistan, the High Atlas of southern Morocco, the Sierra de Gredos in Spain were probably all places where Arab Muslims were seldom seen. It was only in the two or three centuries that followed the initial conquest that Muslim missionaries, merchants and adventurers entered these lands and began to spread the new religion and news about the new political authorities. There was no incentive for the people of these areas to resist the invaders, because the invaders simply bypassed them.

As we have repeatedly seen, the Muslim conquerors put little or no pressure on the recently subjected populations to convert to Islam. Any attempt at compulsory conversion would probably have provoked widespread outrage and open hostility. As it was, the Muslim authorities established working relationships with the heads of the churches and other religious institutions that were now in their power. Conversion when it came was partly the result of fiscal pressures, the desire to escape the hated poll tax, but also because conversion provided an opportunity to escape from existing social constraints and to become a part of the new ruling class. Being a Muslim had always been essential for anyone who wanted a career in the military. By the tenth century, and before in some areas, it had become very difficult to have a successful career in the civil bureaucracy without becoming a Muslim. Attraction, not coercion, was the key to the appeal of the new faith.

During the first century, the Muslim Empire was a fairly open society. The elite of the new empire were the Muslims and Islam claimed to be a religion for all mankind. No would-be convert could be denied membership of this new elite. In contrast, Roman citizenship or membership of Persian aristocratic families was an exclusive, privileged position to be defended by those who enjoyed it. By converting to the new religion of Islam, conquered people could move to being conquerors, members of the new ruling class and, at least theoretically, equal to all other Muslims. Of course, problems soon arose and there were prolonged and violent clashes between old Muslims and new Arab and non-Arab Muslims, but this could not undermine the fact that Islam was open to all.

This is the other side of the collapse of the old social order and class boundaries lamented in aristocratic Persian sources of the period.

There were some spectacular examples of this mobility. Nusayr was a prisoner of war, probably of humble Aramaean origin, captured in one of the early Arab campaigns in Iraq. He converted to Islam and his son Mūsā went on to become governor of North Africa and supreme commander of the Muslim forces in the conquest of Spain. At a humbler level, the peasants who refused to obey the orders of the Persian landowner in Iraq, the Copts who chose to stay in North Africa rather than being forced to return to their native Egypt, or the local men who served with the Arab armies in Transoxania may all have seen the coming of the Muslims as an opportunity to better themselves, taking advantage of the freedom and opportunities offered by the new order.

The early Muslims brought with them a great cultural self-confidence. God had spoken to them through His Prophet, in Arabic, and they were the bearers of true religion and God's own language. It is interesting to compare this with the Germanic invaders of western Europe in the fifth century. When they occupied the lands of the Roman Empire, they abandoned their old gods and converted to Christianity, the religion of the empire they had just conquered, and, as far as we know, no one claimed that God spoke German. This cultural self-confidence meant that Arabic became the language of administration and the language of the new high culture. Anyone who wished to participate fully in government or intellectual activity had to be literate in Arabic and preferably a Muslim. Again the contrast with the Germanic west is revealing. Here Latin remained the language of administration and high culture until at least the twelfth century, the new ruling class adopted Latin titles like duke (*dux*) and count (*comes*), and the Germanic languages survived only as vernaculars. The Muslim titles, caliph (*khalīfa*), *amīr* and *wālī* (governor) were all Arabic in origin.

Nonetheless, conquest was the prelude to conversion. It established the political and social framework within which the much slower, incremental processes of changing to Islam could take place. By the year 1000, it is likely that the majority of the population in all the different areas that had been conquered by 750 were Muslim.[3] The conquest did not cause conversion but it was a major prerequisite: without it Islam would not have become the dominant faith in these areas.

The success of the Muslim conquests was the product of a unique set of circumstances and the preaching of a simple new monotheistic faith. There were many features of Islam that would have made it approachable to Christians and Jews. It had a Prophet, a Holy Book, established forms of prayer, dietary and family laws. Abraham and Jesus were both great prophets in the Muslim tradition. From the very beginning Islam established itself as a new faith, but it was one that claimed to perfect rather than destroy the older monotheistic ones. It had none of the strangeness of, say, Buddhism. These similarities, this common tradition, must have aided and encouraged conversion.

In many ways acceptance of Muslim rule was the result of Muslim policy towards the enemy: it was almost always preferable to surrender to the invaders and to make terms and pay the taxes than to resist to the last. The Islamization and Arabization that followed conquest over the next two or three centuries would not have occurred if political conquest had not already succeeded, but they were not a direct and inevitable consequence of that conquest. Instead, it was a gradual, almost entirely peaceful result of the fact that more and more people wanted to identify with and participate in the dominant culture of their time.

In the final analysis, the success of the Muslim conquest was a result of the unstable and impoverished nature of the whole post-Roman world into which they came, the hardiness and self-reliance of the Bedouin warriors and the inspiration and open quality of the new religion of Islam.

NOTES

PREFACE

1. See S. Brock, 'North Mesopotamia in the late seventh century: Book XV of John Bar Penkaye's *Rīs Melle*', *Jerusalem Studies in Arabic and Islam* 9 (1987): 51–75.

FOREWORD: REMEMBRANCE OF THINGS PAST

1. For this change and its importance, see J. Bloom, *Paper before Print: The History and Impact of Paper in the Islamic World* (New Haven, CT, 2001).
2. See the discussion of this and other military topoi in A. Noth with L. I. Conrad, *The Early Arabic Historical Tradition: A source-critical study*, trans. M. Bonner (Princeton, NJ, 1994), pp. 109–72.
3. P. Crone and M. A. Cook, *Hagarism: The Making of the Islamic World* (Cambridge, 1977).
4. E. Landau-Tasseron, 'Sayf ibn Umar in medieval and modern scholarship', *Der Islam* 67 (1990): 1–26.
5. J. Fentress and C. J. Wickham, *Social Memory* (Oxford, 1992).

6. Ibn Abd al-Hakam, *Futūḥ Miṣr*, ed. C. C. Torrey (New Haven, CT, 1921), pp. 74–6.
7. Sebeos, *The Armenian History*, trans. R. W. Thomson, with notes by J. Howard-Johnston and T. Greenwood, 2 vols. (Liverpool, 1999).
8. John of Nikiu, *The Chronicle of John (c. 690 AD) Coptic Bishop of Nikiu*, trans. R. H. Charles (London, 1916).
9. See J. Johns, 'Archaeology and the history of early Islam: the first seventy years', *Journal of the Economic and Social History of the Orient* 46 (2003): 411–36.

1. THE FOUNDATIONS OF CONQUEST

1. On Rusāfa and the cult of St Sergius, see E. K. Fowden, *The Barbarian Plain: Saint Sergius between Rome and Iran* (Berkeley, CA, 1999).
2. Quoted in A. Jones, *Early Arabic Poetry*, 2 vols. (Oxford, 1992), I, p. 1.
3. C. Lyall, *The Dīwāns of ʿAbīd ibn al-Abras, of Asad and ʿĀmir ibn at-*

Tufayl, of ʿĀmir ibn Saʿsaʿah
(London, 1913).
4. Lyall, Dīwāns, p. 106.
5. For the best introduction to the
history of the south Arabian
kings, see R. Hoyland, Arabia and
the Arabs: From the Bronze Age to
the Coming of Islam (London,
2001), pp. 36–57.
6. G. W. Heck, 'Gold mining in
Arabia and the rise of the Islamic
state', Journal of the Economic and
Social History of the Orient 42
(1999): 364–95.
7. Mughīrah b. Zurāra al-Usaydī;
Tabarī, Ta'rīkh, ed. M.J. de Goeje
et al. (Leiden 1879–1901), I, pp.
2241–2.
8. Al-Nuʿmān b. Muqarrin; Tabarī,
Ta'rīkh, I, pp. 2239–40.
9. G. M. Hinds, 'Maghāzī',
Encyclopaedia of Islam, 2nd edn.
10. This discussion of jihād is based
on R. Firestone, Jihād: The
Origin of Holy War in Islam
(Oxford, 1999).
11. See R. P. Mottahedeh and R. al-
Sayyid, 'The idea of the jihād in
Islam before the Crusades', in
The Crusades from the Perspective
of Byzantium and the Muslim
World, ed. A. E. Laiou and R. P.
Mottahedeh (Washington, DC,
2001), pp. 23–39.
12. Al-Nuʿmān b. al-Muqarrin;
Tabarī, Ta'rīkh, I, p. 2240.
13. Quoted in F. M. Donner, The
Early Islamic Conquests
(Princeton, NJ, 1981), p. 67. See
also M. Lecker, 'The estates of
ʿAmr b. al-ʿĀs in Palestine',
Bulletin of the School of Oriental

and African Studies 52 (1989): pp.
24–37.
14. Quoted in Lecker, 'Estates', p. 25
from Ibn Abd al-Hakam, Futūh,
p. 146.
15. On this, see Donner, Early Islamic
Conquests, p. 81
16. Firestone, Jihād, pp. 124–5.
17. Donner, Early Islamic Conquests,
p. 135.
18. Ibid., pp. 205–9.
19. For the visual images, see D.
Nicolle, Armies of the Muslim
Conquests (London, 1993);
Nicolle, 'War and society in the
eastern Mediterranean', in War
and Society in the Eastern
Mediterranean 7th to 15th
centuries, ed. Y. Lev (Leiden,
1997), pp. 9–100.
20. Tabarī, Ta'rīkh, II, p. 1315.
21. On weapons in general, see H.
Kennedy, The Armies of the
Caliphs (London, 2001), pp.
173–8; on swords, see R.
Hoyland and B. Gilmour,
Medieval Islamic Swords and
Swordmaking: Kindi's treatise 'On
swords and their kinds' (London,
2006).
22. See Kennedy, Armies, pp. 169–72.
23. Tabarī, Ta'rīkh, II, pp. 554–5.
24. See H. Kennedy, 'The military
revolution and the early Islamic
state', in Noble Ideals and Bloody
realities: Warfare in the Middle
Ages, ed. N. Christie and M.
Yazigi (Leiden, 2006), pp.
197–208.
25. On Islamic siege engines, see P.
E. Chevedden, 'The hybrid
trebuchet: the halfway step to the
counterweight trebuchet', in On

the *Social Origins of Medieval
Institutions. Essays in Honor of
Joseph F. O'Callaghan*, ed. D.
Kagay and T. Vann (Leiden,
1998), pp. 179–222.

26. Tabarī, *Ta'rīkh*, I, pp. 2427–8.
27. Tabarī, *Ta'rīkh*, I, p. 2237,
ascribed to al-Mughīra b. Shuʿba.
28. Tabarī, *Ta'rīkh*, I, p. 2309.
29. Awf b. Hārith, quoted in
Firestone, *Jihād*, p. 114.
30. Tabarī, *Ta'rīkh*, I, p. 2271,
ascribed to Ribʿī b. ʿĀmir.
31. Tabarī, *Ta'rīkh*, I, p. 2289.
32. Tabarī, *Ta'rīkh*, I, p. 2365.
33. Tabarī, *Ta'rīkh*, I, pp. 2302–3.
34. Tabarī, *Ta'rīkh*, I, pp. 2293–4.

2. THE CONQUEST OF SYRIA
AND PALESTINE

1. A. Cameron, 'Cyprus at the time
of the Arab conquests', *Cyprus
Historical Review* 1 (1992): 27–49,
reprinted in *eadem, Changing
Cultures in Early Byzantium*
(Aldershot, 1996), VI.
2. Balādhurī, *Futūh al-Buldān*, ed.
M. J. de Goeje (Leiden, 1866,
repr. Leiden, 1968), p. 129.
3. Tabarī, *Ta'rīkh*, I, p. 2156.
4. Donner, *Early Islamic Conquests*,
p. 119.
5. For this chronology, based on *The
Chronicle of 724* see Donner, *Early
Islamic Conquests*, p. 126;
Balādhurī, *Futūh*, p. 109.
6. 'Doctrina Jacobi Nuper
Baptizati', ed. with French trans.
V. Déroche in *Travaux et
Mémoires* (Collège de France,
Centre de recherche d'histoire et
civilisation de Byzance) 11

(1991): 47–273, cap. V, 16 (pp.
208–9).
7. See N. M. El Cheikh, *Byzantium
Viewed by the Arabs* (Cambridge,
MA, 2004), pp. 39–54.
8. Tabarī, *Ta'rīkh*, I, pp. 1561–2.
9. Tabarī, *Ta'rīkh*, I, pp. 2108–25,
Balādhurī, *Futūh*, pp. 110–12;
Ibn Athʿam al-Kūfī, *Kitāb al-
Futūh*, ed. S. A. Bukhari, 7 vols.
(Hyderabad, 1974), vol. I, pp.
132–42; al-Yaʿqūbī, *Ta'rīkh*, ed.
M. Houtsma, 2 vols. (Leiden,
1883), vol. II, pp. 133–4.
10. See Donner, *Early Islamic
Conquests*, pp. 119–27 for the best
discussion.
11. Tabarī, *Ta'rīkh*, I, pp. 2113–14.
12. P. Crone, 'Khālid b. al-Walīd',
Encyclopaedia of Islam, 2nd edn.
13. Tabarī, *Ta'rīkh*, I, pp. 2097,
2114–15; Balādhurī, *Futūh*, p.
112.
14. This account is based on the
chronology worked out by Ibn
Ishāq and al-Wāqidi, two
important eighth-century
authorities, and described in
Donner, *Early Islamic Conquests*,
pp. 128–34. For alternative
chronologies, see ibid., pp. 134–9
(Sayf b. Umar) and pp. 139–420.
15. Tabarī, *Ta'rīkh*, I, pp. 2398–401.
16. Fredegar, *The Fourth Book of the
Chronicle of Fredegar with its
Continuations*, trans. J. M.
Wallace-Hadrill (London,
1960), p. 55.
17. Sebeos, *The Armenian History*,
trans. R. W. Thomson, with
notes by J. Howard-Johnston and
T. Greenwood, 2 vols.
(Liverpool, 1999), I, p. 97.

380 THE GREAT ARAB CONQUESTS

18. Tabarī, *Ta'rīkh*, I, pp. 2145–6, 2157.
19. Tabarī, *Ta'rīkh*, I, p. 2152.
20. Balādhurī, *Futūh*, p. 121.
21. Tabarī, *Ta'rīkh*, I, p. 2154.
22. Tabarī, *Ta'rīkh*, I, p. 2393.
23. See, for example, Tabarī, *Ta'rīkh*, I, p. 2099.
24. W. E. Kaegi, *Byzantium and the Early Islamic Conquests* (Cambridge, 1992), p. 127.
25. Donner, *Early Islamic Conquests*, p. 133. Kaegi, *Byzantium*, p. 121, has the climax of the battle on 20 August without citing any sources.
26. Tabarī, *Ta'rīkh*, I, p. 2091.
27. Tabarī, *Ta'rīkh*, I, pp. 2091–2.
28. See L. Caetani, *Annali dell'Islam* (Milan, 1905–26), III, pp. 491–613, and the discussion in Kaegi, *Byzantium*, pp. 122–3, esp. n. 23.
29. The account that follows is based on Kaegi, *Byzantium*, pp. 119–22 and the map on p. 113.
30. Tabarī, *Ta'rīkh*, I, p. 2099.
31. Tabarī, *Ta'rīkh*, I, p. 2092.
32. Tabarī, *Ta'rīkh*, I, p. 2100.
33. Fredegar, *Chronicle*, p. 55.
34. Quoted in Kaegi, *Byzantium*, p. 141.
35. Tabarī, *Ta'rīkh*, I, pp. 2390–93; Balādhurī, *Futūh*, pp. 130–31 for the fall of Homs.
36. Balādhurī, *Futūh*, p. 131.
37. Balādhurī, *Futūh*, p. 131 and Yāqūt, *Mu'jam al-Buldān*, ed. F. Wüstenfeld (Leipzig, 1886), 'Homs'.
38. Tabarī, *Ta'rīkh*, I, pp. 2393–5.
39. Balādhurī, *Futūh*, pp. 139–40.
40. Tabarī, *Ta'rīkh*, I, p. 2396.
41. Balādhurī, *Futūh*, p. 137.
42. Tabarī, *Ta'rīkh*, I, p. 2396
43. Michael the Syrian, *Chronicle*, ed. with French trans. J.-B. Chabot, 4 vols. (Paris, 1899–1924), II, p. 424.
44. Balādhurī, *Futūh*, p. 131: *muqallisīn*, 'a mime, a mummer, one who beats the Arabian drum (*daf*) and meets or goes before kings and other great men with that and other musical instruments on triumphal occasions'.
45. Ancient Adhri'āt; Balādhurī, *Futūh*, p. 139.
46. Balādhurī, *Futūh*, p. 142.
47. Balādhurī, *Futūh*, pp. 132–3.
48. Balādhurī, *Futūh*, p. 127.
49. For the map, see H. Donner, *The Mosaic Map of Madaba: An introductory guide* (Kampen, 1992).
50. Translated in R. Hoyland, *Seeing Islam as Others Saw It: A Survey and Evaluation of Christian, Jewish and Zoroastrian Writings on Early Islam* (Princeton, NJ, 1997), pp. 72–3.
51. Donner, *Early Islamic Conquests*, pp. 151–2.
52. Tabarī, *Ta'rīkh*, I, pp. 2405–6.
53. Sa'īd ibn Batrīq, *Das Annalenwerk des Eutychios von Alexandrien*, ed. M. Breydy in *Corpus Scriptorum Christianorum Orientalium*, vol. 471 Scriptores Arabici, t. 44 (Leuven, 1985); see also R. L. Wilken, *The Land Called Holy: Palestine in Christian History and Thought* (New Haven, CT, 1992), pp. 233–9.
54. C. F. Robinson, *Empire and Elites*

after the Muslim Conquest: The Transformation of Northern Mesopotamia (Cambridge, 2000), p. 34.

55. On the sources for the conquest and the problems they raise, see Robinson, *Empire and Elites*, pp. 1–32.
56. Balādhurī, *Futūh*, pp. 172–3.
57. Balādhurī, *Futūh*, p. 176.
58. Balādhurī, *Futūh*, p. 123.
59. Balādhurī, *Futūh*, p. 126.
60. For the documents, see C. J. Kraemer, Jr, *Excavations at Nessana*, vol. 3: *Non-Literary Papyri* (Princeton, NJ, 1958), pp. 175–97.

3. THE CONQUEST OF IRAQ

1. For a general history of the Sasanian Empire, see A. Christensen, *L'Iran sous les Sassanides* (rev. 2nd edn, Copenhagen, 1944); *Cambridge History of Iran*, vol. III: *The Seleucid, Parthian and Sasanian Periods*, ed. E. Yarshater (Cambridge, 1983); M. Morony, 'Sāsānids', in *Encylopaedia of Islam*, 2nd edn, with full bibliography; Z. Rubin,'The Sasanian Monarchy', in *Cambridge Ancient History*, vol. XIV: *Late Antiquity: Empire and successors, A.D. 425–600*, ed. A. Cameron, B. Ward-Perkins and M. Whitby (Cambridge, 2000), pp. 638–61; for Iraq under Sasanian rule, see M. Morony, *Iraq after the Muslim Conquest* (Princeton, NJ, 1984).
2. For Zoroastrians in Iraq, see

Morony, *Iraq*, pp. 281–300.
3. For Christians and Jews, see ibid., pp. 306–42.
4. On the history of agriculture and settlement in central Iraq, see R. McC. Adams, *The Land behind Baghdad: A history of settlement on the Diyala Plain* (Chicago, IL, 1965).
5. Morony, *Iraq*, pp. 185–90.
6. On the Aramaens, see ibid., pp. 169–80.
7. *Maurice's Strategikon: handbook of Byzantine military strategy*, trans. G. T. Dennis (Philadelphia, PA, 1984), pp. 113–15.
8. The following account is based on R. N. Frye, 'The political history of Iran under the Sasanians', in *Cambridge History of Iran*, vol. III: *The Seleucid, Parthian and Sasanian Periods*, ed. E. Yarshater (Cambridge, 1983), pp. 168–71.
9. Adams, *Land behind Baghdad*, pp. 81–2.
10. Donner, *Early Islamic Conquests*, pp. 170–73.
11. Ibid., p. 178. For Khālid's campaigns in Iraq, see Balādhurī, *Futūh*, pp. 241–50.
12. Donner, *Early Islamic Conquests*, p. 179.
13. Balādhurī, *Futūh*, pp. 242–3.
14. Balādhurī, *Futūh*, p. 243.
15. The excavations, led by D. Talbot Rice were published as 'The Oxford excavations at Hira, 1931', *Antiquity* 6.23 (1932): 276–91 and 'The Oxford excavations at Hira', *Ars Islamica* 1 (1934): 51–74. Sadly there were no further campaigns on the site.

16. Balādhurī, *Futūh*, p. 244.
17. Balādhurī, *Futūh*, p. 243.
18. Balādhurī, *Futūh*, pp. 247–8.
19. Tabarī, *Ta'rīkh*, I, p. 2159.
20. Balādhurī, *Futūh*, pp. 251–2.
21. Tabarī, *Ta'rīkh*, I, p. 2178.
22. Tabarī, *Ta'rīkh*, I, pp. 2174–5.
23. Tabarī, *Ta'rīkh*, I, p. 2179.
24. Balādhurī, *Futūh*, p. 254.
25. Balādhurī, *Futūh*, p. 255.
26. Firestone, *Jihad: The Origin of Holy War*, p. 106.
27. Donner, *Early Islamic Conquests*, p. 206.
28. Ibid., p. 221.
29. Ibid., p. 205.
30. Balādhurī, *Futūh*, pp. 255–62.
31. Tabarī, *Ta'rīkh*, I, p. 2377.
32. Sebeos, *The Armenian History*, pp. 98–9, 244–5; Movses of Dàsxuranci, *The History of the Caucasian Albanians*, trans. C. J. F. Dowsett (Oxford, 1961), pp. 110–11.
33. Christensen, *L'Iran*, pp. 499–500.
34. Especially Tabarī, *Ta'rīkh*, I, pp. 2247–9.
35. Firdawsi, *Shahnāmah*, trans. D. Davis (Washington, DC, 1998–2004), Vol. III, pp. 492–6.
36. Tabarī, *Ta'rīkh*, I, pp. 2269–77.
37. Tabarī, *Ta'rīkh* I, p. 2270.
38. The word used is *tarjumān*. With the 'j' pronounced as a hard 'g' in Egyptian dialect, this became the dragoman, the term used by eighteenth- and nineteenth-century travellers in the Levant to describes their local guides and agents.
39. Tabarī, *Ta'rīkh*, I, p. 2269, names al-Sarī and Shuᶜayb.
40. Balādhurī, *Futūh*, pp. 259–60.

41. Firdawsi, *Shahnāmah*, III, p. 499.
42. Balādhurī, *Futūh*, p. 258.
43. Tabarī, *Ta'rīkh*, I, p. 2421.
44. Tabarī, *Ta'rīkh*, I, p. 2411.
45. Nā'il b. Juᶜsham al-Aᶜrajī al-Tamīmī; Tabarī, *Ta'rīkh*, I, pp. 2422–4, trans. Juynboll.
46. Morony, *Iraq*, p. 186.
47. Tabarī, *Ta'rīkh*, I, p. 2425.
48. Tabarī, *Ta'rīkh*, I, pp. 2429–30. Juynboll suggests the identification of Ifridūn but it is not certain. The general sense of the remarks is, however, entirely clear.
49. Tabarī, *Ta'rīkh*, I, pp. 2433–4.
50. Tabarī, *Ta'rīkh*, I, p. 2438.
51. Balādhurī, *Futūh*, p. 263.
52. Tabarī, *Ta'rīkh*, I, p. 2451.
53. Tabarī, *Ta'rīkh*, I, pp. 2441, 2451.
54. Tabarī, *Ta'rīkh*, I, pp. 2450–56.
55. Tabarī, *Ta'rīkh*, I, p. 2445.
56. Tabarī, *Ta'rīkh*, I, p. 2446.
57. Tabarī, *Ta'rīkh*, I, pp. 2446–7.
58. Tabarī, *Ta'rīkh*, I, p. 2453. The Persian tradition of carpet weaving is very ancient but no trace of carpets from this period survives. The oldest existing Persian carpets date from the fifteenth century and the earliest full-size masterpieces such as the Ardabil carpet from the sixteenth. Descriptions like this make it clear that such magnificent artworks were heirs to a thousand years of tradition.
59. Tabarī, *Ta'rīkh*, I, pp. 2453–4.
60. Balādhurī, *Futūh*, p. 264; Tabarī, *Ta'rīkh*, I, p. 2445.
61. Tabarī, *Ta'rīkh*, I, pp. 2442–3.
62. Tabarī, *Ta'rīkh*, I, p. 2457.
63. Tabarī, *Ta'rīkh*, I, p. 2459.

64. Ṭabarī, *Ta'rīkh*, I, p. 2463.
65. Ṭabarī, *Ta'rīkh*, I, pp. 2462–3.
66. Donner, *Early Islamic Conquests*, p. 213, estimates the numbers.
67. Balādhurī, *Futūḥ*, p. 341.
68. Koran, 4:15–16.
69. Balādhurī, *Futūḥ*, p. 345.
70. On this text, see C. F. Robinson, 'The conquest of Khuzistan: a historiographical reassessment', *Bulletin of the School of Oriental and African Studies* 67 (2004): 14–39.
71. Ṭabarī, *Ta'rīkh*, I, pp. 2567–8.
72. Ṭabarī, *Ta'rīkh*, I, pp. 2464–6.
73. Ṭabarī, *Ta'rīkh*, I, p. 2567.
74. Khuzistān Chronicle and Ṭabarī, *Ta'rīkh*, I, pp. 2554–5.
75. Ṭabarī, *Ta'rīkh*, I, pp. 2557–9; Ṭabarī, *Ta'rīkh*, I, p. 2560, gives a variation with a slightly different trick.
76. On the Hamra, see Morony, *Iraq*, pp. 197–8; M. Zakeri, *Sāsānid Soldiers in Early Muslim Society. The origins of 'Ayyārān and Futuwwa* (Wiesbaden, 1995), pp. 116–20.
77. Ṭabarī, *Ta'rīkh*, I, p. 2261.
78. Balādhurī, *Futūḥ*, p. 280; Morony, *Iraq*, p. 197.
79. See Morony, *Iraq*, p. 198; Zakeri, *Sāsānid Soldiers*, pp. 114–15.
80. Balādhurī, *Futūḥ*, p. 280.
81. Ṭabarī, *Ta'rīkh*, I, p. 2484.
82. Donner, *Early Islamic Conquests*, p. 229.
83. Ṭabarī, *Ta'rīkh*, I, p. 2488.
84. For the mosque, see Ṭabarī, *Ta'rīkh*, I, pp. 2488–94; H. Djaït, *Al-Kūfa: naissance de la ville islamique* (Paris, 1986), pp. 96–100.

85. Ṭabarī, *Ta'rīkh*, I, p. 2494.
86. Ṭabarī, *Ta'rīkh*, I, pp. 2490–91.
87. Ṭabarī, *Ta'rīkh*, I, p. 2492.
88. Ṭabarī, *Ta'rīkh*, I, pp. 2491–5.
89. Djaït, *Naissance*, pp. 102–3, rejects Sayf's narrative without giving any convincing reasons: the fact is, we simply do not know.
90. Djaït, *Naissance*, p. 108–111.
91. On this, see Donner, *Early Islamic Conquests*, p. 230.
92. See H. Kennedy, *The Armies of the Caliphs* (London, 2001), pp. 60–74.
93. Balādhurī, *Futūḥ*, p. 332. For the origins and early development of Mosul, see Robinson, *Empire and Elites*, pp. 63–71.
94. Morony, *Iraq*, p. 175.

4. THE CONQUEST OF EGYPT

1. For Egypt in the early seventh century, see W. E. Kaegi, 'Egypt on the eve of the Muslim conquest', in *Cambridge History of Egypt*, vol. I: *Islamic Egypt, 640–1517*, ed. C. Petry (Cambridge, 1998), pp. 34–61.
2. In this chapter, I have followed the 'tentative chronology' worked out in Kaegi, 'Egypt on the eve', pp. 60–61.
3. Ṭabarī, *Ta'rīkh*, I, pp. 2579–95.
4. Ibn Abd al-Hakam, Abū'l-Qāsim 'Abd al-Rahmān b. 'Abd Allāh, *Futūḥ Miṣr*, ed. C. C. Torrey (New Haven, CT, 1921). For critiques of this work, see R. Brunschvig, 'Ibn ᶜAbdal-hakam et la conquète de l'Afrique du Nord par les Arabes: etude critique', *Annales de l'Institut des*

Etudes Orientales 6 (1942–7): 108–55, and W. Kubiak, *Al-Fustāt, Its Foundation and Early Urban Development* (Cairo, 1987), pp. 18–22. Both see Ibn Abd al-Hakam as a jurist looking for legal precedents rather than as a historian. I think the historical content is more significant and Kubiak certainly exaggerates when he says (pp. 18–19) 'that its primary intention was not to transmit knowledge of bygone facts and events to posterity or to apothesize the warriors of the first generation of the Islamic conquerors, but to give a plausible historical explanation for a number of obscure juridico-religious traditions concerning the conquest of Egypt and North Africa'.

5. Kubiak, *Al-Fustāt*, p. 19. The earliest collector of traditions about the conquest seems to have been Yazīd b. Abī Habib (d. 745).

6. John of Nikiu, *The Chronicle of John (c.690 AD) Coptic Bishop of Nikiu*, trans. R. H. Charles (London, 1916).

7. See the second edition by P. M. Fraser (Oxford, 1978).

8. For Ancient Egypt, see R. E. Ritner, 'Egypt under Roman rule: the legacy of ancient Egypt', in *Cambridge History of Egypt*, vol. i: *Islamic Egypt, 640–1517*, ed. C. Petry (Cambridge, 1998), pp. 1–33.

9. Kaegi, 'Egypt on the eve', p. 33.

10. For Egypt in this period, see R. Bagnall, *Egypt in Late Antiquity* (Princeton, NJ, 1993).

11. On which see the discussion in Butler, *Arab Conquest*, pp. 401–25.

12. Ritner, 'Egypt', p. 30.

13. Kaegi, 'Egypt on the eve', p. 34.

14. Quoted in Butler, *Arab Conquest*, p. 72.

15. See Kaegi, 'Egypt on the eve', pp. 42–4.

16. On Benjamin, see his biography, in Sawīrus b. al-Muqaffa, 'Life of Benjamin I the thirty-eighth patriarch A.D. 622–61', in *History of the Patriarchs of the Coptic Church of Alexandria*, trans B. Evetts *(Patrologia Orientalis* I.4, 1905), pp. 487–518.

17. Sawīrus, 'Life of Benjamin', p. 496.

18. Butler, *Arab Conquest*, pp. 176–9.

19. Ibid., p. 183.

20. Sawīrus, 'Life of Benjamin', pp. 491–2.

21. Nikephorus, Patriarch of Constantinople, *Short History*, trans. C. Mango (Washington, DC, 1990), pp. 72–5.

22. This reconstruction is based on R. Hoyland, *Seeing Islam as Others Saw It*, pp. 574–90, which uses non-Arab sources, notably the Byzantine Chronicle of Nicephorus, to produce a plausible reconstruction; cf. the blunt dismissal of this possibility that Cyrus paid tribute by Butler, *Arab Conquest*, pp. 207–8.

23. Balādhurī, *Futūh*, p. 213; Ibn Abd al-Hakam, *Futūh*, pp. 56–7.

24. Ibn Abd al-Hakam, *Futūh*, p. 58.

25. Butler, *Arab Conquest*, pp. 209–10.

26. Ibid., p. 211.

27. Ibn Abd al-Hakam, *Futūh*, pp. 58–9.
28. Ibn Abd al-Hakam, *Futūh*, pp. 59–60.
29. Ibn Abd al-Hakam, *Futūh*, p. 60.
30. The rather confusing story in John of Nikiu, *Chronicle*, pp. 179–80 was used by Butler in his account (*Arab Conquest*, pp. 222–5), on which I have based this narrative.
31. *apud* Ibn Abd al-Hakam, *Futūh*, p. 61, but see also the other figures in Butler, *Arab Conquest*, p. 226, where he remarks that 'there is no sort of confusion not found among the Arab historians'. John of Nikiu speaks of 4,000 new men.
32. Ibn Abd al-Hakam, *Futūh*, p. 64.
33. Butler, *Arab Conquest*, p. 228.
34. John of Nikiu, *Chronicle*, p. 181; Ibn Abd al-Hakam, *Futūh*, p. 59; Butler, *Arab Conquest*, pp. 228–33.
35. See Butler, *Arab Conquest*, pp. 238–48, with a plan at p. 240; Kubiak, *Al-Fustat*, pp. 50–55.
36. John of Nikiu, *Chronicle*, pp. 186–7.
37. Ibn Abd al-Hakam, *Futūh*, p. 63; see Butler, *Arab Conquest*, p. 259 n. 1, in which he discusses other, later variants of this story and the 'invincible confusion' of the Arabic sources. See also Butler, 'Treaty of Misr' (published with separate pagination (1–64) and index at the end of Butler, *Arab Conquest*), pp. 16–19.
38. Balādhurī, *Futūh*, p. 213.
39. Yāqūt, 'Fustāt', Butler, *Arab Conquest*, p. 270, n. 3.

40. John of Nikiu, *Chronicle*, pp. 186–7.
41. The text is given Tabarī, *Ta'rīkh*, I, pp. 2588–9: it is discussed in Butler, 'Treaty of Misr'.
42. Butler 'Treaty of Misr', pp. 46–7.
43. D. R. Hill, *The Termination of Hostilities in the Early Arab Conquests AD 634–656* (London, 1971), pp. 34–44.
44. Balādhurī *Futūh*, pp. 214–15.
45. Yāqūt, 'Fustāt'.
46. Ibn Abd al-Hakam, *Futūh*, p. 73.
47. John of Nikiu, *Chronicle*, p. 188; Ibn Abd al-Hakam, *Futūh*; Butler, *Arab Conquest*, pp. 286–7.
48. Balādhurī, *Futūh*, p. 220.
49. Ibn Abd al-Hakam, *Futūh*, p. 74.
50. Butler, *Arab Conquest*, pp. 291–2, and the description of the city based largely on Arabic sources in ibid., pp. 368–400.
51. The free use of 'Palestine' to describe all of greater Syria is typical of late nineteenth-century scholarship, e.g. G. Le Strange, *Palestine under the Moslems: A description of Syria and the Holy Land from A.D. 650 to 1500* (London, 1890).
52. As Butler notes, 'these obelisks it was reserved for British and American vandalism to remove from Egypt: one is now on the Thames embankment, one in New York ... their height, about 68 feet, would enable at least their tops to be seen from some little distance without the walls'.
53. M. Rodziewicz, 'Transformation of Ancient Alexandria into a Medieval City', in *Colloque international d'archéologie*

islamique, ed. R-P. Gayraud (Cairo, 1998), pp. 368–86.

54. John of Nikiu, *Chronicle*, pp. 192–3.

55. See Hoyland's reconstruction of the 'common core' of the Syrian chronicle tradition in *Seeing Islam*, pp. 577–8.

56. Kubiak, *Al-Fustāt*, p. 71.

57. R.-P. Gayraud, 'Fostat: évolution d'une capitale arabe du VII au XII siècle d'après les fouilles d'Istabl ʿAntar', in *Colloque international d'archéologie islamique*, ed. R.-P. Gayraud (Cairo, 1998), pp. 436–60.

58. Ibn Abd al-Hakam, *Futūh*, p. 102.

59 I have estimated on the basis of the proposition that many of the men would have been single and married local women, but of course all these figures are very speculative.

60. Butler, *Arab Conquest*, p. 361.

61. Ibid., pp. 439–446, discusses the restoration of Benjamin.

62. Sawīrus, 'Life of Benjamin,' p. 500.

63. Ibid., pp. 496–7.

64. Ibn Abd al-Hakam, *Futūh*, pp. 180–82.

65. John of Nikiu, *Chronicle*, p. 200.

66. Three million is the conservative estimate given by Kaegi, 'Egypt on the eve', p. 34: 100,000 is an extrapolation of the figure of 40,000 men given by Ibn Abd al-Hakam, *Futūh*, p. 102, as the maximum number in the *dīwān* in early Umayyad times (see above, pp. 141, 162).

67. Butler, *Arab Conquest*, pp. 305–7.

68. Ibid., p. 534.

69. John of Nikiu, *Chronicle*, p. 182.

70. Ibid., p. 184.

5. THE CONQUEST OF IRAN

1. For a general account of the fall of the Sasanian Empire and the Muslim conquest of Iran, see A. Christensen, *L'Iran sous les Sassanides* (rev. 2nd edn, Copenhagen, 1944), pp. 497–509.

2. Tabarī, *Ta'rīkh*, I, pp. 2596–633; Balādhurī, *Futūh*, pp. 302–7; Ibn Aʿtham al-Kūfī, *Kitāb al-Futūh*, ed. S. A Bukhari, 7 vols. (Hyderabad, 1974), II, pp. 31–59. On the sources, see A. Noth, 'Isfahan-Nihāwand. Eine quellenkritische Studie zur frühislamischen Historiographie', *Zeitschrift der Deutschen Morgenländischen Gesellschaft* 118 (1968): 274–96.

3. Tabarī, *Ta'rīkh*, I, p. 2616.

4. Tabarī, *Ta'rīkh*, I, p. 2618.

5. Tabarī, *Ta'rīkh*, I, p. 2617.

6. Tabarī, *Ta'rīkh*, I, p. 2632.

7. Balādhurī, *Futūh*, p. 303.

8. Tabarī, *Ta'rīkh*, I, pp. 2623–4.

9. Tabarī, *Ta'rikh*, I, p. 2626.

10. Tabarī, *Ta'rīkh*, pp. 2627, 2649–50.

11. Balādhurī, *Futūh*, p. 305.

12. For the conquest of Hamadan, see Balādhurī, *Futūh*, p. 309.

13. S. Matheson, *Persia: An Archaeological Guide* (2nd rev. edn, London, 1976), p. 109.

14. For the conquest of Isfahan, see Balādhurī, *Futūh*, pp. 312–14.

15. Tabarī, *Ta'rīkh*, I, p. 2642.

16. Abu Nuʿaym al-Isfahānī, *Geschicte Isbahans*, pp. 15–16.
17. Tabarī, *Taʾrīkh*, I, pp. 2639–41.
18. P. Pourshariati, 'Local histories of Khurasan and the pattern of Arab settlement', *Studia Iranica* 27 (1998): 62–3.
19. Tabarī, *Taʾrīkh*, I, pp. 2650–711. See 'Bahrām VI Cobin' in *Encyclopaedia Iranica*, ed. E. Yarshater (London, 1985–), III, pp. 519–22.
20. Tabarī, *Taʾrīkh*, I, pp. 2653–5.
21. Tabarī, *Taʾrīkh*, I, p. 2659.
22. Tabarī, *Taʾrīkh*, I, p. 2635.
23. Tabarī, *Taʾrīkh*, I, p. 2667.
24. This account is based on the meticulous work of G. M. Hinds, 'The first Arab conquests in Fars', *Iran* 22 (1984): 39–53, reprinted in *idem, Studies in Early Islamic History*, ed. J. L. Bacharach, L. I. Conrad and P. Crone (Princeton, NJ, 1996).
25. Al-Istakhrī, *Kitāb Masālik waʾl-Mamālik*, ed. M. J. de Goeje (Leiden, 1927).
26. Balādhurī, *Futūh*, p. 388.
27. Balādhurī, *Futūh*, p. 389.
28. Balādhurī, *Futūh*, p. 389.
29. Balādhuri, *Ansab al-Ashraf*, I, ed. M. Hamidullah (Cairo, 1959), p. 494.
30. For the initial conquest of Sistan, see Balādhurī, *Futūh*, pp. 293–4.
31. For discussion, see Christensen, *Iran*, pp. 506–9.
32. Balʿami, quoted by Christensen, *Iran*, p. 507.
33. For Arabic accounts, see Balādhurī, *Futūh*, pp. 315–16.
34. My account is based on Firdawsi, *Shahnāmah*, trans. D. Davis, vol.

III: *Sunset of Empire* (Washington, DC, 1998–2004), pp. 501–13.
35. Tabarī, *Taʾrīkh*, I, p. 1322.
36. Tabarī, *Taʾrīkh*, I, p. 1318.
37. Tabarī, *Taʾrīkh*, I, p. 1320; Balādhurī, *Futūh*, pp. 335–6.
38. Balādhurī, *Futūh*, p. 335.
39. Tabarī, *Taʾrīkh*, I, pp. 1320–22, 1328.
40. Tabarī, *Taʾrīkh*, I, p. 1328.
41. *Taʾrīkh Jurjān*, pp. 56–7; see also P. Pourshariati, 'Local histories of Khurasan and the pattern of Arab settlement', *Studia Iranica* 27 (1998): 41-81.
42. On the Islamization of Gurgān, see R. Bulliet, *Islam: The View from the Edge* (New York, 1994).
43. For this campaign, see C. E. Bosworth, 'Ubaidallah b. Abi Bakra and the "Army of Destruction" in Zabulistan (79/698)', *Der Islam 1* (1973): 268–83.
44. Balādhurī, *Ansāb al-Ashrāf*, ed. Ahlwardt, p. 314.
45. Balādhurī, *Ansab*, p. 315–16. The translation is based on that of Bosworth, slightly simplified.
46. Tabarī, *Taʾrīkh*, I, pp. 1038–9.
47. Tabarī, *Taʾrīkh*, I, pp. 1043–7.
48. Tabarī, *Taʾrīkh*, I, pp. 1054–5.

6. INTO THE MAGHREB

1. The secondary literature on the conquest of North Africa is not extensive. For a narrative account

based on a careful reading of the meagre Arabic literary source, see A. D. Taha, *The Muslim Conquest and Settlement of North Africa and Spain* (London, 1989). V. Christides, *Byzantine Libya and the March of the Arabs towards the West of North Africa*, British Archaeological Reports, International Series 851 (Oxford, 2000), is also based on the Arabic texts but provides some additional material from hagiographical and archaeological sources.

2. Muqaddasī, *Ahsan al-Taqāsim: The Best Divisions for Knowledge of the Regions*, trans. B. Collins (Reading, 2001), p. 224.

3. See A. Cameron, 'Byzantine Africa – the literary evidence', in *Excavations at Carthage 1975–1978*, ed. J.H. Humphrey, vol. VII (Ann Arbor, MI, 1977–78), pp. 29–62, reprinted in *eadem, Changing Cultures in Early Byzantium* (Aldershot, 1996), VII.

4. M. Brett and E. Fentress, *The Berbers* (Oxford, 1996), pp. 79–80, quoting Procopius, *Bellum Vandalicum* IV, xiii, pp. 22–8.

5. C. J. Wickham, *Framing the Early Middle Ages: Europe and the Mediterranean, c. 400–c. 800* (Oxford, 2005), p. 641.

6. Ibid., pp. 709–12, 725.

7. A. Leone and D. Mattingly, 'Landscapes of change in North Africa', in *Landscapes of Change: Rural evolutions in late antiquity and the early Middle Ages*, ed. N.

Christie (Aldershot, 2004), pp. 135–62 at pp. 142–31;

8. I. Sjöström, *Tripolitania in Transition: Late Roman to Islamic settlement: with a catalogue of sites* (Aldershot, 1993), pp. 81–5.

9. Ibn Abd al-Hakam, *Futūh*, p. 170.

10. Ibn Abd al-Hakam, *Futūh*, p. 170, details the movement of Berber tribes to the west.

11. Sjöström, *Tripolitania*, p. 26.

12. Ibid., p. 40. See also D. Mattingly, 'The Laguatan: a Libyan tribal confederation in the late Roman Empire', *Libyan Studies* 14 (1983): 96–108; D. Pringle, *The Defence of Byzantine Africa from Justinian to the Arab Conquest*, British Archaeological Reports, International Series 99 (Oxford, 1981).

13. The chronology here follows Christides, *Byzantine Libya*, pp. 38–9.

14. Ibid., p. 15.

15. Ibn Abd al-Hakam, *Futūh*, p. 173.

16. Ibn Abd al-Hakam, *Futūh*, p. 184; Taha, *Muslim Conquest*, p. 57; Christides, *Byzantine Libya*, pp. 42–3.

17. Taha, *Muslim Conquest*, p. 58.

18. Yāqūt, *Muʿjam al-Buldān*.

19. Maslama b. Mukhallad al-Ansārī.

20. Ibn al-Athīr, *Al-Kāmil fi'l Taʾrīkh*, ed. C. J. Tornberg, 13 vols. (Leiden, 1867, repr. Beirut, 1982), III, p. 465, where he explicitly says he is basing his account on North African sources (*ahl al-taʾrīkh min al-maghāriba*) because they were better informed than Tabarī.

Yāqūt, *Mu'jam al-Buldān*, IV, pp. 212–13.

21. Taha, *Muslim Conquest*, pp. 61–2.

22. Following Taha, *Muslim Conquest*, pp. 63–5, here.

23. The sources for Uqba's great expedition are all much later than the events they purport to describe and the fullest account is that of Ibn Idhārī, *c.* 1300. This has led some, like Brunschvig, to doubt the historicity of the whole episode. Levi-Provençal has argued convincingly, however, that the narrative derives from a Maghrebi-Andalusi tradition and should be treated seriously. In support of this, he provides a translation of an account attributed to one Abū ʿAlī Sālih b. Abī Sālih b.ʿAbd al-Halīm, who lived in Naffis in the High Atlas in about 1300. The edition of the Arabic text, promised by Levi-Provençal in the article, seems to have been aborted by his death in 1954. See E. Levi-Provençal, 'Un récit de la conquête de l'Afrique du Nord', *Arabica* 1 (1954): 17–43.

24. Ibn Idhārī, *Bayān*, II, p. 26.

25. Wickham, *Framing*, p. 336.

26. Ibn Idhārī, *Bayān*, II, pp. 26–7.

27. Ibn Idhārī, *Bayān*, II, pp. 25–6.

28. Ibn Idhārī, *Bayān*, II, p. 26.

29. Ibn Idhārī, *Bayān*, II, p. 27.

30. Ibn Idhārī, *Bayān*, II, pp. 30–31.

31. Taha, *Muslim Conquest*, p. 68.

32. Ibn Idhārī, *Bayān*, II, p. 35.

33. Ibn Abd al-Hakam, *Futūh*, p. 200.

34. Bakrī, *Description de l'Afrique septentrionale*, ed. Baron de Slane (Algiers, 1857), p. 37.

35. Gibbon, *Decline and Fall*, III, p. 300.

36. Following the chronology proposed by Talbi in *Encyclopaedia of Islam*, 2nd edn.

37. Some accounts ascribe the foundation of Tunis to later governors; see Taha, *Muslim Conquest*, pp. 72–3.

38. Ibn Abd al-Hakam, *Futūh*, p. 40.

39. Ibn Idhārī, *Bayān*, II, p. 41.

7. CROSSING THE OXUS

1. The best account of the Muslim conquests of Central Asia remains H. A. R. Gibb, *The Arab Conquests in Central Asia* (London, 1923), on which I have drawn extensively. See also V. Barthold, *Turkestan Down to the Mongol Invasions*, trans. H. Gibb (London, 1928, rev edn, Gibb Memorial Series, V, London, 1968), pp. 180–93.

2. *The Fihrist of al-Nadīm*, trans. B. Dodge, 2 vols. (New York, 1970), pp. 220–25. See also the comments in T. Khalidi, *Arabic Historical Thought in the Classical Period* (Cambridge, 1994), pp. 64–5; C. F. Robinson, *Islamic Historiography* (Cambridge, 2003), p. 34.

3. For this analysis, see Gibb, *Conquests*, pp. 12–13.

4. For the historical geography of this area, see the classic account in Barthold, *Turkestan*, pp. 64–179.

5. For Khwārazm, see the excellent article by C.E. Bosworth,

'Khwārazm', in *Encyclopaedia of Islam*, 2nd edn.

6. *Ibn Fadlan's journey to Russia: a tenth-century traveler from Baghdad to the Volga River*, trans. R. Frye (Princeton, NJ, 2005), p. 29.

7. Narshakhī, *History of Bukhara*, trans. R. Frye (Cambridge, MA, 1954), pp. 9–10.

8. E. de la Vaissiere, *Sogdian Traders: A History* (Leiden, 2005), p. 176.

9. There is a vast literature on the origins and early history of the Turks. For a clear introduction, see D. Sinor, 'The establishment and dissolution of the Türk empire', in *Cambridge History of Early Inner Asia*, ed. D. Sinor (Cambridge, 1990), pp. 285–316, with bibliography pp. 478–83.

10. Trans. Sinor in *Cambridge History of Early Inner Asia*, p. 297.

11. *Maurice's Strategikon: Handbook of Byzantine military strategy*, trans. G. T. Dennis (Philadelphia, PA, 1984), pp. 116–18.

12. Tabarī, *Ta'rīkh*, II, p. 394. Gibb, *Arab Conquests*, is doubtful that these meetings ever occurred.

13. Balādhurī, *Futūh*, p. 412.

14. Silah b. Ashyam al-ʿAdawī; Tabarī, *Ta'rīkh*, II, p. 393.

15. Gibb, *Arab Conquests*, pp. 22–3.

16. Tabarī, *Ta'rīkh*, II, pp. 394–5.

17. Tabarī, *Ta'rīkh*, II, pp. 490–97.

18. Tabarī, *Ta'rīkh*, II, p. 447.

19. Tabarī, *Ta'rīkh*, II, p. 594.

20. Al-Harīsh b. Hilāl al-Qurayʿi.

21. Tabarī, *Ta'rīkh*, II, p. 596.

22. Tabarī, *Ta'rīkh*, II, p. 98.

23. Tabarī, *Ta'rīkh*, II, p. 696.

24. Tabarī, *Ta'rīkh*, II, pp. 831–5.

25. Tabarī, *Ta'rīkh*, II, p. 1022.

26. ʿAttb b. Liqwa al-Ghudānī had his debts paid by Bukayr b. Wishāh al-Saʿdī; Tabarī, *Ta'rīkh*, II, pp. 1022–3.

27. Tabarī, *Ta'rīkh*, II, p. 1029.

28. Tabarī, *Ta'rīkh*, II, p. 1024.

29. Tabarī, *Ta'rīkh*, II, pp. 1024, p. 1031.

30. Tabarī, *Ta'rīkh*, II, p. 1041; Gibb, *Arab Conquests*, pp. 26–7.

31. Tabarī, *Ta'rīkh*, II, p. 1144, gives Muhammad b. al-Mufaddal (al-Dabbi) (d. 784–5) as a source, but it is not clear whether he is the source for the bulk of the saga. Mufaddal was a philologist from Kūfa who joined the rebellion of Ibrahim the Alid in 762 but was pardoned by Mansūr and taken in to the service of Mahdi. He collected the anthology of pre-Islamic poetry known as the *Mufaddaliyat* but is not recorded as having written any historical works.

32. Tabarī, *Ta'rīkh*, II, p. 1147.

33. Tabarī, *Ta'rīkh*, II, pp. 1162–3.

34. Tabarī, *Ta'rīkh*, II, pp. 1146–7. The story is reminiscent of the story of the priest-kings of the Lake of Nemi with which James Fraser begins *The Golden Bough* (New York, 1922).

35. Tabarī, *Ta'rīkh*, II, p. 1147.

36. Tabarī, *Ta'rīkh*, II, pp. 1148–9.

37. Tabarī, *Ta'rīkh*, II, p. 1151.

38. Tabarī, *Ta'rīkh*, II, p. 1152.

39. Tabarī, *Ta'rīkh*, II, pp. 1080–81.

40. Tabarī, *Ta'rīkh*, II, p. 1153.

41. Tabarī, *Ta'rīkh*, II, p. 1153.

42. Tabarī, *Ta'rīkh*, II, p. 1154.

43. The name is given in the text as
Hashūrā or variations on that but
it has yet to be identified.
44. Tabarī, *Ta'rīkh*, II, pp. 1159–60.
45. Mufaddal b. al-Muhallab b. Abī
Sufra; Tabarī, *Ta'rīkh*, II,
p. 1162.

8. THE ROAD TO SAMARQAND

1. Koran 3: 169.
2. Tabarī, *Ta'rīkh*, II, p. 1179.
3. Tabarī, *Ta'rīkh*, II, pp. 1290–91.
4. Tabarī, *Ta'rīkh*, II, pp. 1185–6.
5. Barthold, *Turkestan*, p. 117.
6. Narshakhī, *History of Bukhara*,
p. 44.
7. Tabarī, *Ta'rīkh*, II, pp. 1185–90;
Narshakhī, *History of Bukhara*,
pp. 43–5.
8. Tabarī, *Ta'rīkh*, II, p. 1188.
9. Narshakhī, *History of Bukhara*, p.
45 and note B.
10. Tabarī, *Ta'rīkh*, II, pp. 1198–9.
11. Tabarī, *Ta'rīkh*, II, p. 1202.
12. Narshakhī, *History of Bukhara*,
p. 63.
13. Ibid., pp. 47–9.
14. Ibid., p. 52.
15. Tabarī, *Ta'rīkh*, II, p. 1206.
16. Tabarī, *Ta'rīkh*, II, p. 1207, but
cf. p. 1218, where it is only a few
brigands.
17. E. Knobloch, *The Archaeology and
Architecture of Afghanistan*
(Stroud, 2002), p. 162 and Plates
7 and 17.
18. Tabarī, *Ta'rīkh*, II, p. 1221.
19. Tabarī, *Ta'rīkh*, II, p. 1226.
20. Tabarī, *Ta'rīkh*, II, p. 1230.
21. Gibb, *Arab Conquests*, p.42.
22. Tabarī, *Ta'rīkh*, II, pp. 1229–30.
23. Tabarī, *Ta'rīkh*, II, p. 1235.

24. Tabarī, *Ta'rīkh*, II, pp. 1240–41.
25. F. Grenet and C. Rapin, 'De la
Samarkand antique à la
Samarkand islamique:
continuities et ruptures', in
*Colloque international d'archéologie
islamique*, ed. R.-P. Gayraud
(Cairo, 1998), pp. 436–60.
26. Tabarī, *Ta'rīkh*, II, p. 1245. See
trans. n. 635 for different figures
given in Balʿamī and Ibn
Aʿtham.
27. Tabarī, *Ta'rīkh*, II, p. 1252.
28. Gibb, *Arab Conquests*, p. 45.
29. Tabarī, *Ta'rīkh*, II, pp. 1256–7.
30. Gibb, *Arab Conquests*, pp. 52–3.
31. Yaʿqūbī, *Ta'rīkh*, II, p. 346.
32. Gibb, *Arab Conquests*, p. 50.
33. Tabarī, *Ta'rīkh*, II, pp. 1277–8.
34. Tabarī, *Ta'rīkh*, II, p. 1286. The
word used for pass is *jawāz*, the
modern Arabic word for
passport.
35. Tabarī, *Ta'rīkh*, II, p. 1287.
36. Tabarī, *Ta'rīkh*, II, p. 1288.
37. Tabarī, *Ta'rīkh*, II, p. 1291.
38. Tabarī, *Ta'rīkh*, II, p. 1291.
39. Tabarī, *Ta'rīkh*, II, p. 1290.
40. Tabarī, *Ta'rīkh*, II, pp. 1294–5.
41. Tabarī, *Ta'rīkh*, II, p. 1300.
42. Al-Asamm b. al-Hajjāj; Tabarī,
Ta'rīkh, II, p. 1304. The
translation is based on that of D.
S. Powers in trans. xxiv 28,
slightly amended.
43. On the Turks in the warfare of
this period, see E. Esin, 'Tabarī's
report on the warfare with the
Türgis and the testimony of
eighth-century Central Asian
art', *Central Asiatic Journal* 17
(1973): 130–34.
44. Tabarī, *Ta'rīkh*, II, p. 1431; see

also the poem in Tabarī, *Ta'rīkh*, II, p. 1432.

45. Tabarī, *Ta'rīkh*, II, pp. 1421–8.
46. Tabarī, *Ta'rīkh*, II, p. 1430.
47. On the documents, see F. Grenet and E. de la Vaissiere, 'The last days of Penjikent', *Silk Road Art and Archaeology* 8 (2002): 155–96; I. Yakubovich, 'Mugh l I revisited', *Studia Iranica* 31 (2002): 213–53.
48. Tabarī, *Ta'rīkh*, II, pp. 1446–8, in which Dīwashtīch is called Dawāshīni.
49. De la Vaissiere, *Sogdian Traders*, p. 272.
50. Tabarī, *Ta'rīkh*, II, p. 1518.
51. Tabarī, *Ta'rīkh*, II, p. 1521.
52. Sibāᶜ b. al-Nuᶜmān al-Azdi; Tabarī, *Ta'rīkh*, II, pp. 1524–5.
53. Al-Junayd b. ᶜAbd al-Rahmān al-Murrī; Tabarī, *Ta'rīkh*, II, p. 1527.
54. Tabarī, *Ta'rīkh*, II, p. 1638.
55. Yazīd b. al-Mufaddal al-Huddānī; Tabarī, *Ta'rīkh*, II, p. 1537.
56. Muhammad b. ᶜAbd Allah b. Hawdhān; Tabarī, *Ta'rīkh*, II, p. 1537.
57. Al-Nadr b. Rāshid al-ᶜAbdī; Tabarī, *Ta'rīkh*, II, pp. 1537–8.
58. Tabarī, *Ta'rīkh*, II, p. 1538.
59. Tabarī, *Ta'rīkh*, II, p. 1539.
60. Al-Mujashshir b. Muzāhim al-Sulami; Tabarī, *Ta'rīkh*, II, p. 1543.
61. Tabarī, *Ta'rīkh*, II, pp. 1546, 1557–8.
62. For the mainly negative evidence for this state of affairs, see Gibb, *Arab Conquests*, p. 79.
63. Ibid., p. 89.

64. Tabarī, *Ta'rīkh*, II, pp. 1688–9.
65. Tabarī, *Ta'rīkh*, II, pp. 1717–8.
66. Tabarī, *Ta'rīkh*, II, p. 1697, slightly abbreviated.
67. Gibb, *Arab Conquests*, p. 92.
68. Ibid., pp. 95–6.

9. FURTHEST EAST AND FURTHEST WEST

1. The best modern account of the events of the Arab conquest of Sind remains F. Gabrieli, 'Muhammad ibn Qāsim ath-Thaqafī and the Arab conquest of Sind', *East and West* 15 (1964–5): 281–95; a broader view is provided by A. Wink, *Al-Hind: The Making of the Indo-Islamic World*, vol. 1: *Early medieval India and the expansion of Islam, 7th–11th centuries* (Leiden, 1990).
2. Balādhurī, *Futūh*, pp. 431–41.
3. Alī b. Hāmid al-Kūfī, *Chāchnāmah: An Ancient History of Sind*, trans. M. K. Fredunbeg (Lahore, 1995).
4. On this work, see Wink, *Al-Hind*, pp. 194–6.
5. Al-Kūfī, *Chāchnāmah*, p. 115.
6. Wink, *Al-Hind*, p. 51.
7. Muqaddasī, *Ahsan al-Taqāsim*, p. 474.
8. Ibn Hawqal, *Kitāb Surat al-Ard*, ed. J. H. Kramers (Leiden, 1939), p. 328.
9. Wink, *Al-Hind*, p. 153.
10. Ibid., p. 182.
11. M. J. De Goeje, *Mémoire des migrations des Tsiganes à travers l'Asie* (Leiden, 1903), pp. 1–2.

12. Balādhurī, *Futūḥ*, p. 436.
13. Gabrieli, 'Muhammad ibn Qāsim', pp. 281–2.
14. Balūdhurī, *Futūḥ*, pp. 426–7. The same story is given, with fictitious additions in *Chāchnāmah*, pp. 81–4.
15. *Sumaniyayn*, on which see Balādhurī, *Futūḥ*, glossary s.v. *smn*.
16. Balādhurī, *Futūḥ*, pp. 437–8. Al-Kūfī, *Chāchnāmah*, pp. 91–3, 103–4, also stresses the role of the Samani.
17. Al-Kūfī, *Chāchnāmah*, pp. 93–5.
18. For the battle see the account in Wink, *Al-Hind*, pp. 204–5, based on details in Balādhurī, *Futūḥ*, pp. 438–9, and Al-Kūfī, *Chāchnāmah*, pp. 135–9.
19. Al-Kūfī, *Chāchnāmah*, pp. 125–6.
20. Balādhurī, *Futūḥ*, p. 438.
21. Al-Kūfī, *Chāchnāmah*, pp. 153–4.
22. Al-Kūfī, *Chāchnāmah*, p. 164.
23. Al-Kūfī, *Chāchnāmah*, p. 176.
24. The *Chāchnāmah* confuses Hindus and Buddhists on many occasions. This is partly because the Persian word *butkhana* is clearly derived from 'House of Buddha' but comes to be applied to all temples with 'idols' in them. The protestors may well have been Hindus, a position suggested by their apparent association with the Brahmins.
25. Al-Kūfī, *Chāchnāmah*, p. 170.
26. Al-Kūfī, *Chāchnāmah*, pp. 194–5.
27. Al-Kūfī, *Chāchnāmah*, pp. 178–80.
28. Balādhurī, *Futūḥ*, pp. 439–40.
29. Gabrieli, 'Muhammad ibn Qāsim', p. 293.
30. Balādhurī, *Futūḥ*, p. 440; Al-Kūfī, *Chāchnāmah*, p. 191, has a parallel text in which the figures are 60,000 and 120,000 respectively.
31. De Goeje, *Mémoire*. For a general survey of the history of the Gypsies, see A. Fraser, *The Gypsies* (2nd edn, Oxford, 1992). See also A. S. Basmee Ansari, 'Djat', and C. E. Bosworth, 'Zutt', in *Encyclopaedia of Islam*, 2nd edn.
32. The name Gibraltar is derived from Jabal Ṭāriq or 'Ṭāriq's Mountain'.
33. Ibn Abd al-Hakam, *Futūḥ*, p. 205, translated in O. R. Constable, *Medieval Iberia: Readings in Christian, Muslim and Jewish Sources* (Philadelphia, PA, 1997), pp. 32–4.
34. E. Levi-Provençal, *Histoire de l'Espagne Musulmane*, vol. i: *La Conquête et l'émirat hispano-umaiyade (710-912)* (Paris, 1950), pp. 19–21, prefers the River Barbate.
35. Anon., *The Chronicle of 754*, in *Conquerors and Chroniclers of Early Medieval Spain*, trans. K. B. Wolf (Liverpool, 1990), pp. 28–45, 111–58 at p. 131.
36. The main Arabic account is Ibn Idhārī, *Bayān*, II, pp. 4–9, based largely on the work of Rāzī.
37. Ibn Idhari, *Bayān*, II, pp. 9–10.
38. *Chronicle of 754*, cap. 52, p. 131.
39. Ibn Abd al-Hakam, *Futūḥ*, p. 206, in Constable, *Medieval Iberia*, p. 34.
40. Ibn Abd al-Hakam, *Futūḥ*, p. 208, in Constable, *Medieval Iberia*, pp. 34–5.

41. Constable, *Medieval Iberia*, pp. 37–8.
42. Ibn Abd al-Hakam, *Futūh*, pp. 211–2.
43. Anon., *Conquerors and Chroniclers*, pp. 164–8.
44. Levi-Provençal, *Histoire*, I, p. 55, based on Ibn Hayyān.
45. Ibid., p. 56, based on Makkarī.
46. For recent discussions of the battle and the campaigns that led up to it, see I. Wood, *The Merovingian Kingdoms 450–751* (London, 1994), pp. 281–4; P. Fouracre, *The Age of Charles Martel* (London, 2000), pp. 84–8; E. Manzano, *Conquistadores, Emires y Califes: los Omeyas y la formación de al-Andalus* (Barcelona, 2006), pp. 83–4. The military aspects of the battle are discussed in B. Bachrach, *Early Carolingian Warfare: Prelude to empire* (Philadelphia, PA, 2001), esp. pp. 170–77.
47. Gibbon, *Decline and Fall*, III, p. 336.
48. Bachrach, *Early Carolingian Warfare*, pp. 170 and 352, n. 45.
49. For this translation, and a critique of the older but very influential translation by J. M. Wallace-Hadrill, see Fouracre, *The Age of Charles Martel*, pp. 148–9.

10. THE WAR AT SEA

1. G. F. Bass and F. H. Van Doorninck, *Yassi Ada*, vol. 1: *A Seventh-century Byzantine Shipwreck* (College Station, TX, 1982).
2. For an overview of naval warfare in the Mediterranean from the mid sixth to the mid eighth centuries, see J. H. Pryor and E. M. Jeffreys, *The Age of the Dromon: The Byzantine Navy ca. 500–1204* (Leiden, 2006), pp. 19–34. For a detailed narrative of the early Islamic period, see E. Eickhoff, *Seekrieg und Seepolitik zwischen Islam und Abendland: das Mittelmeer unter byzantinischer und arabischer Hegemonies (650–1040)* (Berlin, 1966).
3. See P. Crone, 'How did the quranic pagans make a living?', *Bulletin of the School of Oriental and African Studies* 63 (2005): 387–99 at p. 395.
4. On Cyprus at this time, see A. Cameron, 'Cyprus at the time of the Arab conquests', *Cyprus Historical Review* 1 (1992): 27–49, reprinted *in eadem, Changing Cultures in Early Byzantium* (Aldershot, 1996), VI. For the Arab attacks, see A. Beihammer, 'Zypern und die Byzantinisch-Arabische Seepolitik vom 8. bis zum Beginn des 10. Jahrhunderts', in *Aspects of Arab Seafaring*, ed. Y.Y. al-Hijji and V. Christides (Athens, 2002), pp. 41–61.
5. Cameron, 'Cyprus', pp. 31–2.
6. Balādhurī, *Futūh*, pp. 152–3.
7. Balādhurī, *Futūh*. p. 154; Tabarī, *Ta'rīkh*, III, p. 709.
8. For the problems of the sources and the difficulties in working out what was attacked when, see L. I. Conrad, 'The Conquest of Arwād: A source-critical study in the historiography of the early

medieval Near East', in *The Byzantine and Early Islamic Near East, vol. I. Problems in the literary source material* (Papers of the First Workshop on Late Antiquity and Early Islam), ed. A. Cameron and L. I. Conrad (Princeton, NJ, 1992), pp. 317–401.

9. See A. N. Stratos, 'The Naval engagement at Phoenix', in *Charanis Studies: Essays in honor of Peter Charanis*, ed. A. E. Laiou-Thomadakis (New Brunswick, 1980), pp. 229–47.

10. Ibn Abd al-Hakam, *Futūh*, pp. 189–9; Ibn al-Athīr, *Kāmil*, p. 119–20.

11. Ibn Abd al-Hakam wrongly calls him Heraclius.

12. V. Christides, 'Arab–Byzantine struggle in the sea: naval tactics (AD 7th–11th centuries): theory and practice', in *Aspects of Arab Seafaring*, ed. Y.Y. al-Hijji and V. Christides (Athens, 2002), pp. 87–101 at p. 90.

13. For the use of Greek fire, see Theophanes, ed. de Boor, I, pp. 353–4; Eickhoff, *Seekrieg*, pp. 21–3; J. Haldon, *Byzantium in the Seventh Century* (Cambridge, 1990), pp. 63–5. Also J. Haldon and M. Byrne, 'A possible solution to the problem of Greek fire', *Byzantinische Zeitschrift* 70 (1977): 91–9.

14. Abridged translation of the text in D. Olster, 'Theodosius Grammaticus and the Arab Siege of 674–78', *Byzantinoslavica* 56 (1995), pp. 23–8; C. Makrypoulias, 'Muslim ships

through Byzantine eyes', in al-Hijji and Christides, *Aspects*, p. 179–90.

15. Theophanes, *Chronographia*, pp. 396–8.

16. Theophanes, *Chronographia*, p. 399.

17. Balādhurī, *Futūh*, p. 235; Eickhoff, *Seekrieg*, pp. 16–17.

18. Eickhoff, *Seekrieg*, pp. 28–9.

19. A. M. Fahmy, *Muslim Naval Organisation in the Eastern Mediterranean from the Seventh to the Tenth Century A.D.* (2nd edn, Cairo, 1966), p. 66.

20. Eickhoff, *Seekrieg*, p. 37.

21. Balādhurī, *Futūh*, pp. 117–8. See the Glossary for this usage of *Mustaghal*.

22. J. Wilkinson, *Jerusalem Pilgrims before the Crusades* (rev. edn, Warminster, 2002), pp. 245, 247.

23. Ya'qūbī, *Buldān*, p. 327.

24. Muqaddasī, *Ahsan al-Taqāsim*, pp. 163–4.

25. Muqaddasī, *Ahsan al-Taqāsim*, pp. 162–3

26. Tabarī, *Ta'rīkh*, III, p. 2200

27. Tabarī, *Ta'rikh*, III, p. 2250

28. Wilkinson, *Jerusalem Pilgrims*, pp. 196–8

29. Ibn Abd al-Hakam, *Futūh*, pp. 191–2

30. Fahmy, *Muslim Naval Organisation*, pp. 36–7

31. Qudāma b. Ja'far, *Al-Kharāj wa Sinā'at al-Kitāba*, ed. Muhammad Husayn al-Zubaydī (Baghdad, 1981), pp. 47–50.

32. For the design of warships in this period, see Pryor and Jeffreys, *The Age of the Dromon*, pp. 123–61, and F. M. Hocker, 'Late

Roman, Byzantine and Islamic fleets', in *The Age of the Galley: Mediterranean Oared Vessels since Pre-classical Times*, ed. R. Gardiner (London, 1995), pp. 86–100. See also Makrypoulias, 'Muslim ships through Byzantine eyes'.

33. For these technical innovations, see Pryor and Jeffreys, *The Age of the Dromon*, pp. 123–61.
34. Hocker, 'Late Roman, Byzantine and Islamic fleets', pp. 99–100.
35. Ibid., p. 99.
36. Fahmy, *Muslim Naval Organisation*, pp. 102–3.
37. Ibid., p. 84.

11. VOICES OF THE CONQUERED

1. The indispensable source for non-Muslim views of early Islam is Hoyland, *Seeing Islam as Others Saw It*.
2. For Sophronius and his writing, see Wilken, *The Land Called Holy*, pp. 226–39; Hoyland, *Seeing Islam*, pp. 67–73.
3. For a general introduction, see P. J. Alexander, *The Byzantine Apocalyptic Tradition* (Berkeley, CA, 1985).
4. Hoyland, *Seeing Islam*, p. 258.
5. For a translation of the text described here, see *The Seventh Century in Western-Syrian Chronicles*, trans. A. Palmer (Liverpool, 1993), pp. 222–42, and the discussions in G. J. Reinink, 'Ps.-Methodius: A concept of history in response to the rise of Islam', in *The Byzantine*

and Early Islamic Near East, I. Problems in the literary source material, ed. A. Cameron and L. I. Conrad (Papers of the First Workshop on Late Antiquity and Early Islam) (Princeton, NJ, 1992), pp. 149–87; Hoyland, *Seeing Islam*, pp. 263–7.

6. On Gabriel and the history of Qartmin in general, see A. Palmer, *Monk and Mason on the Tigris Frontier* (Cambridge, 1990), esp. pp. 153–9.
7. Quoted in S. Brock, 'North Mesopotamia in the late seventh century: Book XV of John Bar Penkaye's *Rīs Melle*', *Jerusalem Studies in Arabic and Islam* 9 (1987): 51–75, p. 57 note b.
8. Sawīrus, 'Life of Benjamin', p. 492.
9. Sawīrus, 'Life of Benjamin', p. 494.
10. John of Nikiu, *Chronicle*, pp. 184, 200.
11. John of Nikiu, *Chronicle*, p. 186.
12. John of Nikiu, *Chronicle*, p. 179.
13. John of Nikiu, *Chronicle*, p. 188.
14. John of Nikiu, *Chronicle*, p. 182.
15. John of Nikiu, *Chronicle*, p. 195.
16. John of Nikiu, *Chronicle*, p. 182.
17. John of Nikiu, *Chronicle*, p. 181.
18. *The Chronicle of 754* in *Conquerors and Chroniclers of Early Medieval Spain*, trans. K. B. Wolf (Liverpool, 1990), pp. 28–45, 111–58.
19. Brock, 'North Mesopotamia', p. 63.
20. *Chronicle of 754*, cap. 31, p. 123.
21. *Chronicle of 754*, cap. 80, pp. 143–4.

22. *Chronicle of 754*, caps. 85–6, pp. 148–50.
23. Hoyland, *Seeing Islam*, pp. 308–12, 526–7.
24. Daniel 11:39.
25. Text and translation in H. W. Bailey, *Zoroastrian Problems in the Ninth-Century Books* (Oxford, 1943), pp. 195–6; see also the comments in Hoyland, *Seeing Islam*, pp. 531–2.
26. For Firdawsi's life, with full bibliography, see D. Khaleghi-Motlagh, 'Ferdowsi', in *Encyclopaedia Iranica*, ed. E. Yarshater (London, 1985–) vol. ix, pp. 514–23.
27. See Firdawsi, *Shahnāmah*, trans. D. Davis, vol. iii: *Sunset of Empire* (Washington, DC, 1998–2004), pp. 494–5.
28. For the text and its context, see Hoyland, *Seeing Islam*, pp. 246–8.

12. CONCLUSION

1. On this frontier, see J. F. Haldon and H. Kennedy, 'The Arab–Byzantine frontier in the eighth and ninth centuries: military organisation and society in the borderlands', *Zbornik radove Vizantoloskog instituta* 19 (1980): 79–116, reprinted in H. Kennedy, *The Byzantine and Early Islamic Near East* (Aldershot, 2006), VIII.
2. C. Foss, 'The Persians in Asia Minor and the end of antiquity', *English Historical Review* 90 (1975): 721–47, reprinted in *idem, History and Archaeology of Byzantine Asia Minor* (Aldershot, 1990), I.
3. For the classic discussion of conversion to Islam, see R. Bulliet, *Conversion to Islam in the Medieval Period. An Essay in Quantitative History* (Cambridge, MA, 1979). See also *idem, Islam: The View from the Edge* (New York, 1994), pp. 37–66, for the processes of conversion.

BIBLIOGRAPHY

HISTORICAL AND GEOGRAPHICAL SOURCES IN ENGLISH TRANSLATION

Muslim Sources

Alī b. Hāmid al-Kūfī, *Chāchnamah: An Ancient History of Sind*, trans. M. K. Fredunbeg (Lahore, 1995).

Al-Bakrī, *Description de l'Afrique septentrionale*, trans. Baron William Mac Guckin de Slane (Paris, 1859).

Al-Balādhurī, *The Origins of the Islamic State*, trans. P. Hitti and F. Murgotten, 2 vols. (New York, 1916–24).

Ibn Fadlan's Journey to Russia: A tenth-century traveler from Baghdad to the Volga River, trans. R. Frye (Princeton, NJ, 2005).

Firdawsi, *Shahnāmah*, trans. D. Davis, vol. i: *The Lion and the Throne*; vol. ii: *Fathers and Sons*; vol. iii: *Sunset of Empire* (Washington, DC, 1998–2004).

Ibn Ishāq, *The Life of Muhammad*, trans. A. Guillaume (Karachi, 1955, repr. 1967).

Al-Muqaddasī, *Ahsan al-Taqāsim: The Best Divisions for Knowledge of the Regions*, trans. B. Collins (Reading, 2001).

Narshakhī, Muhammad b. Ja'far, *History of Bukhara*, trans. R. Frye (Cambridge, MA, 1954).

Al-Tabarī, *Ta'rīkh: The History of al-Tabarī*, ed. Y. Yarshater, 39 vols. (Albany, NJ, 1985–98).

Christian Sources

Anon., *The Chronicle of 754* in *Conquerors and Chroniclers of Early Medieval Spain*, trans. K. B. Wolf (Liverpool, 1990).

Anon., *The Chronicle of Zuqnin Parts III and IV A.D. 488–775*, trans. A. Harrak (Toronto, 1999).

Fredegar, *The Fourth Book of the Chronicle of Fredegar with its Continuations*, trans. J. M. Wallace-Hadrill (London, 1960).

John of Nikiu, *The Chronicle of John (c. 690 AD) Coptic Bishop of Nikiu*, trans. R. H. Charles (London, 1916).

Maurice's Strategikon: Handbook of Byzantine military strategy, trans. G. T. Dennis (Philadelphia, PA, 1984).

Movses of Dasxuranci, *The History of the Caucasian Albanians*, trans. C. J. F. Dowsett (Oxford, 1961).

Nikephorus, Patriarch of Constantinople, *Short History*, trans. C. Mango (Washington, DC, 1990).

Sawīrus b. al-Muqaffa, 'Life of Benjamin I the thirty-eighth Patriarch AD 622-61', in *History of the Patriarchs of the Coptic Church of Alexandria*, trans B. Evetts *(Patrologia Orientalis* I.4, 1905), pp. 487–518.

Sebeos, *The Armenian History*, trans. R. W. Thomson, with notes by J. Howard-Johnston and T. Greenwood, 2 vols. (Liverpool, 1999).

Theophanes, *The Chronicle of Theophanes the Confessor: Byzantine and Near Eastern History AD 284–813*, trans. C. Mango and R. Scott (Oxford, 1997).

Various, *The Seventh Century in Western-Syrian Chronicles*, trans. A. Palmer (Liverpool, 1993).

OTHER PRIMARY SOURCES

Ibn Abd al-Hakam, Abū'l-Qāsim 'Abd al-Rahmān b. 'Abd Allāh, *Futūh Misr*, ed. C. C. Torrey (New Haven, CT, 1921).

Anon., 'Doctrina Jacobi Nuper Baptizati', ed. with French trans. V. Déroche in *Travaux et Mémoires* (Collège de France, Centre de recherche d'histoire et civilisation de Byzance) 11 (1991): 47-273.

Ibn Aᶜtham al-Kūfī, *Kitāb al-Futūh*, ed. S. A Bukhari, 7 vols. (Hyderabad, 1974).

Ibn al-Athīr, 'Izz al-Dīn, *Al-Kāmil fi'l-Ta'rīkh*, ed. C. J. Tornberg, 13 vols. (Leiden, 1867, repr. Beirut, 1982).

Al-Bakrī, *Description de l'Afrique septentrionale*, ed. Baron de Slane (Algiers, 1857).

Al-Balādhurī, Ahmad b. Yahyā, *Futūh al-Buldān*, ed. M. J. de Goeje (Leiden, 1866, repr. Leiden, 1968).

Al-Balādhurī, Ahmad b. Yahyā, *Ansāb al-Ashrāf*, vol. XI, ed. W. Ahlwardt (Greifswald, 1883).

Al-Dīnawarī, Abū Hanīfa Ahmad b. Dāwüd, *Al-Akhbār al-Tiwāl*, ed. V. Guirgass and I. I. Krachkovskii (Leiden, 1912).

Ibn Hawqal, Abū'l-Qāsim, *Kitāb Sūrat al-Ard*, ed. J. H. Kramers (Leiden, 1939).

Isfahānī, Abu Nuᶜaym, *Geschicte Isfahans*, ed. S. Dedering (Leiden, 1931).

Al-Istakhrī, Abū Ishāq Ibrāhīm b. Muhammad, *Kitāb Masālik wa'l-Mamālik*, ed. M. J. de Goeje (Leiden, 1927).

Ibn Khayyāᶜ Khalīfa, *Ta'rīkh*, ed. Akram Diyā' al-'Umarī (Beirut, 1977).

Al-Kindī, Muhammad b. Yūsuf, *Kitāb al-Wulāt*, ed. R. Guest (London, 1912).

Al-Kindī, Ya'qūb b. Ishāq, *Al-Suyūf wa Ajnāsiha*, ed. Abd al-Rahman Zaki, *Bulletin of the Faculty of Arts*, Cairo, vol. 14 (1952), Arabic section, pp. 1–36.

Al-Mas'ūdī, 'Alī b. al-Husayn, *Murūj al-Dhahab*, ed. C. Pellat, 7 vols. (Beirut, 1966-79).

Michael the Syrian, *Chronicle*, ed. with French trans. J.-B. Chabot, 4 vols. (Paris, 1899–1924).

Al-Nadīm, Muhammad b. Ishāq, *Fihrist*, ed. G. Flügel (Leipzig, 1871–2). Note that in this book, page references are to *The Fihrist of al-Nadīm*, trans. B. Dodge, 2 vols. (New York, 1970).

Narshakhī, Muhammad b. Ja'far, *Ta'rīkhi Bukhārā*, ed. Muhammad b. Zafar b. Umar (Tehran, 1972).

Qudāma b. Ja'far, *Al-Kharāj wa Sinā'at al-Kitāba*, ed. Muhammad Husayn al-Zubaydī (Baghdad, 1981).

Sa'īd ibn Batrīq, *Das Annalenwerk des Eutychios von Alexandrien*, ed. M. Breydy, in *Corpus Scriptorum Christianorum Orientalium*, vol. 471: *Scriptores Arabici*, t. 44 (Leuven, 1985).

Al-Tabarī, Muhammad b. Jarīr, *Ta'rīkh al-Rusul wa'l-Mulūk*, ed. M. J. de Goeje et al., 3 vols. (Leiden, 1879–1901)

Al-Ya'qūbī, Ahmad b. Abī Ya'qūb, *Kitāb al-Buldān*, ed. M. J. de Goeje (Leiden, 1892).

Al-Ya'qūbī, Ahmad b. Abī Ya'qūb, *Ta'rīkh*, ed. M. Houtsma, 2 vols. (Leiden, 1883).

Yāqūt, Ya'qūb b. 'Abd Allāh, *Mu'jam al-Buldān*, ed. F. Wüstenfeld (Leipzig, 1886).

SECONDARY READING

Adams, R. McC., *The Land behind Baghdad: A history of settlement on the Diyala Plain* (Chicago, IL, 1965).

Alexander, P. J., *The Byzantine Apocalyptic Tradition* (Berkeley, CA, 1985).

Bachrach, B., *Early Carolingian Warfare: Prelude to empire* (Philadelphia, PA, 2001).

Bagnall, R., *Egypt in Late Antiquity* (Princeton, NJ, 1993).

Bailey, H. W., *Zoroastrian Problems in the Ninth-century Books* (Oxford, 1943).

Barthold, V., *Turkestan Down to the Mongol Invasions*, trans. H. Gibb (London, 1928, rev. edn, Gibb Memorial Series, n.s. V, London, 1968).

Bashear, S., 'The mission of Dihyā al-Kalbī', *Jerusalem Studies in Arabic and Islam* 14 (1991): 64–91, reprinted in *idem, Studies in Early Islamic Tradition* (Jerusalem, 2004), VIII.

Bass, G. F. and F. H. Van Doorninck, *Yassi Ada*, vol. 1: *A Seventh-century Byzantine Shipwreck* (College Station, TX, 1982).

Behbehani, H., 'Arab–Chinese military encounters: two case studies 715–751 AD', *Aram* 1 (1989): 65–112.

Behrens-Abouseif, D., 'Topographie d'Alexandrie médiévale', in *Alexandrie médiévale* 2, ed. C. Décobert (Cairo, 2002), pp. 113–26.

Beihammer, A., 'Zypern und die Byzantinisch-Arabische Seepolitik vom 8. bis zum Beginn des 10. Jahrhunderts', in *Aspects of Arab Seafaring*, ed. Y.Y. al-Hijji and V. Christides (Athens, 2002), pp. 41–61.

Bloom, J., *Paper before Print: The History and Impact of Paper in the Islamic World* (New Haven, CT, 2001).

Borrut, A., 'Architecture des espaces portuaires et réseaux défensifs du littoral syro-palestinien dans les sources arabes (7–11 siècle)', *Archéologie Islamique* 11 (2001): 21–46.

Bosworth, C. E., *Sistan under the Arabs from the Islamic Conquest to the Rise of the Saffarids (30–250/651–864)* (Rome, 1968).

—— ᶜUbaidallah b. Abi Bakra and the "Army of Destruction" in Zabulistan (79/698)', *Der Islam* 1 (1973): 268–83.

—— 'The city of Tarsus and the Arab–Byzantine frontiers in early and middle Abbasid Times', *Oriens* 33 (1992): 268–86.

—— *The New Islamic Dynasties* (Edinburgh, 1996).

Bowersock, G. W., P. Brown and O. Grabar (eds.), *Interpreting Late Antiquity: Essays on the Postclassical World* (Cambridge, MA, 2001).

Brett, M. and E. Fentress, *The Berbers* (Oxford, 1996).

Brock, S., 'Syriac views of emergent Islam', in *Studies on the First Century of Islamic Society*, ed. G. H. A. Juynboll (Carbondale, 1982), pp. 9–21, 199–203, reprinted in *idem, Syriac Perspectives on Late Antiquity* (London, 1984).

—— 'North Mesopotamia in the late seventh century: Book XV of John Bar Penkaye's *Rīs Melle*', *Jerusalem Studies in Arabic and Islam* 9 (1987): 51–75.

Brunschvig, R., 'Ibn ᶜAbdal-hakam et la conquête de l'Afrique du Nord par les Arabes: étude critique', *Annales de l'Institut des Etudes Orientales* 6 (1942–47): 108–55.

Bulliet, R., *The Camel and the Wheel* (Cambridge, MA, 1975).

—— *Conversion to Islam in the Medieval Period. An Essay in Quantitative History* (Cambridge, MA, 1979).

—— *Islam: The View from the Edge* (New York, 1994).

Busse, H., '"Omar b. al-Khattāb in Jerusalem', *Jerusalem Studies in Arabic and Islam* 5 (1984): 73–119.

—— 'ᶜOmar's image as the conqueror of Jerusalem', *Jerusalem Studies in Arabic and Islam* 8 (1986): 149–68.

Butler, A. J., *The Arab Conquest of Egypt*, 2nd edn, ed. P. M. Fraser (Oxford, 1978).

Caetani, L., *Annali dell'Islam*, 10 vols. (Milan, 1905–26).

Cambridge History of Early Inner Asia, ed. D. Sinor (Cambridge, 1990).

Cambridge History of Egypt, vol. i: *Islamic Egypt, 640–1571*, ed. C. Petry (Cambridge, 1998).

Cambridge History of Iran, vol. iii: *The Seleucid, Parthian and Sasanian Periods*, ed. E. Yarshater (Cambridge, 1983), vol. iv: *The Period from the Arab invasion to the Saljuqs*, ed. R. Frye (Cambridge, 1975).

Cameron, A., 'Byzantine Africa – the literary evidence', in *Excavations at Carthage 1975–1978*, vol. vii, ed. J. H. Humphrey (Ann Arbor, MI, 1977–78), pp. 29–62, reprinted in *eadem, Changing Cultures in Early Byzantium* (Aldershot, 1996), VII.

—— 'Cyprus at the time of the Arab conquests', *Cyprus Historical Review* 1 (1992): 27–49, reprinted in *eadem, Changing Cultures in Early Byzantium* (Aldershot, 1996), VI.

Chevedden, P. E., 'The hybrid trebuchet: the halfway step to the counterweight trebuchet,' in *On the Social Origins of Medieval Institutions. Essays in Honor of Joseph F. O'Callaghan*, ed. D. Kagay and T. Vann (Leiden, 1998), pp. 179–222.

Christensen, A., *L'Iran sous les Sassanides* (rev. 2nd edn, Copenhagen, 1944).

Christides, V., *Byzantine Libya and the March of the Arabs towards the West of North Africa*, British Archaeological Reports, International Series 851 (Oxford, 2000).

—— 'Arab–Byzantine struggle in the sea: naval tactics (7th–11th C AD): theory and practice', in *Aspects of Arab Seafaring*, ed. Y.Y. al-Hijji and V. Christides (Athens, 2002), pp. 87–101.

Cole, D. P., *Nomads of the Nomads: the Āl Murrah Bedouin of the Empty Quarter* (Arlington Heights, 1975).

Collins, R., *The Arab Conquest of Spain: 710–797* (Oxford, 1989).

—— *Visigothic Spain, 409–711* (Oxford, 2004).

Cook, M., *Muhammad* (Oxford, 1983).

Conrad, L. I., 'The conquest of Arwād: a source-critical study in the historiography of the early medieval Near East', in *The Byzantine and Early Islamic Near East, I: Problems in the literary source material*, ed. A. Cameron and L. I. Conrad (Papers of the First Workshop on Late Antiquity and Early Islam) (Princeton, NJ, 1992), pp. 317–401.

—— 'The Arabs', in *Cambridge Ancient History*, vol. xiv: *Late Antiquity: Empire and Successors, AD 425–600*, ed. A. Cameron, B. Ward-Perkins and M. Whitby (Cambridge, 2000), pp. 678–700.

Constable, O. R., *Medieval Iberia: Readings in Christian, Muslim and Jewish Sources* (Philadelphia, PA, 1997).

Crone, P., *Slaves on Horses. The Evolution of the Islamic Polity* (Cambridge, 1980).

—— *Meccan Trade and the Rise of Islam* (Oxford, 1987).

—— 'How did the quranic pagans make a living?', *Bulletin of the School of Oriental and African Studies* 63 (2005): 387–99.

Crone, P. and M. A. Cook, *Hagarism: The Making of the Islamic World* (Cambridge, 1977).

Crone, P. and G. M. Hinds, *God's Caliph: Religious Authority in the First Centuries of Islam* (Cambridge, 1986).

De Goeje, M. J., *Mémoire des migrations des Tsiganes à travers l'Asie* (Leiden, 1903).

De la Vaissière, E., *Sogdian Traders: A History* (Leiden, 2005).

Dennett, D., *Conversion and Poll-tax in Early Islam* (Cambridge, MA, 1950).

Djaït, H., *Al-Kūfa: naissance de la ville islamique* (Paris, 1986).

Donner, F. M., *The Early Islamic Conquests* (Princeton, NJ, 1981).

—— *Narratives of Islamic Origins: The Beginnings of Islamic Historical Writing* (Princeton, NJ, 1998).

Donner, H., *The Mosaic Map of Madaba: An introductory guide* (Kampen, 1992).

Dunlop, D. M., 'A new source of information on the Battle of Talas or Atlakh', *Ural-Altaische Jahrbücher* 36 (1964): 326–30.

Eickhoff, E., *Seekrieg und Seepolitik zwischen Islam und Abendland: das Mittelmeer unter byzantinischer und arabischer Hegemonies (650–1040)* (Berlin, 1966).

El Cheikh, N. M., *Byzantium Viewed by the Arabs* (Cambridge, MA, 2004).

Esin, E., 'Tabarī's report on the warfare with the Türgis and the testimony of eighth-century Central Asian Art', *Central Asiatic Journal* 17 (1973): 130–49.

Fahmy, A. M., *Muslim Naval Organisation in the Eastern Mediterranean from the Seventh to the Tenth Century AD* (2nd edn, Cairo, 1966).

Fentress, J. and C. J. Wickham, *Social Memory* (Oxford, 1992).

Fiey, J. M., 'The last Byzantine campaign into Persia and its influence on the attitude of the local populations towards the Muslim conquerors 7–16 H/628–36 AD', in *Proceedings of the second symposium on the history of Bilad al-Sham during the early Islamic period up to 40 AH/640 AD*, ed A. Bakhit (Amman, 1987), pp. 96–103.

Firestone, R., *Jihād: The Origin of Holy War in Islam* (Oxford, 1999).

Foss, C. 'The Persians in Asia Minor and the End of Antiquity', *English Historical Review* 90 (1975): 721–47, reprinted in *idem, History and Archaeology of Byzantine Asia Minor* (Aldershot, 1990), I.

—— 'The Near Eastern countryside in Late Antiquity: a review article', in *The Roman and Byzantine Near East: Some recent archaeological research*, vol I: *Journal of Roman Archaeology, Supplementary Series* 14 (1995): 213–34.

—— 'Syria in transition, AD 550–750: an archaeological approach', *Dumbarton Oaks Papers* 51 (1997): 189–270.

Fouracre, P., *The Age of Charles Martel* (London, 2000).

Fowden, E. K., *The Barbarian Plain: Saint Sergius between Rome and Iran* (Berkeley, CA, 1999).

Fowden, G., *Empire to Commonwealth: Consequences of Monotheism in Late Antiquity* (Princeton, NJ, 1993).

Fraser, A., *The Gypsies* (2nd edn, Oxford, 1992).

Fraser, J., *The Golden Bough* (New York, 1922).

Gabrieli, F., 'Muhammad ibn Qāsim ath-Thaqafī and the Arab conquest of Sind', *East and West* 15 (1964–65): 281–95.

Gayraud, R.-P., 'Fostat: évolution d'une capitale arabe du VII au XII siècle d'après les fouilles d'Istabl ᶜAntar', in *Colloque international d'archéologie islamique*, ed. R.-P. Gayraud (Cairo, 1998), pp. 436–60.

Gerö, S., 'Only a change of masters? The Christians of Iran and the Muslim conquest', in *Transition Periods in Iranian History. Actes du Symposium de Fribourg-en-Brisgau (22–24 mai 1985), Cahiers de Studia Iranica* 5 (1987): 43–8.

Gibb, H. A. R., *The Arab Conquests in Central Asia* (London, 1923).

Gibbon, E., *The History of the Decline and Fall of the Roman Empire*, ed. D. Womersley, 3 vols. (Harmondsworth, 1994).

Goldziher, I., *Muslim Studies*, ed. and trans. C. R. Barber and S. M. Stern, 2 vols., (London, 1967, 1971).

Grenet, F. and C. Rapin, 'De la Samarkand antique à la Samarkand islamique: continuities et ruptures', in *Colloque international d'archéologie islamique*, ed. R.-P. Gayraud (Cairo, 1998), pp. 436–60.

Grenet, F. and E. de la Vaissière, 'The last days of Penjikent', *Silk Road Art and Archaeology* 8 (2002): 155–96.

Haldon, J., *Byzantium in the Seventh Century* (Cambridge, 1990).

Haldon, J. and M. Byrne, 'A possible solution to the problem of Greek fire', *Byzantinische Zeitschrift* 70 (1977): 91–9.

Haldon, J. F. and H. Kennedy, 'The Arab–Byzantine frontier in the eighth and ninth centuries: military organisation and society in the borderlands,' *Zbornik radove Vizantoloskog instituta* 19 (1980): 79–116, reprinted in H. Kennedy, *The Byzantine and Early Islamic Near East* (Aldershot, 2006), VIII.

Heck, G. W., 'Gold mining in Arabia and the rise of the Islamic state', *Journal of the Economic and Social History of the Orient* 42 (1999): 364–95.

Helms, S. W., 'Kandahar of the Arab conquest', *World Archaeology* 14 (1982–83): 342–51.

Hill, D. R., *The Termination of Hostilities in the Early Arab Conquests AD 634–656* (London, 1971).

Hinds, G. M., 'The banners and battle cries of the Arabs at Siffin (657 AD)', *Al-Abhath* 24 (1971): 3–42.

—— 'The first Arab conquests in Fars', *Iran* 22 (1984): 39–53, reprinted in *idem, Studies in Early Islamic History*, ed. J. L. Bacharach, L. I. Conrad and P. Crone (Princeton, NJ, 1996).

Hocker, F. M., 'Late Roman, Byzantine and Islamic fleets', in *The Age of the Galley: Mediterranean Oared Vessels since Pre-classical Times*, ed. R. Gardiner (London, 1995), pp. 86–100.

Hönigmann, E., *Die Ostgrenze des byzantinischen Reiches: von 363 bis 1071 nach griechischen, arabischen, syrischen und armenischen Quellen* (Brussels, 1935).

Hoyland, R., *Seeing Islam as Others Saw It: A Survey and Evaluation of Christian, Jewish and Zoroastrian Writings on Early Islam* (Princeton, NJ, 1997).

—— *Arabia and the Arabs: from the Bronze Age to the Coming of Islam* (London, 2001).

Hoyland, R. and B. Gilmour, *Medieval Islamic Swords and Swordmaking: Kindi's treatise 'On swords and their kinds'* (London, 2006).

Johns, J., 'Archaeology and the history of early Islam: the first seventy years', *Journal of the Economic and Social History of the Orient* 46 (2003): 411–36.

Jones, A., *Early Arabic Poetry*, 2 vols. (Oxford, 1992).

Kaegi, W. E., 'Initial Byzantine reactions to the Arab conquest', *Church History* 38 (1969): 139–49.

—— *Byzantium and the Early Islamic Conquests* (Cambridge, 1992).

—— 'Egypt on the eve of the Muslim conquest', in *Cambridge History of Egypt*, vol. i: *Islamic Egypt, 640–1517*, ed. C. Petry (Cambridge, 1998), pp. 34–61.

—— *Heraclius, Emperor of Byzantium* (Cambridge, 2003).

Keenan, J. G., 'Egypt', in *Cambridge Ancient History*, vol. xiv: *Late Antiquity : Empire and Successors, AD 425–600*, ed. A. Cameron, B. Ward-Perkins and M. Whitby (Cambridge, 2000), pp. 612–37.

Kennedy, H., 'From Polis to Medina: urban change in late antique and early Islamic Syria', *Past and Present* 106 (1985): 3–27, reprinted in *idem, The Byzantine and Early Islamic Near East* (Aldershot, 2006), I.

—— *Muslim Spain and Portugal: a Political history of al-Andalus* (London, 1996).

—— 'Syria, Palestine and Mesopotamia', in *Cambridge Ancient History*, vol. xiv: *Late Antiquity: Empire and Successors, AD 425–600*, ed. A. Cameron, B. Ward-Perkins and M. Whitby (Cambridge, 2000), pp. 588–611.

—— *The Armies of the Caliphs* (London, 2001).

—— ed., *An Historical Atlas of Islam* (2nd rev. edn, Leiden, 2002).

—— *The Prophet and the Age of the Caliphates* (2nd rev. edn, London, 2004).

—— 'Military pay and the economy of the early Islamic state', *Historical Research* 75 (2002): 155–69, reprinted in *idem, The Byzantine and Early Islamic Near East* (Aldershot, 2006), XI.

—— 'The military revolution and the early Islamic state', in *Noble Ideals and Bloody Realities: Warfare in the Middle Ages*, ed. N. Christie and M. Yazigi (Leiden, 2006), pp. 197–208.

Khalidi, T., *Arabic Historical Thought in the Classical Period* (Cambridge, 1994).

Knobloch, E., *The Archaeology and Architecture of Afghanistan* (Stroud, 2002).

Kraemer, C. J., Jr, *Excavations at Nessana*, vol. 3: *Non-Literary Papyri* (Princeton, NJ, 1958).

Krasnowalska, A., 'Rostam Farroxzād's prophecy in Sāh-Nāme and the Zoro-astrian apocalyptic tests', *Folia Orientalia* 19 (1978): 173–84.

Kubiak, W., 'The Byzantine attack on Damietta in 853 and the Egyptian navy in the 9th century', *Byzantion* 40 (1971): 45–66.

—— *Al-Fustāt, Its Foundation and Early Urban Development* (Cairo, 1987).

Kulikowski, M., *Late Roman Spain and Its Cities* (Baltimore, MD, 2004).

Lancaster, W., *The Rwala Bedouin Today* (Cambridge, 1981).

Landau-Tasseron, E., 'Sayf ibn Umar in medieval and modern scholarship', *Der Islam* 67 (1990): 1–26.

Le Strange, G., *Palestine under the Moslems: A description of Syria and the Holy Land from AD 650 to 1500* (London, 1890).

—— *Lands of the Eastern Caliphate* (Cambridge, 1905).

Lecker, M., 'The estates of ʿAmr b.al-ʿĀs in Palestine', *Bulletin of the School of Oriental and African Studies* 52 (1989): 24–37.

Leone, A. and D. Mattingly, 'Landscapes of change in North Africa', in *Landscapes of change: Rural evolutions in late antiquity and the early Middle Ages*, ed. N. Christie (Aldershot, 2004), pp. 135–62.

Levi-Provençal, E., *Histoire de l'Espagne Musulmane*, vol. I: *La conquête et l'émirat hispano-umaiyade (710–912)* (Paris, 1950).

—— 'Un récit de la conquête de l'Afrique du Nord', *Arabica* 1 (1954): 17–43.

Lings, M., *Muhammad: His life based on the earliest sources* (rev. edn, London, 1991).

Little, L. (ed.), *Plague and the End of Antiquity: The Pandemic of 541–750* (Cambridge, 2006).

Lyall, C., *The Dīwāns of ʿAbīd ibn al-Abraṣ, of Asad and ʿĀmir ibn at-Ṭufayl, of ʿĀmir ibn Saʿsaʿah* (London, 1913).

Makrypoulias, C., 'Muslim ships through Byzantine eyes', in *Aspects of Arab Seafaring*, ed. Y. Y. al-Hijji and V. Christides (Athens, 2002), pp. 179–90.

Manzano, E., *Conquistadores, Emires y Califes: los Omeyas y la formación de al-Andalus* (Barcelona, 2006).

Matheson, S., *Persia: An Archaeological Guide* (2nd rev. edn, London, 1976).

Mattingly, D., 'The Laguatan: a Libyan tribal confederation in the late Roman Empire', *Libyan Studies* 14 (1983): 96–108.

Mayerson, P., 'The first Muslim attacks on southern Palestine (AD 633–640)', *Transactions of the American Philosophical Association* 95 (1964): 155–99.

Morony, M., *Iraq after the Muslim Conquest* (Princeton, NJ, 1984).

Mottahedeh, R. P. and R. al-Sayyid, 'The idea of the *Jihād* in Islam before the Crusades', in *The Crusades from the Perspective of Byzantium and the Muslim World*, ed. A. E. Laiou and R. P. Mottahedeh (Washington, DC, 2001), pp. 23–29.

Mourad, S., 'On early Islamic historiography: Abū Ismāʿil al-Azdī and his *Futūḥ al-Shām*', *Journal of the American Oriental Society* 120 (2000): 577–93.

Nicolle, D., *Armies of the Muslim Conquests* (London, 1993).

—— 'War and society in the eastern Mediterranean', in *War and Society in the Eastern Mediterranean 7th to 15th centuries*, ed. Y. Lev (Leiden, 1997), pp. 9–100.

Noth, A., 'Isfahanī-Nihāwand. Eine quellenkritische Studie zur frühislamischen Historiographie', *Zeitschrift der Deutschen Morgenländischen Gesellschaft* 118 (1968): 274–96.

Noth, A. with L. I. Conrad, *The Early Arabic Historical Tradition: A source-critical study*, trans. M. Bonner (Princeton, NJ, 1994).

Olster, D., 'Theodosius Grammaticus and the Arab siege of 674–78', *Byzantinoslavica* 56 (1995): 23–8.

Palmer, A., *Monk and Mason on the Tigris Frontier* (Cambridge, 1990).

Pourshariati, P., 'Local histories of Khurasan and the pattern of Arab settlement', *Studia Iranica* 27 (1998): 41–81.

Pringle, D., *The Defence of Byzantine Africa from Justinian to the Arab Conquest*, British Archaeological Reports, International Series 99 (Oxford, 1981).

Pryor, J. H., 'From Dromon to Galea: Mediterranean bireme galleys AD 500–1300', in *The Age of the Galley: Mediterranean Oared Vessels since Pre-classical Times*, ed. R. Gardiner (London, 1995), pp. 101–16.

Pryor, J. H. and E. M. Jeffreys, *The Age of the Dromon: The Byzantine navy ca. 500–1204* (Leiden, 2006).

Reinink, G. J., 'Ps.-Methodius: a concept of history in response to the rise of Islam', in *The Byzantine and Early Islamic Near East, I. Problems in the Literary Source Material*, ed. A. Cameron and L. I. Conrad (Papers of the First Workshop on Late Antiquity and Early Islam) (Princeton, NJ, 1992), pp. 149–87.

Retsö, J., *The Arabs in Antiquity: Their History from the Assyrians to the Umayyads* (London, 2003).

Ritner, R. E., 'Egypt under Roman rule: the legacy of ancient Egypt', in *Cambridge History of Egypt*, vol. i: *Islamic Egypt, 640–1517*, ed. C. Petry (Cambridge, 1998), pp. 1–33.

Robinson, C. F., *Empire and Elites after the Muslim Conquest: The Transformation of Northern Mesopotamia* (Cambridge, 2000).

—— *Islamic Historiography* (Cambridge, 2003).

—— 'The conquest of Khuzistan: a historiographical reassessment', *Bulletin of the School of Oriental and African Studies* 67 (2004): 14–39.

Rodziewicz, M., 'Transformation of ancient Alexandria into a medieval city', in *Colloque international d'archéologie islamique*, ed. R.-P. Gayraud (Cairo, 1998), pp. 368–86.

Rubin, U., *The Eye of the Beholder: The Life of Muhammad as viewed by early Muslims: a textual analysis* (Princeton, NJ, 1995).

Rubin, Z., 'The Sasanian monarchy', in *Cambridge Ancient History*, vol. xiv: *Late Antiquity: Empire and Successors, AD 425–600*, ed. A. Cameron, B. Ward-Perkins and M. Whitby (Cambridge, 2000), pp. 638–61.

Schick, R., *The Christian Communities of Palestine from Byzantine to Islamic Rule: A historical and archaeological study* (Princeton, NJ, 1995).

Shaked, S., *From Zoroastrian Iran to Islam: Studies in religious history and inter-cultural contacts* (Aldershot, 1995).

Shoufani, E., *Al-Riddah and the Muslim Conquest of Arabia* (Toronto, 1973).

Sjöström, I., *Tripolitania in Transition: Late Roman to Islamic Settlement: With a catalogue of sites* (Aldershot, 1993)

Stratos, A. N., 'The naval engagement at Phoenix', in *Charanis studies: essays in honor of Peter Charanis*, ed. A. E. Laiou-Thomadakis (New Brunswick, 1980), pp. 229–47.

408   THE GREAT ARAB CONQUESTS

Taha, A. D., *The Muslim Conquest and Settlement of North Africa and Spain* (London, 1989).
Talbot Rice, D., 'The Oxford excavations at Hira, 1931', *Antiquity* 6.23 (1932): 276–91.
—— 'The Oxford excavations at Hira', *Ars Islamica* 1 (1934): 51–74.
Von Grunebaum, G. E., 'The nature of Arab unity before Islam', *Arabica* 10 (1963): 5–23.
Walmsley, A., 'Production, exchange and regional trade in the Islamic east Mediterranean: old structures, new system?', in *The Long Eighth Century. Production, Distribution and Demand*, ed. I. L. Hansen and C. J. Wickham (Leiden, 2000), pp. 265–343.
Watt, W. M., *Muhammad at Mecca* (Oxford, 1953).
—— *Muhammad at Medina* (Oxford, 1956).
—— *Muhammad, Prophet and Statesman* (Oxford, 1961).
Wellhausen, J., *The Arab Kingdom and Its Fall*, trans. M. G. Weir (Calcutta, 1927).
Wickham, C. J., *Framing the Early Middle Ages: Europe and the Mediterranean, c. 400–c. 800* (Oxford, 2005).
Wilken, R. L., *The Land Called Holy: Palestine in Christian History and Thought* (New Haven, CT, 1992).
Wilkinson, J., *Jerusalem Pilgrims before the Crusades* (rev. edn, Warminster, 2002).
Wink, A., *Al-Hind: The Making of the Indo-Islamic World*, vol. 1: *Early Medieval India and the Expansion of Islam, 7th–11th Centuries* (Leiden, 1990).
Wood, I., *The Merovingian Kingdoms 450–751* (London, 1994).
Yakubovich, I., 'Mugh I revisited', *Studia Iranica* 31 (2002): 213–53.
Zakeri, M., *Sāsānid Soldiers in Early Muslim Society. The origins of 'Ayyārān and Futuwwa* (Wiesbaden, 1995).·

In addition the reader should refer to the two editions of the *Encyclopaedia of Islam*. The first edition, 4 vols. (Leiden, 1913–42), is still useful but many of the articles are now outdated. The second edition, 12 vols. (Leiden, 1954–2004), is now complete. It is also accessible on CD-ROM. A third edition is planned. Many of the articles are of great scholarly value and the *Encyclopaedia* should always be used to supplement other reading. Another important reference tool is the *Encyclopaedia Iranica*, ed. E. Yarshater (London, 1985–), which contains descriptive articles and is still incomplete. For further bibliography, readers should use *Index Islamicus: A bibliography of books, articles and reviews of Islam and the Muslim World from 1906* (published 1958 onwards and available on CD-ROM).

INDEX

Abarkāwān 182
Abbasids 97, 273, 292, 326
Abd al-Azīz b. Marwān 24–7, 222,
   223
Abd al-Azīz b. Mūsā b. Nusayr 313,
   314–16, 333
Abd al-Malik, Umayyad caliph 11,
   13, 90, 197, 215, 216, 222, 241,
   249
Abd al-Rahmān al-Ghāfiqī 321–2
Abd al-Rahmān b. al-Ashʿath 197–8,
   249
Abd al-Rahmān b. Muslim al-Bāhilī
   256, 258–60, 267, 268, 270, 275
Abd Allāh b. Āmir 183–4, 185, 186–7
Abd Allāh b. Mūsā b. Nusayr 342
Abd Allāh b. Khāzim al-Sulamī
   238–41, 243, 247
Abd Allāh b. Mubārak 50
Abd Allah b. Saʿd b. Abī Sarh 164,
   207, 327, 328, 352
Abgar, King of Edessa 94
Abraham 44, 148, 376
Abū Bakr, Caliph 46, 51, 52, 54–5,
   72–4, 76–7, 80–81, 105, 358
Abū'l-Hayyāj 134
Abū'l-Muhājir, *mawla* Maslama
   211–12
Abū Mūsā al-Ashʿarī   125, 126, 136,
   137
Abū Muslim 294–5
Abū Sufyān b. Harb 53, 70–71, 74

Abū Ubayd al-Thaqafi 106
Abū Ubayda b. al-Jarrāh 20, 75, 79,
   81, 83, 85–6, 87, 88
Acre 335, 335–6
Afāriqa, the 204
Afghanistan 3, 99, 185–7, 194–8, 228,
   294, 296, 307, 364, 372
African Red Slip 33, 201, 203
Aghmāt 213
Ahriman 99
Ahvāz 126, 131, 134, 182
Ai Khanum 229
Ain Tamr 105
Ajnādayn, battle of 78–9
Akk tribe 147–8
Al-Rūr 297–8, 304–6
Alā b. al-Hadramī 181
Aleppo 34, 87, 95, 373
Alexander the Great 3, 128, 141, 143,
   175, 176, 187, 214, 229, 276, 296
Alexandria 20, 24–7, 69, 101, 141–8,
   151, 154–60, 162–6, 200, 216, 218,
   244, 337, 344, 346, 351–3
Algeciras 310, 313
Algeria 201, 202, 203, 208, 211, 212,
   219, 222, 224
Alī, Caliph 135, 164
Alī b. Hāmid al-Kūfī 296–7
Alor 304–5
Alqama 318
Amida (Diyarbakr) 95
Āmir b. al-Tufayl 41–2

Amr b. al-Ās 52–3, 56, 71, 73, 78–9,
  83, 88, 92, 96, 146–52, 154, 155,
  158–60, 162–4, 206–7, 209, 211,
  216, 371–2
Amr b. al-Hurayth al-Qurashī 173
Anahita, goddess 182–3
Anastasius, St 85
Anatolia 87, 94, 102,143, 179, 337,
  363, 365, 367
anwatan 19–20
Anbār 105, 132
Anbasa b. Sulaym al-Kalbī 320
Andronicus 144
ansār, the 52, 54, 106
Antony, St 141
Antioch 20, 31, 66–7, 69, 74, 82, 87,
  88, 93, 156, 307, 367
Apamea 69, 88
Aphrodito 333–4, 341, 343
Aquitaine 319
Arabian peninsula 2, 7, 34–5, 42–5,
  48, 59, 70, 171, 186, 205, 364
Aramaeans 100–101, 375
Aramaic 3, 28, 67, 100, 103, 106, 118,
  230
Achaemenids 128, 129, 182
archery 57–8, 59, 112, 115, 234, 266
Arculf 93, 337
Ardashīr I, Shāh 118, 130
Ardashīr III, Shāh 102
Arfaja b. Harthama al-Bāriqī 181
Armenia 68, 76, 95, 101–2, 109, 180,
  318–19, 369
Armenians 20, 23, 29, 80, 82, 101,
  107, 109, 180, 319, 369
armour 21, 58, 59, 61, 63, 98, 106,
  189, 234, 240, 259, 284, 286, 288,
  321
Arnold, Matthew 227
Arrajān 170, 183
Artemios, Emperor 330–31
Asad b. Abd Allāh al-Qasrī 64, 226,
  289–90, 291, 294

Asāwira, the 132
Astorga 314
Aswan 142–3, 163, 364
Atā b. Rāfi 333, 343
Atlas mountains 201, 213, 223
Aurelian, Emperor 35
Aurès mountains 212, 214, 216,
  219–22
Avars 61, 324, 369
Avignon 319
Ayyāsh al-Ghanawī 266
Azd tribe 10, 181, 226, 243, 274, 285,
  297–8
Azerbaijan 102, 123, 174, 179–80,
  374

Bāb al-Abwāb 180, 365
Babylon, Egypt 61, 140, 143, 144,
  149–54, 157, 160, 162, 166, 343,
  353
Babylon, Iraq 116
Baʿalbak 32, 66, 82, 326, 329
Bactria 229
Badakhshān 229
Badhghīs 257
Badr, battle of 46, 62, 108
Bāghāya 212, 220
Baghdad 16–17, 27, 97, 99, 105, 108,
  137, 139, 226, 361, 366
Bāhila tribe 226, 255, 281
Bahira, monk 77
Bahnasā 150
Bahrām Chūbin 122, 176
Bahrām Gūr, Sasanian Shāh 298, 359
Bahrayn 181
Bakr b. Wā'il tribe 238
Balādhurī 9, 16, 153, 183, 296, 297,
  299, 301
Balkh 229, 255, 257, 260, 263, 264,
  266, 273, 284, 289, 290, 305, 364
Balqā 71
Bam 185
Bamiyan 229

Banbhore 298
Bandi Qaysar 129
Barcelona 314, 319, 320
Barqa 205–9, 215, 216, 220
Basra 39, 97, 121, 125, 126, 132, 136,
    137, 160, 171, 182–4, 193, 195,
    197, 211, 226, 237, 239, 240, 256,
    274, 373
Bāzagharī 281–2
Bede, the Venerable 23–4, 320
Beirut 89
Benjamin, patriarch of Alexandria
    144, 146, 149, 160, 163–4, 167,
    351–2
Berbers 3, 64, 205–12, 213–17,
    218–24, 308–10, 314, 317, 323,
    334, 355, 370
Bet She'an 32
Bilbays 149
Biqa valley 82
Bishapur 170, 182, 183
Bisitun 170, 171
Bistām 116, 177
Bitlis 95
Black Death 68
booty 15, 20–21, 38–9, 52, 58, 64, 69,
    71, 78, 80, 103, 121, 123–4, 135,
    171–4, 177, 181, 193, 198, 207–8,
    212, 214, 216, 218, 222–3, 242,
    259, 273, 277, 287, 292, 307, 309,
    313–14, 317, 322, 333–5, 337, 343,
    366–7
Bordeaux 321
Bostra 70, 77–8
Brahmanābādh 302
Brahmins 298, 302–6, 370
Bridge, battle of the 106–7
bubonic plague 68, 87, 96, 143, 366
Buddhism 188, 229, 258, 300–301,
    303, 305, 306
Bukayr b. Abd Allāh al-Laythī 179
Bukhara 185, 225, 230–31, 238, 242,

    245, 249, 252, 258–63, 269, 271,
    277, 280–81, 292
Bumin 233
Būrān 102, 117
Burgundy 320
Burs 115
Burullus 338
Bust 186, 196, 364
Butler, Alfred 4, 22, 140, 145, 148,
    148–9, 156, 163, 166, 167
Byzacena 200, 204
Byzantine Empire 7–8, 24–7, 36–7,
    66, 68–70, 89–90, 98, 99, 101–2,
    143, 144–6, 202–6, 324, 363,
    365–6, 367–8
Byzantine forces 68–70, 78, 82–3,
    83–5, 101–2, 149, 150, 151, 152–3,
    155, 159–60, 166, 207–8, 217–18,
    367–8, 368–9, 372
Byzantine naval forces 216, 327–9,
    330–31, 334, 337–8, 339–40, 364

Caesarea 72, 73, 88, 89
Caetani, Leone 84
Cairo 97, 149, 151, 160, 161, 366
Carcassonne 319
Carmona 313
Carthage 156, 200–201, 203–4,
    207–8, 211, 212, 215–18, 333, 346,
    367
Caspian Sea 16, 131, 177–80, 188,
    192, 193, 365, 374
Catalonia 315
Caucasus 1, 29, 144, 179, 180–81,
    365
Ceuta 201, 202, 310
Chāch, king of Sind 298, 303
Chāchnāmah 296–7, 300–302, 304
Chalcedon, Council of 67, 142,
    145–6, 351
Chalcedonian Church 8, 67, 145,
    349, 352–3, 367
Chalkis 76, 86–7, 95, 373

Charjui 227
Charles Martel 319, 320, 321
China 225, 231–2, 232–3, 271–2,
    276–7, 291, 293–4, 294–5,
    360–62
Chosroes I, Shāh 178, 235, 369
Chosroes II, Shāh 69, 98, 102, 118,
    171, 176, 351, 368
Christianity 7, 8–9, 66–8, 94, 99–100,
    141–3, 202, 362, 370
Chronicle of 754 29, 308, 311, 312,
    321, 322, 353–5
Chronicle of Alfonso III 317–18
Cilicia 365
coins 11, 14, 316–17
Constans II, Emperor 327, 328
Constantine IV, Emperor 209
Constantinople 8, 28, 36, 66, 69, 70,
    74, 87, 95, 97, 101, 129, 143–6,
    150, 160, 162, 186, 202, 209, 308,
    324, 328–32, 324, 345, 346, 367
Continuator of Fredegar 322
Cook, Michael 22
Copts 8, 36–7, 140, 142, 144–6,
    148–9, 152, 155, 162, 167–8, 221,
    332, 337, 341, 350–53
Cordova 308, 311–12, 314, 317, 353,
    355
corsairs 334, 343
Covadonga, battle of 318
Crassus 185, 367
Creasy, Edward 320
Crete 1, 2, 343, 363
Crone, Patricia 22
Ctesiphon 61, 99, 102, 109, 116–22,
    132–3, 137–8, 144, 177, 196, 206
Cyprus, 146, 157, 160, 325–7
Cyrenaica 200, 201, 208, 209, 216,
    217, 220, 223, 224, 352
Cyrrhus 93
Cyrus, Patriarch of Alexandria 129,
    144–6, 152, 157–9, 160, 163, 166,
    351, 352

Dabūsiya 280, 283
Dāhir, king of Sind 298, 299, 301–2,
    304–5
Damascus 10, 20, 28, 32, 35, 61, 73,
    75, 79–80, 82, 83, 85–9, 96–7, 105,
    137, 153, 156, 165, 197, 211, 222,
    241, 275, 284–5, 290–91, 303, 312,
    314, 344, 363, 372
Daniel, prophet 129
Damietta 337–8
Darābjird 183
Darᶜa 84, 88
Dashti-Lut, the 170, 186
Dastgard (Daskara) 69, 102, 170, 368
Dāthin, battle of 73
Daybul 61, 297, 299–300
Daylamites 176, 318–19
Derbent 180, 365
Dihistān 193
Diophysite Church 8, 9, 67–8, 142
Dīswashtīch 279–80
Domentianus 155, 158
dromon, the 339–40
Dūmat al-Jandal 75
Dunhuang 232
Dushanbe 265

Ecija 311
Edessa 87, 94, 95
Elburz mountains 177
Empty Quarter, the 34, 43
Ethiopians 43
Eudes, Duke of Aquitaine 319, 321
Euphrates river 37, 87, 94, 95, 98,
    103, 104, 124, 126, 132, 133, 320,
    366, 371

Fannazbūr 299
Faramā 148–9, 337
Farghāna 232, 258–9, 271, 280,
    292–5
Farrukhzād 188, 189

Fars 6, 110, 123–4, 170, 171; 174, 179–85, 195, 298
Fayruzān 116, 171, 173
Fayyum, the 149–50, 158, 166, 353
Fentress, James 24
Fezzan, the 208
Firdawsi 110, 185, 188, 199, 357
fire-temples *see* Zoroastrian
France, invasion of 319–23
Fraxinetum (Fréjus) 343
Fredegar 78, 75, 322
Fustāt 26, 32, 39, 158, 160–62, 164–5, 211, 218, 317, 338, 341, 343, 352

Gābis 221
Garigliano river 343
Garonne 321
Gaza 43, 70, 73, 78, 88, 89, 146
Genghis Khan 3, 229
Gerasa, *see* Jerash
Ghadāmis 209
Ghassānids 36–7, 45, 82, 83, 95, 216, 368
Ghūrak 230, 267, 269–70, 277, 289
Gibbon, Edward 218–19, 221, 320
Gijon 314, 318
Girona 319
Gobi Desert 232
Goeje, M. J. de 308
Golan Heights 36, 83, 84
Greek fire 329, 331, 334, 339, 341
Gregory, Exarch of Africa 207
Gregory of Tours 23–4
Guadalajara 313
Guadalete river 311
Gūrgān 177–8, 192–4
gypsies 307–8

Hajjāj b. Yūsuf al-Thaqafī 196, 197, 198, 243, 249, 255, 259, 271, 273, 297, 299, 302, 306, 307
Hakam b. Abī'l-Ās al-Thaqafī 181

Hamadhan 173–4
Hamra, the 131–2
Hanīfa tribe 55, 56
Harīsh b. Hilāl al-Qurayᶜī 239–40
Hārith b. Surayj 289
Hārūn al-Rashīd, Abbasid caliph 326–7, 336
Hassān b. al-Nuᶜmān al-Ghassānī 216–17, 220–22
Hawāra 205
Hayyān al-Nabatī 257, 274, 275
Hazarasp 268
Heliopolis, battle of 151
Helmand river 185, 195
helmets 59, 250, 283
Heraclius, Emperor 9, 69, 70, 74, 79, 82, 87–8, 93, 101–2, 144–6, 150, 152–3, 202, 203, 324, 345, 351, 368
Herat 238, 239, 364
Herbadh 173, 183
Herod the Great 89
Hijaz, the 41, 44, 47, 53, 56, 89, 95, 107, 108, 125, 297, 371
hijra, the 46, 55, 108
hilm 53
Himyar 35, 43
Hindus 306–7
Hippo 202
Hīra 37, 103, 104–5
Hishām, Umayyad caliph 276, 290, 292, 335
History of Bukhara 226
Homs 74, 76, 79–82, 85–6, 89, 95, 373
Hudaybiya 46
Hulwān 170
Hungry Steppe, the 232
Hurayth b. Qutba 248–51
Hurmuzān 116, 127, 130–31

Ibn Abd al-Hakam 24–7, 139–40, 149, 204, 206, 217–18, 308, 309–10, 312–13, 316, 327, 328

Ibn Abī Sarh *see* Abd Allah b. Saᶜd b. Abī Sarh
Ibn al-Athīr 327
Ibn Hawqal 174, 298, 306
Ibn Idhārī 213, 217–18, 220–21
Ibn Rashīq 40
Ibn Ṭūlūn 335–6
Ifrīqīya 209–10, 211, 217, 220, 221
Imru'l-Qays b. Amr 35–6
India 48, 59, 195, 228, 231, 298–9, 306–7, 356
Indian Ocean 297
Indus river 292, 294, 296, 297, 298, 300–301, 307
Isfahan 171, 174
Isfandiyādh 179
Ishtemi 233, 235
Ishtīkhān 270
Israel 31, 73, 84, 97, 353, 356
Istakhr 6, 32, 170, 182–5, 184
Iyād b. Ghanam al-Fihrī 94–5

Jabal Akhdar mountains 200
Jabala b. Ayham al-Ghassānī 82
Jābiya 36–7, 83, 84, 91, 95, 147
Jacob Baradaeus 8
jāhiliya (time of ignorance) 15, 40, 42, 63, 238
Jalūlā, battle of 123–4, 131, 138
Jannāba 171
Jarīr b. Abd Allāh al-Bajalī 107, 108
Jats 298, 303–4
Jayy 175
Jaxartes 232
Jazira, conquest of the 94–5
Jerash 32, 66
Jerusalem 32, 51, 69, 70, 74, 78, 90–93, 96, 143, 146, 147, 153, 156, 336, 344–6, 348
Jews 50, 67, 73, 89, 92–3, 96, 100, 137, 175, 306, 311, 355–6, 362, 370, 376
jihād 48–51, 62, 97, 221, 223, 237,

244, 256, 266, 269, 270, 334, 337, 361
John bar Penkāye 1, 349–50, 354, 366
John of Damascus, St 28
John of Nikiu 29, 140, 149, 150, 153, 155, 157, 158, 158–9, 163, 165, 166, 167, 352–3
Julfar 181
Julian, governor of Ceuta 213, 310, 313, 314
Junayd b. Abd al-Rahmān al-Murrī 284–9, 372
Junday-shapur 126, 127–8, 131
Jūr 182, 184
Jurjah 76, 82
Justinian, Emperor 88, 90, 98, 202

Kabul 229, 263–4
Kaᶜb b. Abhar 93
Kāhina 218–21
Kamarja, siege of 280–84
Kandahār 194
Kara Kum, the 227
Karkuya 186
Karun river 126
Karyūn 155
Kashgar 232, 271, 295
Kāth 268
Kavād II, Shāh 102
Kazakhstan 232, 294
Kāzirūn 183
Khābūr river 69
Khālid b. al-Walid 20, 52, 56, 71, 74–82, 83, 84–5, 87, 92, 103–5
Khandaq (Trench), battle of the 46
Khāristān, battle of 290
Khātūn, queen of Bukhara 231, 238
Khawlān, tribe 26
Khazars 365
Khurasan 59, 169, 171, 176–9, 187, 189, 193, 228, 236–43, 249, 250, 252–3, 255–6, 264, 273–5, 278,

284, 289, 290, 292–3, 296, 307, 357, 373
Khurrazādh 268
Khusraw the miller 190–91
Khusraw, Shāh see Chosroes
Khusrawshunūm 174
Khuttal 229, 249
Khuzistān 116, 126–31, 170
Khuzistān Chronicle 23, 127–30, 136
Khwārazm 225, 229–30, 238, 268, 269, 271, 273, 292
King's Spring, the 122
Kirman 175, 182, 185–6, 192
Kish 243, 246–8, 252, 271, 285–9, 292
Kizil Kum 227, 230
Koran, the 16, 25, 26, 37, 48–51, 125–6, 129, 141, 223, 256, 262, 320, 325, 327
Kos 324, 327
Kubadhiyān 229
Kūfa 23–4, 97, 121, 132, 132–6, 137, 138, 161, 171, 211, 362, 373
Kūm Sharīk 155
Kurds 170, 179
Kūrsūl 277, 278, 284, 290
Kusayla 212, 214, 215–16

Laguatan, the 205
Lakhmids 37, 45
Latakia 89
Lebanon 89–90, 330–31
Leo III, Emperor 331–2
Leon 314
Leptis Magna 201, 205, 207
Lerida 314
Lyon 319

Maʿlūlā 28
Madāʾin see Ctesiphon
Madāʾinī 27, 226, 244, 297, 301–2
Maghreb see North Africa
Mahuy 189, 190–91

Makrān 296, 299
Malatya 365
Manbij 93
Mansūr, Abbasid caliph 83, 215, 361
Manuel 162
Mar Gabriel 344, 350
Marib dam 43
Maslama b. Abd al-Malik 331–2
Masts, battle of the 327–9
Maurice, Emperor 3, 69, 101, 233–5, 367
mawāli 105, 248, 257, 273
Maximus Confessor 345
Mecca 16, 32, 44, 46, 51–6, 70, 73, 76, 86, 90, 93, 97, 106, 108, 121, 125, 160, 181, 183, 186, 195, 208, 286, 324
Media 109, 123, 173, 176
Medina 16, 21, 44, 46, 51, 52, 54–7, 73, 80, 81, 90, 97, 98, 104–6, 108–9, 122, 124–5, 130–31, 133, 160, 164–5, 174, 181, 324, 368, 372
Medina Sidonia 311, 313
Mediterranean Sea 33, 43, 66, 72, 94, 96, 143, 162, 201–2, 216, 324–5, 327, 333, 337, 339, 347, 363, 364
Menas 145–6, 158
Merida, siege of 313
Merv 170, 185, 187–92, 211, 225, 227–8, 237, 238, 241–2, 252, 255–7, 260, 263–4, 267, 269, 273, 289, 291, 293, 373
Mervrūd 240, 263
Methodius of Olympus, Bishop 346
Mīds 298
Mihrān 123, 298
Mims 216
Misr, Treaty of 153–4
Monastir 212
Mongols 185, 229, 373
Monophysites 8–9, 36–7, 67, 142, 144, 145, 167, 349, 369

Monothelitism 9
Morocco 201, 202, 208, 212–213, 219, 224, 364, 371, 374
mosques 32–3, 97, 121, 128, 134, 135, 160–61, 174, 182, 192, 194, 214, 261, 316, 326, 357, 361
Mosul 137, 373
Moussais la Bataille 321
Mu'āwiya b. Abī Sufyān, Umayyad caliph 89, 91, 164, 212, 326, 327, 328, 349
Mudar 238, 241
Mughīra b. Shu'ba al-Thaqafī 113–14, 125–6
Mughīth 311–12
muhājirūn 46, 52, 54–5
Muhallab b. Abī Sufra 226, 243
Muhammad, the Prophet 2, 3, 14, 22, 38, 41, 43, 45–8, 51, 52–5, 66, 70–72, 74, 76, 77, 80, 102, 107, 108, 114, 137, 150, 154, 208, 236, 239
Muhammad Ali 157
Muhammad b. Qāsim al-Thaqafī 297, 299–308, 314
Multān 297, 305, 306, 307, 364
Munnuza 321
Muqaddasī 335–6
Murcia 315–16
Mūsā b. Abd Allāh b. Khāzim 240–41, 241, 243–54
Mūsā b. Nusayr 105, 222–3, 313–15, 319, 333, 354
Musayyab b. Bishr al-Riyāhī 278–9
Muslim Empire 363–6
Mu'ta, battle of 71
Mutawwakil 157, 335
Muthannā b. Hāritha 103–4, 105–7, 108

Naffīs 214
Nā'il 116–17
Nakhla 76

Narayāna 277
Narbonne 314, 319, 320
Narshakhī 226, 231, 262
Nasaf 252, 271
Nasr b. Sayyār al-Kinānī 226, 290–94
naval warfare 324–43
Nayzak 249, 259–60, 263–5
Negev 73, 86, 96, 97
Nemara 35–6
Nessana 96
Nestorians 8–9, 100, 104, 186
Nestorius, Patriarch of Constantinople 8–9
Nicea, Council of 327
Nihāvand 116, 171–3, 179, 182
Nikiu 155
Nile Delta 29, 161, 168
Nile river 143, 149, 151, 154, 155, 158, 160, 151, 227, 230, 298
Nile valley 72, 141–2, 145, 148–50, 168, 205, 320, 338, 341–2, 364
Nimes 319–20
Nineveh, battle of 102
Nīrūn 297, 300
Nisibis 94
Nistarot 355–6
North Africa 2, 3, 6–11, 27, 43, 64, 66, 69, 70, 200–224, 296, 318, 323, 327, 331–4, 337, 345, 363, 364, 367, 370, 371, 375
Noth, Albrecht 22
Nubians 154, 364
Nu'mān b. Muqarrin 172, 179
Nusayr 105, 374–5

Ohrmazd 99
Oman 34, 42, 48, 56, 181
On 151
Oppa, bishop 318
Oviedo 314
Oxus river 198–9, 225–30, 232, 235, 237, 242, 244–6, 249, 255, 257, 258, 263–5, 268, 273, 284

Pachomius, St 141
Palestine 31–2, 36, 66–97, 143, 146, 148, 156, 205, 325, 337, 344, 348, 363
Palmyra 32, 35, 66, 75
Pantelleria 333
Paykand 6, 258–9
Pelayo 317–18
Pella 78
Pelusium 143, 148
Penjikent 230, 279, 280
People of the Book 50, 306
Persepolis 128, 182, 184
Persian Gulf 181
Persians see Sasanian Persians
Petra 35, 66, 71, 77
Phocas, Emperor 156, 203
Picos de Europa mountains 314, 317–18
Poitiers, battle of 289, 295, 320–22, 354–5
Portugal 3, 308, 315, 364
pseudo-Methodius 346–50, 356
Ptolemies, the 141–2
Punjab, the 307
Pyrenees, the 317, 319, 321, 364

Qādisiya, battle of 4, 19, 21, 22, 57, 63, 83, 108–16, 130, 131, 138, 171, 179, 188, 277, 357
Qarqīsīya 124
Qartmin 350
Qasr al-Bāhilī, siege of 278–9
Qasri Shīrīn 170
Qayrawān 209–12, 214–16, 218, 220–21, 222–4, 314, 317, 333, 373
Qinnasrin see Chalkis
Qubā, siege of 293
Qumm 175–6, 192
Quraysh tribe 26, 44–8, 52–5, 95, 108, 146, 173, 183, 208, 371
Qurra b. Sharīk 341–3

Qutayba b. Muslim 193, 225, 226, 255–7, 258–67, 268–76, 293
Quthm b. Abbās 236–7

Rabīʿa tribe 238
Rāfi b. Umayr al-Ṭāʾī 75
Raqqa 95, 327
Rashahr, battle of 182
Ravenna 98
Rayy 109, 119, 176–7, 179, 189, 192
Rhodes 327, 330
Rhône valley 319, 320
Ribʿi b. Āmir al-Tamīmī 111–14
ridda wars 55–7, 76, 81, 103, 104, 105, 107, 181
Rodrigo, Visigoth king 303, 309, 310, 311, 313, 316, 317
Roman Empire 66, 101, 141–2, 200–201, 363, 366, 371, 375
Rosetta 337
Rusāfa 37
Rustam, Persian general 62, 64, 100, 106–7, 109–15, 125, 130, 357–60
Rustam, legendary hero 185–6, 227, 250
Ruzbān 178
Rūzbih b. Buzurgmihr 135

Sabra 207
Saʿd b. Abī Waqqās 61, 63–4, 108, 111, 115, 116–17, 118, 119, 121, 133, 135, 136, 371
Saʿid al-Harashī 279
Saʿid Khudhayna 278, 279
Saʿid b. Batrīq 92–3
Saghāniyān 229, 257
Sahara, the 201, 205, 208, 219, 364
Sajāh 55, 103
Sajūma 223
Sakas 185
Sālih b. Muslim al-Bāhilī 269, 275
Saljuk Turks 57
Salm b. Ziyād 237–8

Samarqand 61, 185, 189, 225, 230,
    236–8, 245–6, 263, 267, 268–70,
    273, 277, 279–81, 283–5, 287, 289,
    292, 294
Samh b. Mālik al-Khawlāni 319
Sanutius 163, 352–3
Sarat, the 107
Sardinia 333–4
Sasanian forces 21, 68–70, 101, 106,
    107, 115–17, 119–21, 123, 138,
    171–3, 344–5
Sasanian Persians 36, 37, 56, 68–70,
    98–9, 100–102, 109–16, 118,
    121–2, 143, 171–2, 356–60, 367–8,
    369
Sasanian wars 68–70, 101–2, 367–8
Sawād 62–3
Sawīrus b. al-Muqaffa 351
Sawra b. al-Hurr al-Tamīmī 284,
    287, 288
Sayf b. Umar 23–4, 114, 116, 132,
    135
Sbeitla 207
Scythopolis 95
Sebeos 23, 29, 78, 107
Segermes 204
Seleucia 118
Seleucus Nicator 176
Seville 313, 317
Shāhi Zinda, the 237
Shahnāmah 110, 115, 117, 185, 188,
    199, 227, 357
Shahrak 182
Shahrbarāz 102, 180
Shāhriyār 116–17
Shapur I, Shāh 129, 170, 182
Shapur II, Shāh 128
Sharīk b. Shuway 155
Shāsh 232, 271, 292, 293
Shaybān tribe 56, 103–4
Shayzar 88
shields see weaponry

shipbuilding 330, 331, 334, 338, 339,
    343
Shiraz 183, 299
Shīrzād 117, 118
Shiz 69, 368
Shūmān 257, 265–7
Sicily 2, 66, 209, 215, 332, 334, 363
Sidi Okba 208; see also Uqba b. Nāfi
Sidon 89
siege engines 61–2, 118, 152, 184,
    266, 300
siege warfare 61–2, 79–80, 184, 258
Silk Road, the 231–2, 258, 271–2
Sind 3, 61, 296–8, 299–308, 364,
    369–70
Sindered, Archbishop of Toledo 312
Sinkiang 232
Sirjān 185
Sistan 179, 185–7, 192, 194, 197, 249,
    267–8
Sīwīstān 300–301
Siyāvush 176
slaves 105, 206, 214–15, 288, 367
Soghdia 225, 230–32, 238, 242, 243,
    245–6, 258–9, 270–71, 276–7,
    278, 279–80, 292–3
Sophronius, Patriarch of Jerusalem
    90–91, 344, 344–6, 349
Stephen, St 186
Straits of Gibraltar 200, 201, 223,
    268, 296, 308, 309, 320
Strategikon 101, 233–5, 369
Su-Lu 277
Subeita 86
Sufyān, Arab naval commander 331
Sulaym tribe 44, 265
Sulaymān b. Abd Malik, Umayyad
    caliph 273, 276, 306
sulhan 19–20
Sūs al-Aqsā 213–14, 214, 223
Susa 128–9
Suwayd b. Muqarrin 177, 180
Syracuse 334

Tāb river 171
Tabarī 16–17, 21, 27, 30, 72, 109,
    133, 135, 139, 226
Tabaristān 177–8, 187, 192–4
Tabensi 158
Tabūk 71
Tahert 212
Tā'if 53, 181, 195
Tajikistan 228
Tajiks 228
Talas, battle of 225, 294–5
Tāliqān 264
Tamīm tribe 38–9, 63, 239, 260
Tangier 201, 213, 223, 224
Tāqi Bustān 98, 170
Taraz see Talas
Tāriq b. Ziyād 223, 309–13, 313–14,
    314–15, 319
Tarkhūn 189, 245–6, 249, 252–3,
    263, 267
Tarsus 336–7, 365
Tashtakaracha Pass, battle of the 285
Tawwaj 182
taxation 7, 8, 19–20, 43, 117, 124,
    136, 138, 154, 179, 291, 302–3,
    362, 373
Thābit b. Qutba 248–52
Thaqafīs 297
Thaqīf 53, 106
Theodemir 315–16
Theodora Empress 98
Theodore 151, 155, 159, 160
Theodore Trithurios 82, 150
Theodosius Grammaticus 329–30
Theophanes 28, 207, 327, 328, 330,
    331
Theophilus 141
Thessalonica, siege of 61
Tiberias 96
Tigris river 94, 117, 119–20, 126
Tikrit 124
Timgad 201, 203
Tinnis 338

Tirmidh 229, 241, 244–5, 246–7,
    249–53, 255, 260
Tlemcen 212
Tobna, battle of 221
Tokra 206
Toledo 309, 312–13, 313–14, 367
Toulouse 319
Tours 321
Trajan, Emperor 77, 151
Transjordan 97
transliteration 9–10
Transoxania 27, 62, 193, 225–28,
    232–7, 243, 247–53, 257, 263–9,
    275–89, 289–95, 296, 305, 316,
    363–9, 371–5
tribute 6, 8, 12, 19–20, 47, 50–51, 80,
    103, 105, 122, 128, 146, 154, 159,
    187, 196, 206, 214, 231, 236, 243,
    249, 257, 258, 260, 261, 263, 266,
    267, 270, 272, 303, 316, 326, 348,
    350, 372
Tripoli 89–90, 96, 200, 206–7, 209,
    215, 219, 20, 328
Tripolitania 200, 204–5, 208, 224
Tu Huan 360–61
Tubna 214
Tughshāda 262, 277
Tukhāristān 225, 228–9, 257, 263–5,
    289–90, 292, 294
T'ung Yabghu 236
Tunis 217, 221, 333–4
Tunisia 200, 204, 223–4
Türgesh 277, 288
Türgesh Kaghan 236
Turkey 1, 69, 144, 169, 232, 350, 363
Turkmenistan 3, 99, 178, 191, 193,
    230
Turks 178, 188–90, 192–3, 225, 226,
    232–6, 247, 250–53, 259–61,
    276–89
Tus 187, 357
Tustar 23, 126, 128, 129–30, 138
Tyre 89, 335, 336

Ubāda 152
Ubayd Allāh b. Abī Bakra 184, 195–7, 372
Ubulla 124, 127
Uhud, battle of 46, 76
Umar I b. al-Khattāb, Caliph 21, 46, 51–4, 57, 75, 76, 81, 88, 91–3, 105–6, 107, 108, 124, 125–6, 129, 130–35, 147, 160, 171, 173, 181, 325, 356, 372
Umar II b. Abd al-Azīz, Umayyad caliph 276, 332
Umar Khayyām 189
Umayya b. Abd Allāh b. Khālid b. Usayd 241–2, 247
Umm Dunayn, battle of 149
Umm Jamīl 125–6
umma, the 38, 48, 51, 56, 351
Umayyad Caliphate 73, 97, 137, 198
Uqba b. Nāfi 207, 208–15, 222, 223, 371
Ushtum 338
Utba b. Ghazwān al-Māzinī 124–5
Uthmān b. Abī'l-Ās al-Thaqafī 181, 182
Uthmān b. Affān, Caliph 46, 51, 89, 164, 207, 299, 326, 349, 368
Uzbekistan 230, 232
Uzbeks 228

Valerian, Emperor 129, 183
Vandals, the 202, 203
Visigoths 309, 310–11, 313, 315–16, 319
Volubilis 201, 212, 213

Wadi'l-Ruqqād 84, 85
Wadi Araba 73
Wadi Dra 213, 214, 223
Wadi'-l'Allān 85
Wadi Maskiyāna, battle of 220
Wadi Natrun 164
Wāj al-Rūdh 176

Wakī al-Tamīmī 261, 274–5, 278
Walīd I, Umayyad caliph 222, 273, 276, 306, 314
Walīd II, Umayyad caliph 326
Walīla see Volubilis
Wardān-Khudā 154, 260
warships 339–41, 343
weaponry 58; bows 59, 234; crossbows 59; naval 341; shields 82, 111, 112; spears 59, 111; swords 58–9, 111, 112, 114, 234
Wickham, Chris 24, 203
Willibald, St 335
Witiza 309–10

Yahūdiya 174–5
Yamāma 44, 52, 55
Yāqūt al-Hamawī 172–3, 209–11
Yarmūk, battle of 19, 22, 57, 76, 81, 83–5, 87, 89, 347
Yassi Adi wreck 324–5, 340
Yazdānfar 175
Yazdgard III, Shāh 47, 102, 107, 109–10, 117, 119, 120, 123, 132, 171, 182, 185–6, 187–91, 225, 281, 368
Yazīd I, Umayyad caliph 212, 215, 238
Yazīd II, Umayyad caliph 276, 329
Yazīd III, Umayyad caliph 326
Yazīd (Mūsā supporter) 252
Yazīd b. Abū Sufyān 53, 73, 79, 83, 87, 350, 354
Yazīd b. al-Muhallab 192–4, 226, 249
Yemen 24–7, 35, 42, 43, 44, 48, 56, 59, 107, 108, 147, 149, 161

Zacharia 155
Zaghwān 222
Zagros mountains 99, 123, 124, 126, 132, 137, 169–71, 174, 177
Zanāta tribes 218–21, 223
Zarafshan river 185, 230

Zarafshan valley 258, 280, 285
Zaragoza 314, 317, 364
Zaranj 186–7
Zarq 190
Zenobia, Queen 35
Zeugitania 200
Zinābi 177
Zionists 32
Ziyād b. Abī Sufyān 125, 134, 135, 237
Zoroastrianism 99–100, 144, 173, 178, 183, 184, 186, 187, 190, 195, 229, 306, 344, 356

Zoroastrian fire-temples 99, 100, 118, 174, 183, 188, 195, 261, 262, 270, 306, 356
Zubayr 136
Zubayr b. al-Awwām 150–51, 152, 153, 154
Zuhayr b. Dhu'ayb al-Adawī 240–41
Zuhayr b. Qays 215, 216
Zunbīl 195–8, 267–8
Zutt 298, 301, 307–8
Zuwayla 209